A. Q. Faizí

In the garden of thy heart plant naught but the rose of love,
and from the nightingale of affection and desire loosen not thy hold.

– The Hidden Words of Bahá'u'lláh

Calligraphy by A. Q. Faizí

Penned by A. Q. Faizí

This volume is a collection of some of the books,
pamphlets, transcripts and essays penned by
Hand of the Cause of God Abu'l-Qásim Faizí

It is dedicated to all the people in every
corner of the world who loved him

Compiled by Naysán & Zohreh Faizí

Edited by Naysán & Zohreh Faizí
with invaluable assistance from Rosanna Smith

GR

George Ronald
Oxford

George Ronald Publisher Ltd
Oxford
www.grbooks.com

The following works are reprinted with
the permission of the copyright holders:

A Day When the Faithful Rejoiced
(National Spiritual Assembly of the Bahá'ís of the United Kingdom)

Stories from The Delight of Hearts:
The Memoirs of Ḥájí Mírzá Ḥaydar-'Alí
(Kalimát Press)

A Flame of Fire and
Explanation of the Symbol of the Greatest Name
(from *Bahá'í News*, 432/March, 433/April and 451/October.
National Spiritual Assembly of the Bahá'ís of the United States)

A catalogue record for this book is available
from the British Library

ISBN: 978-0-85398-637-9

Book design by Naysán & Zohreh Faizí

The pens and cases depicted on the cover belonged to Mr Faizí
and were used by him extensively in his calligraphy

Contents

Introduction	1
All the Seas Shall Have Pearls	3
A Day When the Faithful Rejoiced	9
Divine Education	15
Explanation of the Symbol of the Greatest Name	27
A Flame of Fire	45
From Adrianople to 'Akká	61
A Gift of Love	83
Glory of the Sand	115
The Hidden Words	119
Mesbah	133
Milly	141
Narcissus to 'Akká	171
Once Upon a Time	179
The Prince of Martyrs	183
Stories from the Delight of Hearts	223
Three Meditations on the Eve of November the Fourth	345
A Village Scriptorium	363
The Wonder Lamp	367
Photographs	381

Publisher's note:

This book contains pieces of Mr Faizí's writings that were produced at different times and in various styles, many of them previously published by different Bahá'í publishing houses around the world. Effort has been made to reproduce these collected writings as closely to the originals as possible, therefore it was decided to avoid applying a blanket style and format across the whole book but rather to strive for consistency within each piece and allow some variations in style and convention between the texts as they appeared.

Introduction

Those whom my father embraced with his love experienced such warmth and closeness to him that they felt they had a special place in his heart. This was the uniqueness and mystery of my father's love and affection – it would envelop all those who shared even a few moments with him. What people felt was, in fact, true. Each and every one had a very special place in my father's boundless affection.

When in England at boarding school, I would cherish the times I was able to be with my father, whether in Haifa during the summer school holidays or when he would visit in between his extensive travels around the world. These visits continued after Zohreh and I got married and had our children, Cherry Gloria and Aram Amoz.

My father's knowledge of the Bahá'í Faith and of comparative religion, as well as the arts and philosophy, was vast. Fellow Hand of the Cause* William Sears once said: 'A. Q. stands for "Answers questions"'. For all the years that we were together, unlike his friends (who, in person and by mail, would ask him to clarify or explain particular extracts from any given book), I rarely asked him any questions – it seemed that my job was to make him laugh, especially when he was engaged in some important conversation on the phone. I was young and foolish but, given those moments again, I would do exactly the same thing – the memory of his laughter warms my heart.

My father never asked anything of me; however, during one of our visits – knowing that both Zohreh and I were graphic designers – he mentioned that he would like to have his works collected in one volume. It took us some 40 years to make a start and, with the encouragement of my sister, May, and some close friends, Zohreh and I were able to collect and compile some of his published works, the result of which is this volume.

The way my father structured the English language, both in the spoken as well as the written word, had a certain sweetness unique to itself and, when appropriate, a subtle sprinkling of humour.

In preparing this book, as I was reading his words, I could hear his voice and his laughter, sense his smile, and feel the warmth of his embrace.

My thanks go to Zohreh, with whom I designed this book, and to Cherry and Aram for helping me realize the request my father made of me so many years ago.

– Naysán Faizí

NOTES

* The Hands of the Cause of God, Hands of the Cause, or Hands (informally) were a select group of Bahá'ís, appointed for life, whose main function was to propagate and protect the Bahá'í Faith. The title is no longer conferred.

– The copyright of all my father's works, whether transcribed, published in print or online, is held by myself and my sister, May Moore.

– Where the word 'man' is used to denote humanity rather than the male gender, it is written with a capital M – 'Man'.

– Martyrdom in the Bahá'í Faith is the act of sacrificing one's life in the service of humanity and in the name of God. While the Bahá'í Faith exalts the station of its martyrs, Bahá'ís are discouraged from pursuing martyrdom as a public declaration of devotion.

All the Seas Shall Have Pearls

Publisher's note:

In this commemorative essay written two years after the tragic death of Hand of the Cause of God Dorothy Baker in 1954, Mr Faizí creates a beautiful analogy for her untimely passing through combining and reimagining elements of two Greek myths, the legend of Europa and the legend of the Golden Ram.

The passage from Bahá'u'lláh quoted by Mr Faizí in the Notes and References section is from *The Seven Valleys* which has since been retranslated by the Bahá'í World Centre and can be found in the 2019 publication *The Call of the Divine Beloved.*

The beloved Guardian initiated the first International Conferences in 1953. The Bahá'í communities throughout the world were moved and thrilled, and those who could travel made their way to one or more of these Conferences.

The one held in India was the most picturesque. A great variety of colourful dresses added beauty and atmosphere to the assemblage of friends who were seated under a large tent, in semicircular files. East and West met each other in perfect unity and mutual understanding. People of different colours with varying racial, religious, and cultural backgrounds, came together for the first time and tasted the beauty and felt deeply the joy of knowing one another. And for the first time they truly comprehended that they were members of one body, still unfortunately separated by the cruel forces of prejudice, hatred, and ignorance. Now under the canopy of love and unity, they shed tears of joy and often their feelings were uncontrollable.

All the speakers responded to this feeling of unprecedented joy. Their voices sometimes broke with emotion. Deeply touched by the rapture of those moments, I wrote down the beautiful words of the speakers; but when Dorothy Baker started to speak, my pen would not move. I could take no notes.

She stood elegantly upon the stage and when she spoke she seemed to abandon her physical temple. A certain mysterious power caused eloquent words to flow from her lips with the clarity and unerring direction of a mountain stream as it moves swiftly over small pebbles. Her soft penetrating voice had the ring of indescribable music. Her face received fresh lights of joy from the worlds beyond.

She continuously spoke about the beloved Guardian, but never, during her visit to India, did she speak about her pilgrimage to the Holy Land. I remained with her during her entire stay in New Delhi, even to the last moment when she was settled in her train compartment. Accompanied by her adopted son, <u>Sh</u>ahriyár, she continued her journey, making trips to other states of India. She bade me farewell as I stood on the pavement beside her train; the last thing I could see was her hand waving goodbye.

After finishing her mission in India she proceeded to Pakistan, where, in Karachi, she had meetings with representatives of religious and civil institutions of the country.

I followed her by prayers and received news of her tremendous victories on all fronts. Yet something in her life has remained a mystery to me. What passed in her dear heart during those last days, and what urged her to talk to the friends in Karachi of her sweetest reminiscences? Why did she share, on that particular visit, the memory of her four-day pilgrimage, about which she made no mention in India? Was it the ecstasy of her soul that prompted her to speak? Was she feeling within the very essence of her heart that her meeting in Karachi would be her last chance to be with the people of this world? Could her soul no longer endure separation from her Lord? She sang her last song, then began her flight to Europe.

'Welcome, a thousand welcomes, my martyr pilgrim' were the first words of the Guardian when she entered his room. She sat enraptured with the joy of beholding the countenance of the Sign of God on this planet. Overcome with the emotion of the moment, she tried desperately to speak, but she could only ask, 'Why martyr, beloved Guardian?' The sweet consoling words of the Guardian brought a blissful peace to her soul: 'Because you asked three times to come on pilgrimage, and three times I sent you to different fields of teaching and you accepted the mission with radiant acquiescence.'

In her address to the friends in Karachi she emphasized the fact that human souls were like pieces of sponge. The presence of the Guardian was like an immense ocean. When the tiny pieces of sponge were placed in the ocean, they absorbed water according to their capacity and no more.

Almost twenty hours after her memorable meeting in Pakistan, the Bahá'í world was shocked to hear that our precious Dorothy Baker had drowned in the Mediterranean Sea, between the coasts of Italy and France.

According to ancient mythology, the beautiful Europa was taken up into the air on the back of the Golden Ram. There, amongst the immensely glorious clouds, shining from the rays of the sun, she watched the wonderful works of God and, in her ecstasy and joy, she could no more hold fast, and fell into the depths of the Mediterranean Sea.

Her disappearance moved the hearts of the people of the ancient world so greatly that they called one whole continent after her: Europe.

Two years ago, our wonderful Dorothy Baker also was flying over the Mediterranean on her return from the four glorious banquets that were spread so generously by the beloved Guardian of the Bahá'í Faith in the four corners of the globe.

She had witnessed how lovingly the Bahá'ís invited the scattered members of the human race to unite and participate in the joyful ceremonies of the Kingdom of God and, with a heart brimful with profound sadness, she lamented the stubbornness with which mankind deprived itself of all these manifestations of love and spiritual regeneration.

As a brilliant member of the Hands of the Cause of God, she did all in her power to awaken this heedless and corrupt generation and guide them to the path of God. Her sorrow was indeed great when she perceived how, in their pride and ignorance, they disregarded the Divine Teachings and spent their God-given talents and energies in acts of brutal destruction and savagery. She was deeply aware of the impending disaster which, because of Man's heedlessness, was bound to overtake the world.

We cannot know for certain what was in the mind and the heart of this beloved servant as she winged her way towards what she no doubt believed would be further fields of service. But we see dear Dorothy in our mind's eye, fresh from the fields of victory which she had so deservedly won, radiant with that inner spirit we had so recently witnessed on her tour of India. Perhaps just before the plane dropped so abruptly from the sky, she read once again that beautiful and soul-stirring supplication: 'Lord! Give me to drink from the chalice of selflessness; with its robe clothe me, and in its ocean immerse me.'

Thousands might chant this prayer each day but only for her was the plea for eternal freedom and everlasting joy answered so dramatically. For although her body entered the majestic blue 'sepulchre' of the Mediterranean, her soul continued its upward flight through unlimited worlds of God, to shine forever from the horizon of service and self-sacrifice. Hereafter, all the dwellers of the seven seas and seven oceans shall receive and accept the message of the Day of God and all the seas shall have pearls.

To understand the sweet reference of the beloved Guardian, we must recall the following: When the beloved Master reached the most desperate moments of His eventful life, one of the enemies went to His house and very cruelly announced to Him, 'The decree is issued. You will be either exiled to the deserts of Africa or hanged in Jerusalem or be drowned in the Mediterranean Sea.' The Master listened in perfect silence and proved so calm and resolute that His enemy, who announced all such revengeful events, became angry. The Master, amazingly, said, '... Mediterranean Sea! What an immense sepulchre!'

This is the reason why the beloved Guardian said that now this immense sepulchre belongs to Dorothy Baker and all seas shall have pearls.

NOTES AND REFERENCES

– O Brother! Not every sea hath pearls; not every branch will flower, nor will the nightingale sing thereon. Then, ere the nightingale of the mystic paradise repair to the garden of God, and the rays of the heavenly morning return to the Sun of Truth – make thou an effort, that haply in this dustheap of the mortal world thou mayest catch a fragrance from the everlasting garden, and live forever in the shadow of the peoples of this city. And when thou hast attained this highest station and come to this mightiest plane, then shalt thou gaze on the Beloved, and forget all else.

– Bahá'u'lláh, The Valley of True Poverty and Absolute Nothingness

– When Loulie Matthews spent a day with the Guardian in Haifa in February 1954, they talked about Dorothy's death and about Loulie's book, *Not Every Sea Hath Pearls.* Shoghi Effendi's gaze wandered out toward the sea. He grew quiet, then said, 'Now the Mediterranean has the blessing of the pearl that was Dorothy.'

– Dorothy Freeman Gilstrap, From Copper to Gold

A Day When the Faithful Rejoiced

Publisher's note:

This is an account of the first Bahá'í World Congress held in 1963 in London, where the nine members of the Universal House of Justice, who had just been elected for the first time at the first International Convention in Haifa, were presented. The Congress was also a celebration of the 'Most Great Jubilee', or the Centenary of the Declaration of Bahá'u'lláh in the Garden of Riḍván in 1863, referred to by Shoghi Effendi as the 'Ascension of Bahá'u'lláh to the throne of His sovereignty'.

A gigantic container of pearls and jewels, with multifarious forms and hues, was the Royal Albert Hall,[1] when more than 6,000 Bahá'ís assembled to celebrate the centenary of Bahá'u'lláh's Ascension to the Throne of Glory.

To give the full account of that memorable event is beyond one man's power and capacity. It is a task to be fulfilled by the collective activity of many friends around the world.

This is only to give some highlights of the Congress in the shade of historical events and stimulate our imagination to correlate the early events of the Cause with the fruitful results of today's achievements.

First of all, our precious pioneers – those luminous souls who forsook their homes and friends and scattered far and wide and settled amongst people of many kinds – after all the years of separation from their friends, kith and kin, now once more came together.

Like unto sailors who, after many dangers and perils, found themselves safely ashore, they were ready to tell the wondrous stories of their travels and inspire the friends to do more.

Like unto lamps, shattered in parts and empty of fuel, once more in that atmosphere of love and unity they were refilled and were ready to return with more vigour and hope to their lonely and solitary posts.

As they sat in that hall and gazed upon the old familiar faces and the faces of their many new brothers and sisters from all over the planet, they remembered the many, many unendurable hours which they had suffered. Their shoulders were then lined with the garlands of the grateful appreciation of the Bahá'í world. Tears of joy, tears of profound memories of their years of loneliness, filled their eyes, but the King of Heaven and Earth wiped their tears away.

My eyes feasted upon the faces of many of them and found them all full of vigour and enthusiasm, but the one which impressed me most was that of our valiant pioneer to one of the islands off the shores of Africa. She is the oldest believer of the United States and has given in the path of God all that God had graciously bestowed upon her. Alone, with trembling hands and frail body, she kept the standard of the Faith unfurled for all these years in that solitary island. With eyes wide open she looked at me and said, ‘Now I am at rest and am going to my pioneering post and am ready to welcome death with joy and peace’.

Now let us go back to the first year of the Bahá’í Era. There was no other topic to be discussed throughout the length and breadth of Persia except the advent of a certain young man who claimed to be the Promised One.

To create fear and wrath in the hearts of the people, the governors, hand in hand with the religious authorities, decreed the demolition and confiscation of the properties of all who even appeared to be adherents of the new Faith.

One day, crowds of people gathered in the streets of Shíráz to watch a procession. The cruel and impious ruler of the town had reviled and cursed three men, stripped them of their clothes, burned their beards, scourged one of them with one thousand lashes, pierced their noses and passed cords through the incisions with which the three men were led through the town. These three heroes were: Quddús, Mullá Ṣádiq Muqaddas and Mullá ‘Alí Akbar Ardestání.

Now what has this to do with our story?

The daughter of no less a person than Mullá ‘Alí Akbar Ardestání was amongst the 6,000 friends who attended the Congress. Though extremely old and frail, and very weak in her eyes, she attended all the sessions. Though she did not understand a word of English, she sat there from morning till evening feeling exalted and happy beyond description by just being in that atmosphere so much imbued with the love of a Faith for the promulgation of which her father suffered so greatly.

What visions passed her mind and what waves of joy covered her aching heart when she sat in that hall?

The noble and graceful image of her illustrious father amidst vicissitudes, tribulations and painful humiliations, appeared in the far off horizons shedding light on the blissful course of love, well trodden by the lovers of God, and suddenly the quickening spirit of that Congress changed all the wild clamours of the mobs and the scornful laughter of the streets of Shíráz into the most penetrating chanting of the Greatest Name by our dearly beloved friends of Africa.

Then she remembered that not long ago the irresponsible farmers of a certain village near Ṭihrán attacked most ferociously the apple of her eye, her most beloved son, and tore him into pieces. No voice was raised against these atrocities and no signs of justice were ever manifested in the whole country. Through the torrents of tears shed in remembering the sad, sad hours of bereavement and silent sufferings, she witnessed the supreme legislative body of the Bahá'í World give new light to the whole of the world. Those nine precious and valiant souls stood there like unto a fortress in the heart of which the Cause of God would forever remain protected. 'Do you see your grandson?'[2] her daughter whispered in her ear. 'Do you see him there, one of the nine members of the Universal House of Justice?' A faint smile appeared on her lips and a sigh of relief took away the burden of one century of suffering from her loving heart. Verily it was the day when the faithful rejoiced.

NOTES AND REFERENCES

1 1963, London, England

2 Húshmand Fatḥ-i-A'ẓam is the great-grandson of Mullá 'Alí Akbar Ardestání, and his wife Shafíqih Khánum is the great-granddaughter of his fellow sufferer, Mullá Ṣádiq Muqaddas. The story of his father's martyrdom and life is carried in *The Bahá'í World*, Vol. XII, pp. 690–692.

Divine Education: The Root of Knowledge

The essence of all that
We have revealed for
thee is Justice, is for man
to free himself from
idle fancy and imitation,
discern with the eye of
oneness His glorious
handiwork, and look
into all things with a
searching eye.

The Journey of Truth Seeking

Of all the basic principles of Bahá'u'lláh for the safeguarding of the world order and unity of mankind, this principle of independent investigation of truth is one of the few which is directed solely to the individual, while the others are basically collective and primarily involve a social change.

For example, individuals are not responsible to adopt the international language or to formulate a universal system of education, but they do have to investigate the truth and to conduct the investigation independently of others. It is equally significant for us to realize that this principle is a two-edged sword; one edge separates falsehood from the truth, the other protects the individual believer against his own ego when confronted with divine tests.

It is important to know that this principle applies not only to man's spiritual life, but equally to whatever he desires to do. He goes through this process of investigation in all his major and minor actions. It is indeed inevitable and one of the most fundamental prerogatives of every individual.

The question is whether the attitude of Bahá'í parents toward their children should be to bring them up as Bahá'ís or to leave them to themselves, on the very wrong assumption and slender hope that the children would find the Faith on their own.

The latter is a misinterpretation of Divine Utterances and one of the greatest factors that contribute to the decrease in numbers, the spiritual destruction of Bahá'í families, and the lack of progress in the work of the Faith in many lands.

It is indeed unfortunate that some newly enrolled believers, due to their lack of knowledge about our all-comprehensive Faith, and in their desire to tread the path of least resistance, and to silence the voice of their conscience, misconstrue the very fundamental principle of Man's eternal life. Thus the gift of God entrusted to us, to be used as a torch which casts its rays through the obscure paths of life, is changed into a fire which consumes every fibre of our spiritual entity and allows nothing to survive except the skeleton of our physical creation, destined to be transformed into dust. I found to my utter grief that some Bahá'í families, though themselves active members of different Bahá'í communities, due to their grave misunderstanding of this fundamental principle, have not uttered even a word to their children about our eternal legacy – the glorious Faith.

Unmindful of the consequences of this ignorance in all the hearts and minds of their dear ones, they act as if they belong to a secret society. There is not a single token of the Faith in their well-furnished houses. I even found some of them ashamed to mention their religious affiliation. Thus the Faith remains unknown to their children who, I am sure, will disperse from their homes never gazing at the immense horizon floodlit with the rising Sun of Truth.

When asked, the parents have invariably answered: 'We want them to find it by themselves and investigate it independently.'

Such answers brought so much sorrow to my heart that I could not find adequate words and expressions to pour out my feelings.

'To find it by themselves'. What a false dictum. How will they find it? Through whom and from where, if not in their own homes, from their own parents' loving and vigilant directions? If we do not pity our children and we throw them to the devouring waves of this turbulent ocean called 'society', how do we expect others to pity them, hold their hands, save them and set them on the shores of safety and security?

If this is what we mean by 'independent investigation', why do we then exert our utmost to arrange schools for them, register their names well ahead of time, even many years in advance, for attendance at universities? Why do we keep on urging them to attend all their classes, and encouraging them to do better work and take pride in their daily advancement in what is called arts and sciences? Why do we not leave them free to find their own way to educational institutions and abandon them to their own choices, never asking them whether they spent their days in schools, or in bars and gambling houses?

For material education, we surely urge our children to go into special training, to acquire discipline, and we are vigilant to see that they will never lose any opportunity. But alas! In this, the most vital matter, which is like unto sunshine in all the aspects of the lives of our dear ones, and which ensures their eternal happiness, we remain heedless, nonchalant and carefree.

Should our intention be limited to raising ourselves from the distress of unbelief, doubt and scepticism to the condition of recognition, faith and certitude in the truth of the Mission of Bahá'u'lláh, when we reach this ultimate goal and recognize Him as the Divine Educator, then our journey ends.

It means that, thereafter, every act of Bahá'u'lláh and every utterance revealed by Him will have to be accepted as the manifestation of truth; and the spirit of investigation will help the traveller who has embarked on this journey to discard the impurities of falsehood from the gems of truth and advance on this path until every member of his physical temple and even every hair will find tongues to proclaim the light of the faith ignited in his heart and soul.

But the journey is not ended. Having reached the station of faith, the traveller is at the shore of an endless and fathomless ocean of divine utterances. He has to plunge into it, not to examine the truth of every word, principle or precept. Nay, on the contrary, with a heart full of certitude and an attitude of utter humility and supplication, the believer will meditate and pray and then seek to discover pearls of wisdom, and will behold beauty and innumerable mysteries enshrined in every word.

THE OBJECT OF ALL KNOWLEDGE

Before turning to the main subject of this essay, let us refer to the following two extracts from the immortal narrative of Nabíl to refresh our memory of the glorious deeds of the heroes and saints of our beloved Cause. These illustrate the two aspects of the problem at hand and will, I feel sure, shed much light on our research.

> As soon as the Call from Shíráz reached his ears, Ḥujjat deputed one of his disciples, Mullá Iskandar, in whom he reposed the fullest confidence, to enquire into the whole matter and to report to him the result of his investigations. Utterly indifferent to the praise and censure of his countrymen, whose integrity he suspected and whose judgment he disdained, he sent his delegate to Shíráz with explicit instructions to conduct a minute and independent enquiry. Mullá Iskandar attained the presence of the Báb and felt immediately the regenerating power of His influence. He tarried forty days in Shíráz, during which time he imbibed the principles of the Faith and acquired, according to his capacity, a knowledge of the measure of its glory.

With the approval of the Báb, he returned to Zanján. He arrived at a time when all the leading 'ulamás of the city had assembled in the presence of Ḥujjat. As soon as he appeared, Ḥujjat enquired whether he believed in, or rejected, the new Revelation. Mullá Iskandar submitted the writings of the Báb which he had brought with him, and asserted that whatever should be the verdict of his master, the same would he deem it his obligation to follow. 'What!' angrily exclaimed Ḥujjat. 'But for the presence of this distinguished company; I would have chastised you severely. How dare you consider matters of belief to be dependent upon the approbation or rejection of others?'

Receiving from the hand of his messenger the copy of the Qayyúmu'l-Asmá, he, as soon as he had perused a page of that book, fell prostrate upon the ground and exclaimed 'I bear witness that these words which I have read proceed from the same Source as that of the Qur'án. Whoso has recognized the truth of that sacred Book must needs testify to the Divine origin of these words, and must needs submit to the precepts inculcated by their Author. I take you, members of this assembly, as my witnesses: I pledge such allegiance to the Author of this Revelation that should He ever pronounce the night to be the day, and declare the sun to be a shadow, I would unreservedly submit to His judgment, and would regard His verdict as the voice of Truth. Whoso denies Him, him will I regard as the repudiator of God Himself.' With these words he terminated the proceedings of that gathering.[1]

It was in those days that his special envoy, Ma<u>sh</u>hadí Aḥmad, whom he had confidentially despatched to <u>Sh</u>íráz with a petition and gifts from him to the Báb, arrived at Zanján and delivered into his hands, while he was addressing his disciples, a sealed letter from his Beloved. In the Tablet he received, the Báb conferred upon him one of His own titles, that of Ḥujjat, and urged him to proclaim from the pulpit, without the least reservation, the fundamental teachings of His Faith. No sooner was he informed of the wishes of his Master than he declared his resolve to devote himself to the immediate enforcement of whatever injunction that Tablet contained. He immediately dismissed his disciples, bade them close their books, and declared his intention of discontinuing his courses of study. 'Of what profit', he said, 'are study and research to those who have already found the Truth, and why strive after learning when He who is the Object of all knowledge is made manifest?[2]

Every human temple, regardless of race, colour, country or clime, is considered by Bahá'u'lláh as a mine in which God has, through His inscrutable wisdom and boundless love, deposited gems which are to be discovered, polished and cultured through the process of proper, divine, all-embracing education.

These gems are the latent powers and talents with which every individual is endowed. When these powers and talents are discovered and correctly trained, the world of humanity will become the mirror of Heaven in which all divine perfections are gloriously reflected.

DIVINE EDUCATION – THE ROOT OF KNOWLEDGE

The vast subject of Bahá'í education has many ramifications stretching over all aspects of Man's life, and our Bahá'í literature is replete with elucidations which reveal to our eyes the most obscure corners of the human soul. How lamentable that mankind stubbornly abandons these abundant divine bounties and chooses the path of disgrace and perdition!

It is still more lamentable if those who believe in the Supreme Manifestation of God deprive themselves of following His loving advice. Until such time as we will have authorized classifications and translations of the holy texts, I shall limit myself in this essay to the references on parents' obligations toward their children.

We must first know that there is a vast difference between education, in the sense of character training, and instruction. The beloved Master has emphasized that education must always have priority over mere accumulation of knowledge.

To know many facts, to memorize numerous formulae and to repeat, parrot-like, theories of science is not honour for Man. True honour lies in Man's education and moral conduct which enable him to be the mirror of divine perfections and shine like unto a guiding star, ready to die rather than to apply his knowledge for the destruction of mankind.

It is toward this ultimate goal that we are encouraged to advance. Divine education is considered by Bahá'u'lláh to rank as the 'most weighty' amongst His commandments and is a great protection for the Cause of God. Educational institutions must first instil divine laws and precepts in the hearts and minds of children. Thus the children grow up to worship God and to love one another as His sons and daughters. Immediately after giving us this commandment, Bahá'u'lláh warns us against excess of any system which, individually or collectively, inculcates prejudice and intolerance in the innocent hearts of our children.

PARENTAL RESPONSIBILITY

Let us take a lesson from nature. When a mother conceives, nature creates a certain condition in her physical temple which forms the growing foetus. In that proper atmosphere the physical growth of the child starts. The parents, though intensely eager to behold the face of their little one, never force its birth. On the contrary, they patiently await the approach of the hour appointed by providence and keep every other thing in perfect harmony with the natural process. When that blessed moment comes through the operation of natural forces, the child is born into this immense world.

Now let us apply the same rule to the second home of the child, into which it is introduced through its physical birth.

By divine education at home, we mean the creation of an atmosphere in which the child can breathe the spiritual powers of this Age, and in due time like unto a rose, may blossom out, unfold, and proclaim his or her existence in the garden of God under the care and protection of the Divine Gardener. This cannot be achieved by force or by any form of compulsion, just as the child's birth cannot be realized by outside forces. We never try to pull the flower out of its stem in winter. The flowers will adorn the stems in due time, according to rules and regulations especially conferred upon the plants by the Creator.

Let us illustrate this by giving an example. The children who grow up in homes where the music of Mozart or Beethoven is often played surely grow to enjoy that kind of music. This is achieved because the atmosphere of the home was filled with such melodies. The child has breathed them in. As a matter of fact, this united aim becomes a focus which brings parents very close to each other.

Should the parents read the Writings each morning and evening as commanded by the Ancient Beauty; hold firesides in their homes where they show love, respect and reverence to the people regardless of race, class and creed; recite the obligatory prayers; fast; attend the Nineteen Day Feasts; celebrate the nine Holy Days; and, in all of these commemorations, have the children comprehend the importance and significance of each act, then there remains nothing for the parents to fear.

They will proudly watch the growing flowers in their own homes. Thus the spirit of the Cause will fill every layer in the atmosphere of the house.

The warmth and light of this divine love, emanated from such a home, will definitely help the little ones to grow into fruitful trees in the Garden of God, and, in due course, they will proclaim, not only by their words but also by the sanctity of their deeds, that they are gathered under the banner of the Greatest Name; committed to be soldiers in the army of life, winning victories in the forefront of the battle lines of teaching, consolidation and pioneering fields of service.

Our Writings further indicate that expectant mothers are advised to recite the words of God to foster the spiritual growth of the conceived children. After the birth of the child, the mother is exhorted to say prayers as she puts her dear ones to bed.

The influence of these words on the infants' hearts has been described as the influence of the light and the heat of sunshine on the growing flowers. As the children grow, the parents are called on to teach them the Words of God. At the age of five, they are to be gathered together to receive divine education.

We clearly observe that education is emphasized and is given the first rank in the order of importance. It is explicitly recommended to first teach the children courtesy and reverence, after which comes the acquisition of knowledge.

NEED FOR EARLY SPIRITUAL TRAINING

Knowledge must go hand in hand with divine education, otherwise Man's learning will be governed by greed and lust. These qualities will change science into a disgrace and bring about the eternal destruction of all Man's achievements. 'Abdu'l-Bahá, in His love for children, begs the friends to do their utmost to give proper Bahá'í education to their dear ones so they may understand the importance of the practice of its precepts in their lives.

He promises that the children trained in the divine gardens of love and in homes imbued with the Bahá'í spirit, will learn in one month what others will learn in twelve. He urges the parents to be diligent in directing the frail steps of their little ones to the path of eternal glory. All of this should be done with tender affection, loving care and kindness.

He warns us against beating the children and making them the victims of tongue lashings and rebukes. Experience shows that such treatment is detrimental to the proper growth of the child's mental, spiritual and even his physical powers; it dams the opening and inflow of their latent powers. In addition, they grow to hate their home and all that pertains to it.

We must always remember this fundamental principle of the Master, affirming that education of the child who is more than fifteen is extremely difficult and, in some cases, impossible.

Can we straighten a branch when it has become hard and stiff? Such children, we are warned by the Master, will be left in the abyss of misery, the victims of inequity, arrogance, pride and ignorance, and very often of mental deficiencies.

They will be despised and humiliated, sick and invalid, and forever ashamed of themselves. They will barely pass the tests of life. What will they think of their parents who had the torch of guidance and did not try to show it to their loved ones?

Parents who thus reduce their offspring to such depths of misery through their negligence will surely be responsible to God. We are emphatically warned by the Ancient Beauty that He will charge the parents with this negligence and will consider this as a great sin – a sin which will never be forgiven.

The injunction of Bahá'u'lláh to parents about the divine education of their children is so emphatic that, as pointed out by Him, those who ignore such a responsibility are, in the sight of God, deprived of their rights of parenthood.

I appeal to the hearts of the parents who desire nothing but the welfare of their children, the apples of their eyes, or, as the Arabs say, 'the fragments of their hearts which walk on earth', I supplicate them to ponder upon the conditions prevailing in the world and find out for themselves whether children need protection or whether they should be left to themselves and to the cruel influence of life.

That the world is too much with us and that society is overcome by many social diseases, no sound mind can ever deny. Pollution has penetrated into all the pores of Man's existence and the swamps of moral corruption have flooded the farthest and driest deserts and the most remote corners of every barren waste. Carnal desires and animal passions are unleashed and all aim to be gratified. Gratification of this beast of lust is to be fulfilled by all means – at the risk of breaking every sacred standard in Man's life. To accede to the desires of self has become a universal verdict.

Plunged into this overtly immoral world, where the raging beast of lust is the domineering monarch, caught in the throes of its devilish machinations, unable to separate the diabolical from the divine, and almost insensible to benevolent love, pity and reverence, our children, our poor children, find themselves engulfed by their own urges within and hypnotized by their dazzling and alluring lights. Don't they need lamps at their feet, an inherent and powerful force to enable them to live as true human beings, to walk with celestial pride and to lead a clean, a holy and pure life as a prelude to the eternal one?

PROTECTION OF BAHÁ'U'LLÁH'S TEACHINGS

Whatever the explanation the world may give and however it justifies its present plight, it is crystal clear to the adherents of our Faith that the road projected by Bahá'u'lláh through this world enveloped in darkness is illumined by the protective measures of His teachings.

The unpardonable forgetfulness and negligence of parents in their attitude toward their children are the result of wrong deductions and will, ultimately, bring the children to the abyss of disgrace and shame and, in the life to come, will hold them subject to God's justice.

If we live in a house without a lamp, the consequences of unseen troubles and even disasters will no doubt await us. If we do not ignite the fire of faith in the hearts of our little ones, the decline of their mental, physical and spiritual lives will immediately set in. Where there is light everything is properly placed and clearly seen; and the residents of the house can use everything with proper perspective. The same thing is true of the light of faith when ignited in the hearts and souls of children. Then all their God-given gifts, talents and capacities will function harmoniously and efficiently.

As the immense horizon of life stretches in front of our children's eyes, we see them torn between two forces. The one pulls them down to the point where all their pleasures turn into agony; and the other, symbolized by a voice within them, seeks to lift them to summits of splendours where even death is changed into glory and eternity. Look at them with their expectant, innocent and bewildered eyes, undecided amidst the controversial and devouring forces of life. Do we sit comfortably in our seats as Roman spectators and watch human lives thrown into the mouths of beasts? Or, as honest parents, do we help them, guide them, and assist them to raise their eyes and behold the rising Sun of Glory?

BACKBITING QUENCHES THE SPIRIT

From my experience, I know of one calamity which pitilessly brings gradual death to the growing spirit of our children. This disaster is very often an undesired guest, but alas, sometimes is invited, given the best seats – our hearts – and is offered the sweetest moments of our precious lives. It is like the freezing breeze of midwinter which passes through almond groves, kills the blossoms and leaves the poor farmers, who were comfortably settled in their warm rooms, poverty-stricken and sorrowful.

This hideous intruder is backbiting. No matter how much we endeavour to bring up our children in the spirit of the Faith, to teach them its laws, principles and precepts, if there is the slightest whisper of backbiting in our homes, let us be sure that our dear little ones are gone forever and irretrievably lost.

The perilous effects are so imperceptible that one's own ego is not warned and the parents are not alerted to the symptoms of the spreading spiritual ailment. One of the old teachers of the Cause used to say that we try to pull a very heavy load to the top story of the house, and when the load is up, an ignorant man applies the sharp edge of his knife to the rope carrying the load. The downfall is sure. All the efforts of the many labourers who pulled the load are lost forever and in one instant. The same thing is true of the poisonous atmosphere created by this hideous guest in our own abode.

We think the children are playing with their toys and are not paying attention to what we are saying. It may be true that they do not consciously respond to the conversation of their elders, but their eyes see and their ears hear and register things within. The children's hearts and souls are like clean mirrors or containers of pure, crystal and translucent water. Every word uttered by us against other friends, like a drop of ink, sinks deep into their transparent hearts.

At the beginning, the colour may not seem to have changed, but we know that it is absorbed with all its poisonous effects. Should the drops of the poison be repeated, the child's whole existence becomes victim to a spiritual disease, the first symptoms of which are reluctance to attend Bahá'í classes, grudges, and even sometimes hatred, toward other Bahá'ís.

What do we expect our children to do when we as elders sit in our homes and talk against our fellow Bahá'ís, members of committees and local Spiritual Assemblies, and perhaps the secretary or a member of the National Assembly?

The children look up to these divine institutions and we lower them to the dust in their growing minds and loving hearts. Then when they are of age, they do not feel any sense of security and safety in the friends' homes, nor do they trust Bahá'í committees, local Spiritual Assemblies or the National Spiritual Assembly. That is why, when we ask them to attend classes or summer schools, their reaction is obviously antagonistic. It is exactly as if we paralyse the child and then ask him to run, or starve him and then demand the performance of athletic feats.

NOTES AND REFERENCES

1 *The Dawn-Breakers, Nabíl's Narrative*, pp. 178–179
Bahá'í Publishing Committee, New York, 1932, 1953 edition.

2 ibid. pp. 532–533

Explanation of the Symbol of the Greatest Name

Publisher's note:

In this explanation by Mr Faizí, he refers on page 36 to the recitation of the Greatest Name (Alláh-u-Abhá) 95 times a day, which is mentioned in the Kitáb-i-Aqdas. This text was first published in 1968, before Shoghi Effendi's *A Synopsis and Codification of the Laws and Ordinances of the Kitáb-i-Aqdas* was published in 1973, or the first official English translation of the Kitáb-i-Aqdas was released in 1992. As such, this requirement was not universally applied at the time and, as Mr Faizí notes, Shoghi Effendi had said it was 'not absolutely binding'. In their letter of 28 December 1999 however, the Universal House of Justice announced that a number of laws from the Aqdas regarding obligatory prayer and fasting were to be universally implemented and applicable to all, including the recitation of the Greatest Name 95 times each day.

From eternity Thou hast been removed far above the reach
and the ken of the comprehension of Thy servants,
and immeasurably exalted above the strivings of Thy
bondslaves to express Thy mystery.

– *Bahá'u'lláh*

The identity of the Greatest Name – a mystery concealed from time immemorial 'behind the mystic veil' and preserved in the treasure house of the knowledge of God, was to be revealed and manifested to Men's eyes at its appointed time in accordance with the Divine Plan, like the other manifold and basic truths of the New Age.

Allusions had been made to it by the Messengers of old, under the impact of whose Revelations Man has made spiritual progress and gradually attained a clearer understanding of its hidden meanings. Like a brilliant sun wrapt in clouds, the Greatest Name remained hidden and unknown. Those who longed to catch a glimpse of its splendour drew close, but enjoyed only a dim vision of its radiance. Throughout past centuries, in accordance with the inscrutable wisdom of God's progressive revelation of truth, the veils remained until gradually, one by one, they were removed from this precious and all-embracing Name.

ANTICIPATED IN PAST RELIGIONS

The eager followers of past religions, in their deep desire to witness a flickering of the approaching majestic dawn, found that the new Name of the Great One to come meant 'light', 'splendour' and 'glory'. The followers of Krishna, for instance, expected His return under the name of *Vishnu Yasha*, which in Sanskrit means 'Glory of God'. The last chapter of the *Shrimad Bhagawad* of the Hindu Scripture states: 'Vishnu Yasha will possess great energy, intelligence and prowess … He will restore order and peace in this world … Man in general will begin to honour and practise truth.'[1]

One of the Bahá'í scholars in the Middle East, whose father had formerly superintended a Buddhist Temple, and who was himself well-versed in the writings of that Faith, told me that many times he had read the entire Gospel of Buddha in Sanskrit, every word of which he had understood with the exception of the meaning of a word composed of 'b', 'h' and 'a', which occasionally appears in Buddhist Scripture. When he learned of the Bahá'í Faith, the mystery was solved. The letters, joined together, formed the name of 'Bahá'.

The references by Buddha are exceptionally clear. Ananda, one of His disciples, asked Him: 'Who shall teach us when Thou art gone?' Buddha replied in these clear terms:

> I am not the first Buddha who came upon earth, nor shall I be the last. In due time another Buddha will arise … He shall reveal to you the same eternal truths which I have taught you. He will preach to you His religion, glorious in its origin, glorious at the climax and glorious at the goal, in the spirit and in the letter.[2]

It is most interesting to note that in Buddhist Scripture, particularly in the Amitayus Sutra, clear reference is made to *Amitabha* as the 'Infinite Light of Revelation', the 'Unbounded Light' and the 'Source of Wisdom, of Virtue and of Buddhahood'. When giving the qualities of a 'true follower', Buddha stated that it was he who 'relies with his heart upon Amitabha … the unbounded Light of Truth'.[3]

The Jewish mystics knew of the significance of the two letters 'b' and 'h' and attached much importance to them. Their spiritual leaders and philosophers wrote commentaries and drew the attention of seeking souls to these letters. There is a legend among the Jews about Solomon's Seal, a seal said to have carried the Greatest Name from which it reputedly derived its power over all creation, including the animal world.

In Isaiah, we read, '… Lebanon is ashamed and hewn down; Sharon is like a wilderness; and Bashan and Carmel shake off their fruits'.[4] Isaiah also says, 'The glory of Lebanon shall be given unto it, the excellency of Carmel and Sharon; they shall see the glory of the Lord and the excellence of our God.'[5]

It is interesting to compare this last verse with its Arabic version which, when translated literally into English, reads as follows: 'God will render to Lebanon its glory: the Bahá of Carmel and Sharon shall be manifested, and they shall see the glory of God, the Bahá of our Lord.'[6] When Jesus spoke to the Jews who were familiar with these terms, He told them that He would return 'in the glory of the Father'.

As the Islamic Faith immediately preceded the New Day, followers of Islám found that the veils covering this hidden treasure had become more diaphanous, allowing the heavenly rays of light to penetrate deeper, and to reveal in sharper detail the reality of this mystery. Explicit references had been made to the Greatest Name, and, as the seekers found clear indications of these references, they became encouraged to persevere in their search.

The words of the Imáms and divines of Islám served to draw the longing souls to the fountainhead of true knowledge. There is a very powerful prayer which the Shí'ih Muslims chant as a dawn prayer during the month of the fast. The faithful believer awakens at dawn to catch the melody of its tune as it is chanted from the minarets of mosques or, in these days, is broadcast from the radio stations. In introducing this prayer, Imám Riḍá has said, 'I swear by God that the Greatest Name is found in this prayer. Had you known this, you would have fought with swords to possess this prayer.'[7] The opening words of this prayer read as follows: 'O God! My God! I beseech Thee by Thy Bahá, Thy Bahá in its entirety. I beseech Thee by all Thy Bahá.' The prayer then goes on mentioning other Names of God including 'Beauty', 'Splendour', and all the Names which are a part of the Bahá'í calendar.

ACCLAIMED BY POETS

Poets and philosophers found this mystic secret and openly acclaimed it. At the time of Sháh 'Abbás, the Persian King and contemporary of Queen Elizabeth I, the greatest of all the divines of that age went to Persia from Lebanon and established his residence in Iṣfahán which was then the royal seat and the country's capital. This man had an encyclopaedic mind and he wrote outstanding books on the arts, sciences, the literature and philosophy of his age. There are many stories about him and his unique erudition and genius. It is even said that he had invented a machine which reproduced voices from distant lands. One of his discoveries was the Greatest Name, and he adopted the name of 'Bahá'í' for himself. Shaykh Bahá'í is unquestionably the most renowned of all Persian divines. In one of his poetical works he says, 'The Greatest Name is unknown to man, but in the list of all the Names of God it stands first.' No doubt he had in mind the dawn prayer mentioned above which opens with the name of Bahá.

Mawlaví, the greatest of all the mystic poets of the East, whose poems are known for their elucidations of the spiritual journey of Man and his attainments in the realms of God, has stated, 'We have found Bahá and we hasten to offer our life as a sacrifice to Him. He is our ransom.'[8]

Ḥáfiẓ, the most renowned of all lyric poets of the East, addressed Persia, saying, 'May this land remain forever prosperous. From its sacred soil at every breath the breezes of the Merciful are wafted. Glad tidings to the glorious Kings of Persia! Glad tidings for a blissful ending! The power of the Greatest Name has stayed away the hand of evil from that country.'

While I was in Arabia, I examined the manuscript of a book on mystic philosophy from one of the learned men there. In one chapter the author speaks of the conditions to be observed by the seeker of the path to God, and says, 'Those who tread the path and knock at the door of the knowledge of the Light are sincere and forbearing. They stand face to face with angels who greet them, cleanse, and purify them. They pour for them water from the fountainhead of Bahá. When they open their eyes they behold God passing by with great majesty. His name appears above the horizon of the Kingdom. Those people, though they wander on earth, have their hearts attached to the Exalted Spot[9] and the dwellers in the Great Tabernacle.'

MADE KNOWN TO BÁBÍS

With the inauguration of the New Age and the appearance of its Herald, the Báb, the remaining veils were torn asunder through the movement of His Exalted Pen. The people began to know more and more clearly that 'Bahá' was, without any shadow of doubt, the name so dearly treasured and destined to be manifested with all splendour and majesty. The explicit nature of the Báb's reference to Bahá'u'lláh and the glowing terms with which He praised Him made 'Bahá' the focus of adoration.

The Báb singled out the Greatest Name in the manuscript copies of His matchless Writings. Years ago, I had the honour to read three volumes of His Writings before they were despatched to the beloved Guardian. The books were written down by Mullá 'Alí Akbar Ardestání[10] in the first year of the Báb's Dispensation. These books were written in black ink, but whenever the many references were made to 'Bahá', this word always appeared in red. During the very first year of His ministry, the Báb had instructed His amanuensis to write in this manner in order that those who had no time or patience to read all His Writings would be helped to see this Name.

There are innumerable references to 'Bahá' in all the Writings of the Báb and to quote them all here is beyond the scope of this essay. It is sufficient to note that He has said, 'Well is it with him who fixeth his gaze upon the Order of Bahá'u'lláh and rendereth thanks unto his Lord.'[11]

When the followers of the Báb gathered under special circumstances at Badasht, it was there that everyone received a new name. It was then that they knew this shining diadem of majesty and might found its eternal manifestation, not on the forehead of one who was clad in the garments of the learned; but shone instead on that of a Youth who was majestic in appearance, glorious in gait and manners, and godly in every atom of His being. So exalted was He in the eyes of the people, so highly respected and adored that, out of sheer homage and love, they did not dare to mention His name. Instead He was referred to as *Íshán*.[12]

The Letters of the Living and the early believers now knew the Bearer of this Name and recognized in Him such heavenly attributes that, even though they had quaffed from the newly found stream of life, they prayed and longed for the even more glorious day when they could be drowned in the powerful, celestial ocean of the Utterance of this Great One.

Ṭáhirih, in one of her epistles, says, 'O my God! O my God! The veil must be removed from the face of the Remnant of the Lord. O my God! Protect Ḥusayn the mystery of Muḥammad and advance the day of reunion with him … Make the point of Bahá, O my God, to circulate … O my God! Protect all who circumambulate the twin points and keep them steadfast in Thy most Great Cause, so that they might behold the point sending forth light upon them.'

It was no wonder that so many hundreds of learned and outstanding divines of the East sacrificed their lives with devotion and faith in the path of the promulgation of the Greatest Name. They waited for its advent, waited for the moment when the effulgences would emanate from it. The instant they felt it was ascending toward the dawning point, they burned themselves in its light and rose like glowing lamps. They became the Dawn Breakers.

There are numerous references to the name, the place of birth, the date of declaration, the places of banishment, the imprisonment and the fate of the Central Figures of our Faith. For the purposes of this essay it is sufficient to know this great, authentic Islamic tradition: 'All the followers of the Promised Qá'im shall be put to death except One whose face shall shine with Abhá beauty in the plain of 'Akká.'

From this introduction we gather that the Greatest Name is 'Bahá'. This point should be well understood and borne in mind as we proceed to fathom, with our limited means, this tremendous divine mystery. It will be necessary to proceed slowly and patiently, step by step, in order to discuss each phase of this essential theme, so that we might have a full grasp of all the problems pertaining to the subject.

The Báb adored the name 'Bahá' and used it profusely in all His Writings. He even made many derivatives from this one word and wrote them out in a Tablet which had the form of a five pointed star, symbolizing the human temple.

Far from attempting to make an exhaustive study of this subject, we merely set forth a few points at random to pave the way for a clearer understanding of this theme, the 'Symbol of the Greatest Name'.

THE SYMBOL OF THE GREATEST NAME

Our explanation of the symbol of the Greatest Name is based mainly on Tablets revealed by the beloved Master and will cover the topics as follows in this article.

WHO DESIGNED THE SYMBOL?

One of the believers who had the bounty and privilege of attaining the presence of the beloved Master has recorded one of His oral statements which shows that this emblem was initiated by Him. No less a person than ‘Abdu’l-Bahá could have designed this emblem, for who else could have condensed so much of the divine mystery into so little space and into so few letters! Some of the mystic divines among the Israelites have emphatically drawn the attention of their followers to the two letters ‘b’ and ‘h’ indicating that they have some idea about the Greatest Name.

It has been said that the Greatest Name was the leading decoration of the Temple. The Muslims were better acquainted with it but not in this form and finality. One finds in the Islamic laws governing worship and reverence that whoever possesses a ring bearing the symbol of the Greatest Name, must wear the ring on their right hand.

The friends are not obliged by Bahá’u’lláh to wear a ring carrying this emblem since there is no specific law by Bahá’u’lláh in the Aqdas or in His Tablets regarding this. The beloved Master told the friends in the West that the ring should be placed on the right hand, which is a perpetuation of the Islamic law referred to above.

SOME DERIVATIVES OF THE NAME 'BAHÁ'

BAHÁ Light or Glory	بهاء
ABHÁ Most Glorious	أَبهىٰ
AL-ABHÁ (sometimes used as El-Abhá) The All-Glorious – The Most Glorious.	أَلأَبهىٰ
BAHÍYYIH Full of Glory The Greatest Holy Leaf	بهيّه
ALLÁH-U-ABHÁ God, the All-Glorious. This is a Bahá'í greeting initiated and used since the days of Adrianople.[13] Its use, ninety-five times each day, according to an instruction written on behalf of the beloved Guardian, 'is not absolutely binding'. 'Alláh-u-Abhá' is to be repeated in the long obligatory prayer where instructions call for use of the Greatest Name.	أَللّٰهُ أَبهىٰ

YÁ BAHÁ'U'L-ABHÁ

This is an invocation.
It means 'O Glory of the All-Glorious'.
In this connection, we recall the soul-stirring message of the Guardian in 1953 to the Intercontinental Conferences, where he refers to 'Yá Bahá'u'l-Abhá' and 'Yá 'Alíyyu'l-A'lá' as the 'battle cry' of the pioneers and teachers in the many fields of this world-embracing spiritual Crusade.

The first, as already stated, means 'O Glory of the All-Glorious', while the second means 'O Exalted of the Most Exalted One' (The Báb). There is nothing in the Writings which says we have to repeat such an invocation a specific number of times each day. However, what a thrill it would be for us in times of dire need, to seek God's guidance, His support and strength, by addressing Bahá'u'lláh and the Báb directly with these beautiful invocations! Yá Bahá'u'l-Abhá is symbolized above.

EXPLANATIONS

We will begin with the basic pattern of the design and, as we proceed, the picture will be complete. This part of the symbol comprises three levels, each level indicated by a number. Together they represent the underlying belief which is the basis of all the religions of God. They are as follows:

(1) THE WORLD OF GOD – THE CREATOR 

(2) THE WORLD OF THE PROPHETS OR MANIFESTATIONS – CAUSE, OR COMMAND 

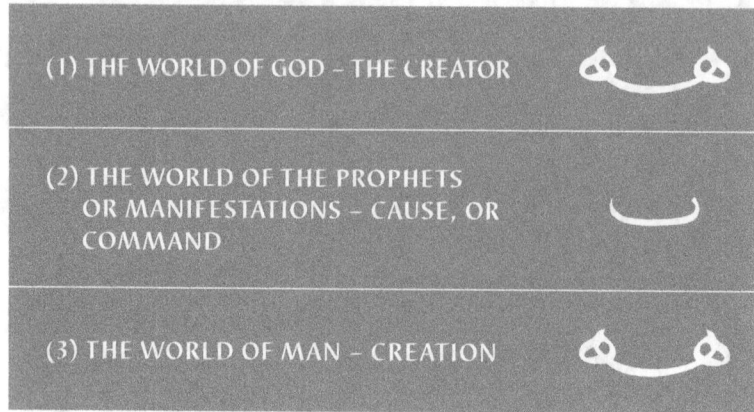

(3) THE WORLD OF MAN – CREATION 

The followers of all religions believe that Man, left to himself, can never recognize God and attain His presence; nor is Man able to fathom the mystery and purpose of his own creation. God, in His unlimited bounty has singled out His Chosen Ones, and will continue to do so, sending Them to mankind at different times and ages in order to grant humanity penetrating insight and to enable them to have a glimpse of the unfading glories of the innumerable worlds beyond.

The Prophets accept descent from their realms on high and suffer the abasement of living in human temples, walking amongst Men and speaking their languages. The Manifestations are invariably denied, ridiculed, humiliated and even put to death. Were it not for Their spiritual upliftment and leadership, Man would have continued to live as wild beasts and would have been eternally doomed to deprivation and loss.

These functions of the Prophets are clearly demonstrated in the design of the Greatest Name by having the world of the Prophets (shown in horizontal line) repeated in a vertical line, thus joining the world of the Creator to that of His creation.

Contrary to this, mystics believe in only two worlds: the world of God and the world of Man. They proclaim that should Man cleanse himself from all worldly desires and earthly attachments, he will be enabled to attain the presence of his Lord, the Creator. The mystics claim there is no need for an intermediary link between God and His creation. They therefore believe in, and practise, ascetic lives which sometimes takes them to secluded corners of the world, occasionally in the mountains, forests, and jungles. This hermit's life is utterly forbidden by the mighty Pen of Bahá'u'lláh because He desires every Man to be a fruitful member of the society he lives in.

The Bahá'ís believe that no matter what height of spiritual, scientific and material success Man may reach, he is and will forever be in need of divine guidance bestowed upon him by the Prophets of God. It is only through Them that Man can comprehend the secrets of true civilization and recognize the Will of God and His Purpose. The Bahá'ís also believe that it is through a complete understanding and the full establishment of Their highly valued and vital precepts and teachings that Man can attain the highest state of happiness, and eventually rejoice in the presence of his Lord.

Let us ponder once more upon this design and behold with our own eyes the perfect realization of Christ's prayer. The lights of the Kingdom on High are mirrored forth by the Manifestations of God upon the plane of creation, thus fulfilling the promise of the appearance of God's Kingdom on earth, as it is in heaven.

THE LETTERS IT CONTAINS

Let us study the letters in the symbol to discover what they signify. The letters 'b' and 'h' in the original script are written as:

B	ب
H	ه

'B' stands for the name of Bahá and 'H' stands for the name of the Báb.[14]

To grasp the significance and the important implications of this beautiful and artistic combination, we must bear in mind that among the Near-Eastern people, the Phoenicians were the first to sail their boats to distant lands. Wherever they travelled, they established trading centres, and, as traders, found themselves forced to adopt some practical ways of recording their commercial transactions. The characters they adopted became their alphabet and, in the course of centuries, this alphabet developed and gradually became a pattern of alphabets used in both the East and the West. Gibbon says 'Phoenicia and Palestine will forever live in the memory of mankind; since America, as well as Europe, have received letters from the one, and religion from the other.'

'The use of letters was introduced among the savages of Europe about fifteen hundred years before Christ; and the Europeans carried them to America about fifteen centuries after the Christian era. But in a period of three thousand years, the Phoenician alphabet received considerable alterations; as it passed through the hands of the Greeks and Romans.'[15] Will Durant, in his monumental *Story of Civilization*, describes this contribution as the most precious legacy of the ancient cultures.

ANCIENT ALPHABETS

The Phoenicians used their alphabet for both letters and numbers, therefore each letter had a numerical value. Their alphabet starts as follows[16]:

LETTER	A	B	J	D	H	W	Z
NUMERICAL VALUE	1	2	3	4	5	6	7
LETTER	H	T	I	K	L	M	N
NUMERICAL VALUE	8	9	10	20	30	40	50

When the Phoenicians wished to say, 'One house; two years; or nine letters', they would write, 'a house; b years; t letters'. There are some very interesting remnants of the influence exerted by this very ancient people of the Near East still to be found in the western languages of today. The four letters, 'K', 'L', 'M' and 'N' are in the same order in English, French and some other western alphabets just as they appeared in the Phoenician alphabets, illustrated above.

The next stage in the science of numbers was the acquisition of numbers by the Muslims who acquired them from the Indians. Added to the nine digits of the Indians, the 'zero' discovered by the Arabs completed the science of numbers. The world is indebted to the Indians for this very valuable and fundamental contribution. Had it not been for these numbers, the science of mathematics would have stood still, and without mathematics Man could not have progressed in technology, nor could he have fashioned instruments with which he changes the face of the earth today.

The people of the East continued to give numerical values to the letters of their alphabet even though they had the Indian numbers. Today it is still common to find that poets, doctors of religion and writers, convey their thoughts through this symbolic method of letters and their numerical value.

This method was used a great deal by the Báb. He very often gave people and places surnames which had the same numerical value as the original names. For example, He called Máh-kú, *Básit* (open). Máh-kú and Básit have the same numerical value of 72. He called Chihríq, *Shadíd* (Grievous).

Both of these have a numerical value of 318. Likewise, the great author of *The Dawn-Breakers* was named Muḥammad, but surnamed Nabíl; both names have a numerical value of 92. It is this same method which is used for the designs of the symbols of the Greatest Name.

THE NAMES OF THE BÁB AND BAHÁ'U'LLÁH

We repeat that the two letters 'b' and 'h' stand for the names of Bahá'u'lláh and the Báb respectively.

The numerical value of 'Báb' is:

B	A	B	Total
2	1	2	5

The numerical value of 'Bahá' is:

B	A	H	A	Total
2	1	5	1	9

Nine is the perfect number, on the top of the ladder of the numerical progressive elevation. It is very mysterious and, more than any other number, full of special qualities and potencies. The numbers end with nine. After nine, whatever we write in the form of digits is repetition of the same figures. Mankind, throughout the ages, will gradually fathom the mysteries of this special number which is the numerical manifestation of the Greatest Name: Bahá.

ADAM AND EVE ARE INCLUDED

Number nine contains all the digits from one to nine and number five from one to five which when added respectively will be:

1 + 2 + 3 + 4 + 5+ 6 + 7 + 8 + 9 = 45

1 + 2 + 3 + 4 + 5 = 15

Now the names of Adam and Eve in the Oriental scripts are written as follows: ADM (ADAM) and HWA (HAWA), the numerical values of which are as follows, respectively:

A	D	M	Total
1	4	40	45

H	W	A	Total
8	6	1	15

Thus we find that two traditional names, Adam and Eve, God's first two spiritual creations, referred to in the Scriptures of old and held in such reverence and love by Man throughout the ages, are linked with the twin Manifestations referred to in all the Books of God, and whose appearance was promised to be on the Last Day. Thus Adam and Eve are connected with the Báb and Bahá'u'lláh in this great symbol, which becomes a token of oneness between the past and the present.

THE ESSENCE OF SACRIFICE AND THE ESSENCE OF SERVITUDE

The two five pointed stars on both sides of the emblem represent the human body: a head, two hands and two feet. These two stars represent the twin Manifestations of God in this Day. Their advent is the fulfilment of all the writings of God's Prophets in bygone ages, who, emphatically, repeatedly and often, in a language clearer than the light of the sun, assured mankind of the undoubted appearance of these Twin Luminaries, who would rescue the world from the fetters of prejudice and the dictates of self.

In conclusion, may I venture to suggest another approach to the meaning of the two stars. This approach is merely a personal one, therefore not authoritative. Could we not visualize God as manifested in His most resplendent glory in the majestic figure of Bahá'u'lláh, and standing on either side of Him, two towering personalities of unsurpassed beauty: the Báb, the Herald, the incarnation of sacrifice and of self-effacement and the highest expression of true love ever possible in this contingent life; and 'Abdu'l-Bahá, the Centre of the Covenant, the true Exemplar of the teachings and the highest embodiment of servitude. These two exemplify the mysteries of sacrifice and servitude, calling on all men to hasten and offer their potentialities as humble gifts for the establishment of God's redeeming Order, the very reflection of His Kingdom on earth.

NOTES AND REFERENCES

1 Prof. Pritam Singh, *The Second Coming of Shri Krishna*, p. 10.

2 Sermon of the Great Passing.

3 Shírín Khánum, *Lord Buddha and Amitabha*, pp. 13, 17–19.

4 *Isaiah*, chapter 33, verse 9.

5 *Isaiah*, chapter 35, verse 2.

6 *Holy Bible*, Arabic translation, 1881, Third Ed., also: Ishráq Khávarí, *Raḥíq-i-Makhtúm* (The Sealed Wine) pp. 218–219.

7 *Mafatihu'l Jenan*, 'Keys of Paradise', compilation of Muslim Prayers.

8 A Tradition, also referred to in *The Dawn-Breakers*: 'Whoso seeketh Me, shall find Me', p. 72 (1932 edition).

9 *Maqám-i-A'lá* is the name given by 'Abdu'l-Bahá to the Shrine of the Báb. It means 'the Exalted Spot'.

10 *The Dawn-Breakers*, p. 146, footnote no. 3 (1932 edition).

11 Shoghi Effendi, *God Passes By*, p. 25.

12 Honorific form of Persian pronoun for the third person singular.

13 Shoghi Effendi, *God Passes By*, p. 176.

14 Abú-Basír says that he asked the Imám Ja'far as to the meaning of *Besmellah* (in the name of God). The Imám answered, 'The letter 'b' stands for Bahá'u'lláh ...', *Fazilat Besmellah*, p. 44 by Abbass Rezai, Tehran.

15 Edward Gibbon, *The Decline and Fall of the Roman Empire*, Ch. 1, p. 32.

16 The Hebrew alphabet used by Israeli people today is exactly the same.

A Flame of Fire

The Story of the Tablet of Aḥmad

There are two Tablets each bearing the name of Aḥmad: one in Persian and the other in Arabic. The latter is the one used throughout the Bahá'í world, which the beloved Guardian characterized as being imbued with a special potency.

The Persian Tablet[1] is quite a long one and is written to Aḥmad of Ká<u>sh</u>án. Ḥájí Mírzá Jání, who was the first one to embrace the Báb's Faith in Ká<u>sh</u>án, in whose house the Báb sojourned[2] some days and who was finally martyred in Ṭihrán, had three brothers.

One was never moved by his brother's faith, no matter how much the latter endeavoured to teach him. He remained a Muslim and died as such. The second was called Ismá'íl, entitled by Bahá'u'lláh *<u>Dh</u>abíḥ*[3] (sacrificed) and also *Anís* (companion); the third one who went to Ba<u>gh</u>dád was called Aḥmad.

He remained with the Ancient Beauty and had the honour to be amongst those who were chosen by Him as one of the companions in His exile to Istanbul. But unfortunately, in the storms of tests and trials, this Aḥmad departed from the right path and sided with Azal.[4]

He then caused much suffering for the Blessed Beauty, His family and friends. In order to warn this man against such evil deeds and the detrimental consequences for the nascent Faith, Bahá'u'lláh sent him this long Persian Tablet full of exhortations, elucidations of the divine power and advice as to how a true seeker should act and behave. Aḥmad remained heedless, unmoved and unchanged, but when he found out that he could no more live in Turkey, he returned to Iraq where he found his old associates and resumed his iniquitous life with them. One of his worst habits was to insult people and curse them in the most bitter and vile language.

In one of his disputes with his evil friends, he lashed them with his sharp tongue and the victims, to get rid of him, killed him one night.

AḤMAD BEGINS HIS SEARCH

As to the Aḥmad in whose honour the well-known Tablet is revealed, he was born in Yazd (circa 1805) to a very noble and rich family. His father and uncles were the chieftains of the town, but Aḥmad, even at the age of fourteen, showed a great inclination towards mysticism and endeavoured to find new paths to truth. When he was fifteen, he had already started his investigations during which he heard from some of the people that there are saints or holy men who know special prayers which, if read and repeated so many times and in accordance with certain rituals, would definitely enable the reader to behold the countenance of the Promised Qá'im (The Messiah).

This flared up the fire of his ever-growing longings. He began to practise an ascetic life with long prayers, successive days of fasting and secluding himself from people and from the world. His parents and relatives never approved of such practices, nor did they permit him to continue this seclusion which was contrary to their ways of life and ambition.

Such opposition could not be tolerated by a man like Aḥmad who was wholeheartedly searching and striving to reach his heart's desire – reunion with his eternal Beloved. Therefore, one day early in the morning, he made a small bundle of his clothes and belongings and under the pretext of going to a public bath, departed from his father's home and set out on his way to search for God's manifestation.

In a beggar's outfit he roamed from village to village, and wherever he found a *pír* (spiritual leader), with great devotion and rectitude of conduct, he sat at his feet in the hope of finding a path to the mysterious worlds of truth. He invariably begged such people for the special prayer, the reading of which would draw him near the court of his Beloved. Whenever someone would suggest to him any practice, he was so ardent in his search that he would invariably carry out the instructions with absolute sincerity no matter how time-consuming or arduous those practices were. But all of this was of no avail.

Losing hope and faith in such pursuits, he made his way to India, a land so well known for its mystic teachers and hermits with special powers and spiritual gifts. He reached Bombay, and took up his residence there, still looking for someone to give him a glimpse of the glorious court of the Promised One.

He heard that if one would perform a specific ablution, put on spotlessly clean white garments, prostrate oneself and repeat the following verse of the Qur'án, 'There is no God but God' twelve thousand times, he would definitely attain his aim and heart's desire. Not once, but several times, Aḥmad prostrated himself for hours to repeat the above-mentioned verse 12,000 times, but still found himself in darkness. In his dismay he returned to Persia, but did not go to his own hometown of Yazd. He settled in the city of Káshán and started his own craft of cloth-making, in which he was an expert. In no time he became a very successful businessman; but still, in his inmost heart he was restlessly searching.

A STRANGER POINTS THE WAY

'Knock, and it shall be opened unto you.' 'Ask, and it shall be given you.'[5] No true seeker ever returned from His door of mercy deprived or unanswered. It was here in Káshán that the rumours about One claiming to be the Promised Qá'im were heard by Aḥmad. Ceaseless in his efforts and sincere in his search, he asked many people in many different ways. No one ever gave him a clue.

Then one day an unknown traveller arrived in this town and stayed in the same inn where Aḥmad had established his successful business. A certain inner urge drew Aḥmad close to this unknown man. In their conversation, the traveller was asked about the already spreading rumour. 'Why do you ask this question?' he inquired. 'I want to know if it is true. If it is, I shall follow it, with all my might', was Aḥmad's rejoinder.

The traveller, with a smile of triumph on his face, instructed him to go to Khurásán and find a certain famous learned man called Mullá 'Abdu'l-Khaliq who would tell him the whole truth.

The very next day Aḥmad was on his way to the province of Khurásán. The owners of the neighbouring shops were very much surprised when they did not find Aḥmad at his work as usual. 'What passed between him and the unknown traveller?' they asked one another, and no one knew the right answer.

Aḥmad crossed deserts and mountains on foot, and his heart overflowed with joy and longing. Every step he took he found himself nearer to the time when all his efforts would yield the desired fruits – his reunion with his Beloved in the search of whom he spared no effort and found no sacrifice too great.

He reached Mashhad, Khurásán, exhausted and so ill that he had to stay in bed. After two months' struggle to overcome his weakness, he mustered the last ounces of his strength and courage and went directly to the door of the desired house.

Here are his own words as related to his friends and companions of those days:

> When I reached the house, I knocked at the door and the servant of the house came forth. Holding the door ajar, he asked me, 'What do you want?' 'I must see your Master', I answered. The man went back into the house and then the Mullá himself came out. He admitted me to his house and when we stood face to face I explained to him all that had happened to me. When I finished, he at once grasped my arm and told me, 'Do not say such things here!' and he pushed me out of his house.
>
> There was no end to my sorrows. Heartbroken and utterly astounded I said to myself, 'Are all my efforts in vain? To whom shall I turn? Whom shall I approach? ... But I will never leave this man. I will persist till such time as he will open his heart to me and will guide me to the right path of God. It is incumbent upon the one who searches to drain the bitter cup of hardship.'
>
> The next morning I was at the door of the same house. I knocked harder than the previous day. This time the Mullá himself came to the door and the moment he opened it, I said, 'I will not go away, I will not leave you until you tell me the whole truth.' This time he found me earnest and true. He became sure that I had not been at his door to spy or cause difficulties for him and his friends.

Aḥmad was then instructed to attend the evening prayers at a certain mosque where the same Mullá led the congregational prayers followed by a long sermon. He was also told to follow the Mullá after the sermon was over. The next night Aḥmad tried his utmost to find the Mullá after the prayer and the sermon, but crowds of people surrounded him and Aḥmad did not have the slightest chance to even approach him. The next day when the two met again, Aḥmad was instructed to go to another mosque at night and a third person would be there to show him the way. Accordingly Aḥmad was at the mosque at sunset and as promised, after the evening prayers, a certain person came to him and beckoned him to follow. Without hesitation or fear Aḥmad followed. Now the three men started to walk like shadows in the darkness of the night, through narrow and obscure lanes. Aḥmad, a complete stranger, never wavered nor faltered nor fled. He took every step with great determination and was ready for any outcome.

At last they reached a certain house. They knocked at the door very gently and it was opened immediately. The newcomers went in very quickly. They passed through a covered passageway, reached a small courtyard, climbed a few steps and were at the door of an upper chamber where a very dignified figure was sitting.

The Mullá approached that revered personage with great humility and absolute reverence, and courteously whispered, 'This is the man I told you about', and indicated Aḥmad, who had been standing at the threshold with utter respect and high expectation. 'Welcome. Please come in and be seated', said the man. Aḥmad then entered the room and sat down on the floor.

The host was no less a person than Mullá Ṣádiq (truthful), one of the early believers during the Báb's ministry and very distinguished for his erudition, audacity and steadfastness. During Bahá'u'lláh's ministry, the same Mullá Ṣádiq displayed such great ardour and zeal that he was entitled *'Aṣdaq* (the most truthful) by Bahá'u'lláh.[6]

A TREASURE IS FOUND

Aḥmad, who for twenty-five years had been wandering in the valleys of search and had nowhere found even a drop to quench his thirst, now found a path to the main spring. With parched lips and an insatiable longing he drank in the sweet scented stream of the verses of God through His new Manifestation. Three sessions were sufficient and he embraced the Faith with all his heart and soul. So elated, exalted and over-enthusiastic he looked, that Aṣdaq exhorted him to return to his family in Ká<u>sh</u>án and insisted that he should not mention the Faith to the people, not even to his own wife.

Those days were days of extreme danger to the nascent Cause of God. The few followers recruited from the poor people of the world were forever the targets of many atrocities. Even the air was imbued with suspicion, spying and slander. Therefore, the friends had to be very careful lest the slightest unwise deed or even a foolish word would ignite a never-ending conflagration that would consume the believers in its flame.

Aṣdaq, knowing how Aḥmad had suffered, felt that he had no money to go back home; therefore, he gave him some small gifts for his family and the sum of three tumans and again advised him to be very wise.

Commenting upon his return to Ká<u>sh</u>án, Aḥmad has said:

> When I reached Ká<u>sh</u>án, everyone asked what had happened that I had left everything so abruptly. I told them: 'My longing for pilgrimage was too great to resist, and I was right.' What else could take me away from my work, my house and my family except that innermost yearning? The instant I heard these words from the traveller there was no more patience left in me.

In Ká<u>sh</u>án he resumed his work, but longed to teach the Faith. He heard rumours that a certain man by the name of Ḥájí Mírzá Jání had changed his faith and had become the follower of a new obscure religion. He searched for him and when the two found each other, there was no end to their joy and excitement. They became fast friends, constant companions and the first and only Bábís of that town.

One day, Ḥájí Mírzá Jání went to Aḥmad and with great enthusiasm and uncontrollable excitement asked him, 'Would you like to visit the countenance of your Lord?' Aḥmad's heart leapt up. With much joy and ecstasy, he immediately got up from his seat and asked, 'How and when?' Ḥájí explained to him how he had arranged with the guards to have the Báb in his house as a guest for two or three nights.

Therefore, at the appointed hour, Aḥmad went to Ḥájí's house. When he entered, his eyes fell on a face the beauty of which surpassed heaven and earth. A young Siyyid was sitting with such meekness, grandeur and majesty that one could not help but behold the light of God in His countenance. Some of the divines and dignitaries of the town were seated on the floor around and the servants stood at the door.

One of the mullás faced the Báb and said, 'We have heard that a certain young man in <u>Sh</u>íráz has claimed to be the Báb. Is it true?'

'Yes', answered the Báb.

'And does he reveal verses, too?' asked the same man.

The Báb responded, 'And We reveal verses, too'.

Aḥmad has further said,

> This clear and courageous answer was sufficient for anyone who had ears to hear and eyes to see and find the whole truth immediately. His beautiful face and His powerful Words and presence sufficed all things. But when they served tea and a cup was offered to the Báb, He immediately took it, called the servant of the same Mullá and very graciously gave it to him.
>
> The day after, the very same humble servant came to me and, with great sorrow, deplored the stupidity of his master. A little explanation as to the station of the Báb brought him to our fold and our number grew to be three.

This small nucleus started to grow and the number of the adherents increased. This angered the divines who used all their cunning to stop the flow of the already powerful stream of life. They instigated the cruel ignorant mob to plunder, confiscate and kill all those who bore the name of the Báb. Every day they would go to a house, so enraged that they would break its doors and windows, destroy the building and plunder and loot the contents.

In the evening, one would find the bodies of people dead in the streets and lanes and even scattered over neighbouring mountain and plains. This continued and Aḥmad's house was no exception. Aḥmad then had to hide in a tower for forty days and the friends used to take him food and provisions.

JOURNEY TO THE ABODE OF PEACE

Finding life unbearable in Ká<u>sh</u>án and hearing that Bag<u>h</u>dád had become a point of attraction, Aḥmad decided to go there.

'And God calleth to the Abode of Peace (Bag<u>h</u>dád) and He guideth whom He will into the right way.'[7]

In the darkness of the night, Aḥmad emerged from his hiding place and scaled the walls of the city to make his way to Bag<u>h</u>dád. He travelled on foot, full of love, enthusiasm and eagerness to behold the countenance of the One whom God would make manifest. As he was walking, he came across another man travelling in the same direction. Afraid of being molested further, Aḥmad tried to ignore the stranger, uttering not a word, but the man persisted in walking by his side. Taking great care never to even allude to the Faith or the purpose of his journey, Aḥmad and his fellow-traveller reached their destination.

On arrival in Baghdád, they separated and Aḥmad immediately set out searching for the House of Bahá'u'lláh. When he found the House and entered therein, he found, to his utter astonishment, that his companion was there, too. He then understood that his friend was also a Bábí and had been on his way to attain the presence of the Blessed Beauty.

AḤMAD IN THE PRESENCE OF BAHÁ'U'LLÁH

It was a breathtaking experience for a man like Aḥmad who, all through his life, had been searching for this immense spiritual Fountainhead. When, for the first time, he glanced at the youthful countenance of Bahá'u'lláh – a Face full of charm, freshness of colour and penetrating powers, he was overwhelmed. He came to his senses only through the mirthful remark of the Ancient Beauty, 'He becomes a Bábí and then hides in the tower!'

Bahá'u'lláh allowed him to remain in Baghdád and have his residence very close to the House. Aḥmad immediately installed his small cloth-making machine and was the happiest man in the world. What else does one expect? To live at the time of the Supreme Manifestation of God, adore Him, be loved by Him and be so close to Him in heart and soul and even in residence.

When once asked about the events of the years he spent in such close proximity to Bahá'u'lláh, with tears in his eyes he said,

> How innumerable, how great and how immensely mighty were the events of those years. Our nights were filled with memorable episodes. Joyful and at times sorrowful were our experiences, yet beyond the power of anyone to describe.
>
> For example,[8] one day as the Blessed Beauty was walking, a certain government officer approached Him and reported that one of His followers had been killed and his body thrown on the river bank. The Tongue of Power and Might replied, 'No one has killed him. Through seventy thousand veils of light We showed him the glory of God to an extent smaller than a needle's eye; therefore, he could no more bear the burden of his life and has offered himself as a sacrifice.'

When the caliph's decree was conveyed to Bahá'u'lláh and He had to leave Baghdád for Istanbul, He left the town on the thirty-second day after Naw-Rúz for the Riḍván Garden. On that same day the river overflowed and only on the ninth day was it possible for His family to join Him in the Garden. The river then overflowed a second time, and on the twelfth day it subsided and all went to Him. Aḥmad begged Bahá'u'lláh to be amongst His companions in exile, but Bahá'u'lláh did not accede to this request. He chose a few people and instructed the others to stay to teach and protect the Cause emphasising that this would be better for the Faith of God.

At the time of His departure, those who were left behind stood in a row and all were so overcome with sorrow that they burst into tears. Bahá'u'lláh again approached them and consoled them saying: 'It is better for the Cause. Some of these people who accompany me are liable to do mischief; therefore I am taking them with Myself.' One of the friends could scarcely control his anguish and sorrow. He addressed the crowd reciting this poem of Sa'dí: 'Let us all rise to weep like unto the clouds of the Spring Season. On the day when lovers are separated from their Beloved, one can even hear the lamentations of stones.'

Bahá'u'lláh then said, 'Verily this was said for this day.' Then He mounted His horse and one of the friends placed a sack of coins in front of the saddle and Bahá'u'lláh started to distribute the coins to the bewailing poor who were standing by. When they ran to Him and pushed one another, He plunged His hand in the sack and poured all the coins out saying, 'Gather them yourselves!'

Aḥmad saw his Beloved disappear from his sight, headed for an unknown destination. Little did he know that He was like unto the sun rising towards the zenith of might and power. Sad at heart and utterly distressed in soul, he returned to Baghdád, which to him seemed devoid of any attraction. He tried to make himself happy by gathering the friends and encouraging them to disperse and teach the Faith which had just been declared. Though actively serving the Cause, he was not happy. All that could keep him happy was nearness to his Beloved.

THE TABLET IS REVEALED

After a few years he once again left his home and work and set out on foot towards Adrianople, the city of his love and desire. When he reached Istanbul he received a Tablet from Bahá'u'lláh, now well known as 'The Tablet of Aḥmad'. He describes receipt of this Tablet as follows: 'I received the Tablet of "The Nightingale of Paradise" and reading it again and again, I found out that my Beloved desired me to go and teach His Cause. Therefore I preferred obedience to visiting Him.'

He was specially commissioned to travel through Persia, find the old Bábí families and convey to them the new message of the Lord. Hence such glorious references to the Báb in this Tablet. The task was arduous beyond description and therefore such exhortations as, 'Be thou as a flame of fire to My enemies and a river of life eternal to My loved ones, and be not of those who doubt.' The path to be pursued by him would be full of blood, thorns and hardships to be borne, but followed by such soul-stirring promises of victory as 'And if thou art overtaken by affliction in My path, or degradation for My sake, be not thou troubled thereby.'

With this divine amulet in his possession – a small piece of paper which had been 'invested by Bahá'u'lláh with a special potency and significance', and clad in the simple garments of a mendicant, Aḥmad made his way back to Persia. He entered the country from the district where the Báb had been imprisoned and martyred and crossed this region like unto the breeze of life. Many of the Bábís were thus enabled to see the sun then shining from Adrianople and even many of the Muslims embraced the Faith wholeheartedly.

'GLAD TIDINGS OF THE NEARNESS OF GOD'

Aḥmad became the embodiment of his own Tablet. Such persistence, undaunted spirit, tenacity and steadfastness as his are hardly to be found in any annals of the Cause. When he found a contact, although he suffered afflictions and degradations, he would return again and again to finish that which had been left half discussed.

For example, when he was travelling throughout the Province of Khurásán, he went to the house of a very well known Bábí family, the head of which was no less a person than Furúghí[9] – one of the survivors of the Ṭabarsí upheaval. Aḥmad went in and gradually opened the subject and in very frank, vigorous and emphatic terms explained that the One to be manifested by God was none other than Bahá'u'lláh whose light was then shining from the horizon of the 'remote prison' – Adrianople.

Furúghí, who had so audaciously fought in Ṭabarsí, started a fight here, too. The discussion became more intense as the hours went by. Furúghí became very angry, attacked Aḥmad, broke one of his teeth and threw him out of the house.

Aḥmad left broken-hearted; but, undaunted, he later returned, knocked at the door and told them that he would not go until such time as the subject was fully discussed and some definite conclusions reached.

We must bear in mind that the Bábís were in such great danger that even a piece of paper bearing the verses of the Báb found in any house was enough for the house to be demolished and the inhabitants to be sent to prison or even to the field of martyrdom. Therefore, many of the friends hid their books and writings in the walls of their houses. When Aḥmad went to Furúghí's house for the second time to resume the discussion, he said emphatically that the Greatest Name, Bahá, had very often been mentioned by the Báb in all His Writings.

Furúghí challenged the truth of this statement. To prove to Aḥmad that he was wrong, he tore a part of the wall down and brought out a bundle containing the Writings of the Báb, and promised not to say a word against the explicit texts. Aḥmad says, 'The very first one we opened referred to the name of Bahá.' As promised, Furúghí and all the members of his family accepted the Faith of Bahá'u'lláh and became zealous defenders and very outstanding in its propagation and protection.

'A FLAME OF FIRE'

After crossing all the lands of Khurásán, Aḥmad decided to go once more to Baghdád to convey the message of love and greetings on behalf of Bahá'u'lláh to all the friends of that very important city, but unfortunately, on the way he again fell sick and could not reach Baghdád.

In addition, in Ṭihrán, some of the divines of Káshán recognized him and lodged complaints against him at the court of the King, who was ever ready to inflict hardship on the adherents of the new Faith. He was consequently arrested and committed to the hands of a certain young officer who was ordered to investigate the case and, if he was sure that his victim had gone astray, to put him to death immediately.

The young officer did not wish to molest Aḥmad and therefore insisted that he should recant his Faith. Aḥmad says, 'At that moment I was at the height of my faith and enthusiasm and never for one moment even thought of recanting.'

Ever ready to lay down his life in the path of the Cause he served with such self-sacrifice, he insisted that he was not a Bábí, but a Bahá'í, a follower of the Supreme Manifestation. He was detained and while in prison he heard of the sudden and severe illness of the officer's wife. In great fright and in extreme distress, the officer came to Aḥmad and said, 'Should my wife recover, I will release you', and after three days the young man, heedless of the dire consequences to himself, took Aḥmad to the gate of Ṭihrán and set him free.

'A RIVER OF LIFE ETERNAL'

Released like a bird, he first went to the villages where some sifters of wheat were Bábís. They received him with the utmost love and courtesy. They offered him hospitality and he guided them to the right path of God and, in great rejoicing, Aḥmad left them and made his way to the province of Fárs, the capital of which was Shíráz.

He lived in this province for about a quarter of a century. He became the constant companion of the wronged and afflicted ones. He consoled them during times of persecution and gave them hope and vision of the ever-widening horizons of victories and triumphs.

It was through the old people of this district of Persia that this humble servant, the writer, came to hear the distant echoes of a glorious dervish living amongst the villagers, and that he had been to them an angel of protection, guidance and mercy. Such rumours set me to search about for him and then I found out that this adorable individual was our precious Aḥmad – a name now mentioned throughout the world with so much love and devotion.

Aḥmad received many of the travelling teachers who passed through this part of Persia and feasted with them in his humble abode, mentioning God, His Faith, and recounting the experience of the many teachers who had been in those days quickening many souls.

One of the most touching incidents as related by himself was the following:

> One day a man barely clad and almost barefooted came to the door of my house. He was utterly exhausted and worn out. His clothes were stiff and brownish with a mixture of dust and perspiration. He happened to be Ḥájí Mírzá Ḥaydar-'Alí.[10] I immediately helped him to take off his clothes. I washed them and spread them in the sun to dry while he rested, waiting for the friends to come for a meeting.

'STEADFAST IN MY LOVE'

The years passed by full of eventful days, but when the waves of persecution spread all over Persia, the friends in their love and admiration for Aḥmad endeavoured to protect him against fatal attacks and, after long consultations, they suggested to him that he immediately leave that forlorn and forsaken corner of the country for a more populated centre.

Wherever Aḥmad went, the friends suggested the same thing to him. He was so well known through the length and breadth of the country that his mere presence would cause agitation amongst the bigoted Muslims whose first arrows would be aimed at Aḥmad himself. After changing many places of residence many times, he settled in Ṭihrán.

He never wavered, nor was he ever anything but that 'flame of fire' and 'river of life eternal'. After having lived one century, always enjoying good health, he passed on to the presence of his Beloved in 1905 in Ṭihrán.

As to the family of Aḥmad, he had two children: a son called Mírzá Muḥammad and a daughter, Khánum Guhar. When Aḥmad's house was confiscated, Mírzá Muḥammad, his wife and children left the city of Káshán for Ṭihrán. He, his wife and small daughter died on their way to Ṭihrán. The traces of their graves – if any – are lost forever. There remained only their son, Jamál, aged five.

The mule drivers who used to take food from the provinces to Ṭihrán, not knowing that Jamál was a son of Bábís, took pity on the forsaken and homeless child and, placing him on one of the loads, brought him to Ṭihrán. In that great capital, the poor child was left all alone and no one even told him of his glorious ancestry or of the Faith, in the path of which the family had borne so many afflictions and untold hardships.

He was left in this state until his aunt, Khánum Guhar,[11] also went to Ṭihrán. When Aḥmad reached the capital, he came to know of his grandson whom he loved very much. He took him under the wings of his own love and protection and Jamál grew to be an excellent Bahá'í.

Aḥmad's most outstanding characteristic was his iron determination and his indefatigable energy. Nothing could ever deflect this man from the straight path of God, though to him it had always been narrow and strewn with thorns, blood and multifarious plights and calamities.

Towards the end of his life, Aḥmad entrusted the original Tablet to Jamál who, in turn, out of the purity of his heart and his devotion to the Faith of God, offered it as a gift to Hand of the Cause, Trustee of Ḥuqúq, the son and brother of two illustrious martyrs, Jináb-i-Valíyu'lláh Varqá.[12]

When Jináb-i-Varqá, according to the instructions of the beloved Guardian, attended the opening ceremony of the Temple in Wilmette during the Intercontinental Conference of 1953, he brought this most precious Tablet as his offering to the archives of the Bahá'ís of the United States. Now the beloved friends of that country are the trustees of this great gift of God to humanity.

SOURCES

- A letter written on the same subject by Jináb Ishrágh Khávarí at the request of Mrs Amelia Collins in 1958.
- Manuscripts sent to the author by Mírzá Faḍlu'lláh Shahídí of Khurásán.
- Personal investigations from the Djamálís, descendants of the immortal Aḥmad in Iran.

NOTES AND REFERENCES

1 Selections from this Persian Tablet appear in *Gleanings from the Writings of Bahá'u'lláh*, section CLIII, p. 323.

2 *The Dawn-Breakers*, pp. 217–222.

3 See *Gleanings from the Writings of Bahá'u'lláh*, section CXV, p. 240.

4 Mírzá Yaḥyá

5 Matthew 7:7

6 *The Dawn-Breakers*, p. 100.

7 Qur'án 10:25

8 *God Passes By*, p. 136.

9 One of the members of this family is listed with eighteen others as *The Apostles of Bahá'u'lláh* by the beloved Guardian. This list appears in *The Bahá'í World*, Volume III, p. 80 where the Guardian says, 'Mírzá Maḥmúd: an indomitable spirit and zealous defender of the Faith'.

10 The man who was entitled by the beloved Master as *The Angel of Mount Carmel.*

11 As to Khánum Guhar, the glorious daughter of Aḥmad, she was a very active Bahá'í. The story of such a daring woman's history has only been briefly recorded. Such a mirror-like heart is rarely to be found. For example, during the lifetime of Bahá'u'lláh there were some outstanding teachers who were almost worshipped by the friends. One of them, who had so many exalted letters from the Blessed Perfection, often went to Khánum Guhar's house and she respected him so much as to clean his shoes. It seems that such titles and extraordinary respect had turned the heads of some of them. They thought of assuming an independent rank in the Faith of God. One such person went to Khánum Guhar's house after the Ascension of Bahá'u'lláh. When the hostess brought tea and sweets and stood at the door with folded hands in absolute respect and homage she found that the man had not taken any of the refreshments. He seemed to be gloomy and pensive. Khánum Guhar asked for the reason. 'I must go to the Holy Land', he said, 'and see to the affairs of the Cause myself. The Faith is left in the hands of a young man.' He pronounced the last phrase with indignation and pride. Upon hearing these words, Khánum Guhar raised her voice saying, 'Do you think Bahá'u'lláh did not know whom to appoint after Himself?' She then entered the room and collected the tray of tea and sweets and in a very emphatic tone ordered the haughty and arrogant man to immediately leave the house. She then went to the neighbouring Bahá'í families and advised them to be most careful about him till such time as they should receive definite instructions from the Most Great Branch.

The following example illustrates her purity of heart. She heard that a very young girl belonging to a Bahá'í family was in bed with severe illness. She went to her bedside and prayed to God saying, 'O, my Lord I have had my share of life. Please take me and leave this child for her parents.' The very same night she died and the patient became well.

12 His picture appears amongst other Hands appointed by the beloved Guardian in *The Bahá'í World*, Volume XII, p. 110.

From Adrianople to ‘Akká

A talk by A. Q. Faizí
to the Oceanic Conference, held in
Palermo, Sicily, August 1968.

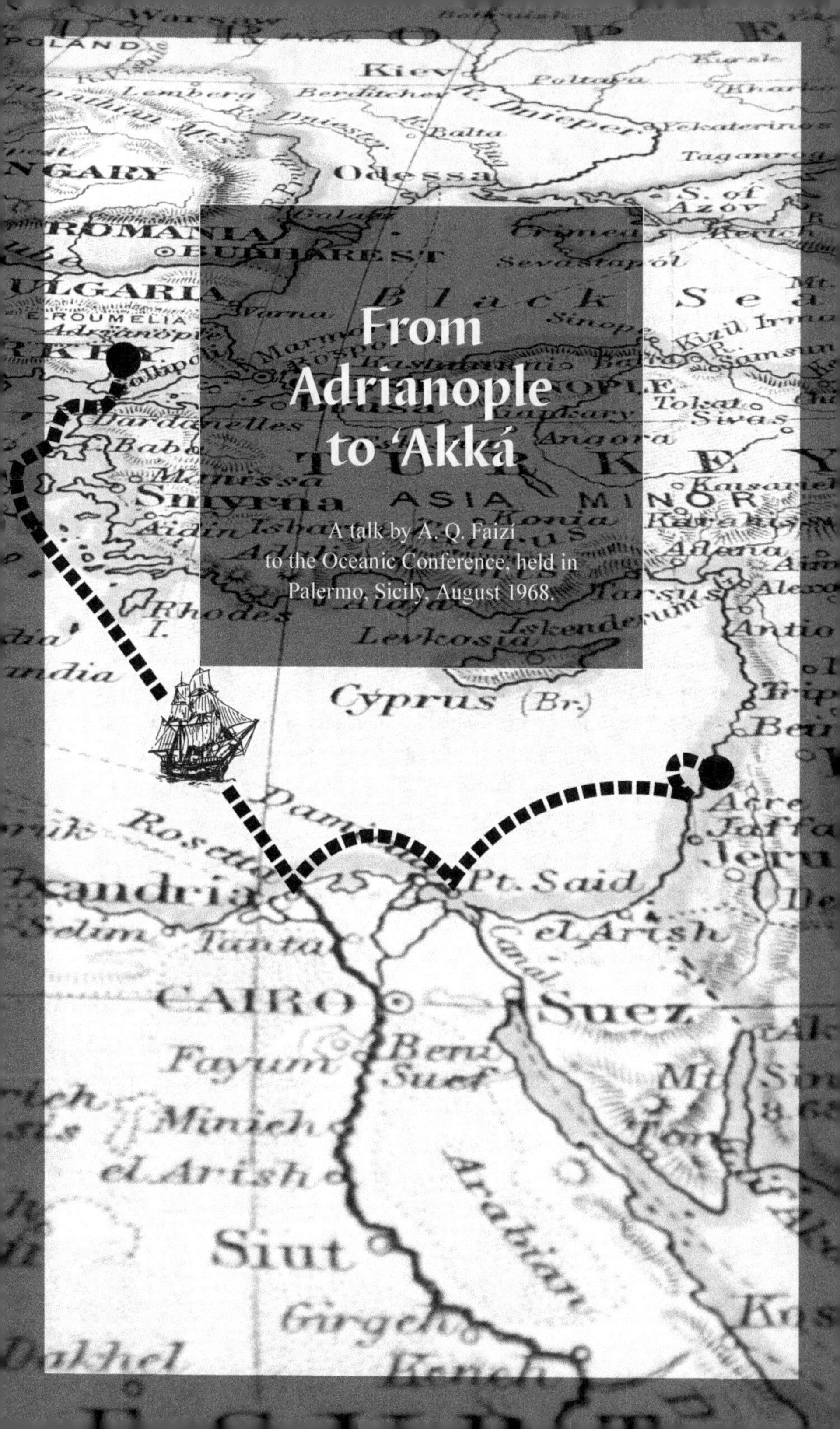

INTRODUCTION

The glorious Sun of Truth rising from its homeland had ascended in its orbit and, in the years of banishment in Adrianople, had mounted to its zenith of all-conquering majesty and might.

As Bahá'u'lláh rose in His power and grandeur, believers from all walks of life abandoned their homes and sought haven and shelter in His nearness. When faced with tests, trials and ordeals, rather than renounce their faith, the true companions of Bahá contented themselves with the bare necessities of life, intensified their spiritual fervour, welcomed any calamity in His path and through the sweat and strain of suffering offered their very lives as humble tokens of love at the sacred altar of the Lord of the Age.

There were also those who, immersed in the trivialities of life, unmitigated in their hatred, enslaved by their own corrupt inclinations and assisted by persons drunk with pride and power, arose, with all the energy, evilness and bitterness of their sinful souls, to challenge the nascent and already vigorously-growing Cause of God. The devastating effects of such deeds created clouds of suspicion, hatred and wrath that dimmed the radiant fame of the Greatest Name.

Never should we think of Bahá'u'lláh as one amongst many. Though He appeared in a physical human temple, He remained always far above – immeasurably far above – the reach and ken of men. No tempest could move the hem of His garment. No waves of calamities could ever sprinkle a drop in His serene presence. How can mortal Man ever cover the face of the Sun with the veil of his evil plottings? The sun shines above all clouds and eventually disperses them. So was to be the destined mission of the Ancient Beauty throughout His eventful life. Though sorely tried, He remained lofty and unshaken. Though relentlessly calumnized, He was never resentful or vindictive. The evil deeds of the world could never be commensurate with His intense longing to save the children of Men, to redeem their souls and to put them on the right path to God.

No ingratitude, no lack of virtue could minimize His love. No depths of infamy could prevent the seemingly hopeless and unrepentant humanity from receiving the open treasures of His clemency and compassion.

In the innermost shrine of His own Being, He remained calm and serene. He continued emitting rays of His redeeming light through the clouds of accumulated vice which had covered the sin-stained souls of Men.

With these thoughts in mind, let us review the events that marked the different stages of Bahá'u'lláh's banishment from Adrianople to the Fortress of 'Akká.

THE LATTER DAYS IN ADRIANOPLE

The followers of Azal, long-standing enemies of Bahá'u'lláh, finding all their attempts to destroy the Faith abortive, tried to tarnish the lustre His Cause had achieved through Himself, His family and His followers.

First they sent people to the Court to complain that they had insufficient means of livelihood, blaming the Blessed Perfection for this. Then Áqá Ján-i-Kaj-Kuláh, instigated by Siyyid Muḥammad, wrote letters to the dignitaries and government representatives containing the false accusation that Bahá'u'lláh had made an alliance with Bulgaria, and had gathered together many people under His sway for the sole purpose of conquering Constantinople.

The Persian Ambassador in Constantinople, who had always been prepared to initiate or support any plot against Bahá'u'lláh and His followers, took advantage of the disturbance in Turkey and immediately informed the Persian Consuls in Egypt and Iraq that the Turkish Government had withdrawn its protection of the Bábí Sect. This news convulsed both countries and unleashed the hidden forces of malice and mischief.

'Abdu'r-Rasúl-i-Qumí, one of the exceptional souls and a true and enthusiastic lover of the Ancient Beauty, who had suffered long years of imprisonment in Ṭihrán, had, after his release, visited Bahá'u'lláh in Adrianople and was residing in Baghdád. Every day he brought water in skin bags from the Tigris River and watered the roses in his Beloved's garden. Thus he had become well known and a target of the Muslims' cruel attacks. One day, at the hour of dawn, a number of these people, rushing out from their hiding places, stabbed him from all sides. Though fatally wounded, with blood gushing forth in profusion, he succeeded in dispersing his attackers, retained his balance and dragged himself to the garden of his Beloved where, for the last time, he watered the flowers of the House before yielding his last heroic breath.[1]

It was also during these latter days that Nabíl arrived in Adrianople after a very long, exhaustive, and successful teaching tour in Persia and Iraq. He became very sad when he looked upon the countenance of the Ancient

Beauty. He found Him as if suspended in boundless space, attacked with swords and spears by the whole world. Bahá'u'lláh had no shelter except His Most Great Branch Who, like a compass, never ceased to turn to, and circle around, His Lord.

Bahá'u'lláh's true and faithful brother, Mírzá Músá, with the permission of Bahá'u'lláh, had been living in Smyrna. Yaḥyá lived in Adrianople, unreasonably filled with fear because of the majesty and power with which the Tablets to the Kings had been revealed. Such was the extent of his fear that he ventured to suggest to Bahá'u'lláh that it would have been better if Bahá'u'lláh's address to the Sulṭán described the Divine Message as a humble provision offered to the King. Bahá'u'lláh's reply was that if He were the Divine Messenger, He would describe His message as nothing short of abundant provision.

Nabíl was commissioned to deliver a Tablet of Bahá'u'lláh to His brother, Mírzá Músá, also known as Áqáy-i-Kalím. On arriving at Smyrna, Nabíl gave the Tablet to him who, after reading it, said, 'The days of hardships are approaching. At times of suffering I do not like to be away from His Holy Presence.' He therefore accompanied Nabíl on his return to Adrianople. On the way they received the news that some of the believers had already been arrested. 'These are the first waves of the ocean of calamity' was Kalím's immediate remark as he heard the news.

It was in the middle of winter and snow had covered the mountains and plains when our two precious travellers arrived in the Land of Mystery, only to find it in a state of confusion. Bahá'u'lláh had encouraged the friends to disperse as He did not want more hardships to be inflicted on them nor did He desire them to be exiled or imprisoned. He would rather have them scattered around the world to propagate the Word of God and to win victories for His struggling Faith in various lands. But those who lived in His nearness were so enthralled by His love that they remained heedless of His warnings, preferring hardship to separation from Him.

Bahá'u'lláh instructed Nabíl to proceed to Egypt and appeal to the Khedive on behalf of the friends who had been unjustly treated.

It was during these days also that the loving heart of the Supreme Manifestation was turned towards His persecuted friends in different parts of the world. The shadow of the dark days ahead was slowly approaching and He could see the sorrow and grief of His lovers who, at times, were utterly cut off from any news of Him and His family. Therefore He revealed several brief Tablets to be dispatched to the friends. These Tablets are extremely touching, intimate and uplifting. They were meant to strengthen His oppressed followers so that they would not lose heart if they did not hear from or about Him for a long time.

The contents of these Tablets are sources of delight and encouragement to all the friends throughout eternity. In them He praises God and offers thanksgiving and gratitude for this further humiliation suffered in the path of God. In one instance He addresses Himself and says that He should remember God and bear in mind His promise[2] that He would stand with Him forever and would help and assist Him under all conditions.

The Ancient Beauty addresses the people of the earth in one of these Tablets, and lamentingly asks them how and when they could prevent the Divine Youth from mentioning the All Knowing God. He asserts the utter failure of all the united forces of the world to extinguish the fire of His Faith. He seeks to awaken in the hearts of men the consciousness that no power in the universe can prevent the blowing of winds, and that He Himself, like unto a leaf, is powerless to stir except when the winds of the Will of God are blowing. In several places He exhorts the friends never to forget Him even if the cruel ones of the earth should cast Him in fathomless pits because, in such a state, the fire of His love would burn more intensely than before.

This fire was of such a nature that if all the seas were poured on it, it would continue to burn. In some places He explicitly mentions that the Prisoner of Adrianople says that the place of His incarceration is the Fortress of ‘Akká, well-known for its putrid air and foul water. He furthermore points out that though the sole aim of such banishments is to humiliate the Manifestation of God, the friends should, under no circumstances, feel sad and despondent, because such sufferings in the path of the Lord are like unto the showers of rain on the plains, and serve as fuel for the celestial Lamp. Were His head to adorn the point of the spear, His tongue would continue to proclaim the name of the All-Merciful.

At the end of one of these Tablets, He says that the Divine Youth is prevented from writing. His enemies had imprisoned Him and His pen. The latter was more unbearable to Him. Had it not been for such restrictions He would have sent a message to every one of the believers throughout the world.

Thus He wrote His Tablets, and thus He dispersed His friends. He sent the pilgrims away, He strengthened the hearts of His lovers in all lands, and He remained as ever contented and prepared to welcome the shafts of the enemy.

EVENTS PRECEDING HIS EXILE

The people in Turkey, and especially those who were privileged to live near Bahá'u'lláh, such as the inhabitants of Adrianople, had the highest respect and reverence towards Him and, in the course of time, they came to know and love Him from the depths of their beings. The successive local governors of the city, one after the other, paid their homage to the Blessed Beauty.

Amongst them the noble and honest K͟hurs͟híd Pás͟há shines as the radiant sun from the horizon of faithfulness. In answer to reports from Constantinople, he courageously refuted the unjust accusations heaped upon Bahá'u'lláh. As long as he was governor he visited Bahá'u'lláh on the occasions of Feasts and, whenever he went, he openly declared that nothing except sanctified words and holy deeds emanated from His Holy Presence. He never approved of, or agreed with, the presumptuous deeds of the unjust rulers in the capital. Bahá'u'lláh praised him in one of His Tablets by characterizing him as the strongest pillar of the Ottoman Government whose hearts enshrined the greatest amount of love. Yet, Bahá'u'lláh continues, even to him no word was mentioned about personal affairs. To Bahá'u'lláh this would have been the lowest of deeds.

K͟hurs͟híd Pás͟há was very sad and disheartened when the authorities in Constantinople would not handle the affairs of Bahá'u'lláh with justice and faith. When the hour struck and he found matters beyond his control, he felt so ashamed of such cruel treatment towards such a great Person, that he abandoned his official responsibilities and left everything in the hands of a Registrar.

The inhabitants of Adrianople were well acquainted with the friends and knew of the detached way they had lived amongst them. The people really loved them and very much desired that they would be allowed to continue living in their town. The news of the unexpected decrees, therefore, surprised and grieved them. As they met in mosques, coffee-houses or markets, they invariably asked one another, 'Why should these people be victims of such cruel treatment? We have not seen anything from them except honesty and truthfulness.' When they found that Bahá'u'lláh and His companions were to be forced to depart, they all wept and bewailed.

Not only did the people, dignitaries and authorities in Adrianople show their grief and sorrow, but the representatives of European countries were also moved and astounded. Some of them sought the presence of Bahá'u'lláh and pleaded with Him to utter one word when they would arise to help Him and His friends and rescue them from their difficulties. They even said that they would inform and appeal to their respective governments to resolutely prevent the perpetration of such inhuman deeds.

To all of them Bahá'u'lláh replied that He sought no remover of difficulties save God and would turn His face in supplication to no place except to His Threshold. He then showered His love and bounties upon them and sent them away from His presence resigned and contented.

Meanwhile, contradictory rumours had been spread which lent their share to the convulsion and confusion of affairs. Some said that only those whose names had been registered in Government books could accompany their Lord.

Others reported that Bahá'u'lláh and His brothers and families would be taken to different destinations, the rest being sent to their own respective countries. In the words of one of the companions, 'I well remember as though it were only yesterday, the fresh misery into which we were plunged, to be separated from our Beloved; and He, what new grief was in store for Him? He accepted all vicissitudes with His calm, beautiful smile, cheering us with wonderful words.'[3]

Those who had lived day and night in or near His house, found separation the most unbearable of all sufferings. They decided, therefore, that they would undergo any bitter test rather than be deprived of His presence.

One night, the friends were gathered in a house and naturally discussed the prevailing rumours of the city. Ḥájí Ja'far-i-Tabrízí, one of the staunch followers of Bahá'u'lláh, was also there. In the middle of their conversation they heard a faint voice from under the window – the voice of someone struggling for breath. They rushed out and found Ḥájí Ja'far in a desperate condition. He had cut his throat with a razor and blood was gushing out. The friends first informed the Master Who immediately sent men to fetch a surgeon and a *Qáḍí* (a magistrate or judge of a Sharí'a court).

The surgeon's house was near and fortunately he came quickly, treated the cut and enabled Ḥájí Ja'far to talk. When the Qáḍí reached the scene, he asked who had been responsible for the deed. He asked Ḥájí Ja'far several times, and every time he replied, 'When I came to know that I would be deprived of His Holy Presence, I did not desire to live any more.' When asked again he confirmed, 'Feeling lonely and separated from Him prompted me to sacrifice my life.'

The people who loved the Bahá'ís and revered them increased in their wonderment as they witnessed such acts of love, detachment and spiritual consecration. It was remarked by them that the Bahá'ís knew that they would be taken to exile and imprisonment and yet they were ready to meet greater hardships, to offer their lives, and to welcome even death, as they could not bear the thought of separation from their Beloved. What ties held them together? How could they comprehend those mysterious bonds of love, which were beyond the reach of Men's concepts and standards? Ḥájí Ja'far received assurance and treatment and became better. On another day, shortly afterwards, Bahá'u'lláh received him, promised him that he would eventually attain his heart's desire, and exhorted him not to be sad. He must be patient, fix his gaze upon God, feel happy and abide by His Will.

HIS DEPARTURE TO GALLIPOLI AND THE EPISODE OF DHABÍḤ (SURNAMED ANÍS)

One day soldiers were posted at the doors of Bahá'u'lláh's residence in order to guard the House and allow no one to go in or out.

His companions were also arrested, taken to the Governor's office and imprisoned one night. In the course of the investigations, they were asked whether they were followers of Bahá'u'lláh, to which they invariably answered with great courage and audacity, professing their faith in Him. They were then commanded to sell their properties and get ready for departure. Needless to say, the friends auctioned their belongings and lost almost everything they possessed, yet they stood firm and resolute, determined to accompany their Beloved to the ends of the earth.

The day of departure was fixed. Carriages were brought to the house, and the friends helped in loading them with luggage. These went first. Mírzá Yaḥyá and Siyyid Muḥammad also departed on the same day.

One week passed, and then came the turn of Bahá'u'lláh. On the morning of departure, the members of the household took their seats in the carriages. At about noon, Bahá'u'lláh came out of His house.

Throngs of people had gathered at the door to bid Him farewell and look for the last time upon His countenance. Their grief had no end. Signs of anguish and sorrow were witnessed on all faces. They approached the Ancient Beauty and either kissed His hand or knelt and touched the hem of His robe, reverently kissing it too.

They uttered words which expressed their sorrowful state and deprivation. It was indeed a strange day. It seemed that even the walls and the gates of the town were lamenting. Amidst such expressions of profound love and respect, Bahá'u'lláh set out at midday on the last stage of His banishment, depositing 'beneath every tree and every stone a trust, which God will erelong bring forth through the power of truth'.[4]

Thus the Sun of Truth pursued its course towards its setting point.

They spent four days on their way to Gallipoli, a town on the shore of the Marmara Sea. All the captives were to be gathered in this town, whence their journey on the sea would begin.

Jináb-i-Dhabíḥ, afterwards surnamed Anís, and his friends, who had gone to Adrianople during the last days of Bahá'u'lláh's sojourn in that city and were instructed to proceed to Gallipoli, were already there and attained the presence of their Lord.

Here again the companions of Bahá'u'lláh underwent fresh tests by hearing contradictory reports about the possible dispersion of the friends and the extermination of Bahá'u'lláh.

Ḥasan Effendi, the Turkish Captain who had escorted Bahá'u'lláh and His companions to the port, sought His presence in absolute humility and submission to bid farewell. Through him, Bahá'u'lláh sent a verbal message to the Sulṭán in Constantinople: 'Tell the King that this territory will pass out of his hands, and his affairs will be thrown into confusion … Not I speak these words, but God speaketh them.'[5] He then told the Captain that it would have been fair if the Sulṭán had arranged a gathering of the divines where Bahá'u'lláh could ring forth the proofs of His truthfulness.

If the Sulṭán could find anything in the community, which created corruption and upheaval in his domains, then it would be just for him to treat them in the way that he had chosen. What had been done, He affirmed, was according to the desires of those who had grudges in their hearts and followed their passions and base desires instead of the true path of God. They had committed unwarranted deeds without the least proof. The Captain promised to convey Bahá'u'lláh's message to the King. Thus was Ḥasan Effendi sent back to Constantinople. A Major, 'Umar Effendi, replaced him, who brought the confusion created by the rumours to an end. He announced that those whose names had not been registered in the government books could board the ship, provided they would arrange their own affairs.

Before leaving Gallipoli, Bahá'u'lláh informed the friends of the hard days ahead of them and warned them against the divine tests which would befall each and all of the companions. He asked them to ponder His words and to return if they found themselves unprepared. He even warned them against the impossibility of returning in case of remorse.

To reach the Austrian boat, which had anchored far away from the shore, the passengers had to cross in small sailing boats. At the same time that Bahá'u'lláh was entering one of those boats, He was already uttering verses. Jináb-i-Anís and his companions were standing on the shore watching their Beloved on His way to a destination as yet undisclosed; a poignant sorrow pressed their hearts and tears flowed down their cheeks. Bahá'u'lláh, beholding them thus stricken with grief, consoled them and strengthened their hearts by showering His love and compassion upon them. Thus He cheered the burning hearts of His lovers throughout the world in their moments of grief and separation. When He took His seat in the small boat, He assured everyone they would sail in absolute safety even if every wave beat upon the boat or the strongest tempest surround it.

Boarding the Austrian steamer, they found passengers, including some Persians. Bahá'u'lláh did not talk to anyone, but went ahead to a spacious place where several chairs were arranged. He occupied one of these chairs and permitted the friends to take their seats too.

One of the prisoners related:

> In this small boat, we, seventy-two persons, were crowded together in unspeakable conditions for eleven days of horror.
>
> Ten soldiers and two officers were our escort. There was an appalling smell in the boat, and most of us were very ill indeed … We had embarked so hurriedly that we had been unable to provide for the voyage, and a few loaves and a little cheese … was all the food we had for those indescribable days. … There was no vessel … our lack of food had reduced us to a seriously weak state of health.[6]

The steamer sailed in the evening and the next day, at about sunrise, touched the shores of Smyrna.

SMYRNA AND ISMU'LLÁHU'L-MUNÍB

Jináb-i-Munír, surnamed Ismu'lláhu'l-Muníb, was a very handsome and radiant young man from the city of Ká<u>sh</u>án, Persia. Before embracing the Faith, he had led a comfortable life and, having had the opportunity to study, he had become accomplished in many of the accepted and prevailing notions of his time. In calligraphy, which was considered the art par excellence, he was one of the few recognized masters. He had also a melodious and penetrating voice and a gentle temperament. His heart brimmed with infinite love. He was a great soul.

When Bahá'u'lláh was in Ba<u>gh</u>dád, Muníb brought his God-given gifts and offered them at the altar of his Beloved. Thus when the caravan of exiles started on their journey from Ba<u>gh</u>dád to Constantinople with all glory and might, he volunteered to walk beside the steed of the Blessed Perfection. Great had been the honour conferred upon him, and tremendous too were the sufferings, which he willingly accepted with joy and radiant acquiescence. 'Abdu'l-Bahá said that this noble soul traversed the distance between Ba<u>gh</u>dád and Constantinople on foot and, throughout the journey, was in perfect happiness. Day and night he was in a state of prayer.

'Abdu'l-Bahá described him as the companion of His soul and the beloved of His heart. Some nights the Master and Muníb would walk on the two sides of Bahá'u'lláh's steed. Their joy had no end and remained forever beyond words to describe. Some nights, Muníb, with his silvery voice, would sing songs and odes of great Persian poets, such as those of Ḥáfiẓ. His voice resounded through the silence of those memorable nights.

When they reached Constantinople, Muníb was instructed to go on a teaching tour to Persia and Iraq. This he accomplished with distinction, and, after a long and arduous tour, he returned to Turkey in the latter days of Bahá'u'lláh's sojourn in Adrianople. The teaching tour had been too exacting, however, and although his health was now in a precarious condition, he begged Bahá'u'lláh to permit him to be included amongst those who had the honour of being exiled with Him. He would not even consider remaining behind to undergo medical care and treatment, his only aim and aspiration being to sacrifice his life in the path of the Ancient Beauty. His request was granted. He was so weak that three persons had to carry him on board the ship, and by the time they reached Smyrna, Muníb's condition had deteriorated.

He was melting away like a candle in the fire of love ignited within him; he could not even utter a word. The Captain forced him to return to shore. When the inevitable moment of separation came, he dragged his frail body until he reached the feet of Bahá'u'lláh, and burst into tears. At that moment, signs of intense grief were seen on the countenance of the Ancient Beauty.

It was clear that there and then, Muníb had reached his exalted paradise of sacrifice and his Beloved had accepted the gift of his life. 'Abdu'l-Bahá has related that He, and those in His company, took him to the hospital in Smyrna and spent one hour with him before returning to the boat. They laid his blessed body in bed and covered him with kisses, but had to leave as soon as the officers bade them return. They were immersed in sorrow as they left him alone in the hospital.[7]

ALEXANDRIA AND NABÍL

Three days the Ancient Beauty had been sailing on the waters of the Mediterranean Sea between Smyrna and Alexandria. In Alexandria, they were to change boats and some were allowed to go ashore to purchase provisions. Muḥammad Ibráhím, one of the companions who catered for Bahá'u'lláh's retinue, was amongst those who went ashore.

This was providential, because one of the most interesting episodes of Nabíl's life took place as a result.

We remember that Bahá'u'lláh ordered Nabíl to go to Egypt. He obeyed, and went there, but after some time he was arrested and put in prison. There he met a certain Christian physician and priest, Fáris Effendi, imprisoned on a charge of an offence in a financial transaction. Nabíl taught him the

Faith and in a short while he became a very ardent and enthusiastic follower of Bahá'u'lláh.

Because of this, the sorrow of being in prison was changed into joy and both felt extremely happy. Sometimes they would sit at the window of their cell watching the people passing by, and one day, when Nabíl was alone at his window, he was astounded to see Muḥammad Ibráhím passing by. He called to him. When Muḥammad Ibráhím saw Nabíl he was even more surprised. Nabíl asked him what had brought him there. Ibráhím related the story of Bahá'u'lláh's banishment and pointed out the steamer carrying the Blessed Perfection. Nabíl's sorrows knew no bounds. To be so near and yet so cruelly deprived of beholding the Countenance of the One who was the point of his adoration! This was unbelievable!

After a little while, Fáris Effendi came to the cell and found the happy Nabíl drowned in oceans of sorrow. When he heard the reason, he felt even sadder than Nabíl. He longed for a single glance of Him, but this was utterly impossible. There was only one thing for them to do: to send Him a message of love and loyalty.

This was immediately written; but how to send it was the main problem. God has always His own ways for those who supplicate Him with all their hearts. He will never abandon them. There passed by the window of the cell a young man by the name of Constantine who was known to Fáris Effendi, who at once asked him if he could take a letter to someone on board the Austrian steamer. This was an unexpected and rather arduous task to demand. But the young man agreed to do it, took the letters and made for the steamer.

Nabíl and Fáris were watching intently from their prison cell. They even saw the young man get in a small boat and go out to reach the steamer. But to their utter dismay and grief they heard the siren and saw the steamer sailing away before the small boat had reached her.

What a disappointment to the two prisoners whose letters would not even reach their Beloved! Then that which seemed utterly impossible took place. After proceeding for some distance, the steamer stopped. The small boat reached her. In the afternoon, Constantine returned to the prison shouting: 'By God! My eyes fell on the face of the Father!' Saying these words in great excitement, he gave a small parcel to Nabíl and Fáris Effendi.

Afterwards, the companions of Bahá'u'lláh related that, although they witnessed many extraordinary events while in His Presence, the incident of the steamer in Alexandria was the most astonishing. When the steamer was sailing away, the Captain noticed a sailing boat hastening toward the ship. He immediately anchored. All were astonished at the unexpected halt for such a cause. The passengers stood in a state of bewilderment. They saw a young man climb the companionway and, according to the indications given to him by Nabíl, go directly to the place occupied by Bahá'u'lláh and His retinue.

After the perusal of the letter, a Tablet was immediately dictated by Bahá'u'lláh and, as there was not time to transcribe it, it was sent in the rough penmanship of the amanuensis. The Master and the Purest Branch sent handkerchiefs, flowers and perfume as gifts for Nabíl and his co-prisoner.

When Constantine returned, the steamer resumed its journey.

In his letter, Fáris Effendi had begged Bahá'u'lláh to accept him as one of His devoted servants and confirm him to teach the Faith of God.

The receipt of this letter so pleased Bahá'u'lláh that He has related this story in one of His Tablets to the friends and, at the end, He has quoted the letter of Fáris Effendi. The perusal of such words teaches us to read and study the Writings with the discerning eye of the spirit. Let us ponder the situation of the Ancient Beauty when He received this communication. Though captive in the hands of oppressors, He proclaimed in this Tablet that His banishment had marked the dawn of the day when the divine fragrances wafted throughout East and West, and the pearls of wisdom had been deposited under every stone and, in the fullness of time, would proclaim: 'He is the Beloved of the world'. He then states that when the ship touched the harbour, one of the followers of the Son brought Him a letter from which the fragrance of sanctity could be inhaled, as its writer had been ignited with the fire of the love of his Lord. Anyone who reads his letter will realize how the Almighty God changes the hearts of men.

Here are some fragments of the letter:

> O Thou Glory of the All Glorious, and the Exalted One of the Most Exalted! … I am honoured to write and send this supplication to Thy Presence … They did to Thee what they did to Jesus, the Manifestation of His Wisdom … They became the scattered and lost sheep of the herd … May I entreat Thee to include my people and myself amongst those who are saturated by the bounties of the oceans of Thy grace … Thou art the Ever-Abiding, Ever-Flowing Fountain of Purity and Holiness. … I supplicate Thee by Thy innermost Secret, by Thy Kalím (Interlocutor), by Thy Son, by Thy Ḥabíb (Beloved),[8] and by Thy Forerunner Who embraced the Cross for the sake of His love for Thee … that Thou may not deprive me and my poor family of beholding the light of Thy Countenance.
>
> … Make our faith complete, choose us to serve the chosen ones amongst Thy servants, and accept us as martyrs, who offered their blood for the sake of Thy love … We are weak, ignorant and unworthy, do not make us of the losers … Give us the bounty of love, faith and hope and enable us to tear away from our hearts that which pleaseth Thee not … make us forget ourselves.
>
> We demand no comfort except in that which pleaseth Thee.
> Thou art the Searcher of hearts … a wooden vessel is carrying Thee. How intensely do I long to be in Thy company! … O Sea! What hath befallen thee? I see thee disturbed. Is it because of the fear of thy Lord, the Most Great? O, Alexandria! I see thee sad because of the departure of thy Lord, the Living, the Most Patient. The dilapidated city of ‘Akká is clapping its hands to welcome Thee with great joy. It is rejoicing because it can welcome the Greatest of all Glories.

HAIFA

After a brief stop in Port Sa‘íd and Jaffa, the steamer touched Haifa where extreme consternation struck the party because of the cruel decision to separate some of the friends from Bahá'u'lláh and force them to go to Cyprus with Mírzá Yaḥyá. This news fell like a thunderbolt from the blue on the friends and they recoiled in horror.

‘The friends, though prostrated by sickness, worn out by the wretchedness of the voyage and crushed by this further blow, determined to refuse submission’ as one of the companions reported.

‘The heat of that month of July was overpowering. We were put into a sailing boat. There being no wind, and no shelter from the burning rays of the sun, we spent eight hours of positive misery ...’[9]

A sailing boat was ready to take Bahá’u’lláh across the bay from Haifa to ‘Akká. One of the believers condemned to this separation was ‘Abdu’l-Ghaffár. When he saw the hand of the officer raised to take him away from his Beloved, he cast himself into the sea crying, ‘Yá Bahá’u’l-Abhá’.[10]

Bahá’u’lláh, in a tone of sadness, rebuked the officers responsible for such unnecessary treatment, telling them that their cruel decree resulted in this pitiful situation. He then asked them to immediately rescue ‘Abdu’l-Ghaffár. He was rescued, but pitilessly forced to go to Cyprus where he remained for some time. As soon as possible, however, he travelled to ‘Akká and lived under the shadow of his Lord.

‘AKKÁ

A ‘generation of vipers’,[11] as described by the Son, were gathered on the seashore at ‘Akká to behold the Father. They crowded on the walls of the Fortress and thronged the crooked lanes of the town. Though steeped in the miseries and misfortunes of their fate, they shamelessly raised their voices shouting, ‘God of the Persians!’,[12] as the majestic figure of Bahá’u’lláh emerged from the oceans of His tribulations, passed through the Sea Gate and entered the last stage of His banishment in the Promised Land. The members of His family and His friends followed in the footsteps of their Beloved, marching in with pride and calm. The officers in charge counted them. In the words of one of the prisoners, they were ‘counted as if they were sheep’.

> All the townspeople had assembled to see the arrival of the prisoners. Having been told that we were infidels, criminals and sowers of sedition, the attitude of the crowd was threatening. Their yelling of curses and execrations filled us with fresh misery. We were terrified of the unknown. We knew not what the fate of our party, the friends and ourselves would be. We were described as enemies of God, as the worst kind of criminals. The people were exhorted to shun these vile malefactors.[13]

The Divine procession was led through the dark, crooked and filthy streets of ‘Akká, surrounded by the sneering laughter of the populace, till they reached the Army Barracks.

The moment Bahá'u'lláh stepped into the citadel, He stopped and made a remarkable pronouncement – remarks which will echo throughout eternity in the hearts of all the adherents of His Faith. He pointed out to all who accompanied Him to the Most Great Prison, the exalted position they occupied. He reminded them that, thereafter, their lives would take another form and would have a deeper significance. Even a breath breathed in that atmosphere and a step taken along that path would be immortalized.

He saw a broken branch near His feet. He looked at it and declared that even that broken twig would be mentioned in East and West. Thus He demanded from his family and followers an unswerving rectitude of character and an unflinching devotion to the Cause of God, so that all their words and deeds would become worthy of eternity.

He entered His prison cell, placing the fate of humanity in the balance.

Through His Writings, we realize the significance of His banishments and imprisonment. Through His words we behold the vistas behind all these scenes. He accepted to dwell in the most desolate town of the world so that the citadels of Men's hearts might become pure and prosperous. He carried the burdens of degradation so that the children of men might be glorified and rescued from humiliation. He suffered the chains of captivity so that all the chains of human bondage might be broken asunder.

Drowned in tempests of accusations and calumnies and snared in the traps of dismay and apparent frustration, He raised His clarion call and strengthened the hearts of His persecuted followers throughout the world. He assured them that the drops of the blood of the martyrs, the toils and troubles of the teachers and the pioneers, and the hardships borne by each individual believer in His path, would be amply rewarded.

In the mirror of the knowledge of God a drop would be seen as an ocean and a pebble as a mountain. Thus He proclaimed that His Faith would cover all lands, seas and islands. He assured the friends that, ere long, they would hear the cry of, 'Here am I, here am I',[14] from all sides. He comforted them in their sufferings by giving them the glad tidings of the splendid dawn of a day when no voice would be raised betwixt earth and heaven save in praise of His Cause.

PROPHECIES FULFILLED

Thus we see that when Bahá'u'lláh entered the Most Great Prison, the promises of all ages and religions of the past were fulfilled. The dilapidated city of 'Akká emerged from under the veils of centuries of obscurity and became the 'door of hope' for all mankind. Pilgrims started to move to it. The blessings of the Lord on lands in the neighbourhood of Jerusalem, as foretold in the Qur'án, became known to all. That illustrious Person who was destined to adorn the plain of 'Akká and change it into the Lord's 'Banquet Hall' was drawn to it, by force of the Caliph's farmán, and imprisoned in its fortress.

> Indeed such a consummation, He assures us, had been actually prophesied 'through the tongue of the Prophets two or three thousand years before'. God, 'faithful to His promise', had, 'to some of the Prophets' 'revealed and given the good news that the "Lord of Hosts should be manifested in the Holy Land"'. Isaiah had, in this connection, announced in his Book: 'Get thee up into the high mountain, O Zion that bringest good tidings; lift up thy voice with strength, O Jerusalem, that bringest good tidings. Lift it up, be not afraid; say unto the cities of Judah: "Behold your God! Behold the Lord God will come with strong hand, and His arm shall rule for Him."' David, in his Psalms, had predicted: 'Lift up your heads, O ye gates; even lift them up, ye everlasting doors; and the King of Glory shall come in. Who is this King of Glory? The Lord of Hosts, He is the King of Glory.' 'Out of Zion, the perfection of beauty, God hath shined. Our God shall come, and shall not keep silence.' Amos had, likewise, foretold His coming: 'The Lord will roar from Zion, and utter His voice from Jerusalem; and the habitations of the shepherds shall mourn, and the top of Carmel shall wither.'
>
> 'Akká, itself, flanked by the 'glory of Lebanon', and lying in full view of the 'splendour of Carmel', at the foot of the hills which enclose the home of Jesus Christ Himself, had been described by David as 'the Strong City', designated by Hosea as 'a door of hope', and alluded to by Ezekiel as 'the gate that looketh towards the East', whereunto 'the glory of the God of Israel came from the way of the East', His voice 'like a noise of many waters'. To it the Arabian Prophet had referred as 'a city in Syria to which God hath shown His special mercy', situated 'betwixt two mountains ... in the middle of a meadow', 'by the shore of the sea ... suspended beneath the Throne', 'white, whose whiteness is pleasing unto God'. 'Blessed the man', He, moreover, as confirmed by Bahá'u'lláh, had declared, 'that hath visited 'Akká, and blessed he that hath visited the visitor of 'Akká.'

> Furthermore, 'He that raiseth therein the call to prayer, his voice will be lifted up unto Paradise.' And again: 'The poor of 'Akká are the kings of Paradise and the princes thereof. A month in 'Akká is better than a thousand years elsewhere.' Moreover, in a remarkable tradition, which is contained in Shaykh Ibnu'l-'Arabí's work, entitled *Futúḥát-i-Makkíyyih*, and which is recognized as an authentic utterance of Muḥammad, and is quoted by Mírzá Abu'l-Faḍl in his *Fará'íd*, this significant prediction has been made: 'All of them (the companions of the Qá'im) shall be slain except One Who shall reach the plain of 'Akká, the Banquet-Hall of God.'[15]

CONCLUSION

Now, after the lapse of one century, we can stand in the precincts of the Fortress to gaze at the windows of His prison cell. We remember the dauntless pilgrims who crossed desserts and mountains on foot with the sole aim of beholding the countenance of their Beloved. When they reached those sacred shores some were forbidden to enter; others came in, but could not behold His face, nor were their hearts attracted by hearing His melodious voice. A few – only a few – saw His hand waving from the same windows. They saw little and received physically less, but were so imbued with the spirit of pilgrimage that they returned home and consecrated their lives to the service of the Cause.

We ask ourselves, 'Where are the Caliphs, the Sulṭáns, their ministers and their officers who, hand in hand and with all their material forces, tried to exterminate the Faith of God? We see with our own eyes that the dazzling lights of their vanishing glory have long been extinguished. Their commanding voices have been stilled by the ignominious death they have suffered. Forsaken and forgotten, they are buried in the ruins of their own schemes, intrigues and plots.

Then once more we remember the sweet and assuring words of the Master, uttered in the darkest hour of His precious life when He said that all the plans made by the enemies of the Cause would eventually prove to be nothing more than painting on water. Then we behold the All-Conquering Figure of Bahá'u'lláh emerging from the mists of myriads of crises and upheavals like a beautiful silhouette against the evening sky above – far above the reach of men. We feel His merciful hand raised to wipe away our tears, to touch our fever-laden brows, to comfort our suffering hearts, to assuage our pain and to give reassurance to our struggling souls.

Let us renew the pledge of love and devotion we made to such a compassionate Lord and decide to return home with unflinching determination. Let us disperse; yet, united in our aim and welded together in His love, let us take our place among the rank and file of the Army of Life and with a powerful and animated spirit raise the cry of *Yá Bahá'u'l-Abhá!* in all climes, countries, lands and plains and on all the seas and the mountain tops.

Undaunted by the overwhelming tragedies of the world around us, let us tread the path of love and sacrifice, looking forward to the advent of that promised dawn when the world will bathe in the light and warmth of the Sun of Truth shining with all its God-given splendour, when Man can live in abiding peace and unity and when the earth will become the true mirror of the Abhá Kingdom.

NOTES AND REFERENCES

1 Bahá'u'lláh mentioned him in many Tablets, consoling his mother and relatives and appointed his nephew caretaker of the pilgrims in 'Akká. The nephew served in this post until the days of the beloved Guardian. The Master advised Rasúl's relatives to perpetuate his name.

2 The same promise is mentioned in *Epistle to the Son of the Wolf.*

3 *The Chosen Highway*, Lady Blomfield.

4 *Súriy-i-Ra'ís*

5 *God Passes By*, p. 181.

6 *The Chosen Highway*, Lady Blomfield.

7 Muníb died two or three days after the departure of Bahá'u'lláh from Smyrna.

8 Moses (Thy Kalím), Jesus (Thy Son) and Muḥammad (Thy Ḥabíb).

9 *The Chosen Highway*, Lady Blomfield.

10 *God Passes By*, p. 182.

11 *The Bible*, cited by Bahá'u'lláh in *Gleanings*, section CLXIV.

12 *God Passes By*, p. 186.

13 *Bahiyyih Khánum*, quoted in *The Chosen Highway* by Lady Blomfield.

14 *Gleanings*, section CLXIV.

15 *God Passes By*, p. 183–184.

A Gift of Love

Offered to the Greatest Holy Leaf

PREFACE

Towards the end of his life, my husband, the Hand of the Cause Abu'l-Qásim Faizí, had a great longing to prepare a small booklet on various topics related to the life of the Greatest Holy Leaf, and dedicate it as a gift of love to her memory on the occasion of the fiftieth anniversary of her passing. The Universal House of Justice encouraged him and felt that this was 'a truly highly meritorious project' and a 'noble undertaking'.

But the condition of his health and his failing memory made it impossible for him to concentrate on writing. He started the work many times but could not continue, and this caused him much suffering. Once he wrote,

> O my Lord! Grant me the strength needed to begin this work. For me it is infinitely hard. I am like unto one who is at the edge of a frozen lake and invited to plunge in.

After he passed away, I gathered all the scattered notes he had jotted down at different times for this project, and tried to piece them together. I found that, in order to prepare a coherent whole, it was necessary to decide on an order of topics, to add certain words and phrases of my own and, in some instances, to fill in a few gaps.

The final form this work has taken is, of a necessity, my choice; but it is from my husband's writings and descriptions that the choice has been made. Whenever it was impossible to avoid adding my own words, every effort was made to keep to the original style of the author himself.

It should be mentioned that my husband's personal recollections of the Greatest Holy Leaf were closely linked to his memories of the Guardian of the Cause. Every time that he mentioned the Greatest Holy Leaf, he dwelt at some length on the Guardian and the effect that Shoghi Effendi had on him when he came on pilgrimage to Haifa as a young student from Beirut. His love for the Guardian became the motivating force of his being, and his whole life thereafter became a constant effort to please his beloved.

It was to the Guardian that he and some of his fellow-students from Beirut owed the privilege of meeting the Greatest Holy Leaf, for it was not customary in those days for men to be admitted to the presence of the ladies of the household.

Although my husband met the Greatest Holy Leaf only two times, and no conversation took place between them on those occasions, the impression made by her saintly presence on his sensitive heart was such that the very mention of her name filled him with the tenderest feelings of reverence and devotion.

It is a great pity that he was unable to complete his labour of love in her sweet memory. Even so, what he has left with us captures the imagination and inspires the heart with deep feelings of affection and admiration for the one of whom Bahá'u'lláh has said:

> Verily, she is a leaf that hath sprung from this preexistent Root. She hath revealed herself in My name and tasted of the sweet savours of My holy, My wondrous pleasure. At one time We gave her to drink from My honeyed Mouth, at another caused her to partake of My mighty, My luminous Kawthar. Upon her rest the glory of My name and the fragrance of My shining robe.[1]

– Gloria Faizí
June, 1982

NOTES AND REFERENCES

1 *Bahíyyih Khánum, The Greatest Holy Leaf* (Haifa: Bahá'í World Centre, 1982) p. 5.

Grief-stricken by the sudden passing of our beloved Guardian, I sought shelter beneath the slopes of a far-off range of mountains. I needed a fresh spirit of patience and endurance to withstand the many difficult tests ahead.

A strong and yet mysterious force drew me out of the dust of despondency and opened my tearful eyes to the splendour of God's creation: the indescribable beauty of the firmament above, and the charm of the mountains resting calm and serene on the banks of a lake which stretched endlessly before me.

I inhaled the fresh air of the early hour of dawn. The quiet solitude of that hour and the infinite beauty of the scenery around filled my heart with awe and reverence for the Creator.

I turned my eyes to the majesty of the lofty mountains to learn from them the lesson of steadfastness if sorrows were to darken all horizons. Suddenly a moving image startled me! It was a figure clad in black which seemed to follow the turns and twists of the elevated mountain paths, dim in the morning mist. Was it a vision, or a hallucination caused by my intense grief? Or was it a mental realization of my deep longing to catch one more glimpse of the lost Beloved?

Many a time I had followed that magnetic figure when he climbed the mountain of God, his rhythmic and determined steps enhancing the charm of his royal gait. It was he who had breathed life into my withered bones.

And now an immeasurable distance separated us from each other. In no time the clouds, like a mass of cotton wool, their fringes on fire with the rays of the rising sun, enveloped that distant figure. The mountain peaks concealed him, nature sheltered him and the far-off horizons shielded him from the realm of man, the intruder.

Unbearable pangs of loneliness swept over me. Dazed and dejected, whither could I turn my heart? I asked myself:

Is this all we crave for?
Are these the only gifts we receive:
a swift glance, a sigh, a tear drop?
And when possessions are plundered
and all doors are shut, what remains?
Only dismay which holds fast sway over us.

At that early hour of morning, the lake seemed fast asleep, cradling the mountains in its bosom. Not even a ripple disturbed its serenity. It was like a large mirror reflecting the glory of the firmament and the exquisite beauty of its surroundings.

The sun was slowly rising and one could feel the presence of the birds amongst the thick foliage. It would take them some time to beautify themselves before they made their appearance. A single bird, however, appeared on the topmost branches of a lofty arbour, but before it started singing its morning devotions, it had to make its ablutions. It spread its wings like a pair of ethereal Japanese fans to sustain its equilibrium. Then it swooped down to the water, yet its flight never broke the prevailing silence.

The bird touched the surface of the lake with the tip of a wing and then took its flight to the pinnacle of the heavens above.

By the touch of its wing, the bird, like an accomplished artist, had created ever-widening, harmonious circles which covered and ornamented the vast surface of the lake. The ripples, like well-trained soldiers, hastened to reach the shore. They rolled on and on. They seemed greedy and ready to confiscate the rich banks of the lake, but it was not so. Having reached their destination, they came back unstained by the red soil of the shore. Nor did they carry with them even a blade of grass as they returned, translucent and unsoiled, to the bosom of the lake – now aglow in the first rays of the sun.

The lake finished its game of circles and regained its calm to reflect the image of the rising sun; the mountains remained firm and unshaken, while the bird continued its upward flight. Its morning prayer was a celestial song which reverberated in all directions. The entire creation was awakened by the sweet melodies of that song. The bird soared higher and higher until it was reduced to a tiny dot.

That beautiful bird reminded me of one of the statements of 'Abdu'l-Bahá. The Master said there are souls ushered into this world who keep themselves utterly detached from the defilements of this earthly life and return to their Lord absolutely pure and unsullied. They are like certain birds which swoop down but barely touch the surface of the earth before they fly back to their heavenly nest.

Whenever I ponder upon this wondrous statement of 'Abdu'l-Bahá, my thoughts are immediately drawn to His own beloved sister, the Greatest Holy Leaf, who is to me the exalted personification of all the sublime qualities of detachment. She came from the firmament on High and, though she touched the world of dust, she was not defiled by it. She lived on this planet but was never attached to this world. Though in the physical temple and surrounded by the pressures and cares of earthly life, she remained absolutely detached. Nor did she show any tendency towards the mundane habits of human life or any inclination to its material bonds.

Throughout her tempestuous life, the progress of the Cause of God was her only aim for which she sacrificed all she had. She left no material riches. She had none. But we are imbued by the perfume of her heavenly life which is the celestial legacy she has left for every Bahá'í.

Bahíyyih Khánum, daughter of Bahá'u'lláh and designated by Him as the Greatest Holy Leaf, was born in Ṭihrán in 1846. She was two years younger than her illustrious brother, 'Abdu'l-Bahá, and three years older than the Purest Branch. As I think of her now, my mind goes back to her childhood and, beyond that, to the time when the family of Bahá'u'lláh enjoyed fame and every comfort in their native land, Iran.

The mansion in which Bahá'u'lláh was born is still considered one of the luxurious and magnificent dwelling places raised during the reign of the Qájár dynasty. It is situated in the proximity of the palaces of the Qájárs and the central square of the capital.

This mansion belonged to Mírzá Buzurg-i-Núrí, the father of Bahá'u'lláh, who was a Vazír or Minister of the Sháh. The Vazír traced his lineage to the ancient kings of Iran, and he was distinguished amongst the rest of the courtiers for his literary and artistic merits, especially his exquisite calligraphy. He was a very handsome person and his dignified presence commanded awe and reverence. He attracted people by his generosity, piety and nobility. He was known as the shelter of the oppressed, and victims who suffered the ill treatment of cruel government officials in far away regions of Iran would throng to the doors of his mansion, seeking help and justice.

The residence of the Vazír had a spiritual influence on many people and, at the time of the birth of the Supreme Manifestation of God, Bahá'u'lláh, one of the neighbours dreamed that an extraordinary Child had been born in that exalted abode.

'Abdu'l-Bahá, the Greatest Holy Leaf and the Purest Branch were born into this noble household and they spent the first years of their lives surrounded by every wealth and comfort. But the day came when the solid foundations of the family of Bahá'u'lláh were shaken by severe adversities. They became the target of the wrath of a fanatical mob. Cruel hands were lifted up against them and voices were raised to insult and humiliate them. One day they heard the thunder of drums, bugles and cymbals in the street outside their house; then suddenly, a furious, savage crowd, shouting abuses and cursing the followers of the Báb, broke open the doors and descended upon them. The inhabitants of the house came under the brutal treatment of a mob inflamed with wrath against all Bábís. Like a terrible storm the wild crowd swept through their richly furnished house and, when they had left, there remained nothing but a barren, empty place, the desolate ruins of the beautiful home.

The reason for these disastrous events was to remain a mystery for the small children of Bahá'u'lláh for many years to come. At that time 'Abdu'l-Bahá was not yet nine years old, the Greatest Holy Leaf was six and the Purest Branch was only three.

As long as the members of the family of Bahá'u'lláh had been under the shadow of His protection, they had no worries, but now rumours reached them that Bahá'u'lláh had been chained, taken through the streets of Ṭihrán and finally doomed to enter the most despicable of the prisons of the world – the Síyáh-Chál! His wife and children thought He was lost to them forever.

Bahá'u'lláh had come to be known as the strongest defender of the Báb's religion at a time when the Bábís were unjustly suspected and mercilessly accused of plotting to assassinate the Sháh. The attack on the followers of the Báb was a sudden upheaval which focused on Bahá'u'lláh the attention of all the authorities in the land and the mass of its population.

The Muslim clergy, in the guise of protectors of their Faith, sanctioned monstrous actions and freely issued cruel verdicts against the Bábís, which were contrary to the explicit decrees of their Holy Book, the Qur'án. Blasphemous falsehood became the rule of the day. There was no authority which could control these unbridled priests, nor was there any fair-minded and courageous person in command to punish their glaring disobedience to the texts of the Book they professed to believe in. No wonder that one of the Imáms of their Faith had prophesied that the clergy living in the days of the Promised One would be 'the most wicked of the divines beneath the shadow of heaven'.[1]

We should know that the Shí'ih Muslims had theological institutions to which students were drawn from surrounding areas. The graduates of these institutions became centres of authority around which clustered a large group of individuals. The lives of these people were safe as long as they obeyed such centres of authority, but as soon as a word was uttered against anyone who dared to disobey these religious leaders, that person, his entire family and property, would be in immediate danger. He would be persecuted, his possessions would be plundered and his house razed to the ground.

The influence of the clergy was felt all over the country and the masses were completely under their control. Religious leaders discouraged the opening of schools in Iran because they wished their followers to remain illiterate and offer them blind obedience. Thus they suffocated the people in the dark and poisonous atmosphere of sheer ignorance so as to satiate their own thirst for power. In brief: life and death, wealth and poverty and every detail of the people's lives were under the strict rule of the clergy and they had no right to question the decrees issued by their ecclesiastical leaders.

The sovereign, Náṣiri'd-Dín Sháh, was surrounded by religious potentates. He was afraid of their influence and their satanic plans and, as the Persian proverb goes, 'He did not dare to even drink a glass of water without their sanction.' But after the attempt on his life, the Sháh himself was so enraged that he said if he knew that a tree had been planted by a Bábí he would uproot and burn it! No one dared approach him for the purpose of removing misunderstandings and assuring him that the Bábís had never plotted against him. All doors were shut in their faces, and the followers of the Báb had no chance to prove their loyalty to the Crown.

The clergy needed no further encouragement. They unanimously spread the verdict that the Bábís should be mowed down by the order of the Sháh. They shouted the ugliest and most ignoble accusations against the new Faith from the top of their pulpits in the mosques where thousands of their followers gathered to hear them. They flung down their turbans in indignation and cried, 'Do you call yourselves Muslims? Are you not ashamed to face your Prophet? How can you rest when the Bábís are multiplying around us? Anyone who kills even one of these infidels will reap abundant reward in heaven!'

The illiterate and ignorant followers would unite to please their religious leaders. One of them would cry out, 'Let us go and burn the home of a Bábí', and within a short time the house would be burned down and its inhabitants dispersed on the streets. In those days, friends and neighbours, members of one family or profession were like a rosary in the hands of a clergyman. All of a sudden he would break the thread that held them together and would scatter them in all directions.

The people of Iran had not been ferocious by nature, but their so-called divines changed them into beasts. They were pushed towards insanity and savagery until they became like wolves with an insatiable thirst for blood. Even the youth and children were encouraged to wave banners, beat drums and take part in devilish activities.

All the forces of the government and the clergy now became concentrated against the small Bábí community dispersed in different quarters of Ṭihrán. Exchange of news became impossible and the fate of every believer was unknown in those days of terror.

The tide of hatred spread quickly from the capital throughout the whole country. Blind prejudice and sheer animosity drew bloodthirsty crowds to the home of anyone who was suspected of being a follower of the Báb. That moral force which controls beastly conduct in Man had been slain in these people. They grew rich by plundering the homes of defenceless individuals. They became intoxicated by the sight of the blood of the innocent. At the instigation of the clergy, they went so far as to carry the decapitated heads of their victims through the streets of the town and then throw each head back to the bereaved family.

The account of an incident will suffice to show the attitude of the clergy in those days: A crowd of people captured a man who was branded as a Bábí and took him to the house of a priest so as to obtain a death warrant and be able to kill their victim with a clear conscience. The priest was having his afternoon siesta when he heard the angry crowd clamouring outside his door. He did not so much as sit up to have a look at the man he was about to sentence. He cried out to the mob not to bring him in. If the man was a Bábí, he said, they could kill him. Then he went back to sleep while the savage people tore their victim to pieces in the street.

The clergy in Iran, inflated with pride, established the throne of their might on the corpses of the followers of the Cause of God in order to consolidate the foundations of their supreme authority. Their thirst for the blood of these innocent souls was insatiable and they were determined to avail themselves of every opportunity to claim as many victims as they could.

The early period of our Faith was the ripe season of trials and tribulations. They were replete with severe tests which, like a hurricane, struck down many strong and deeply rooted trees. The religion of God went through the process of purification and His true lovers were called upon to demonstrate their faith.

Thousands of greetings and salutations to those invincible, dauntless and steadfast souls who waxed eloquent in the midst of persecutions, when surrounded by their ferocious enemies. They displayed the utmost courage and, whenever they had the slightest chance, proclaimed the advent of the Beloved of the World and tried to explain the verities of the Cause of God, though they received no response except foul accusations, blasphemous curses and indescribable torture. If they were not cut to pieces with knives and daggers on the streets, they were chained and forced into dark prisons where they were made to drink poison, face bullets or receive the stroke of the sword of the executioner. These heroic souls kept the doors of heaven open for any who were thirsty for the Water of Life. On the day when Bahá'u'lláh was taken to the Síyáh-Chál and the brutal mob looted His house, His relatives and the servants of His household fled the place in terror. Bahá'u'lláh's small children were left alone with their mother, the saintly and gentle lady, Ásíyih Khánum.

To save her children from further assault, Ásíyih Khánum took the youngest in her arms, told the other two to follow her, and hurried through unfamiliar streets and narrow, dusty lanes to a part of the town where they would not be easily recognized.

The writer, in his childhood, lived in the quarter where the mother and her children had taken shelter years before. He recalls how the local inhabitants encouraged their young people to embitter the life of the Bahá'ís by throwing stones at their children and cursing them on their way to the Bahá'í school. He also remembers the streets and lanes through which Ásíyih Khánum and her children must have passed on the day they left their home to find a refuge in another part of the town.

Coming out of the central section of the capital where the palace of the Sháh and the mansions of the ministers are situated, they entered the covered bazaars of Ṭihrán where there is little light even during the day. From the bazaars they emerged into a crowded area where people used to have religious gatherings and, issuing forth from this dangerous section of the road, they came to a large district which is called *Sandilaj*. Here they found a place to stay until their banishment from Iran.

To the end of His life 'Abdu'l-Bahá recalled the courage with which His gracious mother set out to save her children from the ferocious people around them.

Isfandíyár was a gem from Africa, pure and untarnished, and yet firm and steadfast as a diamond under all pressures and persecutions. He manifested his inherent qualities when faced with perils which endangered his life as a Bábí. His wonderful countenance reflected the rays of love and courage.

Isfandíyár was a servant in the house of Bahá'u'lláh and, as a fruitful tree planted in good soil, he yielded a spiritual harvest. His love for Bahá'u'lláh was unlimited and, though many Ministers and other high government officials coveted him as a servant in their household, he remained ever faithful to his own Master.

At the time when the persecution of the Bábís began in the capital and Bahá'u'lláh was taken to the Síyáh-Chál, the enemies of the new Faith were looking for Isfandíyár so that they could force him to betray the followers of the Báb whom he had seen in the house of Bahá'u'lláh. The Sháh had commanded many people to find Isfandíyár and they were searching for him everywhere. But when he heard of the misfortune which had befallen the family of his beloved Master, nothing could keep him away from them.

We can imagine Isfandíyár standing among the ruins of his Master's House, drowned in an ocean of tribulation, his heart heavy with the weight of anguish. He seemed to have lost everything in the world. He did not think of all the rich furnishings, clothes and jewels which had been looted from the house of Bahá'u'lláh. But the thought of his Master in the Síyáh-Chál and the members of that noble family now dispersed and at the mercy of their foes, was more than he could bear. 'Where are the children?' he asked himself. 'What has befallen their saintly mother?' Isfandíyár decided to find them, but there was no trace of the family in the surrounding neighbourhood. No one knew where they had gone or what fresh misfortune had overtaken them.

Isfandíyár pondered, planned and came to a decision; then he rose up like one of the lions of his own continent. But bravery alone was not enough and here is where we discover the purity of his heart. He put his trust in divine guidance and, as he went out to trace the steps of his lost ones, a mysterious force directed his steps and led him to his goal. It seemed as though he had become invisible as he walked on the streets and passed through the marketplace, because no one recognized or molested him.

The joy of the children at their reunion with Isfandíyár was great, for they loved him dearly. Speaking of him years later, 'Abdu'l-Bahá said, 'Whenever I think of Isfandíyár I am moved to tears, although he passed away fifty years ago.'[2]

After her home was looted, Ásíyih Khánum had little to give her children to eat and they went hungry most of the time. She did not know whom to turn to or how to provide for them. Worst of all, she had no more news of her beloved Husband and wondered what had befallen Him in the Síyáh-Chál. She was surrounded by grave danger and in need of assistance and yet, when she saw their faithful servant standing before them, her first thoughts were for his safety. She said to him, 'There are a hundred policemen seeking for you. If they catch you they will not kill you at once but will torture you with fire. They will cut off your fingers. They will cut off your ears. They will put out your eyes to force you to tell them the secrets of Bahá'u'lláh. Go away! Do not stay here.'[3]

Isfandíyár was deeply touched by her noble expressions of true concern, but he refused to go away. He told Ásíyih Khánum he could not leave until he had paid the family debts to shopkeepers from whom he had bought supplies. He could not bear to hear the fair name of his Master belittled in the market-place, and he did not leave until he had sold a few things he had and paid Bahá'u'lláh's debts to the last penny.

'Abdu'l-Bahá spoke most lovingly of Isfandíyár during His tours of Europe and America. He praised him as 'the essence of love, radiant with sanctity and perfection, luminous with light'. He crowned his head with the diadem of eternity when He said, 'If a perfect man could be found in the world, that man was Isfandíyár.'[4]

Ásíyih <u>Kh</u>ánum now lived in an obscure corner of the town where she kept her children by her side all day, fearful for their safety. But one day, when they were hungry and there was no food in the house, she sent her eight-year-old son, 'Abbás, to the house of an aunt to ask for a little money. 'Abdu'l-Bahá recounts how He was recognized as the son of a Bábí and chased by a group of boys on His way back. He had to run for His life and, when He reached home and threw Himself into the house, He was completely out of breath. But He had managed to bring back a small coin which His aunt had tied in the corner of a handkerchief.

The children pined after their Father and longed to have as much as a single glance of His face. 'Abdu'l-Bahá repeatedly begged to be allowed to go to visit His Father until the faithful Isfandíyár volunteered to take Him to the Síyáh-<u>Ch</u>ál.

They went through long, crooked streets and dimly-lit, covered bazaars. They passed the famous district of *Galú-Bandak*, which was the midway point to the prison, and reached a very crowded, busy street at the end of which was the gate to the <u>Sh</u>áh's palace. A few rooms had been built for the royal guards above the arched gateway, and in the evenings primitive musicians beat their drums and blew their trumpets there. Through the palace gate one could see a beautiful, spacious garden and a large pond of crystal-clear water with a fountain in the middle. There was a cannon near this pond which was claimed to be one of the booties of war brought from India by Nádir <u>Sh</u>áh many years before. But the cannon had been gradually elevated in rank and had become a shrine for the ignorant people. Women would tie colourful pieces of cloth to its wheels, make vows and beg the cannon to grant them the realization of their wishes. Such was the depth of the misery and ignorance of the people who failed to see the light of the Sun of Truth which had risen from their country.

The Síyáh-Chál was not far from the palace of the Sháh and, when they reached the place, Isfandíyár was shown the way down to the door of the dungeon. He took 'Abdu'l-Bahá on his strong shoulders and slowly descended the steep, narrow steps. The entrance to the Síyáh-Chál was in complete darkness, but before they could reach it, they heard the commanding voice of Bahá'u'lláh: 'Do not bring the child here.' They had to go up again and wait for the time when the prisoners were taken out for a short while each day.

When they saw Bahá'u'lláh, He was tied to a number of other prisoners and stooped under the weight of an extremely heavy chain which hung around His neck. Lack of food and the absence of the least means of sanitation in that foul prison had left their terrible marks on His body, and 'Abdu'l-Bahá was heart-broken as He looked upon His beloved Father.

His little sister, Bahíyyih, too had her share when, after four long months of suspense, Bahá'u'lláh was released from the Síyáh-Chál. Can we ever imagine the pangs of bitter grief which filled her heart at that tender age when she saw her Father at last? His clothes were torn and soiled, His hair and beard unkempt. He was so weak that He could only walk with great difficulty. His back was bent and His neck was blistered and swollen from the galling weight of the chains He had borne day and night for four months. He was ill from the foul air He had breathed in that dark dungeon and His eyes were not yet accustomed to daylight.

As she looked on unbelievingly, Bahíyyih little realized that, from now on, she would be called upon to share her Father's sufferings. She would be raised and educated in the school of adversity, and the rest of her childhood would be spent as though in a rudderless boat tossed about by the storms raging around them. But, through all those years of repeated exile and persecution, imprisonment, poverty and illness, she stood firm by her Father's side, never wavering in her loyalty and devotion to Him and His Cause.

Bahá'u'lláh had not yet had time to recover from the ordeals He had suffered in the Síyáh-Chál, when He was banished from Iran. It was rumoured that the Sháh could not rest on his throne until Bahá'u'lláh and His family had left the country. The decree of the Sháh was immediately confirmed by the flattering courtiers around him and enthusiastically applauded by all the religious dignitaries of the land. The hysterical cries of these relentless enemies of the Cause were raised from every pulpit.

Their ignoble accusations against the Bábís knew no limits. 'The religion of the Báb', they said, 'is worse than the outburst of a terrifying epidemic sweeping over our country, and the S̲h̲áh is determined to wipe it out.' The news of the banishment of Bahá'u'lláh and His family filled them with joy and excitement. They congratulated each other as they passed on the news: 'The Bábís are banished, and this supreme victory is won by no less a personage than the S̲h̲áh himself!' They showered exaggerated titles upon the sovereign, calling him the Protector of the Religion of God, the Supporter of Islám in the world, the Shield and Shelter of all true believers.

The small band of Bahá'u'lláh's friends were immersed in an ocean of poignant sorrow. They had leaned on Him in their weakness, and had received the light of His guidance. Now that He was leaving them, they did not know whom they could turn to for help.

But the Sun of Truth, which had risen in Iran, was destined to reach its zenith in other lands and shed its light from the prison-city of 'Akká. Bahá'u'lláh was to ascend the throne of fame and glory, while the S̲h̲áh, now filled with pride, was doomed to perish and leave no trace.

The day came when the family of Bahá'u'lláh set out from Ṭihrán, never to return to their homeland. The two older children, 'Abbás and Bahíyyih, had thought that their worries were over now that their Father had come back, but when they realized that their little brother, Mihdí, had to be left behind in Ṭihrán, there was no end to their sorrow. They missed the innocent look of his large black eyes and the sweet smiles which always adorned his heavenly face. Their beautiful mother had surrendered her will to the Will of her Lord and was content to follow her beloved Husband wherever He went, but for her, too, the parting with Mihdí was heart-rending. How could she explain to him the reason for this sudden, cruel separation as he followed her with his eyes?

An Arab poet has said that the ground where lovers bid each other farewell is set aflame by the fire in their hearts.

Once, when I was in a meeting in Bag̲h̲dád, I met a wonderful person. His name was Jalíl. He was tall, well-built and wore a long, spotless, Arab gown. He had a penetrating, warm voice which rang out like a bell when he chanted the Arabic Tablets of Bahá'u'lláh. I was drawn to this man and felt a deep love for him in my heart.

After the meeting, Jalíl approached me with a smiling face and conversed with me in pure, beautiful Persian. I was astonished at his command of the language, and asked, 'How is it that you speak such fluent Persian?' He said, 'Our mother spoke to us in the language of Bahá'u'lláh. If any of her children addressed her in Arabic, she would not answer.'

'Was your mother a Persian?' I inquired. He said, 'No, our mother was born into an Arab tribe.' Then he added, 'When the Ancient Beauty resided in Baghdád, the ladies of His household had to remain inside the house almost all the time. Bahíyyih Khánum was only a child and felt lonely being by herself all day. Our mother, who was a young girl of the same age, became Bahíyyih Khánum's playmate and learned Persian from her.'

I was eager to know more, and Jalíl continued: 'The two girls became inseparable friends. Bahíyyih Khánum called her playmate *Ḥabíbatí* (my dear one). Our mother lived in the house of Bahá'u'lláh almost all the time and her parents were very happy. This went on for almost ten years. Then Bahá'u'lláh and His family were exiled from Baghdád, and Bahíyyih Khánum had to leave for an unknown destination. Ḥabíbatí was heart-broken and no one could console her in her grief.

'After the family left, she became like a bird without wings. She would sit in a corner all day and lament in the anguish of her separation from her beloved companion. She was not embittered. She just sat chanting prayers and reciting sad poetry. Imagine! She was not sorrowing for an ordinary friend. No, the one who had left her was the daughter of Bahá'u'lláh! Even pilgrims who met Bahíyyih Khánum for only a few days grew to love her. Ḥabíbatí, who had been her close companion for many years, could not bear to be parted from her and she suffered from this separation all her life.

'Our mother was illiterate, but she would at times dictate letters for Bahíyyih Khánum. Every word of her letters was a drop of the blood of her heart, a gem of pure love offered to her exalted beloved.'

Jalíl related another moving incident in the life of his mother. He said that they sometimes held meetings in their home. Though their house was very modest and the gatherings quite simple, the friends vied with each other to be present at those meetings. Many prayers and Tablets were chanted and the meetings went on till after midnight.

Ḥabíbatí sat in a small adjacent room by herself and prepared tea and coffee for her guests. One night, when the meeting had come to an end and the friends had dispersed, her children found Ḥabíbatí in physical agony and unable to move from her seat on the floor. 'When I was serving tea,' she told them, 'this large pot of boiling water spilled over my leg.' They removed her clothes and saw that she was severely burned. 'Why did you not call us?' they asked, 'The burn should have been attended to immediately.'

'What!' she said, 'Did you expect your mother to cry out for help and disturb a meeting held in the name of Bahá'u'lláh?'

Ḥabíbatí was blessed with wonderful children who were stalwart, enthusiastic members of the Bahá'í community in Baghdád. She died very peacefully, and her long years of separation from her beloved Bahíyyih Khánum came to an end at last.

Bahíyyih Khánum grew to be a beautiful young woman. By the time she began to carry the load of her mother's family responsibilities, she came to be known as Khánum 'the lady of the household'. Many asked for her hand in marriage but she preferred to remain single. Incessant pleading did not change her plan of life. She was determined to spend all her days and every ounce of her energy in the service of the Cause of God.

Khánum was a solace to her Father and, though she was not physically strong, she followed Him through all the stages of His exile. She faced every deprivation and endured every hardship, firm and unshaken in her faith.

To fathom a life which was lived under the shadow of the Supreme Manifestation of God is indeed beyond the scope of Man's imagination. These inadequate lines written in memory of the most exalted woman of the Universal Faith of Bahá'u'lláh, are put down with the hope that we may become acquainted with the walks of life trodden by great souls and learn the essence and reality of our stupendous Cause. Thus, love will find its way easily into our hearts and show us the road we must follow when bewildered among the many paths of life.

The Greatest Holy Leaf showed magnanimity when confronted with savagery; endurance and perseverance when burdened with sorrows; and never failed to be gentle and loving towards those who poisoned her life. She suffered with absolute acquiescence the bitter stages of exile from country to country, the many changes of residence, the lack of the barest necessities of life and, above all, the merciless acts of cruelty committed by those who were in charge when she and her family were in prison. She remained a moving spirit of detachment and passed through the darkest periods of her life with unparalleled dignity.

In the Most Great Prison where the guards, bereft of any kind of clemency, made conditions as difficult as possible for them, she never complained. The filthy environment and the appalling conditions within the prison walls, and the never-ending sickness around her could not embitter her life or induce her into a state of inactivity. She desired nothing but to follow 'Abdu'l-Bahá in the path of servitude. When their fellow-prisoners were in distress, she tried to alleviate their suffering; when they were ill, she helped 'Abdu'l-Bahá to care for them.

Khánum had boundless love for her younger brother, Mihdí, the Purest Branch. She suffered bitterly when he fell through a skylight in the prison and died in pain before her very eyes. She suffered, too, when the followers of Bahá'u'lláh, who had walked on foot for many months to reach 'Akká, were forbidden to meet their Lord, or when a fellow-prisoner was not allowed to buy a little milk for his dying child. But she suffered in silence.

Years later, whenever pilgrims asked Khánum to tell them of those days, she would smile and say they should talk of happy times, for those sad days were over.

After Bahá'u'lláh passed away, the Greatest Holy Leaf held fast to His Covenant and became 'Abdu'l-Bahá's staunchest supporter. Her greatest joy was to be near Him and assist Him in His work. She demonstrated the same qualities of faith during the Master's lifetime as she had shown in the days of her Father and, in the midst of the fresh calamities heaped upon them through the machinations of the Covenant-breakers, she never wavered from the straight path though the road she trod was strewn with many thorns.

Khánum was a jewel around which revolved the life of every member of the family of 'Abdu'l-Bahá. The Master Himself could not be parted from her for long. We can see this from some of the words He wrote to her when only the distance between Haifa and 'Akká separated them from each other:

> Thou didst leave for 'Akká to remain but two days or so and then return, but now thou hast been gone from us for quite a while. We have stayed behind in Haifa, all alone, and it is very difficult to get along … In any case, no matter how things are, come thou here today, because my heart is longing for thee.[5]

The tender and celestial relationship between 'Abdu'l-Bahá and His sister is beyond description. Their hearts were cemented together in their love for the Ancient Beauty. They shared every joy and, when sorrows abounded, Khánum was ready to lighten her Brother's burden by taking on more than any other person around Him could endure. In a letter to her, the Master writes:

> O my well-beloved sister, O Most Exalted Leaf!
>
> … There is no way but to endure the toil and trouble of God's path. If thou dost not bear these hardships, who could ever bear them?[6]

And again, contemplating the extent of her tribulations, He says:

> Dear and deeply spiritual sister! At morn and eventide, with the utmost ardour and humility, I supplicate at the Divine Threshold, and offer this, my prayer:
>
> 'Grant, O Thou my God, the Compassionate, that pure and blessed Leaf may be comforted by Thy sweet savours of holiness and sustained by the reviving breeze of Thy loving care and mercy. Reinforce her spirit with the signs of Thy Kingdom, and gladden her soul with the testimonies of Thy everlasting dominion. Comfort, O my God, her sorrowful heart with the remembrance of Thy face, initiate her into Thy hidden mysteries, and inspire her with the revealed splendours of Thy heavenly light. Manifold are her sorrows, and infinitely grievous her distress. Bestow continually upon her the favour of Thy sustaining grace and, with every fleeting breath, grant her the blessing of Thy bounty. Her hopes and expectations are centred in Thee; open Thou to her face the portals of Thy tender mercies and lead her into the ways of Thy wondrous benevolence. Thou art the Generous, the All-Loving, the Sustainer, the All-Bountiful.'[7]

The life of the Greatest Holy Leaf cannot be separated from that of either the Master or the Guardian. With the passing of 'Abdu'l-Bahá, Khánum lost the support she had depended on all her life. She was now called upon to shoulder fresh responsibilities which required all her strength. But the love of the Guardian of the Cause surrounded her; and in him she found her joy and comfort.

Ever since Shoghi Effendi's childhood there had always been a very close relationship between him and the Greatest Holy Leaf. When the Master passed away, the Guardian became Khánum's only love in life. Her thoughts were centred in him, and his happiness and comfort was all that she desired.

In the literature of the East, many stories are told about two lovers, Laylí and Majnún. Because of the intensity of his love for Laylí, Majnún could think of nothing else. Once a man went to him and complained about his partner in trade. He talked for hours and explained the details of their dispute. At the end he asked Majnún, 'In your judgement, which of us is right?' Majnún's reply was 'Laylí'. This is given as an example of true love because nothing could distract the lover from the thought of his beloved.

In *The Seven Valleys*, Bahá'u'lláh recounts another story about Laylí and Majnún: Majnún was found looking through a pile of dust. They asked him what he was searching for, and again his reply was 'Laylí'. Such extreme concentration of thought is considered the sublime sign of selfless love.

This was the quality of the love which the Greatest Holy Leaf had for the Guardian. Once, when tea was being served to a group of pilgrims visiting Khánum, the girl who carried the large tray piled with teapots, cups and saucers, dropped it on her way to the room and a terrific noise resounded through the house. Khánum put her hands on her heart and exclaimed, 'Where is Shoghi Effendi?' When she was assured that he was upstairs and all right, she calmed down and told the attendant, 'Do not worry about the cups and saucers. We have others in the house.'

The Guardian reciprocated Khánum's feelings, and the love and reverence he had for her was far beyond anything he showed toward all others.

Every afternoon the Guardian would go up Mount Carmel to visit the Shrines and spend some time with the pilgrims. If he was later than usual in coming back, Khánum would grow restless and send someone to bring her news that Shoghi Effendi was on his way to the house. The Guardian would visit her in the evenings and would often have his dinner in her room.

It was not very long after the passing of the Master when a pilgrim, by the name of Rawḥáníyyih, came to visit the Holy Land. She belonged to a family of early believers from a Jewish background. Rawḥáníyyih was a charming person and she chanted prayers with a voice which was penetrating and full of sweet resonance. Her beautiful chanting brought much comfort to the heart of the Greatest Holy Leaf and, when the Guardian heard of this, he asked Rawḥáníyyih to extend her stay for a few months after the days of her pilgrimage had come to an end.

The sweet stream of Khánum's love purified the hearts and uplifted the souls of those who came in touch with her, and the spell of that love was cast on all the pilgrims who came to the Holy Land.

One of the Persian believers once recounted to the writer that when he came on pilgrimage with a group of fellow-believers, he brought along his wife who was not a Bahá'í. In those days the journey to Haifa was long and difficult. Coming from Iran, they had to travel by car for days and cross a stretch of hot desert between Baghdád and Damascus. Some of the travellers, under the hardships of the journey, grew somewhat short-tempered and were rude to the Muslim woman. She was very sad at heart but did not say anything.

Then the day came when the pilgrims found themselves at the door of the Master's House. It was the custom for the women-folk to be led into a room where they would have the privilege of meeting the daughter of Bahá'u'lláh. But on that day, they found Khánum waiting expectantly outside. The pilgrims hastened to meet her. She greeted them all but was still waiting outside. Waiting for whom? Finally they saw the Muslim woman slowly approaching, full of uncertainty and concern. The Greatest Holy Leaf advanced toward her and took the woman in her arms. Then, holding her by the hand, she led her into the room and invited her to sit next to herself. When all the pilgrims had taken their seats, Khánum took off her own ring and put it on the finger of her guest of honour. This brought tears to the eyes of everyone in the room as they learned a lesson in universal love.

The husband of the Muslim woman told me that his wife did not embrace the Faith, but she would never part with the ring, and she died with the name of Khánum on her lips.

I was a new Bahá'í when I first came to Haifa as a pilgrim in 1927. I was young and inexperienced and my knowledge of the Faith was limited to a few elementary books I had gone through in Bahá'í classes in Ṭihrán.

I waited in the garden of the Master's House to be called to meet the Guardian and it seemed an infinitely long while before someone came to invite me in. The room I entered was beautiful though very simply furnished, and I thought I could sense the heartfelt prayers of countless visitors resounding and vibrating in that place.

I sat facing the door when suddenly the Guardian came in unannounced and without the least ceremony. He was in the prime of youth, with a heavenly countenance and a divine majesty. I was overcome by emotion and could not move. The Guardian, seeing my plight, came forward and said, 'Let us embrace like two brothers.' My head rested on his shoulder and tears filled my eyes as I received my spiritual baptism.

From the moment I saw the Guardian, I lost my heart to him completely. I came to realize how a single glance of the Beloved can change the entire course of a person's life. I understood the meaning of pure love and stepped into a world which cannot be fathomed through the knowledge prevalent among men.

The Guardian showered his love upon me. He asked about my studies at the American University of Beirut and encouraged me to concentrate on the study of English, Persian and Arabic.

The beloved Guardian had advised the Persian Bahá'í youth to come from Iran to Beirut for their higher education and a number of us, coming from different walks of life, gathered in Beirut during the twenties. Most of us were at the American University and we had formed a weekly gathering in the house of the Iqbál family to study Bahá'í history, principles and other aspects of our Faith.

The guide and leader in all our activities was Ḥasan Balyúzí who was indeed a true brother to each one of us. Every word of guidance he uttered was a gem; whatever standards he set, we followed. Ḥasan assumed no rank or title, but he was like a candle which threw light on the path to honour and success. Had it not been for him, I, as a new Bahá'í, would have been lost in my strange environment. His warm, sweet voice still rings in my ears and his love is imprinted on my heart forever.

At Ḥasan's suggestion, the Bahá'í students in Beirut wrote to the Guardian and asked if they might be permitted to come on pilgrimage to Haifa, a few at a time, during their Christmas or Easter holidays. The Guardian graciously granted us this favour and there was no limit to our youthful enthusiasm and happiness.

We came to Haifa each year with hearts brimful with the love of our young Guardian who was himself a fountainhead of love. He welcomed us and inquired about each student's welfare, his studies and the news he had received from his parents. He remembered his own contemporaries at the American University of Beirut. He asked about them from the relatives they had amongst us, and sent them his love. Once he said, 'Tell them that I never forget them.'

The Guardian did his utmost to make us happy and hopeful about our future. He taught us the lesson of detachment and breathed in us the spirit of servitude to the divine Threshold.

We loved him beyond measure and never wanted to part with him. The days we spent in the Guardian's presence were like rays of sunshine penetrating the rest of our dark lives, and the memory of those blissful days is still a source of spiritual nourishment and inspiration.

Every afternoon we would go to the door of the Master's House to wait for the time when the Guardian, exhausted from the burden of his work and heavy correspondence, would come out to go to the Shrines on Mount Carmel. We could discern the signs of fatigue from his tired eyes as he emerged from the house, but his heavenly countenance was always smiling when he greeted us. We followed him up the mountain and listened to the sweet stream of the utterances of the Sign of God as he shared with us news he received each day from the Bahá'ís of the world. He uplifted our spirits with the glad tidings of the progress of the Cause and helped us to understand the grandeur of our Faith.

As we walked through the gardens around the Shrines, the Guardian spoke to the few gardeners, asked after their health and gave them his instructions. One day he told one of the gardeners to gather fruit for us students from the trees around. Then, turning his wonderful gaze on us, he added with a heavenly smile, 'I am sure you must have a good appetite.'

The gardens were not so extensive or developed in those days, but the Guardian had a clear vision of what should be done and he pursued a definite course of action, never wavering in his determination. He did not rest until he had changed the rugged mountainside into a garden of paradise and had completed the construction of the Shrine of the Báb in accordance with the wishes of his beloved Grandfather, 'Abdu'l-Bahá.

What a bounty it was to accompany the Guardian to the Shrines! When he approached the resting places of the Báb and 'Abdu'l-Bahá, it seemed as if he was in Their presence and was advancing towards Them, carrying the hearts of thousands of supplicants with him to Their sacred Thresholds. When he chanted the Tablets of Visitation, it was no ordinary chanting. It was the lamentations of a Nightingale of the Abhá Kingdom caught in the cage of this material world. No one who has heard the Guardian chanting can ever forget that celestial and soul-stirring voice.

After visiting the Shrines, we would accompany the Guardian part of the way back; then he would ask us to go to the Pilgrim House and rest while he himself went back to the pile of work on his desk.

One night we stayed awake, standing on the balcony of the Pilgrim House and watching the light in the upper room of the Master's House where the Guardian worked. We wanted to know when he would go to bed and we stayed up until two in the morning!

The next day when the Guardian met us outside the Master's House, his first remark was, 'You should go to bed early at night. I am sometimes obliged to stay up because I have much to do.' How considerate he was towards others, and how utterly unmindful of his own rest and comfort!

The Guardian, though burdened under the weight of his multifarious obligations, would invariably sacrifice his own few hours of leisure to uplift the spirits of the Bahá'ís around him. In those days there were two meetings for the men in Haifa each week, one in the Pilgrim House close to the Shrines and another in the Master's House.

On Sundays, when the men gathered in the presence of the Guardian in the Pilgrim House, the women would cluster around the Greatest Holy Leaf in another building close by. On Wednesdays, when the Guardian sat with the men in the room where 'Abdu'l-Bahá used to receive His visitors, the Greatest Holy Leaf would often sit in an adjacent room where she could hear the Guardian as he spoke to the friends.

These were wonderful gatherings which we students from Beirut attended as pilgrims. All the Bahá'ís who lived in Haifa and the surrounding areas would be present. The gardeners and caretakers of the Shrines came in very simple, clean, white garments which we knew they had set aside for these meetings and which contrasted well with their weather-beaten, shining faces. Among them were Ustád Abu'l-Qásim, the embodiment of love and detachment, who had served in the Holy Land for many years; Yadu'lláh-i-Saysání, a vigorous young man from Á<u>dh</u>arbáyján; and Ismá'íl Áqá, the faithful gardener of 'Abdu'l-Bahá with whom the Master had shared His sorrows and concerns.

When 'Abdu'l-Bahá passed away, Ismá'íl Áqá could not bear to go on living and he cut his own throat. Fortunately, he was found in time and taken to hospital. There they stitched the wound but Ismá'íl Áqá jerked his head and split the wound open again and again. He had decided that he did not wish to live after his beloved Master had left this world, and the doctors could do nothing about it. When the Greatest Holy Leaf heard of this, she sent him a message saying that she longed to see him working in the Master's garden once more, and he allowed his wound to heal.

We students loved Ismá'íl Áqá and we sometimes gathered around him as he worked in the garden. He would say to us, 'When you are on pilgrimage, fix your attention on your Guardian. There are many others here, but you have only one master.[8] I try to make him happy. The load of work and responsibility on his shoulders is more than one person can carry.'

The meetings in Haifa were often attended by a number of elderly pilgrims from the East who had endured many hardships in the path of God. Indescribable feelings stirred my heart whenever I looked at these veteran soldiers of the Army of Life. These men had been on many fronts and had fought innumerable spiritual battles with courage and self-sacrifice. They had withstood the opposition of fierce enemies of the Cause and had gallantly defended the Faith against the cruel Covenant-breakers in the days of 'Abdu'l-Bahá. And now, after long years of service, they were gathered beneath the shadow and protection of their youthful commander, their beloved Guardian. As they sat in the meeting room with their eyes fixed on the entrance, waiting for his arrival, God knows what waves of memories of bygone days surged within their pure souls.

Some of them had known Shoghi Effendi long before he was appointed Guardian of the Cause, and had realized that he was unique even in his childhood. There seemed to be a mysterious connection between them and the Guardian. Suddenly one would see them arranging their clothes and preparing to stand up to receive him, and then within seconds one would hear the rhythmic footsteps of the Guardian approaching from the hall. Their eyes glittered with the light of pure love, and the rest of the world did not exist for them anymore, when he stepped into the room and lifted up his hand in greeting.

Imagine the spiritual atmosphere prevalent in that heavenly gathering with the Guardian of the Cause present and the Greatest Holy Leaf sitting close by, behind the open door leading to the adjacent room! Those meetings were indeed a sign and token of celestial feasts. Prayers and Tablets were chanted; then the Guardian spoke, encouraging the believers and giving them news of the spread of the Faith of Bahá'u'lláh throughout the countries of the world. Sometimes he would ask the group of students from Beirut to sing Bahá'í songs to cheer the hearts of the friends.

One day, when the meeting had just begun, the beloved Guardian turned to me and said, 'Will you chant something?' I was taken by surprise, but I had to obey him. Fortunately I had a collection of Tablets in my pocket. I took it out and started to chant one of the beautiful, long Tablets of Bahá'u'lláh in which He teaches Man how to tread the path that leads to reunion with the Beloved.

After chanting about two pages, I stopped and whispered, 'It is a very long Tablet.' The Guardian smiled and said, 'Yes, it is one of the early Tablets revealed in Baghdád.' Then he turned to one of the very old believers and remarked, 'Ḥájí Ḥusayn, it is a long time since you heard such chanting!' He addressed me once again and said, 'You have a warm, resonant voice. Do you chant in your meetings in Beirut?'

The day after that, when the group of students was following the Guardian up the Vineyard of God, he said, 'The Greatest Holy Leaf heard your chanting last night and would like to hear you again. Will you all go to her and make her happy?'

This rare, heavenly bounty was offered to us so suddenly that we could not immediately grasp its significance. But our joy was boundless and we spent more than half a day deciding on a suitable programme of prayers, poems and songs which we could present to the daughter of Bahá'u'lláh.

After the elapse of half a century, I still remember very clearly and vividly, the impression of those few blissful hours when I had the bounty of feasting my eyes on the beauteous countenance of the Greatest Holy Leaf.

The tender charm of that personality possessed my entire being. Its fascination has never faded, nor has its influence waned. Every detail is remembered, every nuance of that experience is faithfully retained, untouched and unaltered by the passage of time. This most precious memory scintillates in the treasure-house of my heart and soul as an immortal relic of infinite grace and loveliness.

Whenever the dust of despondency, rising from the path of my life, veils or dims the lustre of my joy, tears of longing shed in remembrance of the Greatest Holy Leaf wash away that dust and cause the light of happiness to shine and envelop my being.

Like a wealthy man who opens his safe at midnight, counts his diamonds with the utmost care and satisfaction, and gently removes the dust from his gold coins, delighting at their touch, I too find happiness in dwelling upon my treasured recollections in the midnight of loneliness and deprivation. I remember those precious incidents of my life and cover them with my tears of thanksgiving and gratitude, thus keeping them forever clear and untarnished.

In the world of my imagination, I once more follow our beloved Guardian up the slopes of Mount Carmel and breathe in the fresh air of the paradise surrounding the Holy Shrines. And I find myself in the presence of the Greatest Holy Leaf – the one who was called upon to tread the path of living martyrdom. Such is my spiritual sustenance. Time and distance have proved too feeble to weaken my grasp from the hem of the Sign of God on earth or to deter my gaze from beholding the beauty of Khánum's celestial countenance.

When our small group of students from Beirut was ushered into the presence of the Greatest Holy Leaf, she was seated at the upper end of a large room, facing the door. The wife of the Master, Munírih Khánum, sat next to her and other ladies of the household sat on either side in a semicircle, but the mother of the Guardian, Ḍíyá'íyyih Khánum, stood behind the Greatest Holy Leaf with her hands resting on the shoulders of her beloved aunt. We students were given seats facing this beautiful audience.

The Greatest Holy Leaf was very frail at that time; the many years of toil and suffering had left their marks on her, but her graceful personality, her delicate smile and her heavenly blue eyes made a lasting impression on us all. For us who had not had the privilege of beholding the majestic countenance of 'Abdu'l-Bahá, seeing the Greatest Holy Leaf was an unexpected bounty because she greatly resembled the Master. Her penetrating eyes, especially, reminded us of 'Abdu'l-Bahá.

Khánum sat still, her lily-white hands resting gently on her lap. She was a queen who inspired love and reverence, and at her throne of grandeur we offered our grateful hearts. Her glance was full of love, but she did not speak to us. The Master's wife, Munírih Khánum, spoke on her behalf. She greeted us when we arrived, and thanked us warmly, in Khánum's name, at the end of our programme of prayers, songs and Bahá'í poems. Then we were served tea and we left the Master's House exhilarated with joy because we had had the honour of creating an hour of rest and pleasure in the life of the Greatest Holy Leaf.

We arrived at the Pilgrim House later in the evening and found that Khánum had sent us boxes of nuts and special sweets. We had known of Khánum's extreme generosity, a trait she had inherited not only from her Father, but from her gracious mother as well. We knew how she always gave gifts to everyone who came to see her, and we remembered having heard that once, when some Arab ladies had arrived unannounced, and Khánum had found her store of gifts empty, she gave them the only thing she could think of – large handfuls of cube sugar – to take away!

The day after we had visited Khánum, when we were walking towards the Shrines with the Guardian as usual, he turned around and asked us, 'Did you go to Khánum yesterday? Did you chant prayers and sing songs for her? Did she like them?' We bowed and answered him. Then, with a celestial smile of contentment he said, 'I, too, had left the door of my room wide open.' We knew that the Guardian had also enjoyed our humble programme.

The next time a group of us were coming from Beirut, we prepared a one-act play called *The Light of Faith in the Darkness of the Dungeon*, which depicted the sufferings of one of the martyrs in Iran. We asked the Guardian in Haifa if he would permit us to show it in the Master's

House. His immediate reply was, 'No, it would sadden the heart of the Greatest Holy Leaf.' Such delicate expressions of concern for Khánum's feelings touched the depths of our hearts because we knew how much the Guardian loved her. But he allowed us to go to the Master's House once more and entertain the Greatest Holy Leaf with songs and poems.

This time we had begged one of our fellow-students to bring his tár[9] with him to Haifa. He had learned to play the instrument from one of the great masters in Iran and he had a lovely touch – 'his fingers were sweet' as we say in Persian. Our friend was very reluctant to bring his tár along and said it was not the proper thing to do, but we managed to persuade him to bring it.

Khánum was delighted with the programme we had prepared for her. Among other things, we sang a group song with the refrain, 'O 'Abdu'l-Bahá, my hand is stretched out in longing to reach Thy robe.' It was a simple, but deeply moving song. I chanted a Tablet revealed by 'Abdu'l-Bahá which is addressed to a man who had suffered all kinds of tribulations in the path of the Blessed Beauty. In the Tablet, 'Abdu'l-Bahá recounts the blessings we have in this Cause, and after each section He repeats, 'Why, then, should we be sad?' When I finished chanting, Munírih Khánum said the Greatest Holy Leaf would like to have a copy of this Tablet. I was very thrilled to know that Khánum was pleased with my choice. Later, in the Pilgrim House, I spent hours in order to choose the right kind of paper and pen with which to write, and made copy after copy before I was pleased with one which was sent to beloved Khánum.

After our programme had come to an end, Munírih Khánum spoke to us on behalf of the Greatest Holy Leaf and told us how much Khánum had enjoyed listening to our chanting, music and songs. Then she said something which touched our hearts and brought tears to our eyes. The Greatest Holy Leaf, she said, would love to hear one of the songs which labourers sing in Iran as they go home in the evenings on their way back from work. She asked if there was anyone among us who knew those songs. We were surprised that Khánum should still remember songs which she must have heard on the streets of Ṭihrán during her early childhood. Perhaps the sight of a group of young Persians, or the music of the tar, had taken her back to those days.

One of us, who sang well, began to sing for her in a beautiful penetrating voice. The songs Khánum had referred to are known as *kúchih-bághí*. They have a sad tune which fills the heart with poignant emotion. Who knows what memories and reminiscences of bygone days that nostalgic tune awakened in Khánum's tender heart that evening! We, too, were carried back to her years of exile and imprisonment, and to the times of sorrow she had known – not so much because of her own deprivations, but because of the tribulations suffered by those she loved.

In my reverie, I saw her as a little girl, clinging to her mother when their house was being looted in Ṭihrán, and crouching in a corner when she had no bed to sleep in during the bitterly cold nights of that terrible, long journey to Baghdád. I saw her as a young girl saying farewell to the loving companion of her childhood when she was taken from Iraq to Turkey; as a gracious woman attending to the needs of her fellow-prisoners in 'Akká; and as a gentle lady comforting 'Abdu'l-Bahá when He was bowed down under the weight of sorrow heaped upon Him by the Covenant-breakers.

The sun had set and the light in the room was fast fading. All I could now see through the mist of tears was the long, delicate white scarf on Khánum's head and the soft, white hands on her lap. Those hands had a strange effect on me. They appeared to me as the wings of a white bird flying over the dark city of 'Akká, bringing the message of strength and courage. I saw Khánum's hands removing the chains placed around her Father's neck, and drying her mother's tears when the Purest Branch was dying. And again I beheld them raised in prayer when she heard the lamentations of Bahá'u'lláh in His cell the night He had offered His beloved son as a sacrifice in the path of God: 'Mihdí, Mihdí!'

Had it not been for all those bitter tests, these hands, as white as a lily, as strong as the grip of destiny, would not have been able to hold the reins of the affairs of the Bahá'ís around the world for almost two years when 'Abdu'l-Bahá had passed away and the Guardian was absent from the Holy Land.

As I bowed my head in gratitude to the daughter of Bahá'u'lláh, I did not realize that this was the last time I would ever see her on this earthly plane.

Our pilgrimage came to an end. Once again it was time for us to part with the Guardian and leave our paradise to go back to studies in Beirut. The hired car was waiting outside the Master's House where we had gathered that morning to say goodbye to Shoghi Effendi. Our hearts were heavy and, as the Guardian entered the main hall, we wept without shame. He put his arms around each of us and whispered words of comfort, 'Do not be sad, you will come back again … Be happy, concentrate on your studies.'

In Beirut, we heard from the Guardian through his powerful messages to the Bahá'í World. These were like a balm for our aching hearts while we counted the days of the year, waiting for the time we could go back to him again.

That was a fateful year. Some months after we left Haifa, the Guardian said his last farewell to the Greatest Holy Leaf when he was going away from the Holy Land for the summer. I have heard that he held her in his arms longer than usual. She asked him to decide on a resting-place for her and he answered that the place had already been assigned. What can one say of the relationship between heavenly souls?

It was the end of summer, and the Guardian was back in Haifa. With throbbing hearts we waited for him at the foot of the stairs in front of the Master's House.

Coming down the steps, the Guardian's first words to us were: 'Do you know that the Greatest Holy Leaf has passed away?' With what depths of sorrow those words were uttered! It seemed as though the Guardian himself was reluctant to believe it. The tone of his voice was a reminder of his great loss, for the last remnant of the Heroic Age of the Bahá'í Dispensation, and the solace of his own life, had left this world.

As he led us up the mountain path this time, the Guardian turned left before coming to the gardens around the Shrine of the Báb. A new garden had sprung up here around the resting-place of the Greatest Holy Leaf. We followed the Guardian as he circumambulated that holy spot. Then we stopped for a few moments of prayer.

The blue Mediterranean stretched out before us and we stood facing, across the water, the Qiblih of the Bahá'í World, the Shrine of Bahá'u'lláh in Bahjí.

NOTES AND REFERENCES

1 *The Kitáb-i-Íqán* (Wilmette: Bahá'í Publishing Trust, 1981) p. 247.

2 *The Promulgation of Universal Peace* (Wilmette: Bahá'í Publishing Trust, 1982) p. 426.

3 ibid. p. 426

4 ibid. p. 426

5 *Bahíyyih Khánum, The Greatest Holy Leaf,* p. 13.

6 ibid. p. 13

7 ibid. p. 8

8 Ismá'íl Áqá was referring to Shoghi Effendi's brothers and cousins who later became Covenant-breakers.

9 A Persian string musical instrument.

Glory of the Sand

A story from the early days of the Faith

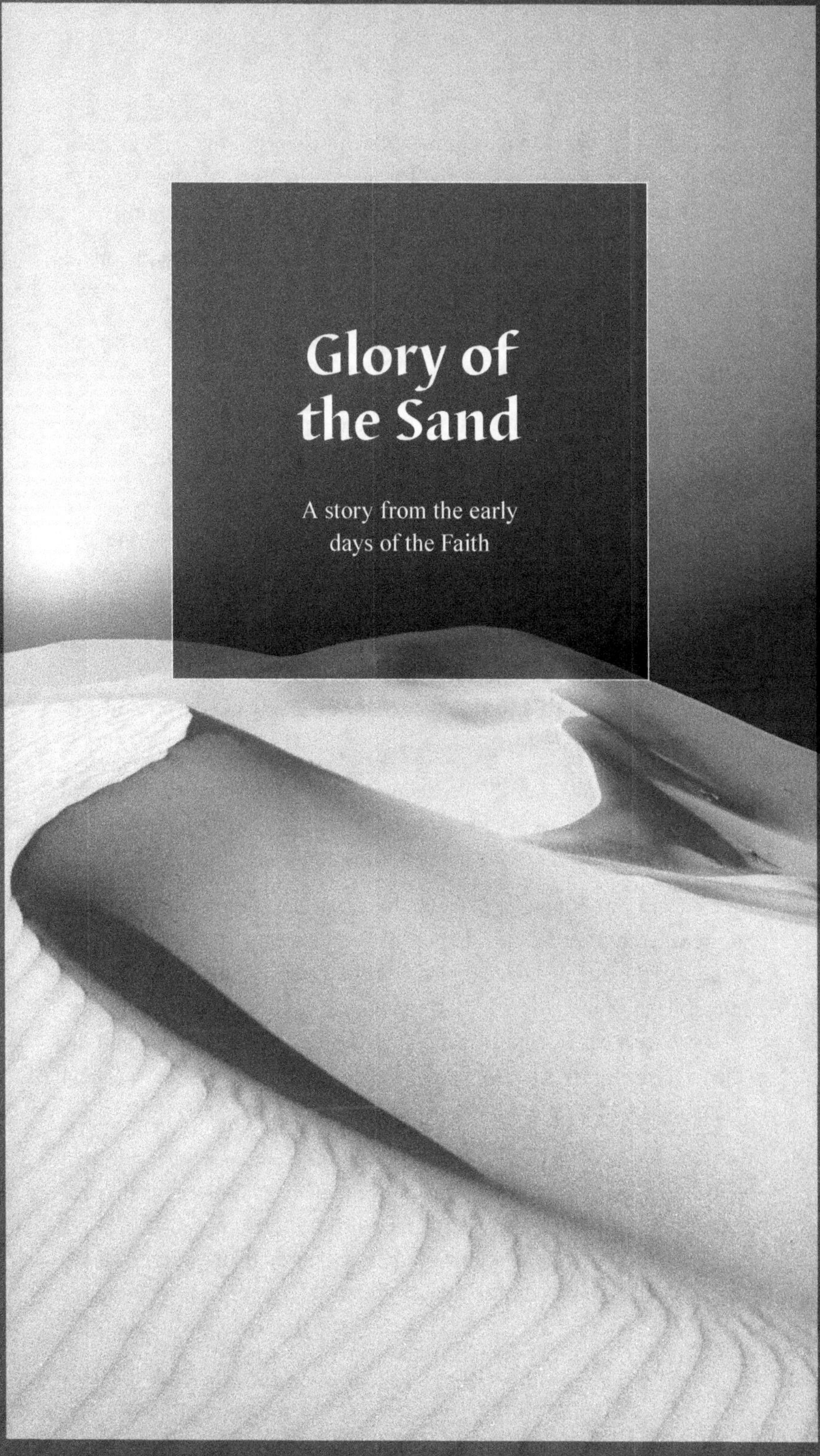

There is no caravan except that which belongs to the famous Bábí' said the servant to his wealthy and learned master, who desired to go on a pilgrimage to the Holy Shrines with all the members of his family.

'No, no,' interrupted the master, 'I can't go on a holy trip with such a profane man who has left Islám and embraced the new cause.'

One week passed and the time for the pilgrimage would come to an end if the master would not make haste.

'But he is the most trustworthy', said the servant. 'Especially if you desire to have your wife and children with you on such a dangerously long journey.'

It took the master some more days to decide, and at last he commanded his servant, 'Go and make arrangements with him and tell him that we will go with him on condition that he should never approach us or touch any of our belongings. His only job is to take care of the caravan.' It was agreed upon, and after a few days, the bells of the mules started to chime and resound in the vast desert as they made their way out of Iran towards the Shí'ih Holy Shrines.

The merchant and his family were comfortably settled on their seats, and the caravan driver was walking far behind them chanting prayers and singing songs in praise of the new Manifestation.

It took them three months to go and return. On their trip back home, they reached a very beautiful spot. The clear water of the spring, the perfume of the flowers, the deliciousness of the fruits and the abundance of the foliage would stop all the passers-by. The learned man decided to stay there for a while, and the caravan driver accordingly stopped all the mules and hurriedly took them away to tether them to some trees and give them some food.

A sudden flash of happiness, gratitude, and satisfaction passed through the mind of the learned man, and in a moment of rest when the cool breeze of the spring passed over his face, he said to himself, 'This man is a Bábí … a Bábí … I do not know what. But all through the journey he has been so kind, so polite and so honest with us all, that he really deserves our heartfelt respect. Besides that, I saw him entering the shrines with perfect homage, love and respect. To compensate all his troubles and his good deeds, I must endeavour to lead him, if he is astray, and shelter him again under the banner of Islám so that in the world to come all his sins may be forgiven by Alláh.'

He then immediately ordered his servant to summon the caravan driver. He first hesitated to approach, but when he witnessed that the merchant himself had been beckoning to him, he drew near and knelt down to take a seat at a reasonable distance.

'I am extremely happy!' exclaimed the learned man. 'I am very grateful to you, due to your honest job and steadfastness, and am, above all, extremely glad that you also entered the shrines of our Imáms in humble faith and perfect devotion. But I have a question for you. You know that I am a wealthy man and grudge no effort to obtain any book dealing with religious subjects, and spend all my time in perusing them. How is it that I, with all my wealth and knowledge, could not comprehend the return of the promised Sun of Truth, and you, an illiterate, simple and plain man, understood it?'

'The answer is extremely simple, sir', replied the caravan driver with a triumphant smile on his lips. 'First of all, at the very beginning of the Holy Qur'án, it is prescribed that the Book is a guidance to the virtuous ones and not to the wealthy and learned people. Second, in the world of existence, people like you are as precious jewels ... diamonds ... emeralds ... rubies ... gold, but people like me are ...' He picked up some sand in his hands and continued, 'We are like these grains of sand strewn everywhere in the desert. Precious objects are not thrown here and there. They are rather wrapped in pieces of cloth, put in boxes, saved in an iron safe, kept in well-built rooms and strongly constructed houses. When the sun rises, it first shines on the sand in the desert that is so easily exposed to the reflection of the sun. Those who are apt to get warm will immediately respond. But, my dear sir, diamonds have to shatter many obstacles and must tear asunder multifarious veils till the time they break down all their enclosures. You also must, once and for all, forget all the earthly learnings and supplicate God to bestow upon you the divine knowledge and celestial love. Then you will not behold anything but the truth.'

The inspired answer of the man penetrated deep into the merchant's heart and made him think and contemplate. He spent the whole night asking questions about the new day of God, and the next day, when the bells of the caravan again started to chime on the way back home, the caravan driver was no more far behind the riders. He was walking beside the master and chanting for him songs and prayers.

The learned master entered his home a newly born man, determined to consecrate his wealth and knowledge and life for the propagation of the new Faith of God.

NOTES AND REFERENCES

1. Another account of this story can be found in *The Revelation of Bahá'u'lláh* vol. 2, (Oxford: George Ronald, 1977) by Adib Taherzadeh, p. 33–34.

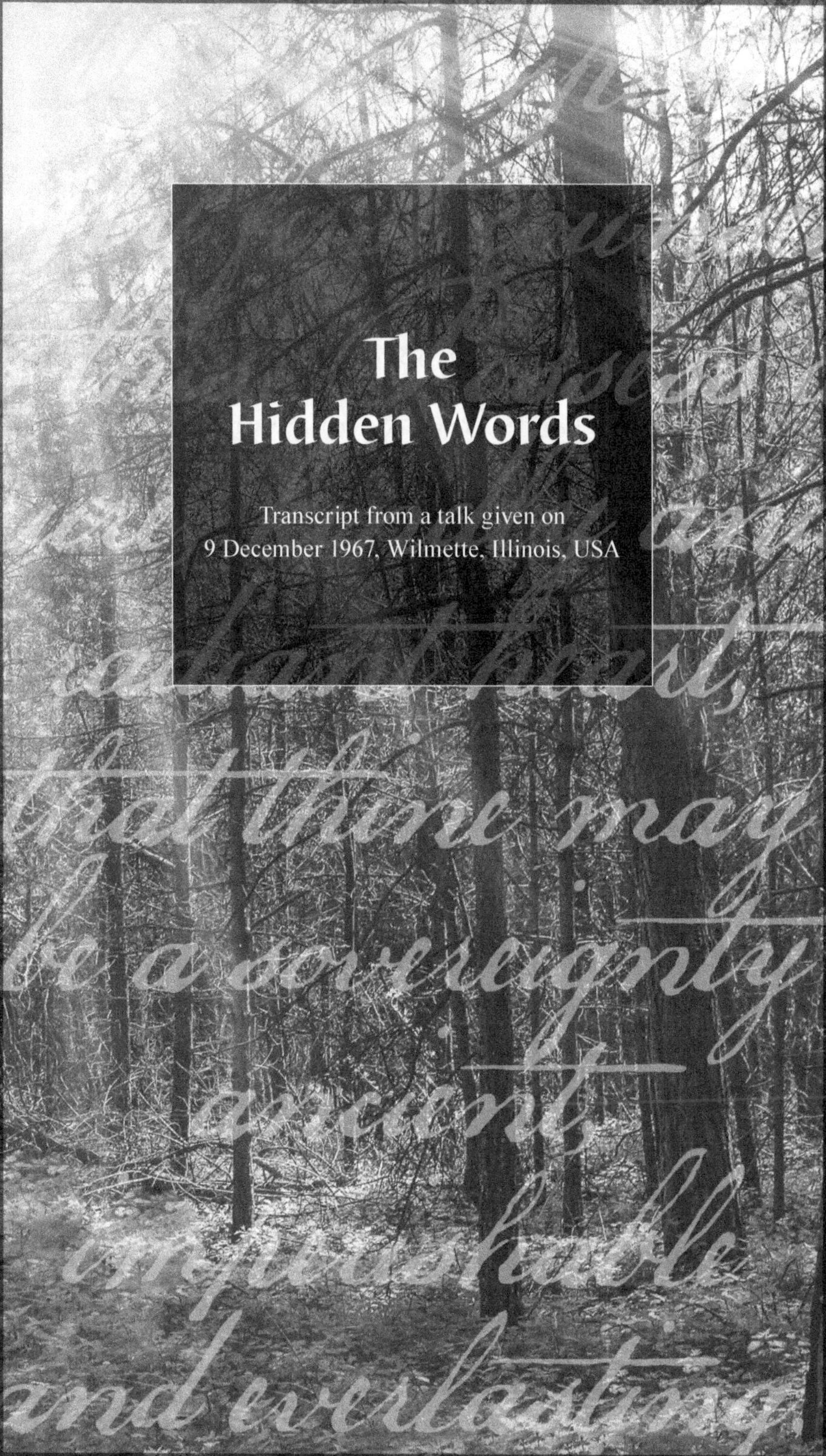

The Hidden Words

Transcript from a talk given on
9 December 1967, Wilmette, Illinois, USA

First of all, a general description of the Hidden Words: When you study the Hidden Words and compare it with other Writings of Bahá'u'lláh, the Writings revealed in Adrianople and later on in the Most Great Prison, you will come to realize that the Hidden Words is the embryonic stage of our Faith. Whatever exists in our Faith exists in the Hidden Words in an embryonic form. By that I mean the general shape of things is given, but it is not very clear, distinct, explicit or detailed. There are those references to many different aspects of our Faith. It is like a seed, which was sown in the city of Baghdád, grew in Adrianople, and reached its fruition in the Most Great Prison. I will give you two examples and the rest you will find by yourselves.

In the Hidden Words, Bahá'u'lláh says, *How can you ever turn from this clear, sweet water to that which is wine?*[1] This is not a prohibition sentence. It's just a statement: how can you turn from this to that? But when it grew, the tree grew in Adrianople, and then, in the city of 'Akká when the Book of Aqdas (The Kitáb-i-Aqdas) was revealed, it was utterly forbidden. It is no more ambiguous. It's explicit and is absolutely forbidden for any Bahá'í under any form.

In another place, He says, *Do you remember that Covenant I made with you in that early morning?*[2] But what is the Covenant? Nobody knew at that time. I said that nobody knew; there were many who knew, even then, that 'Abdu'l-Bahá was the Centre of the Covenant when He was a boy of twelve years. There were many who knew that, but the others did not know. It was ambiguous. But in the city of 'Akká, it was revealed in the Book of Aqdas (The Kitáb-i-Aqdas) that all that is known to you in the books and the Writings regarding this Covenant, that this refers to the Most Great Branch. He then made it explicit and 'Abdu'l-Bahá was introduced. That's why I call it the Revelation of Bahá'u'lláh in its embryonic stage. This is one way to study this book.

The Hidden Words to me is a very glorious sunrise in a beautiful forest. When you study this glorious sunrise and this glorious forest, you must not go and think about one sentence. You will never realize the glory of it, the immensity and majesty of it. You will lose sight of the whole glorious sunrise. Therefore, you stay far away from it, so you can see the whole view in front of you, very clearly, full of colour, full of beautiful references. When you go away from it, you will find it is a world, a plan of life for man.

The lines are beautifully drawn; the roads are perfectly paved, on condition that we will not pay attention to little words here and there, at the beginning. This is a mistake that many of us make with all the Writings; we stick to one sentence, and we stick to it accompanied by doubt.

Now, when you stand at a distance, you will look at it and will find that the Hidden Words is a contract between Bahá'u'lláh and Man. For the sake of those who know the Persian words of it, I would repeat because I want to tell them how this idea dawned upon me – that this is a contract because of one word in the Hidden Words. He says, 'My first counsel' (in Persian or in Arabic), and what He said is the origin of the word 'contract' in the Arabic language. This suggested the idea of this contract between Bahá'u'lláh and Man for this spiritual journey that Man is destined to go through to reach the ultimate aim and goals of his life.

Now, if you have some paper or pieces of paper, put in some columns. The first one will be: 'Why is Man chosen for this spiritual journey, and not other created things in the whole universe?'

The second column will be: 'What are the provisions for this spiritual journey?' Now when Man, accompanied by Bahá'u'lláh, enters the road, he will find it the most beautifully arranged road where there are red lights, through which we must not pass, and green lights, through which we are allowed to go. Therefore, two other columns will be added: the red lights and the green lights.

And the last one: 'What is the ultimate aim, what do we obtain, to where do we reach, what are the results of this spiritual journey?' Therefore, we have five columns, or five pages. First, why is Man chosen for this spiritual journey; second, what are the provisions; third, the red lights; fourth, the green lights; and fifth, the results. If you would like to change the places of the red lights and the green lights, it's according to your own taste.

All right, now when we study the Hidden Words, we find the exalted station of Man. God addresses Man and says, 'I knew My love for thee;

therefore I created thee'.[3] This is one of the reasons why Man is chosen. Please, when you study the writings of the beloved Master, you will find one very interesting point. He has given one definition for three different things. You will find it, please.

Now, a definition of science, of religion and of love: it's extremely important to study this definition. This definition is given in *Some Answered Questions* where it says, 'What is religion?' and then 'Abdu'l-Bahá defines it. The same definition is given for love and the same for science. When we bring it together in the form of a discussion group, or anything else, let us discuss with each other. Why is there one definition for three different things? You will come to understand that these three things, if they are followed in their true sense of meaning and words, will bring you to one end. They are the same rules bringing you to the same end.

The definitions of love, given by 'Abdu'l-Bahá, are these: He says, 'Love is the cause of development to every enlightened man!'[4] If there is any intelligence in man, love will be the cause of its growth. 'Love is the greatest law in this vast universe of God!'[4] There are many laws in the universe, many laws of nature, but this is the greatest law commanding the whole universe. Without it, the universe will fall into pieces. 'Love is the one law, which causeth and controleth order among the existing atoms!'[5]

By this example, we will come to understand how the treasures of Bahá'í literature are full of such gems that the young, aspiring, and ambitious newly-enrolled believers, especially with their enthusiasm, should try to find and collect them together, like a jeweller who puts the same jewels around certain diamonds, to make a beautiful design.

Then Bahá'u'lláh addresses Man again, and says: *You are My fortress, you are My lamp, you are My light, My glory, My dominion, My garment. I made you by the hands of power. I entrusted in you an essence of My light. I created you rich and exalted, and from the essence of My knowledge I manifested you.*[6] These are some of the references in the Hidden Words by the exalted pen of Bahá'u'lláh addressed to Man.

As we go on, please compare this with what is prevailing today, most unfortunately in our educational institutions, propagated by the educators of our children, our youth. They tell them they are a bundle of nerves, passion and desire and that every one of these must find a free channel to express itself. But this is the exalted position of Man. The greatest wrong that we commit in this life, the greatest of all the mistakes that people commit these days is that they apply the laws of the animal world to the human kingdom. It is true that these things should find a free outlet, but this is true of the animal world, not of the human world.

Humanity must be disciplined to have chastity and channel their impulses in the proper way, as prescribed by God, and not by ego and self. See how much the parents are responsible to give strength and power to the children to stand against these current ideas. If they are weak, they will be carried away by these forces. Make them as strong as possible. Give them the spirit of the Faith of Bahá'u'lláh. Make them a fortress so that they can stand against all the currents of conflicting ideas and they can prove they are created as Man and not as animals. We must study these things.

What does it mean when Bahá'u'lláh says, *I have entrusted in you my own mystery, My own light, the essence of My knowledge*?[7] This is not something to be taken easily and lightly. These words should be pondered upon and studied, so that our reality will be manifested. Those talents, those potentialities, which are given and concealed in our human temple, will come out and will be something other than what the others are. Then we can conquer countries, conquer hearts, give light to the souls of the people. If we are like them, we cannot do anything.

There are thousands of candles all dark. If we are dark like them, we'll join them where there is no light. But if one of us is enlightened, we can enlighten others with this enlightened one. And Bahá'u'lláh wants to clearly manifest this power. *Who can ever guess*, Bahá'u'lláh says, *There are eyes that do not see*. If the eyes do not see that there is light here in this lamp, he will never believe it. You ignite it and this lamp will be changed into light. And then He says, *Who can ever think of a man having all these powers, but let him be ignited with the love of God, then he will illumine many souls*. That's why Man is chosen for this spiritual journey. But what are the provisions?

You all know the first one. He says, 'My first counsel is this: Possess a pure, kindly and radiant heart . . .'[8] There are three conditions for this pure-hearted person: pure, kindly and radiant. 'Abdu'l-Bahá has explained this in a most beautiful way. He says, *Suppose this is a container of milk. Milk, in itself,* He says, *is good nourishment for children and for grown ups. From this milk, many things are produced, such as butter, cheese, yogurt and seven or eight other things.*

Now, He says, *this is like a pure heart: when it serves the Cause of God it is good nourishment for the Cause and from it many other things will be produced.* Now, He says, *Pour into this milk a drop of vinegar. The milk itself will be spoiled and nothing will be produced. That drop of vinegar in our soul is our ego.*

If we bring our ego into our services to Bahá'u'lláh, to His Cause, nothing will be produced. We must empty ourselves from our ego and make ourselves a proper channel, a proper instrument, in the Faith of Bahá'u'lláh, and let Him work through us.

When the heart is pure, it must be kind, but also radiant, like the sunshine that is over all, without any discrimination, without any prejudice. This was the greatest praise that 'Abdu'l-Bahá could give. It's very easy to forget this little word 'I' and then we will be relieved from it, once and for all. And then our services will be productive.

It is a spiritual practice, to be kind, loving to all the people of the world, without discrimination. Like the sun: the sun never says, 'I won't shine on Vietnam because there is a war, or on Africa because they are black.' No, it shines everywhere. The clouds rain everywhere. And Bahá'u'lláh says that the Bahá'ís should be like the sunshine and the clouds that rain over all and everywhere. Their love must be pure and radiant.

The Guardian emphasized that you should love your contacts but not for the sake that you will make them a Bahá'í. Just love him or her. If they don't become a Bahá'ís, don't be angry with them, don't change your love, don't say they're hopeless, because we cannot judge the soul of another person.

May I interrupt here to say something about teaching. I am extremely sorry that because of these material comforts and ease that exist in Europe and many other parts of the world, many of our Bahá'í friends have taken the same attitude in teaching. I will give you an example and then perhaps it will be illustrated what I have in mind. When you are in your apartment, you press a button in the elevator and you go to the eightieth story of the building, you press another one, you come down. You take a taxi. You go to the travel agency, get a ticket and next morning you are in Paris. All these things are done within twenty-four hours in the quickest and speediest way. And we believe that when we have a contact sitting in front of us, his heart also has a button, which we can press and push in the Book of Íqán and have the card in hand. This has happened. The Guardian says, *Love your contacts, be patient with them and be wise, and never change your action, because you can never judge the soul of Man.* You are dealing with the soul of Man, not something material. The response of the soul of Man is different in different people.

Now, the second thing that Bahá'u'lláh says is a provision. He asks the person who will accompany Him in this spiritual journey: *Would you like to bring me any gifts as we go on our journey? The most beloved of all things to me is justice. Bring me justice.* Then He says, *As we go along this journey, if you always want to be very happy, you must walk close to Me. But the moment you go away from Me, you will be drowned in oceans of sadness.* This is another provision. And then He says, 'God sufficeth all things'. Don't go after anything else, only search for God. Have God with you always.

Now with these provisions, and some others you will find after studying the Hidden Words, they come to the road they want to take. Now there are two lights: red lights, which means the things you should not do, and green lights. As they walk, He says, *First you must deny your ego.* We always come back to the same thing: the ego. *Comfort is not created for you. Don't ask me for that which I don't like for you.*[9] I want to explain this through another Tablet of Bahá'u'lláh.

He said never insist in your prayers to God that you want something. Just pray, but never insist. He says that out of His bounty, He will give you that which you like, but then it will be followed by tests that you will not be able to bear. Never insist.

Then He gives an example. A father has a glass of liquid in his hand. The child thinks that it is a sweet drink. The father knows that it is poison. It's quinine, it's bitter. The child insists that he wants some of it. Then Bahá'u'lláh says that the father is obliged to put a little bit in a spoon and put it at the tip of his tongue, the bitterness of which he will never be able to suffer. Then He says, *Don't insist, just pray. If He gives it to you, all right, if He doesn't, don't insist.*

As they walk together, this spiritual person, who wants to tread this path, hand in hand with Bahá'u'lláh, becomes a little bit familiar with their Companion, Bahá'u'lláh, and says something which is beyond their reach. Then Bahá'u'lláh says, 'Transgress not thy limits'.[10]

How very often we transgress our own limits. We say things to God that are not within the limitation of Man. We even ask why did Bahá'u'lláh do this, or why did Bahá'u'lláh write that? Why did He say that marriage depends on the consent of parents? We love each other and that's enough. This is beyond our comprehension. These are secret mysteries that Man cannot understand. Therefore, we must leave our affairs in His hands and never transgress our limits.

The companion sees a poor man on the way and walks proudly before him. Bahá'u'lláh immediately says, *Don't wax proud before a poor man.*[11] Now he becomes very familiar and he starts to talk, to gossip, to backbite, and Bahá'u'lláh says, *How is it you have forgotten your own sins and you are telling Me of the sins of others?*

You see how closely He walks with us. How very explicitly He gives us direction. How beautiful and delicate.

Then, in another emphatic way, He says, *Don't ever breathe the mistakes of others, as long as you are a sinner yourself.*[12] This is the most detrimental factor in any community. It has destroyed families, communities, and this is the most unwanted guest in any house. Please, let us never have it. Never in our communities and in our homes. Tomorrow, when we study about the principles of Bahá'í education, perhaps we will deal more with this and the detrimental effects of this in our homes for the education of children.

Then, as they are walking, suddenly they see a man sitting down and getting busy with the material world. Bahá'u'lláh says, *I don't want you to get busy with this world. Come along with Me.* In another place, they see him gathering gold. He says, *You want gold, but I don't want you to have it.*[13] And he goes on. I will explain this afterwards. I know there will be many questions. Let's turn to the green lights; they are better!

First of all, always turn your face to My face. Don't turn it away. Always, have Me in your mind, in your whole life, in your whole daily life. Have Me at the centre of your mind.[14]

Now, here I have a chance to tell you something about our new believers throughout the world. I have gathered many things from them. I have learned many things from them, which are priceless in the explanations of the most mysterious problems of the Cause. Let's not think that these people are coming in masses and they do not understand. On the contrary, to me they are treasure-houses opened by Bahá'u'lláh and they are coming out.

When it was discussed how we can, under all conditions, have our faces turned to God, an Indian woman – a new believer – got up and said: 'Every morning I go to bring water for my house. I have three jugs, one above the other. I fill them with water from the spring. I put them on my head and walk towards my house. I stop at the grocery shop and buy something. I greet my friend and ask him about his home and his children, and so on. I greet a woman and start talking to her. And I do all these things and keep the equilibrium of three jugs on my head. I never let them go. Do the same thing with God. It will be easy.' Could this be explained in a better way? I don't think so.

Then Bahá'u'lláh says, 'Bring thyself to account each day'.[15] See what you have done every day. In the life of our beloved Guardian, we will find this, even when, as a child, he played during the day. Suppose he had hit somebody just by mistake. His father and mother said that he would never go to sleep, as a child, unless and until he would go to the house of that boy and make him happy, and then he would go to sleep. Bahá'u'lláh Himself said that if somebody was sad because of Him, He could never go to sleep unless He would make him happy.

Then we come across one sentence, which I believe is the most important in the whole of the Hidden Words. He says, 'Rejoice in the gladness of thine heart'.[16] It is something that we have utterly forgotten for centuries. The art of meditation, the art of contemplation, the art of dreaming within oneself; and Bahá'u'lláh wants us to start doing this again. First, it means that there is nothing in the world to make you happy, outside of your own heart.

If you possess the whole world, the treasures of the world, the pleasures of the world, they may be momentary pleasures, but they will cause bitter sadness throughout your life. They will never bring you any happiness. People are wrong to change the places of their entertainment and enjoyments from New York to Paris, to Rome, to Africa, to Australia.

They are searching for it, while they are carrying it along with themselves. He says, *Go deep into thy heart.*[17] There is a realm in your heart. There it will spring up with the water of joy, a constant stream of joy will be flowing from your own heart. Nothing will stop it and nothing will be able to give to it except yourselves. This is done by spiritual exercise.

'Abdu'l-Bahá tells the story of one of the prisoners in 'Akká, who had been with Bahá'u'lláh in the Most Great Prison. He said that he had a small rug, a samovar, one cup and a teapot. He said that every afternoon he would sprinkle water somewhere and sweep and then spread this rug, bring his samovar and let the water boil. He would say, 'Listen to it. How it boils. It's better than anything, better than anything else in the world. The weather is most pleasant.' – referring to the weather of 'Akká, which was the most stinking in the whole world. Then he would pour tea for himself. 'Abdu'l-Bahá said that he held the cup, looked at its colour and said that never was there any tea as beautiful. Every day his tea was better than the previous one. And he would drink it with all sorts of happiness and gratitude and praise to God for one cup of tea, which he had made. And he was full of prayer as he was drinking, full of praise, of joy and happiness, because it was something springing up from his own soul.[18]

Now, I saw in a place, in an antique shop, some cups. They told me they belonged to the age of Louis IV. I asked, what is the importance of them. The owner of the shop said, 'They cost $22,000.'

'Six of them?' I asked, 'Would any fool buy this from you?'

He said, 'Many fools hire them from me.'

I asked him how.

He said, 'I have already made more than this from them. Somebody invites a group of friends. He boasts to them that he is giving them tea in the cups of Louis IV.' Just think of the lowness and baseness of people's ambitions. Millions of children are dying of starvation, are deprived of education, of everything in life, and then $2,000 is paid for one afternoon to hire these cups to give tea to some few people, who, when leaving, will make fun of their host.

You know all these things better than I do. Rejoice with the joy of your own heart.

Then Bahá'u'lláh says, *Whatever you do in your life, let it be for the majesty, for the glory of My Cause, then I will glorify you in the Kingdom of God. Never belittle My Cause.* Belittling the Cause of God is to compare it with man-made plans. To compare some of the Writings of Bahá'u'lláh with, for instance, Schweitzer or Einstein. How short-sighted many of us are. We may say, ''Abdu'l-Bahá said this' and then 'It's very interesting. Einstein also said the same thing.' The person never believed in 'Abdu'l-Bahá until he read what Einstein said.

It's very bad. All of these spiritual exercises are needed for us to reach that stage of certitude. When you reach there, you will see everything full of truth, and nothing but truth.

Now, when we pass through all these roads, what will be the result of our journey? Bahá'u'lláh says, *Then you will all walk on one earth. Your ear will become My ear. Your eyes will be My eyes.*[19]

Bahá'u'lláh says, *From every atom of your existence, your deeds, your words, will the signs of the unity of God be manifested. Because I have created you as my treasure-house, in which I have deposited the pearls of mysteries and the essence of my knowledge.*[20] Then towards the end He says, *Now think and ponder upon your affairs.*

This is my humble suggestion, to study the Hidden Words, to have a clear idea to where the Hidden Words will lead us, and I hope that we will come in different groups to discuss this together, in such a way that every session will be an upliftment to our souls.

NOTES AND REFERENCES

- Where the text has been italicized, it denotes paraphrases from the Bahá'í Writings.
- Abbreviations: *AHW*: Arabic Hidden Words; *PHW*: Persian Hidden Words.

1 O Son of Dust! Turn not away thine eyes from the matchless wine of the immortal Beloved, and open them not to foul and mortal dregs. Take from the hands of the divine Cup-bearer the chalice of immortal life, that all wisdom may be thine, and that thou mayest hearken unto the mystic voice calling from the realm of the invisible. Cry aloud, ye that are of low aim! Wherefore have ye turned away from My holy and immortal wine unto evanescent water? *PHW*, No. 62.

2 O My Friends! Have ye forgotten that true and radiant morn, when in those hallowed and blessed surroundings ye were all gathered in My presence beneath the shade of the tree of life, which is planted in the all-glorious paradise? Awe-struck ye listened as I gave utterance to these three most holy words: O friends! Prefer not your will to Mine, never desire that which I have not desired for you, and approach Me not with lifeless hearts, defiled with worldly desires and cravings. Would ye but sanctify your souls, ye would at this present hour recall that place and those surroundings, and the truth of My utterance should be made evident unto all of you. *PHW*, No. 19.

3 O Son of Man! Veiled in My immemorial being and in the ancient eternity of My essence, I knew My love for thee; therefore I created thee, have engraved on thee Mine image and revealed to thee My beauty. *AHW*, No. 3.

4 *Tablets of 'Abdu'l-Bahá*, Vol. 3, p. 525.

5 Know thou of a certainty that Love is the secret of God's holy Dispensation, the manifestation of the All-Merciful, the fountain of spiritual outpourings. Love is heaven's kindly light, the Holy Spirit's eternal breath that vivifieth the human soul. Love is the cause of God's revelation unto man, the vital bond inherent, in accordance with the divine creation, in the realities of things. Love is the one means that ensureth true felicity both in this world and the next. Love is the light that guideth in darkness, the living link that uniteth God with man, that assureth the progress of every illumined soul. Love is the most great law that ruleth this mighty and heavenly cycle, the unique power that bindeth together the divers elements of this material world, the supreme magnetic force that directeth the movements of the spheres in the celestial realms. Love revealeth with unfailing and limitless power the mysteries latent in the universe. Love is the spirit of life unto the adorned body of mankind, the establisher of true civilization in this mortal world, and the shedder of imperishable glory upon every high-aiming race and nation. 'Abdu'l-Bahá: *Selections from the Writings of 'Abdu'l-Bahá*, page 27.

6 See *AHW*, Nos. 10, 11, 12, 13, 14.

7 O Son of Spirit! … Out of the essence of knowledge I gave thee being, why seekest thou enlightenment from anyone beside Me? *AHW*, No. 13.

O Ye Sons of Spirit! Ye are My treasury, for in you I have treasured the pearls of My mysteries and the gems of My knowledge. Guard them from the strangers amidst My servants and from the ungodly amongst My people. *AHW*, No. 69.

8 O Son of Spirit! My first counsel is this: Possess a pure, kindly and radiant heart, that thine may be a sovereignty ancient, imperishable and everlasting. *AHW*, No. 1.

9 O Son of Spirit! Ask not of Me that which We desire not for thee, then be content with what We have ordained for thy sake, for this is that which profiteth thee, if therewith thou dost content thyself. *AHW*, No. 18.

10 O Son of Man! Transgress not thy limits, nor claim that which beseemeth thee not. Prostrate thyself before the countenance of thy God, the Lord of might and power. *AHW*, No. 24.

11 O Son of Spirit! Vaunt not thyself over the poor, for I lead him on his way and behold thee in thy evil plight and confound thee for evermore. *AHW*, No. 25.

12 O Son of Man! Breathe not the sins of others so long as thou art thyself a sinner. Shouldst thou transgress this command, accursed wouldst thou be, and to this I bear witness. *AHW*, No. 27.

13 O Son of Man! Thou dost wish for gold and I desire thy freedom from it. Thou thinkest thyself rich in its possession, and I recognize thy wealth in thy sanctity therefrom. By My life! This is My knowledge, and that is thy fancy; how can My way accord with thine? *AHW*, No. 56.

14 O Son of Utterance! Turn thy face unto Mine and renounce all save Me; for My sovereignty endureth and My dominion perisheth not. If thou seekest another than Me, yea, if thou searchest the universe for evermore, thy quest will be in vain. *AHW*, No. 15.

15 O Son of Being! Bring thyself to account each day ere thou art summoned to a reckoning; for death, unheralded, shall come upon thee and thou shalt be called to give account for thy deeds. *AHW*, No. 31.

16 O Son of Man! Rejoice in the gladness of thine heart, that thou mayest be worthy to meet Me and to mirror forth My beauty. *AHW*, No. 36.

17 O My Brother! Hearken to the delightsome words of My honeyed tongue, and quaff the stream of mystic holiness from My sugar-shedding lips. Sow the seeds of My divine wisdom in the pure soil of thy heart, and water them with the water of certitude, that the hyacinths of My knowledge and wisdom may spring up fresh and green in the sacred city of thy heart. *PHW*, No. 33.

18 In the afternoons he would take his samovar, wrap it in a dark-coloured pouch made from a saddlebag, and go off somewhere to a garden or meadow, or out in a field, and have his tea. Sometimes he would be found at the farm of Mazra'ih, or again in the Riḍván Garden; or, at the Mansion, he would have the honour of attending upon Bahá'u'lláh. Muhammad-'Alí would carefully consider every blessing that came his way. 'How delicious my tea is today', he would comment. 'What perfume, what colour! How lovely this meadow is, and the flowers so bright!' He used to say that everything, even air and water, had its own special fragrance. For him the days passed in indescribable delight. Even kings were not so happy as this old man, the people said. 'He is completely free of the world', they would declare. 'He lives in joy.' It also happened that his food was of the very best, and that his home was situated in the very best part of 'Akká. Gracious God! Here he was, a prisoner, and yet experiencing comfort, peace and joy. 'Abdu'l-Bahá: *Memorials of the Faithful*, p. 25.

19 O Son of the Throne! Thy hearing is My hearing, hear thou therewith. Thy sight is My sight, do thou see therewith, that in thine inmost soul thou mayest testify unto My exalted sanctity, and I within Myself may bear witness unto an exalted station for thee. *AHW*, No. 44.

20 O Ye Sons of Spirit! Ye are My treasury, for in you I have treasured the pearls of My mysteries and the gems of My knowledge. Guard them from the strangers amidst My servants and from the ungodly amongst My people. *AHW*, No. 69.

21 O Son of Him that stood by His Own Entity in the Kingdom of His Self! Know thou, that I have wafted unto thee all the fragrances of holiness, have fully revealed to thee My word, have perfected through thee My bounty and have desired for thee that which I have desired for My Self. Be then content with My pleasure and thankful unto Me. *AHW*, No. 70.

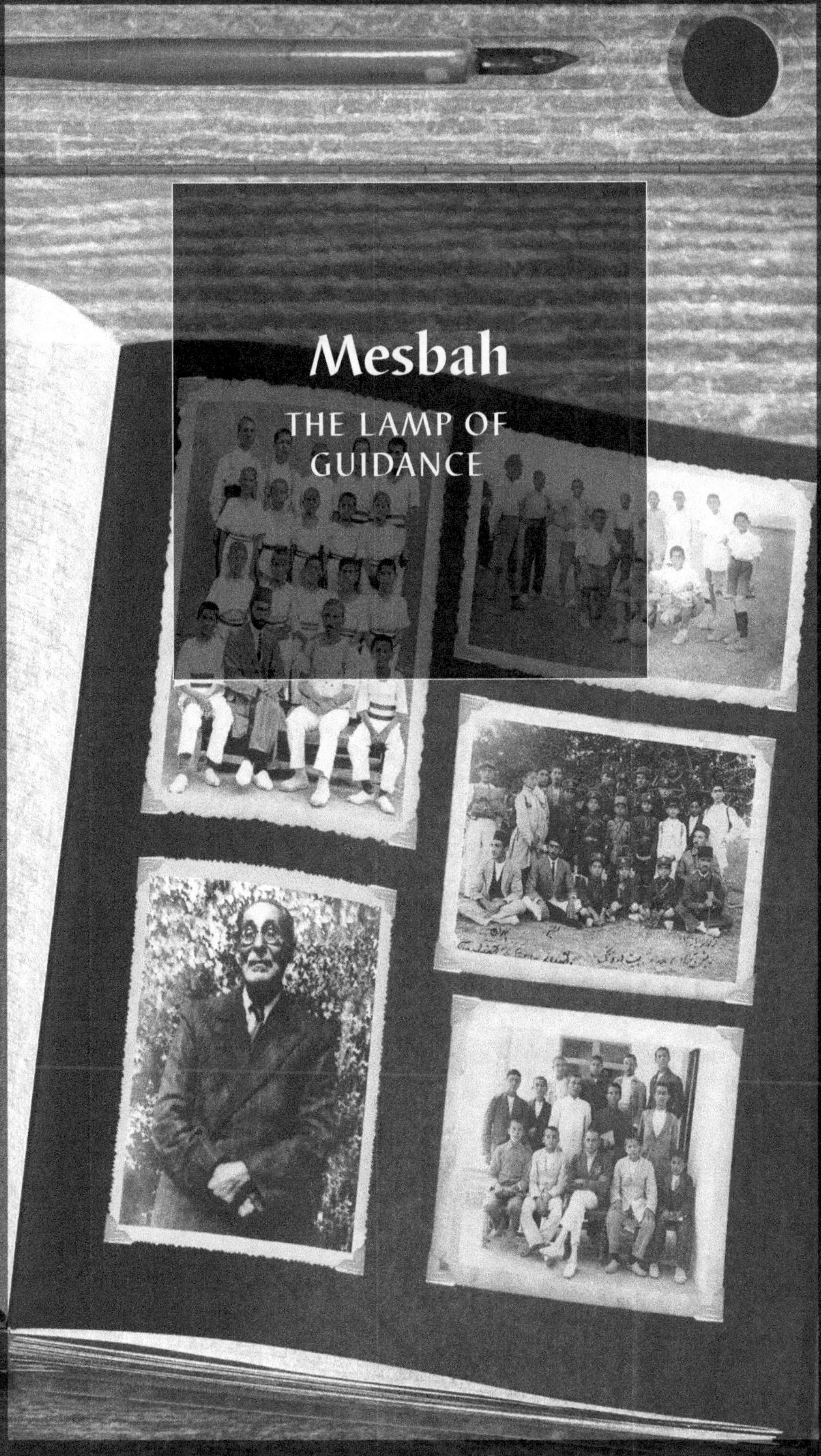
Mesbah
THE LAMP OF GUIDANCE

Publisher's note:

This essay, written by Mr Faizí and his wife Gloria Faizí, pays tribute to Azíz'u'lláh Mesbah, who served as Headteacher of the Tarbíyat Schools in Iran for many years. Mr Faizí attended one of these schools himself as a young boy and first learned of the Bahá'í Faith there.

The Guardian's telegram after the passing away of Mesbah, 'The Lamp of Guidance':

'Deeply grieved passing distinguished promoter faith 'Azíz'u'lláh Mesbah. His magnificent historic services imperishable. Assure relatives, friends fervent prayers advancement his soul Abhá Kingdom. Advise friends hold befitting memorial gatherings loving recognition his manifold achievements. Shoghi Rabbani.'

To possess a saintly life and to purge one's self of all human desires in an age when passions are predominant, and in a country where retrogression and decay have taken it to the abyss of misery and confusion, is a prodigious phenomenon never to be expected except amongst those who are born again through the love of God. Mesbah is forever glorified by such a life.

In the days when the standard of knowledge in Iran was the corrupted theological course of ages gone by, and those who studied the modern arts and sciences were considered heathens, and strongly opposed, Mesbah left his country with the intention of continuing his studies in the French universities of Beirut. There he proved himself not only an ardent scholar and an standard of virtue, but also a very promising poet both in Arabic and Persian. Having gained a firm foundation in French, Arabic and Persian literatures, he went on to Paris where he continued his studies, helped the orientalists in their research works and aided the early believers of that city in translating the Tablets from the Arabic and Persian into the French language.

He crowned all his efforts and services by attaining the presence of the Master, and, in the sunshine of 'Abdu'l-Bahá's love and encouragement, Mesbah's learning bore their finest fruits – the love for and desire to serve mankind.

The Master appreciated his erudition and highly praised his extreme sense of politeness and humility. Having perceived in that youthful countenance the splendid soul of a steadfast servant of God and a staunch promoter of the Cause, He very kindly recommended him to return to Tehran and participate in the Bahá'í educational activities.

Posts of outstanding fame and excellent prospects were already awaiting him when he arrived in Iran, but Mesbah's soul soared beyond all lucrative pursuits, temporary ranks and worldly desires, and above all his one aim was to carry out his Beloved's wishes.

The Spiritual Assembly of Tehran, with whom the Master had instructed Mesbah to consult concerning his future activities, found in him a mighty pillar for their educational institutions.

He entered that glorious field of service and sacrifice, accepting a very scanty salary and carrying the heaviest weight of responsibilities.

During his many years of service as the Headmaster of the Tarbíyat Schools, he was a living example of a martyr's constancy. Endless sufferings and unlimited hardships were inflicted upon him by the many who were too short-sighted to perceive the glorious ideals towards which he was untiringly striving, but these only served to demonstrate the sublimity of his character and the exaltedness of his endurance.

Of what Mesbah had to face during those years, suffice to say that the Tarbíyat Schools, although financially supported by the Bahá'ís themselves, were under strict control of the Persian Ministry of Education – a ministry which was the beehive of the arch-enemies of the Cause and the refuge of the notorious Covenant-breakers, who constantly endeavoured to abate the prestige of the Bahá'í institutions and even encouraged the irresponsible mobs of the streets and the incorrigible children of other schools to cause endless troubles for the students of the Bahá'í schools.

It was the same ministry which caused the publication of certain ignominious books and magazines which were not only the meanest standard of authorship, but also remained as an eternal shame to the press and publishing industry of Iran.

Taking all these difficulties in view, we may realize through what a thorny path Mesbah had to pass and how the Abhá confirmations bestowed upon him those manifold achievements and historical successes.

He defended the schools, protected the children and lifted up the souls of his colleagues. He recruited the ablest teachers and managed to raise the standard of teaching in the Bahá'í schools much higher than other schools, so much so that the graduates of our institutions were envied everywhere for their knowledge as well as for their character.

The constant abortive attempts of the enemies helped to increase their own jealousy, and, pricked to the quick at the lofty prestige of the Bahá'í schools, they did their utmost to raise the hand of their temporarily mighty King against them, and he, ignorant of the Divine Wrath and the efforts of children's supplications to the Almighty, permitted himself to be an instrument in their hands.

No one knows what passed in the heart of Mesbah when he saw his lifetime's work fall into pieces, but this we do know: that he did not give way to disappointment.

Full of certitude in his Master's promises, he brought hope to his scattered and sorrow-stricken children by his repeated and emphatic assertions that ere long from the depth of this ruined nest of hearts, there would arise institutions glorified in the name of God, worldwide in fame, humanitarian in their objectives, scope of scholarship and divine in their eternal salvation of the children of mankind.

Although nothing could weaken Mesbah's mighty soul, his thirty successive years of labour in the schools greatly affected his physical health. His eyes failed him too, and it was only the light of his insight which helped to soften the pains he felt at their loss.

It was hard to believe that our schools were closed, so long as Mesbah was still among us, for in him there was a living school from which the people could learn how to sacrifice their whole lives for a divine ideal, how to hold firm to the hem of the Centre of the Covenant and how to be steadfast in the path of God. After the closing of the schools, Mesbah continued teaching in the classes arranged by the local and national educational committees, and sometimes he went on some most memorable teaching trips in Iran. When the call for pioneers was raised, he encouraged his two elder sons to leave Iran, while he, with the rest of his family, settled in one of the villages around Tehran. There he spent his last days before he took his flight to the eternal Kingdom and, thus to the very end, our Headmaster followed the path of the Beloved Master.

With his passing away, Iran lost a Miltonic grandeur and a Homeric splendour. In his poems one would regain the lost paradise and would hear the far-off echoes of the battle drums of God's heroes who fought the darkness of by-gone ages and broke through the dawn of this new and glorious day of God.

In the midst of his loneliness and constant plights, being of an extremely quiet and forbearing nature, Mesbah took refuge in his Beloved's love, at whose threshold he poured forth his pearls of tears. Scholars and men of genuine understanding have judged his poems as unapproachable by any of his contemporaries and to be placed with the eternal classics of Iranian literature. Yet such was the humility and detachment of Mesbah that none of his poems have been published. But in any meeting or gathering, the friends would request and persuade him to recite to them some lines of his poems. Streams of joyful tears would flow down their cheeks when he enthusiastically sang his love for the Master:

> An effulgence of 'Abdu'l-Bahá's countenance made my sorrow-laden heart the envy of the promised paradise. Out of pure grace, the Divine Cup-Bearer filled my chalice with the wine of His Covenant. Do you consider it madness to be enchanted by such a glorious beauty? Hasten then and fetch my chains! Should the waves of calamities encircle me, my heart never yields to fear and dismay, for His love is my ship and my shore. O, Beloved! Make my heart a shrine of divine mysteries, for the books of the sages and their learnings fail to quench the thirst of my soul.[1]

Fame and praise were shunned by him, but our Beloved has put his name on the wings of fame and made it soar and blaze above the horizons of eternity.

Only a soul illumined by such a stupendous cause of light, a heart brimful with the Master's love and a memory so vastly and beautifully furnished with a tremendously great number of the divine tablets and verses of the previous Holy writings as well as selections from the world's classics, could produce poems such as Mesbah's.

Though the many references make the lines of his poems too deep for a quick understanding, yet the inherent appeal, the music of metre and rhyme and the hue of the highly spiritual subjects attract the souls and possess the hearts of the readers and listeners. The love of Bahá, his soul-inspiring muse, has made each word a shining gem, each line a perfect row of illustrious pearls and each piece a galaxy of eternal stars.

Mesbah was a lighthouse for thousands who were bewildered in the dark and stormy seas of circumstance. The light diffused from such a sublime soul had the most assuaging effect on those who were in spiritual crises. Knowledge, talent and resolution were combined in him with an extreme sense of detachment, humility and pure intention. In the obscure path of life he left traces from which the undisturbed melodies of complete content and utter resignation to the will of God are eternally echoed.

NOTES AND REFERENCES

1 These lines are not the exact translation of Mesbah's verses.

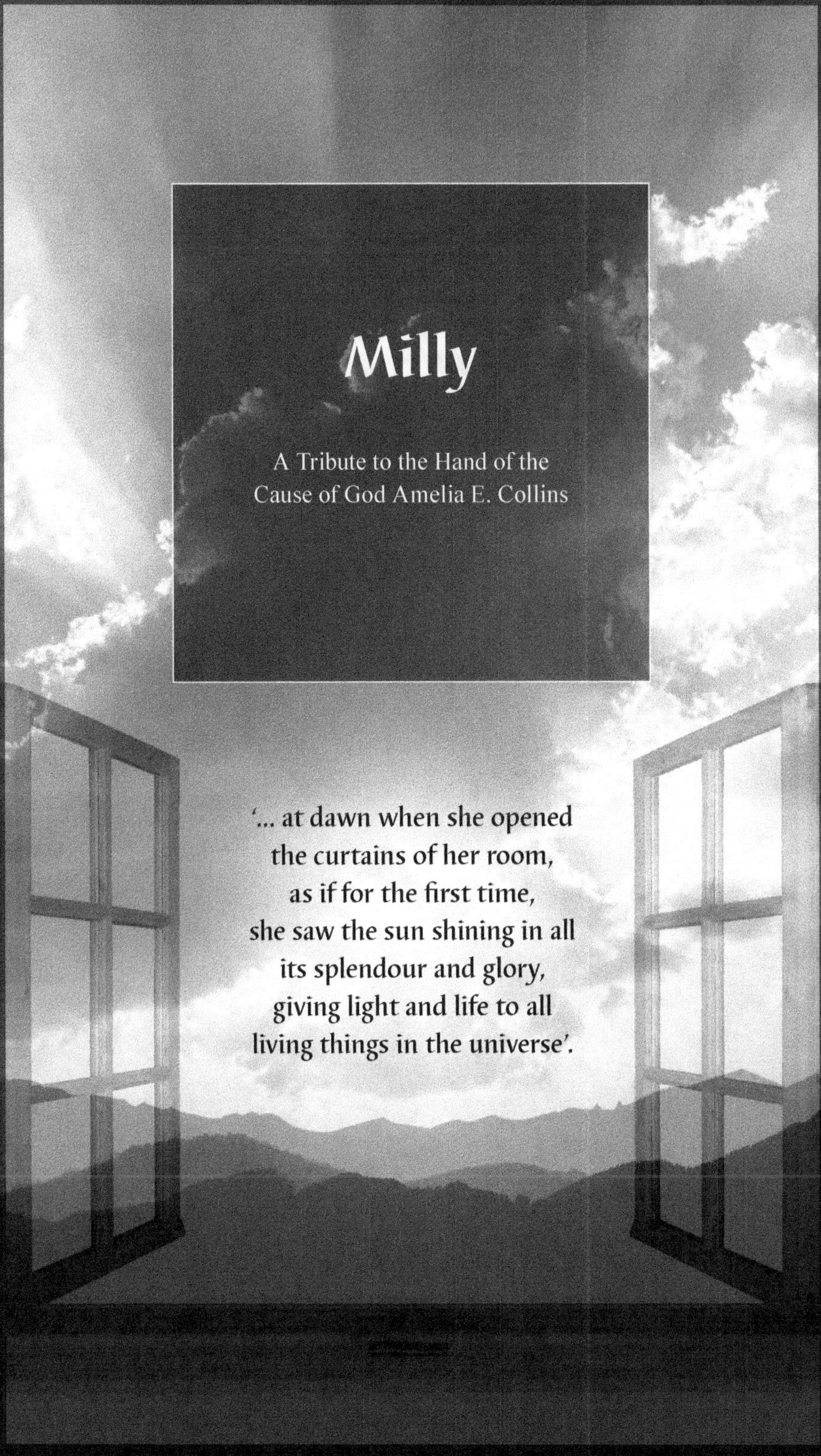
Milly
A Tribute to the Hand of the Cause of God Amelia E. Collins
'... at dawn when she opened the curtains of her room, as if for the first time, she saw the sun shining in all its splendour and glory, giving light and life to all living things in the universe'.

No better name could be chosen for this tribute than that by which she was known to all who loved her: Milly.

FOREWORD

Amelia Collins, the subject of this moving personal tribute, accepted the Faith of Bahá'u'lláh in 1919 and for over four decades gave to it her energetic and single-hearted devotion. The great love she bore for its Guardian, Shoghi Effendi, her loyalty to him and passionate desire to render him any assistance within her power, and to lighten, however slightly, the heavy burden that rested on his shoulders, not only endeared her to him but to all her fellow believers. For many years she was a member of the National Spiritual Assembly of the Bahá'ís of the United States and Canada.[1]

On 9 January 1951, Shoghi Effendi took what he termed an 'epoch-making decision', namely, the formation of the first International Bahá'í Council. This body – whose members were nominated by the Guardian himself and which, he said, was the forerunner of the supreme legislative organ of the world-encircling Bahá'í Administrative Order, namely, the Universal House of Justice – had its seat in Haifa and to it was summoned, as one of its officers, Amelia Collins, whom Shoghi Effendi referred to as its 'highly esteemed Vice-President'. This great and unexpected honour was followed, on 23 December of that same year, by a cable to Mrs Collins informing her that he was 'moved convey glad tidings your elevation rank Hand Cause', and the following day his official announcement to the Bahá'í world of her new position, and the similar rank conferred upon eleven other distinguished Bahá'ís, was made public.

The Hand of the Cause, Abu'l-Qásim Faizí, has made no attempt in these pages to give a biographical history of Amelia Collins. But it is against the setting of her high rank and her distinction as a Bahá'í that this moving tribute to her, as Mr Faizí came to know her in Haifa, must be read.

'You are so precious to us all and ...
a unique asset to the Faith you love so dearly and
have served so valiantly for so many years.'
– Shoghi Effendi

The friends who have had the honour and privilege of pilgrimage to the Holy Shrines may remember a slender, white-haired, very upright, elderly lady who lived in one of the rooms of the Master's House. Her great joy, after the passing of the Guardian, was to go to the Pilgrim House. She often said that such visits to the dear pilgrims were her spiritual intoxication that kept her warm, made her soul happy and her heart strong. She longed to visit the Cradle of the Bahá'í Faith.[2] Whatever was brought to her from Persia she would treasure. To her, these tangible objects were spiritual ties to the Faith she so much loved. She wanted to smell the roses in the Persian gardens and to hear the nightingales at dawn. She often mentioned that it was the desire of her life to go to Máh-Kú and see with her own eyes the fortress where the Báb was left all alone, at night without even the light of a candle.

Time and circumstances did not permit her to do this; therefore, with an endless love, she would come to see the pilgrims. First she would be settled in her seat. For a long time she would gaze into their faces, smile and, as if rejuvenated by their presence, at their request she would give them glimpses into her illustrious life. What you will read in the following pages is largely the record of these beautiful gatherings.

The candle of her faith, ignited by the Hand of God in 1919, stood firm and steadfast; it burned, but did not last to close the first day of the year 1962. In the afternoon of that day the last flame flickered, to be reignited in the Kingdom of God.

Milly – as she was called by the beloved Guardian and by all her friends – began her Bahá'í life with a degree of faithfulness, love and enthusiasm that never lessened to her last breath.

Her first Bahá'í friends in America had told her that she must write a letter to 'Abdu'l-Bahá and beg for confirmation and strength. The night she heard this, she could hardly sleep. Till morning she was contemplating how one should write to such an immensely great Personage. At last she scribbled something, and at dawn when she opened the curtains of her room, as if for the first time, she saw the sun shining in all its splendour and glory, giving light and life to all living things in the universe.

She thought to herself, the sun shines on the world and all that is therein with such grandeur and liberality; does it need a letter? Does He expect us to appeal to Him? The sun shines in the solar system and never needs any such superficial means of communication.

Then she tore up her letter, and in her heart she was certain that the spirit of the beloved Master, 'Abdu'l-Bahá, also would shine upon the world of human beings and grant them faith and love. Like the sun, He had all under His care and protection. There was no need to bother Him with inadequate words and supplications.

She said that days passed. Then, lo and behold, she received a Tablet from the Master. She never showed me that Tablet. She did not at first show it to anyone. It was a secret between the lover and the Loved One, and was sanctified from any kind of pretension.

The only part she revealed to us was this, that the Master addressed her as 'lady of the Kingdom'. But we now know that in that Tablet He stated His 'hope' that she would be confirmed to 'erect a structure that shall eternally remain firm and unshakeable'.

Milly first sought the presence of the Guardian[3] in 1923. Her husband, Thomas H. Collins, though not a Bahá'í, accompanied her. They went to a hotel, but the Guardian invited them to live in the Pilgrim House.

There were several important incidents during her sojourn in the Holy Land; the most significant were the following:

One evening the beloved Guardian gave Milly some papers and asked her to study them.

As she related this incident to us, she explained that before attaining the presence of the beloved Guardian her sole aim was to learn from him some truths about prayer, and purification of the soul and heart. She said:

> To me he was a door to the world beyond, and through him I longed to have a glimpse of that wondrous world. Therefore, with great eagerness and anticipation I hurried to my room, opened the papers, and read and read.
>
> The next day when I saw him, his first question was, 'What did you think of the papers I gave you to read?'

At this point dearest Milly always used to stop to tell us the following:

> I started my spiritual life on a basis of truth and frankness. Whatever I felt in my heart, whether right or wrong, I would say without fear of consequence. Now I was standing before the person who could read the innermost recesses of my heart and soul. How could I speak anything but the simple truth? Those papers contained nothing but explanations and elucidations of the World Order of Bahá'u'lláh and how it should be established in the world. And I desired only to know about prayer and glimpses of the world beyond. Therefore, I could only answer the Guardian's question with these words: 'What shall I say? I did not understand anything!'

Here again, she would pause and look deeply into the faces of the friends, and say,

> Do you think he reproved me for this? Never! On the same day in the afternoon, he told me that the Master had walked often in these lanes and streets near His house, and the Guardian invited me to go walking with him. As we were walking together he spoke of nothing except the same subjects he had written about in the papers he had given me to read. But with what a voice and with what sweetness! Words cannot describe them. He explained the details with such patience, as a father would to a child. But my idea was still lurking in my mind, and I was constantly thinking to myself that soon he would speak the words that would, each one, open a door into the mysteries of prayer and the world of the spirit, which I longed so much to know more about. How can we, insignificant and weak as we are, understand the plans of God?

We are confined to our humble and limited circumstances, unaware of what He may have in store for us. The Guardian, who was beginning to delineate the spiritual foundations, the Kingdom of God on earth, began to educate me in the administrative principles of the Faith in spite of my own desires.

When I returned to America I went directly to the National Convention and arrived during the reading of that very message from the beloved Guardian which he had given me to read in Haifa. I found myself called to the front and the words that I spoke came from some deep well of consciousness. That afternoon's walk with Shoghi Effendi and those exalted statements heard from no less a person than 'Abdu'l-Bahá's successor were like seeds that that dear teacher had implanted in my mind and heart, and now each one was bursting forth into expression of these new ideas.

And later, wherever I went, I found that the friends had received that same letter,[4] and that they, and the members of the Spiritual Assemblies, were busily engaged in discussing it. Sometimes there were clashes of thought and misunderstanding, and these, I found, I had been prepared by the beloved Guardian to explain and throw light upon. I had been given by him that which was necessary for the service and advancement of the Cause, and not that which would satisfy only my own selfish desires.

Two

Many members of my family were Christian clergymen. My father himself was a Lutheran minister. It is a custom among Christians that when a member of the family passes away, he or she is laid to rest in their coffin and, before the lid is closed, those attending the funeral and the members of the family are allowed to have a last look at their deceased loved one and pay their final homage.

I remember that I was a small child when my father passed away and I was taken to the coffin to have a last look at him. I stood there and peeped into the coffin, and this incident remains vivid in my mind.

During my first pilgrimage, one night I dreamt that I was in the very same position, but that my father arose in his coffin as if awakened. This frightened me so much that I woke up very perplexed. The next day I was to meet the Greatest Holy Leaf,[5] and no one can imagine the condition I was in at the prospect. It was no joke for a humble, insignificant creature like myself to enter the presence of the daughter of the King of Heaven and earth. She, immediately, with her loving and keen insight, understood the great agitation I was in. She very gently asked me how I was; did I sleep well? But not once did I think of my dream. Tea was served, and what a delicious feast, but I was still in the same disturbed state. As I was drinking my tea, she asked me, 'Did you have a dream?' She asked me a second time, and suddenly I remembered my dream, and told her about it. She smiled and said, 'Of course, your faith in this Cause has brought your father back to life again.'

Three

My husband was not a Bahá'í, but after two or three days of my pilgrimage he became so enthralled with love for the Guardian that one day, while looking at the new and uncompleted building of the Western Pilgrim House, he became angry and exclaimed, 'How can the Bahá'ís see an unfinished building every day in front of the Guardian's eyes? You will see that the building is brought to completion.'[6]

Mr Collins was also honoured by being able to meet the Greatest Holy Leaf and other members of the household. He was a very sociable man. He would take part in any discussion with perfect freedom and ease. But before entering the Master's House he was so excited that he arranged his tie and smoothed his clothes and repeatedly asked me what he should do when we arrived there. I replied, 'Nothing! In the family of 'Abdu'l-Bahá simplicity reigns and nothing but love is ever accepted.'

When we entered the room, we found the Greatest Holy Leaf sitting in a chair and all the ladies of the household standing reverently and politely around her. We both sat in front of her. Tea was served. Conversation was short and simple. The dignity, the simplicity of the Greatest Holy Leaf, and the atmosphere created by her spiritual station so overwhelmed Tom that he was tongue-tied. Even after we were outside the House, he was absolutely quiet for a long time and, when he did open his mouth, he spoke only words in praise of her, and concerning his own astonishment and wonder.

Four

The beloved Guardian had advised me always to be as kind and loving to my husband as possible. I tried always to follow this advice. Nor did I ever disobey Tom. For his sake I stopped having meetings in my home and even going to meetings. As time passed, gradually his heart changed and he allowed me to attend meetings and to hold Nineteen Day Feasts[7] in our own home. But he never became a Bahá'í in this world.

> On one of our trips to Europe in 1937, he passed away on board ship. I had to take his body back to the United States. At this bitter moment of my life I received such a bounty from the Guardian that all my sorrow came to an end.

Here is the message which the Guardian sent to Milly at this sad time:

> Greatly distressed sudden passing beloved husband. Heart overflowing tenderest sympathy. Offering special prayers. Advising Geyserville summer school hold befitting memorial gathering recognition generous support their institution. May Beloved aid him attain goal he was steadily approaching closing years of his life.

Not long after, when Milly again visited Haifa, the beloved Guardian told her:

> Your husband is in the presence of the Master and is proud of your services.

The Guardian reiterated the same thought a few years later, with even greater emphasis:

> How pleased the Beloved must be, how proud He must feel of your truly great achievements! The soul of dear Mr Collins must exult and rejoice in the Abbá Kingdom. Persevere and be happy.

He also wrote to her:

> The days you spent under the shadow of the holy Shrines will long be remembered with joy and gratitude.

After returning from this trip, Milly was not the same person as before. Though encircled by a great many family problems, she was confirmed to perform such great and distinguished services that the beloved Guardian not only called her an 'outstanding benefactress of the Faith', but addressed her as, 'Dearly-beloved sister', and 'Dear and prized co-worker'.

Over the years, in the many letters he wrote to Milly, Shoghi Effendi prepared her to fulfil her destiny, assured her of her spiritual progress and forecast her elevation to the high rank she would attain. For example, in the early years of his Guardianship he appended, in his own hand, such precious sentiments as these:

> My Spiritual Sister: I never cease praying for you from the bottom of my heart and wish you success in the glorious work that lies before you. It is our duty and privilege to translate the love and devotion we have for our beloved Cause into deeds and actions that will be conducive to the highest good of mankind … Shoghi.

In the year 1926, he wrote:

> My dear and precious fellow-worker: Your steadfastness in service, your selflessness and devotion to the work you are engaged in, greatly encourage me and inspire me in my work. Your many services, past and present, will ever be remembered with praise, gladness, and gratitude. Continue in your magnificent endeavours for the propagation of the Bahá'í Faith and remember always that in me you have a grateful, loving and admiring brother who will never cease to pray for you from the bottom of his heart, Shoghi.

Again, in that same year:

> My dearly-beloved Sister in the Cause: I am inexpressibly touched by this further evidence of your spontaneous and self-sacrificing devotion. I will devote your generous donation to promote such interests of the Cause as are most vital and nearest and dearest to my heart … Your bright and shining example is, I am certain, acclaimed and glorified by the Supreme Concourse in the Abhá Kingdom, and in this world below, you have undoubtedly earned the affection and the admiration of us all. With deepest and truest love to my unforgettable friend and brother Mr Collins. Your grateful brother, Shoghi.

In 1940:

> Dear and prized co-worker: I cannot refrain from adding a few words in person as a further token of my true and abiding appreciation of the ceaseless and most touching evidences of your wonderful devotion to the Cause of God, and of the immense support you have extended, and are still extending, to its divers and evolving institutions, locally, nationally and internationally. How pleased the Beloved must be … Your true and grateful brother, Shoghi.

And in another letter that same year:

> Dearly-beloved co-worker: I was deeply touched by your letter and by the assurances you have so lovingly and spontaneously given me of your eagerness to demonstrate your great love for our beloved Cause. For my part I can unhesitatingly assure you that you have amply and

nobly, and in different fields and over a long period of time, revealed the true character of your faith and the depth of your devotion to the Cause and its manifold institutions. You should rest assured and, with radiant happiness and reverent gratitude, persevere in the path you are treading with such zeal, determination and loyalty. I will pray for you with redoubled fervour. Your true and grateful brother, Shoghi.

In 1942:

> Dear and prized co-worker: Your journey to South America, in these days of stress, of uncertainty and peril, in order to lend further assistance to the sacred, the vital, and manifold interests of our beloved Faith, is a fresh and compelling demonstration of the devotion and zeal that characterize your activities in its service. Your extremely generous contribution on my behalf to the teaching Fund, at this critical hour, is a still further evidence of your unfailing solicitude for its extension and development. I am deeply touched and profoundly grateful. My constant and fervent prayers surround you in your historic and arduous journey, and I pray that the Beloved may guide every step you take and fulfil every hope you cherish for the advancement of the Cause and the glory and consolidation of its institutions. Your true and grateful brother, Shoghi.

In 1945 he wrote:

> Dear and valued co-worker: The work you have achieved in recent years is truly highly meritorious. The reports sent by the believers eloquently testify to its character and significance. I feel truly proud of what you are achieving in so many fields, and with such remarkable results. You should feel so happy, assured, and thankful, for the Beloved is well pleased with you. Persevere in your labours. Your true and grateful brother, Shoghi.

And in 1946 came these words of encouragement:

> Dear and valued co-worker: I am deeply grateful to you as I witness on every side and on an ever increasing scale, the evidences of your solid achievements, your exemplary spirit, your marvellous activity, your beneficent influence, and magnificent labours for the propagation and consolidation of our glorious Faith. My admiration for you grows every day, and I supplicate continually our Beloved to bless, sustain and guide you always, and aid you to win still mightier victories. Your true and grateful brother, Shoghi.

From these letters it is evident that our precious Milly was very close to the beloved Guardian's heart. Wherever the Guardian was, she would write letters to Amatu'l-Bahá Rúḥíyyih Khánum,[8] and answers would come in accordance with his instructions. Often Milly desired to know only whether or not he was in good health.

Sometimes special missions were given to Milly by the Guardian and she, without any ostentation, with great humility and single-hearted devotion, would attend to the work he had entrusted to her and report to him confidentially.

From some of the Guardian's letters written in the 1940s, we can understand that she accomplished great services of a unique and exalted character. She was indeed a heroine because of such services, her achievements being due to her great love for and complete obedience to the beloved Guardian, her vigilance and immediate response to do what was his heart's desire. Thus she received honours attained by no one else. She preserved all these signs of bounty and grace in the treasure house of her heart and did not reveal them to anyone. After the bitter grief of the Guardian's passing, these pearls filled her whole existence with light and assurance.

Let us ponder the following letter from the Guardian to Milly, written in 1947:

> Dear and prized co-worker: With a heart overflowing with profound gratitude I am now writing you these few lines to reaffirm the sentiments, expressed lately on several occasions and in a number of telegrams, of heartfelt and unqualified admiration for your magnificent services, rendered in circumstances so exceptional and difficult as to make them doubly meritorious in the sight of God. You have acquitted yourself of the task I felt prompted to impose upon you in a manner that deserves the praise of the Concourse on high. The high rank you now occupy and which no Bahá'í since the Master's passing has ever held in his own lifetime, has been conferred solely in recognition of the manifold services you have already rendered, and is, by no means, intended to be a stimulus or encouragement in the path of service. Indeed the character of this latest and highly significant service you have rendered places you in the category of the Chosen Nine who, unlike the other Hands of the Cause, are to be associated directly and intimately with the cares and responsibilities of the Guardian of the

> Faith. I feel truly proud of you, am drawn closer to you, and admire more deeply than ever before the spirit that animates you. May the Beloved reward you, both in this world and the next for your truly exemplary achievements. Gratefully and affectionately, Shoghi.

And later in that same year:

> Dear and prized co-worker: The memory of the services, assistance and support you extended to me in my hour of anxiety and stress a year ago, at this time is still vivid, and evokes my deepest admiration and gratitude. Your services in other fields, and in the course of many years, have, moreover, served to deepen my feelings of affection and gratitude for so distinguished a handmaid of Bahá'u'lláh and Hand of His Cause ... Gratefully and affectionately, Shoghi.

In 1949 the Guardian addressed Milly:

> Dear and prized co-worker: I greatly welcome the splendid opportunity you now have of contributing your share – substantial and abiding I am confident it will be – to the progress of the Faith and the edification of the believers in Great Britain, Poland, Switzerland and Germany. I have already informed the German and British National Assemblies, and I am sure the friends will be delighted to meet you, and will be greatly stimulated by the news you will impart to them, as a result of your wide experience, and particularly by the spirit which so powerfully animates you in the service of our beloved Faith. This latest journey you undertake for the spread and consolidation of the Faith, at such important European Centres, constitutes another chapter of the truly remarkable and outstanding record of your eminent international services to the Cause of God. The international Centre of the Faith and its subsidiary institutions are greatly indebted to you for your superb accomplishments. May the Beloved, Whom you serve so diligently, so devotedly and with such distinction, abundantly bless your high endeavours and enable you to realize, in whatever field you labour and at every stage of your journeys, the dearest wish of your heart. Your true and grateful brother, Shoghi.

In a letter the following year he wrote:

> Dear and valued co-worker: I am deeply touched by the repeated evidences of your self-sacrificing labours, exertions and services to our beloved Faith during these momentous days, at so critical an hour in the fortunes of mankind and at so significant a stage in its world-wide evolution and unfoldment of the Cause of God. Your share in consolidating its divers institutions at its world centre, in

> the North American continent, in Latin America, and in Europe, is indeed memorable and outstanding. I will associate your very generous contribution for the Shrine of the Báb with the memory of dear Mr Collins, whose soul will no doubt rejoice and increasingly progress as a direct result of the historic services you have rendered, for so long and so devotedly, to the Cause of Bahá'u'lláh. He surely must feel proud of you, the Beloved is highly pleased with the standard of your achievements, and I am profoundly grateful for all that you have accomplished for the spread and establishment of His Cause. You should be extremely happy for having been so abundantly blessed in your high and meritorious endeavours. Your true and grateful brother, Shoghi.

In 1956 Shoghi Effendi wrote:

> Dear and prized co-worker: I will devote a part of your very generous contribution to the purchase of a few Chinese and Japanese cabinets, panels and ornaments for the International Archives now nearing completion, the exterior and interior of which will, to a very marked extent, be associated, for all time, with your munificent support of the rising institutions of the Faith at its world Centre. I am sure you will be highly pleased, and the spirit of dear Mr Collins will rejoice in the Abhá Kingdom. Your true and grateful brother, Shoghi.

> Dear and prized co-worker: I am deeply touched by these repeated evidences of your great devotion, your unfailing solicitude, and, above all, of the shining spirit of self-sacrifice that prompts you to make these munificent donations for the promotion of the Faith at its World Centre. I am anxiously waiting for the removal of obstacles that prevent you from attaining your heart's desire. I am looking forward very eagerly to the time when we will be able to meet again in the Master's Home. Affectionately and gratefully, Shoghi.

Milly often said that she knew very little about the Writings, but loved to listen to the Tablets and prayers and to hear the stories of the early days of the Cause. She said:

> Out of the immense treasury of all the Writings, I memorized one sentence and did my utmost to follow that one injunction. It served as a lamp of guidance, shedding light on the dark and obscure paths of my life. That phrase is from the Will and Testament of the Master, where He says that the friends should make Shoghi Effendi happy. Whatever step I took in my life, any vote cast in the Assemblies, any trip taken,

> even any thought, I would first ask myself whether my vote, words, trip or thought would make him happy. When I was sure, then I would take action without fear.

When, in 1925, for the first time she became a member of the National Spiritual Assembly of the Bahá'ís of the United States and Canada, she found herself, very young in the Cause, sitting with old, accomplished and learned friends. But her initial fears were soon overcome, and for many years she contributed greatly to the consultations of that important body. A letter from the beloved Guardian in 1941, through his secretary, no doubt had reference to this and her many other administrative services:

> It comforts him greatly to know that you are in a position to help watch over and safeguard the interests of the Cause and the believers. Your calm sanity, your great faith and devotion, are assets of outstanding value to the Faith, especially at present.

She was a member of the National Spiritual Assembly for twenty years, and was always vigilant to tread a path guided by the pleasure and wishes of the Guardian.

If we look around the Bahá'í world, we shall be amazed to note her achievements; her contributions made possible the purchase of Temple sites, Ḥaẓíratu'l-Quds,[9] endowment lands; the translation and publication of books, the support of pioneers in America, the Hawaiian Islands, the islands of the South Pacific, Europe, Africa – all were sustained by her generous, yet unknown gifts. Many a pioneer received her support without knowing it, the fact only to be revealed after her passing. These services were rendered either directly or completely by Milly, or by sharing contributions with others.

It is to be noted with something of awe that this handmaiden of the Lord, in her latter years, aching with arthritis, endeavoured so earnestly and perpetually to participate in laying the foundations of so many pillars of the divine institutions raised in the name of Bahá'u'lláh throughout the world. All these services were performed with complete love and detachment, sanctified from any ostentation, and in perfect order to the last moment of her life.

Here we must emphasize two points.

First, Milly herself never mentioned anything about her generous contributions to the Faith, many of them made directly to the beloved Guardian.

Even after his passing, many of these activities were continued, as she had arranged for them to be, and they were kept confidential, as was her wish. The Hands of the Cause in Haifa came to know about some of them through receiving the minutes of the National Spiritual Assemblies sent to them from all over the world. Whenever Milly would offer a contribution at a meeting of the Hands of the Cause, she would urge us to keep it confidential. 'Just send the money,' she would say; 'don't mention my name.'

Secondly, Milly's eyes were wide open and always bright with longing to see where in the Bahá'í world the friends were confronted with insurmountable difficulties in teaching, pioneering or any other field of activity. At such moments she would say, 'If the Guardian were alive, he would never like to see these tasks unfinished. I am ready to help. But please don't mention my name.'

We need more souls like Milly, dedicated, sensitive and pure. Is there any better way to serve the Cause than to have one's own will, desires and wishes wholly dissolved in the Will of God?

Can we find anywhere a soul purer than hers and a heart more brimfull with divine love? She submerged herself in the ocean of the Guardian's love. She was both generous and shrewd. She never plunged her hands in her pocket to pour out money at random. She was never moved to take any step until she was sure that every penny would be passed along in the channels advised by the Guardian. She did not spend money to please herself. That was not Milly. Her whole aim and purpose was to see her beloved happy and relieved of cares. And when she took a step, she never expected, or wanted, to receive acknowledgement and praise, much less any public announcement.

In her personal habits she was thrifty. She would, every now and then, go to her clothes-cupboard and choose a dress that had been set aside for some reason, and this she would shorten or adjust to make it more in fashion. When I knew her in Haifa she lived in one small room – which had previously been occupied by Mr Maxwell, the father of Rúḥíyyih Khánum – in the utmost contentment and joy, because it was a room in the Master's House, under the same roof as her beloved Shoghi Effendi.

Once she said that the very first time she saw that divine countenance and beheld those beautiful and expressive eyes, so full of eagerness and expectation, she realized that that divine youth was surrounded by many insurmountable hardships and sorrows. His sorrows dwelt in the very depths of his youthful and loving heart, and he trod the path of suffering, as did Bahá'u'lláh and 'Abdu'l-Bahá before him, in quietude and patience. In his look she could clearly discern his need for love and co-operation from those who claimed to love him. And, she said, having sensed these heavenly traces in his gracious manner, his expectant eyes and his selfless tone of voice, she felt a poignant ache in her heart in response to this need.

This pain grew into something that changed her life and her attitude towards him. It was so strong and mysterious, she said, that she could never presume to mention it to the Guardian. One day, after his passing, she said to us:

> You know, I had never had the joy of having a child. Therefore, in my heart and soul, I adopted him as my own son and, in the world of faith and spirit, enthroned him on the throne of certitude where he reigned as the sole sovereign of my soul, the ruler of my destiny and the fashioner of my life. In whatever direction he willed, I would go, with the utmost joy and assurance.

In her daily life, dearest Milly demonstrated this love and faith. Everyone could feel it in the increasing momentum and power of her services, and in her integrity. In the light of this love she remained radiant and glowing. In its consuming flame she stood steadfast with a courageous heart that beat with unprecedented acquiescence. After the passing of the beloved Guardian this love became ever more intense. It was as if she could no longer remain alone in this world. We could almost hear the sorrowful songs of separation as she spoke with words of intense longing for reunion with him. We could behold the fire of her love burning brighter day by day.

The friends should never for a moment misunderstand or think that the cause of such a close and loving relationship was ever due to the large and numerous contributions that she regularly offered at the threshold of his love. That which made her unique was the selflessness and purity of soul and sincere intention with which she offered her wealth to her beloved, to assist him in accomplishing what was dearest to his heart – the progress of the Faith.

There is a large and beautiful wrought-iron gilded gate at the beginning of the path leading to the Shrine of Bahá'u'lláh. The symbol of the Greatest Name surmounts it and it is called the 'Collins Gate'. When the pilgrims approach the Shrine of the Supreme Manifestation of God, they pass through this main gate, which silently stands as a loving remembrance of the one who adored the Guardian of the Faith – Shoghi Effendi, grandson of 'Abdu'l-Bahá, and great-grandson of Bahá'u'lláh.

This gate has a touching story connected with it that goes back to the years of Milly's childhood. This is what she told us:

> As I have said, sometimes I would make a humble offering to Shoghi Effendi. One time I sent him a sum of money and begged that it not be used for the institutions of the Faith or for teaching or pioneering but, in some way, for himself. This humble request was expressed frankly and lovingly, with, one might venture to say, the yearning of a mother's heart.

To such requests, the Guardian would usually reply with a message to the effect that his personal needs were few and limited. This message would be conveyed with such tenderness that Milly never found words to express the feelings that overwhelmed her. But let us go back to the story of the gate:

> Ever since my childhood I had wanted a gate. Even when I was very small and used to build little houses for my dolls, I would try to make a gate for the doll's house. I used little bars of iron and other scraps, but none satisfied my longing. When we built a home in New England, Tom asked me about a gate. I said to him, 'Tom, I do not want to put the money into a gate now.' But nothing could satisfy that deep longing of mine. About this time, I embraced the Faith and forgot about this desire of mine. I had no thought any more for worldly things. After my husband died and I had been called to Haifa to serve, I offered the beloved Guardian a contribution and expressed the hope that the sum be used for his personal needs.
>
> Time passed and one day I received a letter from Shoghi Effendi. It contained a photograph of a gigantic and very beautiful gate and a note asking me how I liked it, and informing me it had been purchased with the money I had offered him! Immediately I sent a message to him, saying, 'Exceedingly beautiful.' One night when some pilgrims were present at the table in the Western Pilgrim House, William Foster was among them. In his love for the Guardian he expressed the wish to be of some service while he was on pilgrimage; he was a builder and

> contractor by profession. The beloved asked him if he could build a gate, and Bill replied, with the greatest delight, that he most certainly could.
>
> The Guardian then said he planned to erect the Collins Gate in the Ḥaram-i-Aqdas.[10]

This was the first time that Milly heard this expression. At that tender moment as she gazed at the beloved Guardian, the Sign of God on earth, who knew her inmost longing, Milly told us, 'He knew that my life had no worth except to offer it at his bidding at any moment. He responded to my look with a heavenly smile.'

The Bahá'ís know that in the last years of His life Bahá'u'lláh made several visits to Haifa. On one of these He went to the extreme western end of Mt Carmel. It is the head of the mountain, in whose heart rests the Shrine of the Báb. The head is indeed beautifully situated. It is a promontory jutting north-westwards into the blue Mediterranean, and the sun rising on one side of it sets on the other. It was while Bahá'u'lláh was visiting this part of the mountain that He revealed the Tablet of Carmel in the vicinity of one of the famous caves where, it is claimed, the Prophet Elijah lived. It is interesting, in view of later events, that the Guardian sent Milly and her husband to visit this historic site during her first pilgrimage.

Many years later Shoghi Effendi very much wished to purchase a piece of land, the highest spot on this promontory, lest it be irretrievably lost to the Faith. His intention was that the future House of Worship in the Holy Land should be erected there. Milly never took any action unless and until she knew definitely that it was the Guardian's desire. As soon as she knew this was his plan, she begged him to allow her to donate the money for its purchase.

This request was granted. She said that if she had ever received any reward in this transient life, this was it. On the day that the transactions for the purchase of this land were completed, she was in her room in the Master's House, when suddenly someone knocked on her door and informed her that the Guardian was waiting for her in his car in front of the House. The purpose of that unprecedented drive was the explanation bountifully given to her about the Temple site by the Guardian himself.

Whatever Milly had offered, in whatever way and for whatever institution, her acts had all been from sheer love; never did she expect, or wish, that what she did should be proclaimed. However, when the Guardian announced her gift of land for the Temple site, she explained to us, 'Who was I to say a word, or to wish otherwise!'

The main purpose in relating these unique and beautiful stories about Milly is to awaken in ourselves an awareness, and to cause us to ponder this point: How many opportunities have we, as individual Bahá'ís, had to make the Guardian happy, but in how many cases have we been heedless and passed them by? Milly was wide awake and alert. Even a word breathed by the Guardian would convey many things to her. She had no desire, no will, no intention other than to fulfil his wishes. She knew very well that if he were happy, he could do more for our great and beloved Cause.

When the Guardian announced to the Bahá'í world his decision to erect the superstructure of the Báb's Shrine, thus fulfilling the wistful desire of the Master, Milly sent a sum of money for this purpose and received the following acknowledgement, written on his behalf by his secretary:

> I am enclosing a receipt, at the instruction of our beloved Guardian, for the sum you so spontaneously and generously sent to him to be used for the construction of the superstructure of the Báb's Holy Tomb on Mt Carmel. He wants you to know that this is the first contribution he has received for this glorious undertaking, and he is not surprised that it should come from you! You lead the way, in devotion, loyalty and self-sacrifice, in many fields of Bahá'í service, and your spirit of dedication to our beloved Faith and its interests greatly endears you to him.

In another instance, when the Guardian's contribution for a specific purpose and her own were received simultaneously, the Guardian cabled her:

> Our recent contributions teaching campaign synchronized evidence our hearts attuned noble Cause.

On one occasion, the Guardian had said that the Bahá'ís should endeavour to purchase as many houses around the Temple in Wilmette as possible. Milly said later that when the Guardian had expressed this wish, it was as if she had not heard him. She had not even grasped the significance of such an instruction. Years passed and one day when, as a member of the National Spiritual Assembly, she was hurrying to the Assembly session – for she always tried to be punctual – she noticed a sign on the property across the street from the Temple which read: 'For Sale'. At that moment Milly remembered the words of the Guardian spoken so many years before, and she immediately telephoned the real estate agent and purchased the property without the least thought of whether or not the price was right. When she reached the session, a little late, the friends could not possibly guess the reason for this delay of one who was always so punctual.

On one occasion, it happened that the Guardian did not meet with the friends for a few days and they came to know that he was not feeling well. This saddened all hearts, and Milly's sorrow had no bounds. The very first night after that, when the Guardian came to dine with the friends in the Western Pilgrim House and all eyes were fixed on him, he announced for the first time the opening of that great 'Spiritual Crusade', 1953–1963.

While listening, Milly remembered being told that the Greatest Holy Leaf had often said the Guardian's hands resembled those of Bahá'u'lláh. That night, when he unrolled his map and showed them all the goals of the World Crusade, Milly's gaze constantly followed the rhythmic movement of his beautiful hands and fingers. She was so overwhelmed by the beauty, power and dexterity of his hands that she was in an ecstasy, and waves of joy and astonishment surged in all hearts at the magnitude of the Guardian's vision. Each one present longed to participate in the fulfilment of the newly-revealed plan. Though old, frail in body and broken in health, Milly could not control the upsurge of her desire to serve, and the words burst out, 'Where can I go?'

The beloved Guardian replied, 'Your place is here.'

As the months passed, following the inauguration of the World Crusade, every night, whenever the Guardian came to dinner to meet the friends, they could detect by an extra light in his eyes that he had received good news. With those beautiful hands he would unfold the cablegrams that had come to him and read out their contents. The news of the pioneers and of the Knights of Bahá'u'lláh[11] arriving at their posts in the first year of the plan poured in to the World Centre regularly. One time the Guardian said:

> The night I explained the details of the Crusade, some of you thought that the goals were unattainable, but now you can all see how the confirmations have descended, and how individuals have been raised up to conquer these goals through the resuscitating power of God.

When the friends entered the dining room to meet the Guardian, he would usually ask, 'How are you, Milly?' She would counter this question by saying 'My condition is not important. How is the Guardian?'

Whenever the Guardian passed through the hall of 'Abdu'l-Bahá's House to go to the Shrine, or returned and was on his way to his own room, Milly might have stood in the hall to have a glimpse of him and receive a word from him. But this was not Milly. Her attitude was utterly different from that of many others. Whenever the Guardian was going to or from his room, she would immediately withdraw to her own room, lest a minute of his precious time should be spent in asking how she was. She kept herself out of sight, never in the way, always self-effacing, courteous and considerate. The Guardian would say of her, 'Day by day she becomes nearer and dearer.'

Never did Milly fail to attend the meetings of the Hands of the Cause in Haifa.[12] The terrible pain she suffered because of arthritis would have put anyone else in bed, but Milly's conscience was extremely powerful and awake. When the pain was too severe to permit her to sit in a chair, she would ask her nurse to give her an injection to appease it, so that she could come to the meetings.

Sometimes when we heard her footsteps on the stairs, we would hasten to reach out a hand to help her. We always noticed that she held her hands together as if holding something between her palms. Coming into the room, with a beautiful and radiant smile she would say, 'The imps are asleep.'

Her presence was a great help. Every word she uttered welled up from a fountain-head of love deep in her pure heart. Her eyes grew wider, bluer and more penetrating when ways and means were found to open up paths towards the fulfilment of one of the goals of the Guardian's Ten Year Plan. Not only her prayers and her wisdom, but also her generous contributions helped to keep such paths open and paved the way to victory.

For several nights one winter, Milly could not attend dinner with the Guardian at the Pilgrim House because of illness. One night, on crossing the street to his home, Shoghi Effendi, accompanied by Rúḥíyyih Khánum, went directly to Milly's room. It was very cold, and he was wearing a delicate light woollen scarf made in Kashmir. After speaking some words of strength and hope to Milly, he removed the scarf from his own neck and wrapped it around hers; then he left, saying he hoped she would soon be all right. Milly said that the scarf carried with it the warmth of his blessed body. It became one of her most treasured possessions.

The beloved Guardian, having been forsaken by all the members of his family, had no intimate companions except his wife, Amatu'l-Bahá Rúḥíyyih Khánum, who he said served as his 'shield' against the Covenant-breakers, and her father, Sutherland Maxwell, as well as a few old and trusted servants to whom he would sometimes open his heart. To such as these Milly was added, becoming often the privileged recipient of the Guardian's confidences, one to whom he could open his heart and reveal his sorrows, and many a sleepless night such confidences brought to Milly's loving heart!

One night, Milly said, he came to her room with Rúḥíyyih Khánum and explained to her the infamous acts of his relatives. Milly could not bear to see the distress and sorrow in his beautiful face. She was heart-broken and could not suppress her tears. The Guardian, with the greatest tenderness, told her not to weep.

The day came when the beloved Guardian would leave the Holy Land for ever. While bidding farewell to Milly, he looked deep into her eyes and said, 'Do not be sad, Milly.'

Every summer Milly left the Holy Land for Arizona, where the climate is hot and dry and enabled her to ease the arthritic pains from which she suffered a great deal. She would always arrange her affairs, however, in such a way as to be back in Haifa before the Guardian returned. This would give her the great joy of welcoming her beloved.

Therefore, in early November 1957, she reached Haifa and had hardly begun to unpack when she received the news of that fateful fourth of November.[13] She left immediately for London.

When I first saw her in London, she was like a comforting shadow as she followed Amatu'l-Bahá in her sorrowful tasks, unbelievably calm and serene. That terrible test which shook the foundations of the world of existence could not destroy Milly. Old and heart-broken though she was, she stood firm as a mountain. She was true to her love and, as ever, obedient. The Guardian's words, 'Don't be sad, Milly', rang in her ears.

During the years after the passing of the Guardian, when I had the privilege of being very near to Milly, I received many lessons of love from her. Many a night she and I would sit in the presence of Amatu'l-Bahá. On those memorable nights I would chant Tablets and poems in Persian and we would reminisce about the days of our beloved Guardian. The poems and prayers would be translated and, although we had so much to attend to during those eventful days, we never felt fatigued or exhausted, even though we sometimes sat until the early hours of the morning.

Gradually our precious Milly became acquainted with many Tablets in Arabic and Persian, and also with some of the Persian poets. Sometimes Amatu'l-Bahá would graciously ask her, 'Now, Milly, what do you want? Ṭáhirih, Ustád Muḥammad-'Alí the Barber, Ḥáfiẓ, or Sa'dí?' When the title of an ode was mentioned, Milly could follow the subject matter.

While the Tablets were chanted or the poems sung, she would close her eyes and go into a world of her own, a world where perhaps she could have a vision of her beloved.

One time I asked her the following question. 'Milly,' I said, 'you are not accustomed to the Arabic or Persian tones of singing or chanting. How is it that you so much want to hear them and are rapt in such ecstasy?'

She replied:

> First of all, for the broken heart of our precious Amatu'l-Bahá, and second, I close my eyes, follow the thoughts and visualize that these songs and prayers and poems had been chanted in almost the same tones in the presence of the Master or the Guardian and even Bahá'u'lláh Himself. This thought gladdens my heart.

In times of distress and sorrow, Milly would often repeat, 'Why? Why?' And when one day she was asked what she meant by that question, she said, 'Why am I alive? I am ill, weak and not able to travel and teach. What is the use of my life?'

It was a winter's day when this conversation took place, in the office of the Hands of the Cause, where a small kerosene stove was burning. I said to her,

'Milly dear, isn't the weather very cold now?'

'Yes', she replied.

‘How is it that we can sit here, hold meetings, read letters, send messages to the Bahá’í world, in such comfort and ease? It is because of that little stove that is burning? It doesn’t say anything. Does it make speeches? Does it travel? Never! The stove burns as long as it has kerosene. It gives its heat to us very generously and, in that warmth, we work. This is true of our physical comfort; then how much more do we need spiritual heat to give us energy and power to go on and carry the load to the year sixty three, when we shall surrender all into the hands of the Supreme Body. Now dearest, you are our spiritual stove. You burn and we speak, write, travel.’

A beautiful smile lighted her lovely face and she reached up her hands to me to signify that I should help her up and accompany her to her room.

On Saturday afternoons Milly and I would meet in her room to review her personal letters and prepare answers. During one of these times she told me of the beginning of her deep relationship with Rúḥíyyih Khánum.

Milly was an old friend of Mrs May Maxwell, the mother of Amatu’l-Bahá Rúḥíyyih Khánum; she came to Haifa as a pilgrim in November 1937, after the marriage of the Guardian to Rúḥíyyih Khánum, and this was the beginning of their truly historic relationship to each other as their mutual love for Mrs Maxwell drew them together. Milly told me that when, on one occasion, she saw Mrs Maxwell in New York, Rúḥíyyih Khánum’s mother embraced her and said ‘Take care of Rúḥíyyih Khánum. Take care of Rúḥíyyih Khánum. Take care of her for me.’ Shortly after this Mrs Maxwell left for South America and died in Argentina.

Milly told me that Mrs Maxwell’s words had surprised her very much. How could she take care of the one who had been chosen by the beloved Guardian and was living under his care and protection?

‘But destiny’, said Milly, ‘proved that the heart of her mother had indeed been inspired. Now you see, in this great House of the Master, where all the rooms are left empty and dark, I now live so close to Rúḥíyyih Khánum. My hope and desire is to be with her in these bitter hours of loneliness and separation.’

Milly did her utmost. Whenever Rúḥíyyih Khánum went on a journey, Milly would utter words of encouragement that gushed forth from the very depths of her heart.

‘Rest assured, my darling’, she would say. ‘Rest assured that wherever you go, Shoghi Effendi will be standing next to you, and whatever step you take, he will hold your hand and will guide your steps ...’

In those eventful days and years after the ascension of our Guardian, Milly’s will, determination and absolute certainty of the ultimate victory of the Cause were a great comfort, support and guiding light to her co-workers. Her true comprehension of the greatness of the hour and the exalted significance of the opportunities given to a small group of feeble persons to serve His Cause, inspired us all. She expressed herself very clearly and was extremely frank. Whatever she said had the light and power of conviction.

The passing of the one for whose sake she breathed never changed her love for the Faith, nor her spirit of self-sacrifice and thoughtfulness. In many instances she contributed even more generously than during the lifetime of the Guardian, towards the purchase of Bahá’í centres, the publication of books, sustaining pioneers and supporting the National Spiritual Assembly of the Bahá’ís of the United States, and, especially, the new National Spiritual Assemblies established according to the plan of the Guardian after his passing. Her financial gifts to them were, in her own words, ‘for the sole purpose of pleasing Shoghi Effendi in the presence of Bahá’u’lláh’.

Milly’s suffering from arthritis had no end, but she suffered in silence. The arthritis became gradually worse; she felt excruciating pains in her feet and joints and her fingers grew increasingly worse. As the Guardian had instructed her to do, she went every summer to Arizona to take advantage of the dry, warm climate.

Before leaving Haifa she would visit the Shrines, and I could see in her beautiful eyes the shadow of sorrow, and could sense her thought, that this might be the last time she would gaze at the resting-place of the Supreme Manifestation of God. On the way to the airport she would watch the waves of the Mediterranean Sea washing the shore at the foot of the Mountain of God.

She would gaze at the mountains and hills of the Holy Land and suddenly exclaim, ‘Won’t you sing poems for me?’

Every year she would write from Arizona or Wilmette that her health had improved, but there came a year when she wrote that there was no change. It was during this year that she fell down the stairs in her home in Wilmette.

We were all very sad, thinking that our precious Milly would not be able to attend the annual meeting of the Hands of the Cause. But there was nothing in the world that could keep her from fulfilling her duties towards the Guardian. She reached Haifa on time, and the joint message sent out by the Hands received her signature.

Milly was now so frail that she could not walk properly and, when she arrived from the airport, ascending the steps of the Master's House was impossible for her. Some of the friends helped her and almost carried her up the steps. Though she was exhausted and in acute pain, her face shone with the light of love, her beautiful blue eyes glowed with joy that she was in the Master's House again and with a motion of her aching hands she sent kisses to those who had come to greet her.

She attended the meeting of the Hands held in the Mansion at Bahjí, even though she had to be carried to the upper floor in a chair, and spoke with great conviction and strength, showering her abounding love upon all her co-workers. At the end of the meeting we all entered the Shrine of Bahá'u'lláh for praise and thanksgiving. She recited a prayer, every word of which took wings to the Abhá Kingdom.

It was very evident that this was the last act in her heroic and dramatic life. On returning to the Master's House, her home, she was confined to bed, and her physician would not permit visitors, leaving all of us in acute anguish and deprivation. No more of the frequent visits to the suffering patient were permitted.

Some of her fellow Hands, whose love for Milly was profound, were permitted to go to her bedside to give her the good news of the progress of our discussions and meetings. Though bedridden, she was always expectant to hear the news, and to see how she could serve. She shone like a brilliant star from the horizon of that House. She read all the letters written by the Hands, and signed them.

The last letter taken to her to sign was about the deputization fund. With trembling and aching fingers she held the pen and wrote 'Am ...', and could do no more. This unfinished signature carries with it the pathos of an unfinished melody – the melody of love to the last breath.

One day, towards evening, Amatu'l-Bahá asked me, 'Do you wish to see Milly?' I longed to see her. God knows with what bitter tears in my eyes and strong feelings I entered her room. I remembered that at one time Milly and I had had a little meeting there together once a week, when I used to show her pictures of the martyrs, of outstanding teachers of the Cause, and of true and faithful servants of Bahá'u'lláh; and would read her private letters and prepare answers.

All these beautiful recollections made my heart very heavy, as I stood there looking at her face which was more beautiful than ever. She opened her generous arms and embraced this humble admirer, as I washed her face with my tears.

At this touching moment, in a very faint voice, she said, 'You used to chant and sing. Won't you do it now?' She placed her hands on her chest, ready to listen. When the prayer was finished, she sighed and, smiling faintly, said, 'You used to translate these for me.'

'It was one of the prayers of the Master,' I said, 'in which He recommends that we open our eyes and behold the grandeur and beauty of the Abhá Kingdom ... when Man's soul spreads its wings and gets ready for the eternal flight, he sees some signs of the majesty of God's creation and the immensity of the world beyond.'

I could sense that moment when her frail body would no longer contain the sublime soul that for so long had been yearning to take its flight.

This was my last visit with that lady whose life proved her worthiness to be the 'lady of the Kingdom', as 'Abdu'l-Bahá Himself had addressed her.

During all these years, Amatu'l-Bahá Rúḥíyyih Khánum and Milly were inseparable, and in the last weeks she remained always with Milly, even to the very end when Milly died in her arms.

The first day of January 1962 was drawing to a close when Amatu'l-Bahá informed all the friends of the passing of our precious Milly. 'Alí Nakhjavání and I hastened immediately to the Master's House to be with Rúḥíyyih Khánum. We were there until midnight, when the three of us went to Milly's room.

She was lying on her bed. A heavenly smile adorned her very beautiful face. All the ailments, distress and suffering had gone. With that lovely smile she was able to tell us more clearly than with any words that she had found her lost beloved.

The hours of separation had taken her to the banquet of reunion with the Guardian, as was clearly evident in the light of her dear face, so full of confidence, assurance and serenity. We chanted prayers and left her alone with her beloved.

Coming out of the room, Amatu'l-Bahá said, 'Now this corner of the House is dark also.' With these words she showed her loneliness more than she ever had before. She felt the history of that House in which 'Abdu'l-Bahá and the Greatest Holy Leaf had passed away, and now wherever she turned, upstairs or down, she found the occupant gone, the door closed and the room dark.

'How beautiful our precious Milly is on her bed', I said.

To which Rúḥíyyih Khánum replied, 'Of course, death is beautiful and makes everyone beautiful.'

I had witnessed many times when, about midnight, Rúḥíyyih Khánum and Milly had said goodnight to each other. How they embraced! What loving words of comfort they exchanged, and what assurances of prayers were given!

As we sat there, the three of us, I thought of Amatu'l-Bahá, who had lost the last person dear to her in this world, and who, from that night on, would have no Milly to embrace her on saying good night, assure her of prayers, give her confidence and a motherly love.

'Alí and I suggested that we stay in the House for the night, but Rúḥíyyih Khánum said, 'Milly is asleep and I will sleep too. You go home. Please take a little rest. Tomorrow we have much to do.'

The next day our dearest Milly was laid to rest in the Bahá'í cemetery, in a spot adjacent to the Afnán, chief builder of the Ishqábád Temple.

NOTES AND REFERENCES

1 In 1948 a separate National Spiritual Assembly was established in Canada.

2 Persia, where the Bahá'í Faith was born.

3 Shoghi Effendi, Guardian of the Bahá'í Faith, from 1921 to 1957.

4 The letter, dated 12 March 1923, was subsequently published in *Bahá'í Administration*, pp. 34–43 (Bahá'í Publishing Trust, Wilmette, Illinois, rev. edn. 1974).

5 The daughter of Bahá'u'lláh and sister of 'Abdu'l-Bahá.

6 Milly, joined by seven other Bahá'ís, contributed the funds needed to complete the Western Pilgrim House, for which, in December 1925, the Guardian expressed his 'heartfelt and abiding gratitude'.

7 Gatherings of the Bahá'ís at the commencement of each Bahá'í month.

8 The wife of the Guardian.

9 The headquarters of Bahá'í administrative activity.

10 The Shrine of Bahá'u'lláh and the surrounding area.

11 The title bestowed by Shoghi Effendi upon those Bahá'í pioneers who would first open to the Faith the 131 countries, territories and islands which, in 1953, had no resident Bahá'ís.

12 After the Guardian's passing, in 1957, until the election of the Universal House of Justice in 1963, the Faith was administered by the Hands of the Cause, whom Shoghi Effendi had appointed in his lifetime, and designated as the 'Chief Stewards of Bahá'u'lláh's embryonic World Commonwealth'.

13 The date of the passing of the Guardian.

Narcissus to ‘Akká

In Iran there are villages where many of the people embraced the Bahá'í Faith in the early hours of the dawn of the Age of Bahá'u'lláh. It is amazing how these illiterate and incredibly impoverished people, ignorant of the outside world, could ever comprehend the significance of this great Cause with its world-embracing power, and its many new principles fitted for an age they could scarcely imagine. However, when one visits these villages to meet these radiant souls, the secret of their early attachment to the Faith is uncovered. In these remote places were a few divinely inspired men who, like unto luminous stars, in the last hours of the night, appeared prior to this glorious dawn and prepared their fellow-men by telling them about the impending advent of the Promised One, and by warning them against heedlessness. Each one of these villages has had its own hero and its own unique history.

Such a village of the dawn is Sayessán, an unpretentious, almost forbidding village of stone and mud in the barren mountains, some forty miles south-west of Tabríz, in Persian Á<u>dh</u>irbáyján, not far from Lake Urumíyyih, its inhabitants Persians of Turkish origin. It is this village whose sons were renowned for their bravery and their loyalty. Today it is renowned for identifying itself as a Bahá'í village dedicated to the Cause of God. In the 1830s here, as in other communities throughout Iran and many other parts in the world, there were men who told of the glad tidings of the glorious dawn soon to be. Their message of promise was the preparation, which the villagers brought to their declarations, services and sacrifices, the moment they heard about the advent of the Promised One.

Mullá Asadu'lláh was the sage who trained and readied his fellow Sayessánís by constantly reminding them of the Great Day, the Day of Judgement, that Day when sons would run away from their fathers, and when mothers would choose to abandon their own children. In his exhortations, he emphasized that each one must purge his heart of all else save the love of the Promised One, so that his penetrating effulgence would accept their mirror hearts as its abode.

One day when Mullá Asadu'lláh, followed by a group of his students from Sayessán, was walking through a narrow lane in Tabríz, a well-known mujtahid of that city passed by. He was Mullá Muḥammad-i-Mamaqání, one-eyed, energetic, a vehement controversialist and traditionalist, a man accorded great respect by the people, who always gave way before his passage. But Mullá Asadu'lláh covered his face with his cloak, refusing to look upon the countenance of this man of high priestly estate.

The companions were astounded, for their mentor was a model of humility and temperate good conduct.

Returning to the village, the young disciples, en route, asked Mullá Asadu'lláh to explain this apparently grave breach of etiquette, this seeming almost-insult to the highly placed leader of religion of great prestige in the city and region. To their even greater astonishment, he replied, with deep feelings of sorrow and anger, 'This man will sign the death warrant of the Promised One, and I didn't desire to see his face. Beware! When you hear the news of His advent, and His martyrdom in Tabríz, you must all respond to his call.'

This saintly soul, his seer's vision having prepared his followers, died before the Advent. But those he trained and sensitized, his faithful disciples remained vigilant, listening for reports of a Great One who would be done to death by the order of the same one-eyed mujtahid and some of his colleagues. Thus expectant, they heard in 1850 of the execution in Tabríz Barracks Square of a certain Siyyid 'Alí Muḥammad of Shíráz, One who called Himself the Báb and who asserted that He was the Qá'im. The Sayessánís gathered all the news of this young man, who threatened the authority of the priests and the governors so gravely that these men of power felt He must be killed. And it was true. The Promised One of their prophecies and of Asadu'lláh's vision had come. In a wave of excitement and conviction, 2,700 of the almost 3,000 inhabitants of the Sayessán area became Bábís, embracing the new Faith of God. Isolated from the central pressures of government, they continued to be bold and fearlessly outspoken in their new Faith, and so became the target of frequent persecutions. Many times daring souls among them were taken prisoner to Tabríz, and even to Ṭihrán. But they never wavered in their constancy and fortitude. And when there came the news to Iran of the declaration of Mírzá Ḥusayn-'Alí of Núr, that greatest Bábí known as Bahá'u'lláh, in Baghdád, all rapidly accepted the new Teacher Who was the fulfilment of the Báb's own Book.

The inhabitants of this village have many Tablets from Bahá'u'lláh. In one of them He refers to a parable spoken by Jesus Christ and recorded in the Bible. It is the parable of a very wealthy man who invited the dignitaries and the notables of the town to a sumptuous banquet; but none appeared. When the owner of the house did not find a proper response from the ambitious, greedy and covetous people, he opened the door of his house for the poor who were pure hearted, needy and grateful. Bahá'u'lláh refers to this and emphasizes the fact that the doors of the kingdom of God were flung open for the sovereigns and potentates but they waxed proud, rejected him and remained heedless; therefore, the same doors are wide open for the villagers, the poor and people who have no one to take care of them except their Lord and creator.

Many persons from Sayessán made their pilgrimage to the Holy Land to see Bahá'u'lláh during the years following His exile to 'Akká in Palestine. Some stayed on in the Holy Land to serve their Loved Ones. Among such was the well-known Ismá'íl Áqá, the trusted and faithful gardener of the Master.

In the early days of his sojourn in the Most Great Prison, 'Abdu'l-Bahá once found him in deep anxiety and concern.

He could not bear the thought of any friend being in trouble or in need; therefore, He summoned him and asked him as to what was wrong. A beautiful smile appeared on his strong and charming face and, in Persian mixed with Turkish, he explained to his Beloved that he wanted to send a message to his friend in Sayessán; but he could not write. 'Abdu'l-Bahá smiled and asked him to dictate and He would write the letter. This is indeed a memorable document, a beautiful letter, and an unsurpassed gesture of love and servitude. The signature is the name of the gardener but on the margin there is a line which says that the letter had been written on behalf of Ismá'íl Áqá by 'Abdu'l-Bahá.

Now we know why the whole world became like a dark narrow cage for such a servant when he lost such an Exalted Master. Therefore, when completely overcome with grief, he sought to commit suicide by gashing his throat behind the Shrine of the Báb, near the Holy Place where Bahá'u'lláh had pitched His tent.

Fortunately, he was found very early by Dr Lotfu'lláh Ḥakím and Mr Curtis Kelsey and was taken by them immediately to the hospital where, exhorted by a loving message from the Greatest Holy Leaf, who expressed her hope and longing to see him once more serving in the garden of the Master's House, he accepted treatment and was healed. Thereafter he served with such love, devotion and utter sincerity that when he passed to the Abhá Kingdom, the Guardian ordered this epitaph to be engraved on his resting place: 'The Sign of Steadfastness and Faithfulness.'

During the days when Bahá'u'lláh was under house arrest, imprisoned in the city of 'Akká, the first small group of Bahá'ís from Sayessán set out on foot, circa 1878. After crossing more than 700 miles of desert and mountains, and enduring many hardships, they, at last, attained to the presence of their Beloved One, radiating such love and simple sincerity, and uttering such innocently provincial remarks, that by their zeal and enthusiasm they brought great happiness to the heart of the Blessed Perfection, saddened by the burdens of His incarceration.

They wore their Sayessání clothing, suited of course to the far more rigorous climate of the north-west mountains of Iran. Their large fur hats became the particular target of the street children in 'Akká; these wild and untrained urchins found them so strange and amusing that they followed the pilgrims in the lanes and streets of 'Akká, jeering, taunting, making fun of them ceaselessly. When they told 'Abdu'l-Bahá of this ridicule, He simply advised them to wear the ordinary fezzes of the men of the country. On the very next day, they came into the Master's presence each wearing a newly acquired red fez. He smiled affectionately and with appreciation called them 'the red-hatted soldiers of the Blessed Beauty'.

Soon the believers from Sayessán became familiar with the prevailing bitter conditions of confinement within the fortress of 'Akká. Their hearts brimmed with sorrow for the Holy Ones, for they were surprised that such inadequate food was given to the exiles, with no fresh vegetables. The bad-tasting water, the poor diet, the prevalence of epidemics of every kind, the barren city with scarcely a blade of grass inside its forbidding double walls, all evoked sadness and deep rage. Worst of all, the Blessed Beauty, with His great love of the open space, of the mountains and the gardens of flowers and trees and all the beauty of the natural world, had not been able to walk abroad for about nine long years. Therefore, one day, when in His presence, the pilgrims opened their hearts and entreated Him:

'Come to our village', they proposed. 'Here in 'Akká it is warm and damp, and there are no trees.'

'We cannot', replied the Beloved.

'We promise that the weather will be more agreeable, and we will do everything we can to make you more comfortable.'

'We cannot. We are imprisoned here.'

'Imprisoned!' they replied with tears in their eyes. 'Imprisoned! Who could ever do that to You? You are the King of this world.'

But the Blessed Beauty could not be released from bondage even by these boldest and most resolute of His followers, for God's destiny had ordained His lifetime stay in the Holy Land, that place of fulfilment of prophecies for all mankind.

One day they knew that they must return, full of sorrow that they could not rescue Him, as they desired. But before their departure, Bahá'u'lláh gave them some of the simple food of the prison, calling their particular attention to the potatoes in the meal. 'Plant this in your village', He ordered. 'It is good.' Since they were farmers by occupation, they learned eagerly from the local growers of the potatoes about this strange vegetable. And on their departure they carried back a stock of seed potatoes for planting in their fields.

There in Ádhirbáyján's soil the potatoes flourished, as the Sayessání Bahá'ís adopted the 'new' crop advised by Bahá'u'lláh. As time passed, the potatoes were adopted by the farmers of the area, and became so staple and vital a food, a supplement for the grains upon which they had perennially depended from time immemorial, that several times the whole province was relieved by the potatoes of Sayessán of the threat of famine, which so often afflicted the province.

The sorrow that all had felt in 'Akká, that grim city, continued throughout the long journey homeward across desert and mountains. It continued during their days of recounting to their fellows what they heard and learned and confirmed during those priceless hours of spiritual bounty. So touched were they by the deprivations of the Blessed Beauty that they resolved to do what they could about it.

Among the villagers who had travelled on that pilgrimage were two who bore the name Muḥammad. As there were no family surnames in those days, to distinguish them one from the other, the friends called them Muḥammad, the first, and Muḥammad, the second. Together they suggested to their fellow Bahá'ís that nothing could be more befitting than flowers for such a Beloved. And what flower better than the fragrant narcissus, in Persia a symbol of purity and love, a symbol too of the coming of the spring and the joyful passing of life out from the darkness and cold of winter.

Some months later, after prayerful preparations, the two Muḥammads again set out afoot for faraway 'Akká. But now each carried precious pots of narcissus bulbs on their shoulders, leaving their scant belongings to be carried by two plodding donkeys. Their way was difficult, for the roads were always perilous from brigands and inclement weather, and the authorities and soldiers waiting for them at the several borders they must cross.

With the light of love in their hearts, these two sturdy brave men overcame the hardships of a journey which the comfort-seeking, safety-conscious modern person might view with trepidation or see as unwise. But where there is the light of love in the darkness of the material world, men are willing, nay joyous, in taking daring steps over every obstacle! Wherever they found fresh water, they first gave the water to their flowers and if any remained, it quenched the burning thirst of our two wonderful Muḥammads.

'Abdu'l-Bahá described the arrival of the bearers of the narcissus to the first group of pilgrims who visited Him at the end of World War I, in 1919:

> When the end of their wearisome journey drew nigh, and the city of 'Akká was unfolded to their expectant eyes, and when their gaze fell upon the majestic mansion which marked the limit of their destination, they forgot in a glance all their suffering and scars, attained the gate with sore feet, swollen and blistered, and falling prostrate on the ground, laid at the feet of the Blessed Beauty the token of their undying devotion, which they carried with such zeal and love.
>
> O, what a shower of blessings and of bounty and of favour was poured upon them! Their gift of living beauty was not only accepted, but was considered to be the most precious gem that could ever be presented – the richest and finest gift in the world. To His bestowals and expressions of acceptance and appreciation, these pilgrims muttered and repeated wholeheartedly their sincere wish of *Janem sanah ghorbanela*! Make me the sacrifice; redeem and save my soul![1]

AFTERWORD

So proud were the families of these two valiant Bahá'ís that they adopted the names *The First* and *The Second* as their surnames when this was legally required. Hence these Sayessáni families are now identifiable throughout the Bahá'í world by their last names: Awwal and Tháni.

In the winter of 1935, in company with dearly loved Davood Toeg, then Chairman of the National Spiritual Assembly of Iraq, and with Raḥmat 'Alá'í of Ṭihrán, the author visited Sayessán, thus following in the footsteps of Martha Root and Keith Ransom-Kehler. Hundreds of young boys and girls, knowing of our coming, walked miles to meet us and, with their colourful dress and high spirits, formed two most attractive and picturesque guide groups taking us to their famous village.

The older Bahá'ís were gathered in the Ḥaẓíratu'l-Quds, awaiting us. Muḥammad the First was still living, but very aged, his eyes failing. When Raḥmat 'Alá'í embraced him, Muḥammad held him firm and whispered in his ear: 'Are you the son of Náẓimu'l-Ḥukamá, who was the court physician?'

Startled by the question, Raḥmat answered: 'Yes, I am; but how did you know me whom you have never seen before?'

A very beautiful smile appeared on the old man's face, and he said: 'When some of us were prisoners because of our Faith, your father, as the court physician, used to come to the prison to see the sick prisoners. We Bahá'ís were in a single room. He used to come and embrace every one of us. I can't see you, but when you embraced me, I smelled his perfume.'

There are those who recognize every perfume: the perfume of good men, the fragrance of the narcissus, but particularly the perfume of the spirit of God in the world.

So remarkable these Bahá'ís are in their love for the friends and hospitality towards them that in their intense longing to remember the blissful occasion of their visits, they name children after their guests. There is no wonder if you see a little charming girl passing by and the people call her 'Miss Martharoot' or 'Mrs Kehler Khánum'.

NOTES AND REFERENCES

1 By the kindness of Dr Lotfu'lláh Ḥakím.

Once Upon a Time

Once upon a time there was a king who did everything to make his subjects happy. Lest they would be entangled with many difficulties, he instructed them as to how to conduct even their private lives. They all loved him and obeyed him from the very depths of their hearts and souls. Their loyalty was based on pure love and not at all on fear.

Due to his efforts, his kingdom was to enter a new era and a very great celebration was to be held. But the king had to stay in the capital to prepare means and provisions for those who were so diligently working in all fields. The people wanted him to be there and his presence would add to the glory, majesty and sacredness of all these celebrations. He would give each one his own blessing in all the joyful gatherings.

Then the king sent them a sealed letter in which he told them that they had to carry on their activities towards that glorious consummation of their efforts and endeavours and he would be kind enough to favour them with the presence of his scion, his own blood and line.

In order to keep his people on the safe side and protect them from being deceived by anyone who claimed to be a representative of their beloved king, he said in the same letter that his representative will be either his own first-born son, or one of the same family.

The latter will be accompanied by nine of his chosen ministers who will sign his credentials, and the assembled friends will recognize the king's representative only in this way and in no other way.

The faithful followers increased their activities. They were dispersed far and wide in the country to prepare all the required foundations of a very strong kingdom.

Their joy knew no end and each felt, in the very depths of their souls, the strength given to them by the love of their king. Some gave money, others worked. Architects, teachers, civilians, military, all in all, hand in hand and unitedly, were doing their utmost in the East and West of the king's realm.

Suddenly a silhouette appeared on the horizon who shouted and claimed that he was the representative of the king.

‘Are you his first born son?’ they asked very plainly.

‘No.’

‘Are you from his lineage?’

‘No.’

‘Have you the signature of his nine ministers?’

‘No.’

‘But then how can we go against the explicit wishes and orders of our powerful and beloved king?’

‘I used to dine with the king’, retorted the presumptuous claimer. ‘I had been appointed by him to be the chief of the Council of his attendants. I had letters and medals and many honours from him …’

‘All these are absolutely true. You may have even more honours showered upon you by our beloved king. But none makes you worthy of such a high station as this, which is to be given only to the king’s first born or one of his own lineage.’

Some of the workers, however, who were not familiar with the contents of the king’s letter and who preferred to have their own ways rather than the king’s explicit instructions, threw down their spades and implements and ran to the old man standing on the verge of the valley of ego and perdition.

He continued to shout and command, ‘Stop all these activities. Do not support the ministers. Stop serving the beloved king. Come and accept me as your chief commander.’

The cry stopped for a while and then again came in a more feeble voice: ‘I command you to stop all these activities. Don’t support the plan.’

‘But this is the plan given to us by our beloved king. If we stop this, what other plan can we follow?’

‘What constructive suggestions do you have?’

No answer came to these plain questions. The labourers in the vineyard of God kept on toiling. They never felt fatigue and, as they approached the climax of their wonderful celebrations, they sang songs of joy.

Their cries of happiness, their voices raised in praise and thanksgiving were so loud, so strong and so penetrating that all other voices were unheard.

The inexorable march of time crushed all obstacles. The caravan, which followed the path paved and illumined by the king, reached home safe and sound. They all entered the tabernacle of love, unity and, above all, justice. The toilsome journey came to an end and the travellers 'tired but blissful' were seated on thrones of eternal glory and fame.

Those who stubbornly chose to forsake the path of the Lord were lost in the wilderness of shame and buried in catacombs of eternal remorse and disgrace.

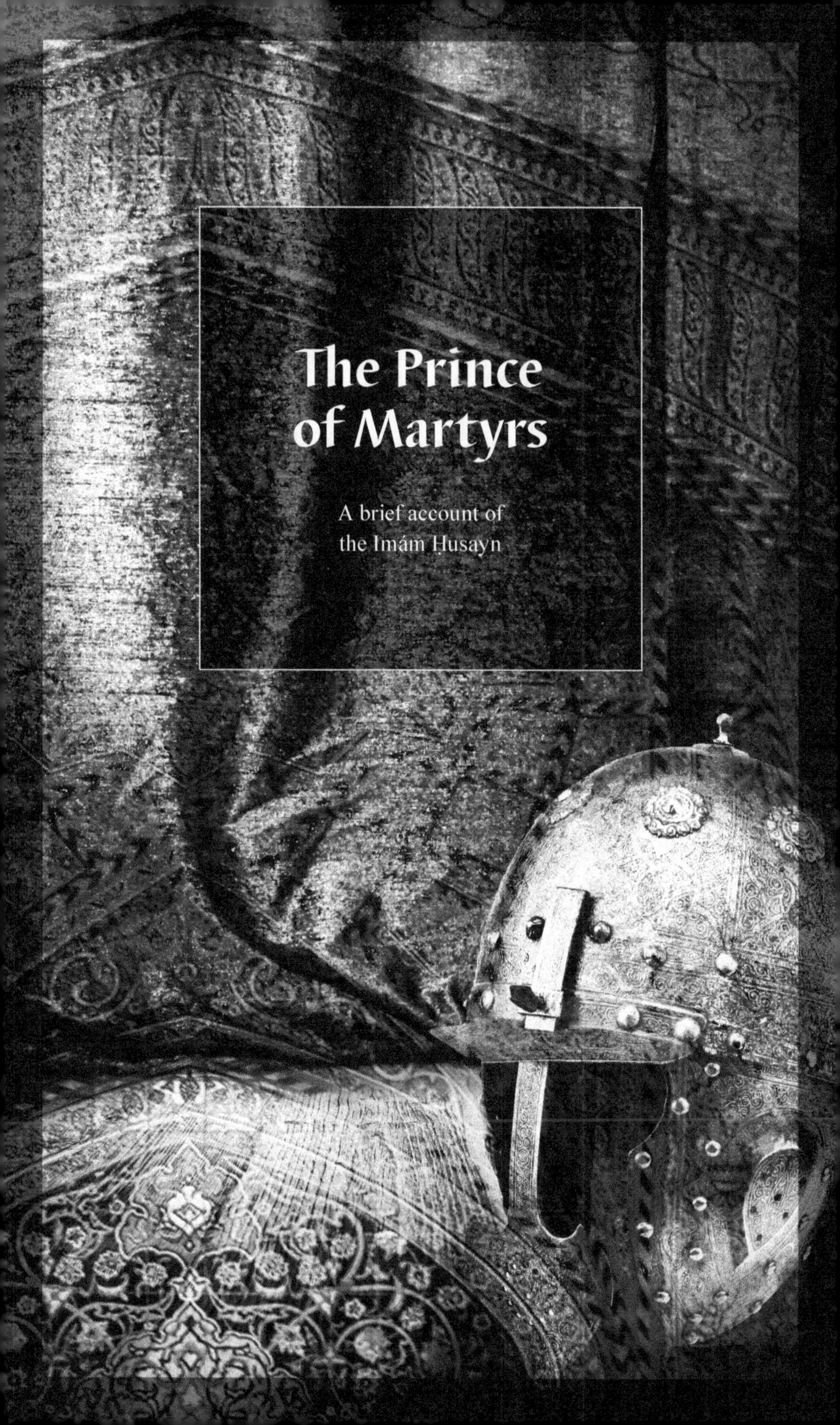

The Prince of Martyrs

A brief account of
the Imám Ḥusayn

Publisher's notes:

Wherever possible, Arabic names in this account have been written using the system of transcription chosen by Shoghi Effendi; however, alternative spellings used in quoted material have been left unchanged (e.g. Abú-Bakr vs. Abubeker).

The statements of 'Abdu'l-Bahá quoted in the final pages of this account are taken from the 1908 edition of *Some Answered Questions* and not the extensively retranslated 2014 edition.

For no warrior could be found on earth more excellent and nearer to God than Ḥusayn, son of 'Alí, so peerless and incomparable was he. 'There was none to equal or to match him in the world.' Yet, thou must have heard what befell him. 'God's malison on the head of the people of tyranny!'...

Furthermore, call to mind the shameful circumstances that have attended the martyrdom of Ḥusayn. Reflect upon his loneliness, how, to outer seeming, none could be found to aid him, none to take up his body and bury it. And yet, behold how numerous, in this day, are those who from the uttermost corners of the earth don the garb of pilgrimage, seeking the site of his martyrdom, that there they may lay their heads upon the threshold of his shrine! Such is the ascendancy and power of God! Such is the glory of His dominion and majesty!

Think not that because these things have come to pass after Ḥusayn's martyrdom, therefore all this glory hath been of no profit unto him. For that holy soul is immortal, liveth the life of God, and abideth within the retreats of celestial glory upon the Sadrih of heavenly reunion. These Essences of being are the shining Exemplars of sacrifice. They have offered, and will continue to offer up their lives, their substance, their souls, their spirit, their all, in the path of the Well-Beloved. By them, no station, however exalted, could be more dearly cherished. For lovers have no desire but the good-pleasure of their Beloved, and have no aim except reunion with Him.

Should We wish to impart unto thee a glimmer of the mysteries of Ḥusayn's martyrdom, and reveal unto thee the fruits thereof, these pages could never suffice, nor exhaust their meaning. Our hope is that, God willing, the breeze of mercy may blow, and the divine Springtime clothe the tree of being with the robe of a new life; so that we may discover the mysteries of divine Wisdom, and, through His providence, be made independent of the knowledge of all things. We have, as yet, descried none but a handful of souls, destitute of all renown, who have attained unto this station. Let the future disclose what the Judgment of God will ordain, and the Tabernacle of His decree reveal. In such wise We recount unto thee the wonders of the Cause of God, and pour out into thine ears the strains of heavenly melody, that haply thou mayest attain unto the station of true knowledge, and partake of the fruit thereof.

Therefore, know thou of a certainty that these Luminaries of heavenly majesty, though their dwelling be in the dust, yet their true habitation is the seat of glory in the realms above. Though bereft of all earthly possessions, yet they soar in the realms of immeasurable riches. And whilst sore tried in the grip of the enemy, they are seated on the right hand of power and celestial dominion. Amidst the darkness of their abasement there shineth upon them the light of unfading glory, and upon their helplessness are showered the tokens of an invincible sovereignty.

– Bahá'u'lláh, from the Kitáb-i-Íqán, pp. 126, 128–130

To write about a man whose martyrdom fortified the foundations of the Islamic Faith, whose blood cleansed the religion of his Grandfather of the detrimental traces of the spirit of the Age of Ignorance,[1] the mere mention of whose name creates waves of poignant sorrow in the hearts of his followers, whose personality towers above even the best of the Imáms, and whose station is so exalted that the hopes and aspirations of the true believers are centred on his 'return', is a difficult undertaking. It is particularly difficult, since so little is known in the West of this incomparable figure, and that little vitiated by prejudicial accounts devoid of true judgement.

Like the waves of a stormy sea, the turbulent events of history constantly surge and swirl, and we are astounded to witness that, amidst the manifold historical episodes associated with the early days of Islám, the most ardent believers, avowed supporters and staunch defenders of the new Faith of Muḥammad were put to the test, fell and vanished in that tempestuous ocean. 'In a distant age and climate, the tragic scene of the death of Hosein will awaken the sympathy of the coldest reader'[2] and indeed, even in that bitter first century of Islám, his death evoked the greatest feeling of sorrow. The martyrdom of Ḥusayn did not occur as a sudden and spontaneous combustion. Nor should we consider it as a simple act of the murder of an individual. It took place as the consequence of deep-rooted animosities and prolonged struggles between the powers of darkness and the army of light.

One must study this tragedy with much devotion and patience. To obtain just a fragmentary outline of the decisive events which so altered the development of Islám, one must look back to the Age of Ignorance, gather the ends of as many threads as possible, and trace their course through the history of Arabia and Islám before and after the Prophet Muḥammad, thus detecting various causes of many of the events recorded. One must also stand at an adequate distance to see how deeply rooted human weaknesses are manifested, how swords are substituted for words, how conquests lead to decline and everlasting fall, and how the sacred blood of devoted adherents is shed to open the way to the ultimate victory of the Word of God.

Though this deathless chapter of world history, which revolves around the central figure of Imám Ḥusayn, is unlimited in scope and fathomless in depth, it is, nevertheless, worthwhile to attempt a study of one who merits both our reverence and love. Bahá'u'lláh, the Báb, and 'Abdu'l-Bahá[3] all made numerous references to the acts of devotion and sacrifice of Imám Ḥusayn, and we find a special visitation prayer revealed for him by Bahá'u'lláh.

This essay is not intended to be exhaustive in scope. It is only a humble attempt to facilitate the study of the Imám's life and achievements. In these events will be found great feats of spiritual ardour and acts of self-sacrifice, the contemplation of which cannot but consolidate one's own faith.

The following outline of persons and happenings will, it is hoped, aid the reader to identify the individuals who played prominent parts in this tragedy and to follow the events in their proper order.

PERSONS AND EVENTS

1. The two outstanding clans of the Quraysh tribe in Mecca

a) The clan of Háshim
b) The clan of Umayyah

2. The first four Caliphs (632–61 AD)

a) Abú-Bakr
b) 'Umar
c) 'Uthmán
d) 'Alí

3. Mu'áwíyah, Governor of Syria, in Damascus, and the first Umayyad ruler (661–80 AD)

a) He stood against 'Alí.
b) After the assassination of 'Alí, he caused 'Alí's son, Ḥasan, to withdraw and retire, and himself became head of the Islamic community.
c) He tried to obtain an oath of allegiance for his son Yazíd to succeed him, instead of Ḥasan's younger brother Ḥusayn, to whom he had promised the succession.

4. Ḥusayn, the third Imám (after 'Alí and Ḥasan)

a) On the death of Mu'áwíyah, he refused to acknowledge Yazíd's succession.
b) He was promised support by the people of Kúfah in Mesopotamia (Iraq).
c) With a small band of about seventy followers and his family, he set out from Mecca in Ḥijáz for Kúfah.
d) Ibn Zíyád was the newly-appointed Governor of Kúfah.
e) Ḥusayn's way was blocked by Ḥurr, a cavalry commander who, at Karbilá, joined Ḥusayn's small company.
f) 'Umar Ibn Sa'd commanded the army of four thousand sent against Ḥusayn.
g) On the plain of Karbilá, Ḥusayn pitched his tents.

5. Ḥusayn's martyrdom, the 10th day of Muḥarram, 61 AH (October, 680 AD)

a) In the ensuing battle, Ḥusayn lost all the male members of his family and companions except his invalid son 'Alí, known as Zaynu'l-'Ábidín.
b) Shimr was the shameless enemy who decapitated the Imám.
c) Ḥusayn's body was trampled by horses.
d) His son 'Alí, and the women and children, were taken captive and conducted, with the heads of their martyrs carried aloft on spears, to Kúfah from whence they were sent to Damascus.
e) Yazíd sent the family from Damascus to Medina with the heads of their martyrs, which they buried in Karbilá forty days after the battle.
f) This tragic event marked the final separation of the spiritual and administrative centres of the Islamic Faith.

The Ka'bah was the first house of worship ever erected in Arabia. It was built by Abraham, aided by his son Ishmael.[4] When they had finished the construction of this cube-like building, they prayed that God would accept their act of service. In the course of centuries, the House became a centre where many idols were placed and preserved by the tribes, each of which had several gods or goddesses to worship. To make the pilgrimage to Mecca was indeed for the sole purpose of worshipping the idols. This pilgrimage had many different stages to be performed over a number of days, and each stage was characterized by rituals, customs and habits which reflected the barbarous life of the Age of Ignorance prevalent in much of the Arabian peninsula.

There were several clans of the Quraysh who were responsible for the care of the pilgrims. The most prominent of their responsibilities were two: 1) The custodianship of the Ka'bah and the keeping of its key; and 2) The administration of Mecca and the provision of water for the pilgrims. Both responsibilities had been vested, in the latter half of the fifth century, in Qusayy, but on his death authority was divided, the second responsibility going to his grandson, 'Abd-Shams, the progenitor of the Umayyads, then passing to his brother Háshim, founder of the Háshimites. This transfer of authority, which engendered ill feelings of rivalry and jealousy between the two clans, became the starting-point of accusations, calumnies, petty strifes and skirmishes which were to stain the pages of Muslim history.

Háshim (d. 510 AD) had been wealthy, generous and of good breeding, as were most of his descendants. But Abú-Sufyán, a merchant in olives and wool, and head of the Umayyads at the time of Muḥammad, was notorious for his infamous character. The popularity of Háshim's descendants could not be endured by Abú-Sufyán. As the years went by, strong feelings of jealous rivalry mounted in his heart. Once such loathsome seeds are sown, they begin to grow and gradually become a deep-rooted tree, the bitter fruits of which are consumed by the members of the tribe. Not only did the elders of Abú-Sufyán's family carry grudges against the Háshimites, but their children also began to hate them. At first, such differences remained within the small circle of Meccan life, but before long their frustrations and ill feelings gushed forth like a flood, inundating all aspects of Muslim life in Arabia and the neighbouring countries.

Now it happened that Muḥammad was singled out by God to act as His Messenger to mankind, and He was of the Háshimites. As His mission began to win adherents, the other clans of the Quraysh, fearing the ultimate victory of the Prophet, rose to persecute Him, His family, His followers and His nascent Faith. The members of Abú-Sufyán's family, under the direction, instigation and evil plotting of their chief, stood impervious to the truth and remained firm against the progress of Islám. So unbearable became the conditions for Muḥammad and His followers that some were forced to leave their country for Ethiopia, and, soon thereafter, the Muslims had to retire to a solitary valley outside Mecca, while the Meccans were commanded by their leaders to abstain from all trade with them. This state of affairs lasted for three years.

Eventually the Prophet decided to change His place of residence from Mecca to Medina, where He was welcomed by a band of followers. With the zeal and enthusiasm of new recruits, the believers won many to His side and soon the Prophet had an army of adherents under His command.

At length, He decided to cleanse the House of God in Mecca, to awaken the Meccans to recognize the dawn of a new day, and to help them understand the truth of Islám and the influence it would have in the world, especially in Arabia which was still under the sway of the abhorred Age of Ignorance.

As the Prophet and His followers approached Mecca in an alarming march of triumph, the very first to embrace Islám was Abú-Sufyán; he was soon followed by the members of his family and a majority of the tribe of Quraysh.

Thus the germ of dissension, which had actively opposed the progress of the Faith of Islám, now entered the body of the Cause of God. It remained hidden but ever ready to emerge, like a virulent disease, to sap the spiritual vitality and strength of the religion of God – that tender young tree – drain enthusiasm and weaken religious affiliation, affect many of the pillars of Islám, put to the test groups of courageous adherents, causing them to fail and, above all, to divide the all-commanding and united power of the newly-established Faith of God. Its evil spell, once cast upon the divine institutions, brought many incorrigible individuals to absolute and ruthless power. Hypocrites found a ready arena for their wicked and arrogant schemes. Military conquests were substituted for spiritual conquests. The exhortations of Islám gave way to the spirit and rules of life prevalent in the Age of Ignorance. And the religion of God became as a dead body deprived even of burial.[5] There was need of a supreme sacrifice to create those mysterious energies which draw people near to their Creator and closer to His religion and His plan for mankind.

Ḥusayn, the grandson of the Prophet, was destined to give the blood of his family and himself for such a spiritual regeneration.

At the death of the Prophet, that poisonous germ began to manifest its evil effects, and its contamination weakened the faith of even the most renowned champions of Islám. It is related that the Prophet, returning home from His last pilgrimage, had gathered His followers together and orally but emphatically designated 'Alí as their master. His mission, He had told them in Mecca, was completed. When He became ill and was bed-ridden, His closest and most stalwart supporters were in his room. He asked for paper and pen to dictate that which would keep them united. 'The man is in delirium,' said one of them; 'sufficient to us is the Book of God.' These words were to cause a disastrous schism in the religion of God that remained irreparable and continually widened as the years went on.

The moment the Prophet laid His head to rest, 'Alí – His cousin and the husband of His illustrious daughter Fáṭimah, who was the second to believe in Him and was the embodiment of nobility, audacity and justice – was left alone to arrange the burial of the Prophet, while those who had heard the penetrating voice of the Prophet, on the day He announced 'Alí as their master, gathered in another place to initiate their own plan, not according to His words, but in accord with the rules of the tribes. Thus the positive forces were robbed of their powers and prerogatives, while the negative ones ruled throughout the decades and centuries.[6] Heedless of this event, which is recorded by almost all the chroniclers of the birth of Islám, many outstanding historians, even those who are Muslims, have disregarded this critical point, creating so many doubts with their own interpretations that the mirror of historical fact has become obscured and darkened.

The tumultuous and heated discussion which ensued, in the effort to choose a successor to their Prophet, 'was appeased by the disinterested resolution of Omar, who, suddenly renouncing his own pretensions, stretched forth his hand, and declared himself the first subject of the mild and venerable Abubeker'. This act was described by Gibbon as an 'illegal and precipitate measure'.[7]

Abú-Bakr, after a rule of two years, designated 'Umar as his successor. 'Umar conquered and ruled for ten years and, before his death, nominated six men from whom one should be chosen to succeed him. 'Uthmán was named by that council.

When 'Uthmán took the reins of affairs in his feeble hands, he appointed the members of his family to be governors of states and judges of provinces. He was a descendant of Umayyah like Abú-Sufyán, and thus the most important office of the Islamic world came under the sway of the Umayyads. 'Uthmán, because of his practice of nepotism, was disliked by the people, and his 'feeble temper and declining age … were incapable of sustaining the weight of conquest and of empire' as described by Gibbon.

From many parts of the Islamic world, delegations were sent to 'Uthmán, to plead with him to exercise justice. Failing to do so, he was assassinated in his own house. 'A tumultuous anarchy of five days was appeased by the inauguration of Ali: his refusal would have provoked a general massacre', although 'Alí 'declared that he would rather serve than reign'. Twenty-four years after the death of the Prophet, the Islamic world acclaimed Imám 'Alí as its leader, and he 'was invested, by the popular choice, with the regal and sacerdotal office'. 'The birth, the alliance, the character of Ali, which exalted him above the rest of his countrymen, might justify his claim to the vacant throne of Arabia', Gibbon has observed. 'The son of Abu Taleb was, in his own right, the chief of the family of Hashem, and the hereditary prince or guardian of the city and temple of Mecca. The light of prophecy was extinct; but the husband of Fatima might expect the inheritance and blessing of her father' who spoke of him as 'vicegerent' and even referred to him as the 'Aaron of a second Moses'.[8]

His two sons, Ḥasan and Ḥusayn, had been very often on the lap of the Prophet receiving special love, and were called 'the chief of the youth of paradise'. He 'united the qualifications of a poet, a soldier, and a saint, his wisdom still breathes in a collection of moral and religious sayings[9] and every antagonist, in the combats of the tongue or of the sword, was subdued by his eloquence and valour'.

In the words of Professor Hitti:

> Valiant in battle, wise in counsel, eloquent in speech, true to his friends, magnanimous to his foes, he became both the paragon of Moslem nobility and chivalry ... and the Solomon of Arabic tradition, around whose name poems, proverbs, sermonettes and anecdotes innumerable have clustered. ... His sabre Dhul Fiqar (the cleaver of vertebrae), ... has been immortalized in the words of the verse found engraved on many medieval Arab swords ... 'No sword can match Dhul Fiqar, and no young warrior can compare with Ali.'[10]

The people knew him as a true believer in Islám, one who would keep to its spirit and never deviate even a hair's breadth from the right path of God. His way of life was simple; he despised the vanities of the world. He showed no favouritism. Even his own brother abandoned him when he received no extra share from the revenues, for 'Alí spared no effort to protect the treasury of the Faith from plunder by covetous individuals.

With the vigour of an undaunted hero and ruler, and the unsurpassed determination of a spiritual leader, he began to purify the administrative institutions of Islám and to dismiss those who were unworthy of position. He wrote beautiful letters to the governors, breathing into them the true spirit of the Faith, and reminding them of the Prophet's lofty standard of justice and tolerance towards the followers of all religions. By such firm steps in the purification of all the channels of affairs, 'Alí conquered the hearts of the people of Mecca; and when they were agitated by the activities of his opponents, he recited the verses of God with so much strength and calmness, and in such a spirit of self-sacrifice, that they came to know his magnanimity in war. On many hazardous occasions, he manifested such determination and truthfulness that the cunning plots of his adversaries were averted and frustrated.

But the Quraysh, in the words of Gibbon, 'could never be reconciled to the proud pre-eminence of the line of Hashem: and the ancient discord of the tribes was rekindled'. Indeed, in all the phases of the history of Islám, we observe the traces of discord and animosity, which started in the Age of Ignorance, penetrating into the very core of the Muslim institutions and dividing the loyalty of the rank and file of its adherents. Like the deadening winds of autumn, disunity swept through all domains and caused the weakening, failure and fall of many of the followers of Islám. 'The mischiefs that flow from the contests of ambition are usually confined to the times and countries in which they have been agitated. But the religious discord of the friends and enemies of 'Alí has been renewed in every age' of Islamic history.[11] Periodical clashes of an intense nature between the army of light and the powers of darkness were one by one unfolded and in all of them we find 'Alí and his illustrious descendants victims in the merciless clutches of the Umayyads.

The Muslim world was shocked when it heard the two influential leaders, aided and accompanied by 'Á'ishah, the wife of the Prophet, had waged war against 'Alí. Upon their defeat, and the death of the two leaders, 'Alí proved most magnanimous. He mourned the deaths of his brave adversaries and the 'venerable captive ... was speedily dismissed to her proper station, at the tomb of Mahomet, with the respect and tenderness that was still due to the widow of the apostle'.

But the most formidable of 'Alí's opponents was in Damascus. Mu'áwíyah, son of Abú-Sufyán, had been appointed by his relative 'Uthmán as governor of Syria. With an insatiable thirst for still higher rank and position, an intense desire to exterminate the last traces of the Háshimites, and motivated by an unmitigated hatred of 'Alí, Mu'áwíyah stood resolutely against the man to whom the Muslim world had promised fidelity and obedience. Mu'áwíyah's intention was to establish himself as Caliph of Islám and to secure for his descendants the throne of a dynasty. He moved against 'Alí, who, by his heroic deeds, had almost won the day, when suddenly he was 'compelled to yield to a disgraceful truce and an insidious compromise'.[12]

After the assassination of 'Alí, in the mosque of Kúfah, Mu'áwíyah had a supreme opportunity to widen the range of his perfidious activities throughout the Muslim domains. He retained the name of Islám as an outer garment, while ceaselessly pouring out his venom of rivalry and jealousy against the Háshimites. Emboldened by the gap created by 'Alí's murder, he revealed his own schemes by vilifying 'Alí in the mosques, minarets and markets. Preachers who would invent traditions against 'Alí were promoted and received gifts of immense value. Those who expressed love and loyalty toward 'Alí and his family were put to death in cruel and insidious ways. Honey mixed with poison was often used. Mu'áwíyah would always say that the army of God is in honey.

Ḥasan, the eldest son of 'Alí, was acclaimed as his successor, but soon he was forced by Mu'áwíyah to withdraw and retire. He was at last poisoned by a slave girl named Ja'dih who poured diamond powder into the Imám's jar of water. She committed this unforgivable sin because of Mu'áwíyah's promise to give her gold coins and arrange her marriage to his son Yazíd, promises which were never fulfilled.

Thus the son of Abú-Sufyán, who had put forth all his efforts to stop the forward progress of the religion of God, was now settled on his throne by ruse and cunning. His nefarious activities were underscored by a now famous motto attributed to him. '"I apply not my sword", he is reported to have declared, "where my lash suffices, nor my lash where my tongue is enough. And even if there be one hair binding me to my fellow men, I do not let it break: when they pull I loosen, and if they loosen I pull."'[13] By giving the people gold, lands and promises of high position, he drew to his court in Damascus persons who were as pillars of Islám; they were put to tests which many failed. He tried by all means to attract men to his court, and threatened those who showed reluctance to approach. He confiscated properties, gouged out the eyes of those who refused to co-operate, hanged them, buried them alive. Such nefarious acts have led certain historians, lacking in judgement and insight, to acclaim Mu'áwíyah as the truest and shrewdest politician of the Arabian peninsula.

We come now to the sad story of that matchless soul, the third Imám, Ḥusayn. As long as his elder brother Ḥasan was alive, Ḥusayn obeyed him as a true believer. But when Ḥasan died, it was Ḥusayn's right and privilege to protect his succession to the caliphate, and his function as the third Imám. It was one of his sayings that should the Faith of his Grandfather require blood to fortify its spiritual foundations, he was ever ready to offer his own.

Mu'áwíyah knew very well that his own son Yazíd would not easily be accepted by the people of Ḥijáz and Iraq as their caliph. Therefore, during his own lifetime, he tried to arrange affairs in such a way as to facilitate Yazíd's succession to the throne of the caliphate. His concern was not that there should be a true successor of the Prophet, one who could be the supreme spiritual example to his people. Rather, his sole aim was to establish a powerful dynasty of his own family, whose domains would rival in scope and wealth the Persian and Roman Empires. But his instruction to the governor of Medina, to obtain pledges of allegiance to Yazíd from Ḥusayn and several other notables, did not succeed before his death.

Yazíd then attempted to obtain submission to his rule, particularly from Ḥusayn and one other notable, and dispatched to Walíd, the governor of Medina, strict orders to this effect. Walíd had no alternative but to summon them, but only Ḥusayn went to the governor's house. There was a man in Walíd's entourage named Marwán. He was an insidious and wicked plotter, who, though a professed Muslim, spied for the infidels.

According to the writer of *Muḥriqu'l-Qúlúb*,[14] he was a dangerous element in the province of Ḥijáz, inspiring evil deeds by his whisperings, promptings and suggestions. As Ḥusayn entered the governor's room, Marwán was sitting there, quiet and malignant as a dead mouse. Ḥusayn asked Walíd about the purpose of his invitation. When the governor disclosed to him the orders he had received from Damascus, Ḥusayn frankly and boldly exclaimed that such oaths should be taken in the mosque and in the presence of the Muslim community, never in private. Having said this, he turned to leave. Marwán whispered to Walíd to capture the Imám immediately, but Walíd ignored this prompting, for he harboured in his heart a certain respect for the family of the Apostle of God.

The idea of obtaining an oath of allegiance from Ḥusayn was pursued by Yazíd with unflagging industry and obstinate ignorance. Such an oath of loyalty by Ḥusayn would have wrapped the dead body of the Faith of God in shrouds of oblivion, and rung a death-knell for the hopes and aspirations of the true believers. But the forces of light remain forever victorious and never reconcilable with the powers of darkness.

Ḥusayn had left the governor's house in Medina for his own, but his mind grappled with deeply disturbing thoughts and poignant sorrows, for he realized that the fate of the religion of Islám was hanging in the balance. To save the covenant of God from irretrievable loss, he decided to go from Medina to Mecca.

It was strange indeed that a perverted and corrupt man such as Yazíd should presume to claim the mantle of the Prophet when his shoulders were already heavily burdened with sins. Harder still is it to think of a drunkard occupying the position of the Prophet, leading the believers at times of prayer and inviting them to the path of spiritual accomplishment. So addicted was he to alcoholic beverages that he could not abstain from drinking, even in the few days of his pilgrimage to Mecca.

Yazíd was absorbed in the frivolities and luxuries of life and was very keen on hunting. He remained oblivious to the fact that his domains were seething with discontent and on the brink of revolt. Imitating the heinous deeds of his father, he also employed many devilish means to achieve his aims. He used poison and fire and bribes, gifts, gold, positions and properties to corrupt the faithful, sheathe the swords of the brave, and silence those with eloquent tongues. He appointed the ignorant as teachers, the ill-famed as missionaries, and the cowards as commanders. A chilling and striking contrast to Ḥusayn! 'The only quality that he lacked', says Sédillot, 'was the spirit of intrigue which characterized the descendants of Ommeya.'[15]

Ḥusayn was aware of the deep-rooted hatred festering in the hearts of the Umayyads. He noticed that they multiplied their chains of control and strengthened them by drawing to their side prominent people in the Islamic world. To enlarge their dominions and to hold them more strictly under their own surveillance, they offered highly-coveted prizes. Even some of the Háshimites joined their ranks, for the temptations were greater than they could resist.

Perplexing news, manifold and magnified, was reaching the court of Yazíd. He sent a special envoy to Mecca to control the pilgrimage. But the pilgrims were attracted to Ḥusayn. As the grandson of their Prophet and in his own right a man of irresistible charm and regal dignity, they acclaimed him with love and reverence beyond the measure of expectation. Yazíd received this news, and the volcano of hatred and jealousy which smouldered within his heart erupted in a stream of awesome calamities directed at Ḥusayn. The sole aim of the tyrant of Syria was to obtain a pledge of obedience from this unique man who was so highly revered by the Muslim world.

When the news reached Iraq, the Muslims, especially those in the city of Kúfah, who in the words of Ameer Ali were 'Eager, fierce, and impetuous, [but] … utterly wanting in perseverance and steadiness',[16] decided to invite Ḥusayn to their own country and to acclaim him as the third Imám, to whom all would remain loyal and obedient. They wrote literally thousands of letters and dispatched them to Mecca, promising their absolute loyalty. In the midst of their excitement, there was one man who addressed the people of Kúfah, begging them to think well before swearing such oaths of fidelity, and not to stake the precious life of Ḥusayn on the venture. But the streams of signed and sealed letters bearing their promises continued to flow to Mecca.

Ḥusayn decided to accept their invitations. Many close friends and even his younger brother advised him not to rely on the inhabitants of Iraq and their pledges. They proposed that, if he intended to go away, he should choose Yemen where the followers of the Prophet were steadfast and truthful. Some of the tribesmen of the desert also warned him against the people of Kúfah, saying, 'Their hearts may be with you, but their spears and swords will be against you.' A Shaykh asked Ḥusayn where he would go. On hearing his reply, 'To Kúfah', in great agony the Shaykh exclaimed, 'They will receive you on the points of their lances and the edges of their swords.' But Ḥusayn was undaunted by danger, choosing to tread the path most acceptable to his Lord and Creator.

The night before his departure, Ḥusayn was in profound meditation, his mind filled with a host of recollections. He knew that he would never look again on the scenes associated with his Grandfather, the Apostle of God; with 'Alí, the ever-conquering lion of God; and with Fáṭimah, his mother, who had been singled out by Alláh as peerless among women in the Islamic Dispensation.

In the ominous calmness of that night, countless memories overwhelmed his sanctified heart. In the all-enveloping darkness, he balanced the behests of his heart and the formidable commands of destiny. Should he choose to stay in Ḥijáz, it would mean taking an oath of obedience to the throne of the despot of Damascus. Such an action would carry Islám to utter destruction. He knew that he could never leave the straight path of his destiny, though it be flooded with adversities and surrounded by calamities. In the words of Gibbon, 'The primogeniture of the line of Hashem, and the holy character of the grandson of the apostle, had centred in his person, and he was at liberty to prosecute his claim against Yazíd, the tyrant of Damascus, whose vices he despised, and whose title he had never deigned to acknowledge.'[17]

Yazíd, aware of the imminent dangers smouldering in Iraq, could visualize the ruin of himself and his dynasty. He began to prepare his soldiers and commanders to commit the most nefarious deeds in his favour. Next he approached Ibn Zíyád, and sent him to replace the unhappy governor of Kúfah. Ibn Zíyád 'was at first styled ibn-Abih [the son of his father] because of the doubt which clouded the identity of his father. His mother was a slave and prostitute in al-Ta'if whom Abu-Sufyan, Mu'awiyah's father, had known. Ziyad was pro Ali.[18] In a critical moment Mu'awiyah acknowledged Ziyad as his legitimate brother.'[19] Upon receiving Yazíd's commission, Ibn Zíyád seized his new responsibility with vigour, malice and inflexible cruelty. He entered the city of Kúfah with his face covered and wearing a black turban resembling that of the family of 'Alí. At first the inhabitants of Kúfah took him for Imám Ḥusayn whose arrival they all expected. But when, in the house of the governor, Ibn Zíyád uncovered his face, they realized they were in the presence of the newly appointed governor of the eastern provinces of the Islamic Empire.

On the morrow of his arrival, Ibn Zíyád ascended the pulpit and in a sudden burst of anger uttered such brazen and terrifying words as to fill the hearts of the populace with horror and numbing fear. Brandishing his whip in one hand and his sword in the other, the new governor threatened to whip to death any who might dare to utter even as much as one word against the prevailing order; and to decapitate those who should venture the slightest gesture of disobedience. He then summoned the notables, the learned and the influential citizens of the town and promised them high positions and costly gifts. Within two days, the inhabitants of Iraq were utterly overtaken by terror on the one hand and by greed on the other. They wavered, and abandoned their expected guest to the hands of his oppressors. Their hearts were changed, and discord and dissension became manifest in words and uncouth forms. Those who had invited Ḥusayn and assured him of their loyalty faltered and fled.

All these events took place while Ḥusayn was on his way to Iraq. Before reaching its hostile and inhospitable confines, he sent his faithful and audacious cousin, Muslim, to examine the situation. Soon Ibn Zíyád came to know of the arrival in Kúfah of the Imám's envoy. His orders were strict and urgent. A slave woman had given shelter and food to Muslim, but how could anyone escape Ibn Zíyád's miserable schemes? Muslim was soon captured and dragged to the governor, who found in his arrest an opportunity to strengthen his rule and to establish in Kúfah his reign of terror. At his behest Muslim was taken to the roof of a house, beheaded, and his corpse thrown down to be crushed on the pavement. The action served its purpose. Thereafter, none dared even to think of love for Ḥusayn, nor was Muslim able to alert the Imám to the ambivalent attitude and infidelity of the people of Kúfah, who had been totally won over to Yazíd by his appointed governor in Iraq.

This done, Ibn Zíyád dispatched soldiers to obstruct the roads to Iraq, Syria and Persia, which Ḥusayn might take. He even installed special guards at wells so that Ḥusayn and his companions would suffer from thirst, aggravated by the blazing sun in the endless desert of Arabia.

He then singled out one of the finest and most energetic of his young cavalry officers, by the name of Ḥurr, and placed him at the head of a thousand skilful soldiers to guard and prevent Ḥusayn from approaching any town or village in Iraq, especially the area surrounding Kúfah. Knowing the perils of afflictive thirst, and aware of the scarcity of water in the desert, Ḥusayn had instructed his friends to store and carry as much water as they could. Ḥurr met the Imám on his way to Iraq, stopped him and explained why he and his soldiers were there. Ḥusayn, in turn, told Ḥurr of the invitations he had received from the people of Kúfah, and even showed him the bag containing more than ten thousand signed letters promising support and allegiance. Ḥurr exclaimed that he knew nothing about such communications and that his mission was to prevent Ḥusayn from advancing into Iraq. This marked the beginning of all the calamities which were to be heaped upon the grandson of the Prophet.

Ḥusayn had no desire to wage war. In his dismay and anxiety, he was overwhelmed by a sense of impending storm. He asked the young officer that he and his followers be allowed to settle anywhere in Arabia. Ḥurr, who had not the slightest desire to be stigmatized as the one to cause difficulties and suffering for the grandson of the Prophet, sent a message to Ibn Zíyád, informing him of the small band of companions of Ḥusayn and of their expressed desire to settle in Arabia.

By this time, Ḥurr's own soldiers and horses were threatened by thirst. When the Imám came to know of this, he immediately provided them with water, generously giving them all that his companions had stored. This magnanimous gesture affected Ḥurr. When the time of prayer came, the commander and his soldiers stood in rows and followed the Imám in prayer.

Ḥusayn and his companions mounted their steeds and rode on, but Ḥurr maintained his watch and controlled their movements, never allowing them to take any road which would lead to the villages or towns of Iraq. Ḥusayn proceeded on until he reached the plain of Karbilá where he pitched his tents and settled. It was the second of Muḥarram[20] in the year 61 after Hijrah.

When Ibn Zíyád received Ḥurr's dispatch and realized that he had shown clemency towards and prayed with Ḥusayn, his rage knew no bounds. He immediately summoned 'Umar Ibn Sa'd and ordered him to prepare and equip an army of at least four thousand soldiers to encounter Ḥusayn and force him to sign a pledge of submission and obedience to Yazíd. He knew very well that for the early Muslims of Arabia, the promised paradise was the country of Persia.

They would undergo endless hardships to reach there and settle in that verdant region, which offered in abundance rivers, orchards, and a mild and desirable climate. Therefore, Ibn Zíyád, after appointing Ibn Sa'd as chief commander of the army, promised him that, in the event of success, he would go to Persia as governor of Ray, the vast and prosperous province where the capital city of Tehran stands today. Those who had sent letters of invitation to Ḥusayn and sworn fidelity to him became the allies of his enemies, rushing to arms in the hope of following their commander to the verdant lands of Persia.

Before the arrival of the newly-recruited and well-armed forces, Ḥusayn arose as a spiritual hero to face the inevitable. He gathered his followers, almost seventy in number,[21] and frankly disclosed to them the hardships and sufferings with which they would be afflicted. He pleaded with them to leave the plain of Karbilá for the peace and security of their own homes, and assured them they would never be considered infidels should they follow this counsel. Though filled with zest for life and sharing the common human aspirations for happiness and tranquillity, none of them abandoned the Imám, but remained firm and steadfast. They even expressed their joy at being able to share in the austerity and hardships of his existence, for they longed to remain in his presence and under his loving leadership. To contribute to the Imám's pleasure and contentment was their highest goal.

The great army under Ibn Sa'd was startled on meeting Ḥusayn's small band. The Imám approached the commander-in-chief and discussed the situation with him. He insisted that he had not the slightest desire to shed the blood of anyone, and proposed that he should be left free to settle in peace in Arabia, be stationed on the borders of Turkey, or go to Damascus to meet Yazíd himself.

Ibn Sa'd, aspiring to become the ruler of Ray, emphatically replied that having entrapped him, they would never allow him out of their sight; his only solution would be to sign a pledge of explicit obedience to Yazíd. Well aware of Ḥusayn's irresistible charm and unyielding spirit, Ibn Zíyád sent, at this time, a contemptible beast in the person of Shimr, to ensure that Ibn Sa'd would not show respect and clemency towards the Imám.

Ḥusayn, in whatever condition he might find himself, would ceaselessly utter words of praise and adoration. Whether in happiness and prosperity, or in the midst of misfortune and adversity, he would offer thanksgiving to his Lord, and he often expressed particular gratitude for being a descendant of the Apostle of God, and enriched by the bounty of the Qur'án. He also thanked his Creator for the members of his family and his friends who, though few in number, demonstrated the most exalted spirit of faith, devotion and steadfastness.

Facing his companions, he prayed for them and supplicated God to grant them His rewards and number them among His near ones. As the eve of the tenth of Muḥarram approached, he addressed his followers and once more stressed that the army of Ibn Sa'd desired no one except himself. They were free to avail themselves of the darkness of the night to go in safety to their own homes and people. He even assured them that, should they choose to withdraw, they would never be counted among those who had broken the covenant of God.

'But this would leave us alive after you', was the unanimous reply of his devoted friends. 'How could we ever pardon ourselves! To leave our beloved in the hands of ferocious beasts and save our own lives is abhorrent to us.' And they all refused to abandon Ḥusayn alone in the midst of his foes.

Throughout that night, Ḥusayn could see the flickering shadows behind the screen of arms and he knew that the eventful day would soon dawn. He decided to exhort his adversaries again in the hope of a peaceful settlement. It was the path, he believed, which the Prophet Himself would have taken. Once more he advanced towards the encampment of Ibn Sa'd and addressed him and his soldiers. His words, jewels of celestial truth, conveyed an enraptured vision of the bounty of God and drew to his side certain brave souls, who offered to mingle their blood with that of the Imám's heroic companions to preserve themselves from breaking the covenant of God.

The most renowned of those repentant souls was the vigorous commander, Ḥurr, who had obstructed all roads to Ḥusayn. His transformation took place in the depths of night, nor could his soldiers believe their eyes when they beheld this man of courage trembling like a leaf in a winter storm. 'But we have never seen you in fear, even in the midst of the most terrifying battles', they cried. 'I find myself between heaven and hell', was Ḥurr's reply. 'My soul cries out and cannot bear these torments of hell.' In the faint light of dawn, he charged his steed towards Ḥusayn, to express his penitence and beg forgiveness. When he had received the Imám's grace and assurance, he faced the army of Ibn Sa'd and chided them in loud tones, hoping to awaken their dormant souls. But alas! Those who were his comrades and under his command, attacked and killed him in an outburst of despicable ferocity.

Even water was denied to the Imám's small band. The sight of the glimmering Euphrates in that barren and waterless desert aggravated their sufferings. Whoever approached the river for a drink, or ventured out to bring a container of water, became the target of spears and javelins.

This was the tragic fate of Ḥusayn's brother, 'Abbás, the standard-bearer of the Imám's camp, renowned as the most handsome of the Há<u>sh</u>imites, and famed as the lion-hearted man of Arabia. In an audacious quest for water, he reached the Euphrates, filled his skin container, and charged his steed toward the tents where children were dying of thirst. Ibn Sa'd flew into a rage when he saw his orders flouted and challenged. His soldiers pursued 'Abbás ferociously, cut off his right hand, then his left, in which he carried the container, pierced its skin, and attacked and killed the water-carrier of Karbilá in a most atrocious way.

With an unswerving rectitude of character, unabated vigour and firmness, Ḥusayn persevered in his readiness to offer all that he possessed as a ransom for the Faith of his Grandfather. Carrying his youngest son who was in the cradle, he held him aloft and asked for water for that suckling child. An arrow lodged deep in the throat of the baby. Ḥusayn tossed the blood of his infant boy into the air. That precious child, it seems, was the last link which fastened his father to life on this planet. After sacrificing him, he became free as a bird, light as the breeze of the morning and ready to take his last flight to the celestial domain. Now, 'alone, weary, and wounded, he seated himself at the door of his tent, … [where] he was pierced in the mouth with a dart'.[22] This was indeed the bitterest moment of his life.

He offered prayers for the dead and reflected upon the losses he had sustained. His sons, the son of his brother Ḥasan, the sons of his sister Zaynab, his followers and their sons – all had been killed in the bloom of their youth.

Vital questions must have flooded Ḥusayn's mind. What would happen to his dear son, Zaynu'l-'Ábidín, who was an invalid and confined to bed? What would be the fate of the women of his family at the hands of the merciless and bloodthirsty soldiers? Who could ever arrest the evil tide of events which was staining the soil of Karbilá? What path would be destined for the Faith of Islám when it fell totally under the sway of the tyrants of Damascus, the beasts from the desert?

At this, the darkest moment of his precious life, when portents and omens clouded his heart, he was ready to bear whatever blows might descend upon him. In his innermost heart he knew his love for God and was confident of God's never-failing triumphs, unblurred and unsullied. He arose as a spiritual giant to proclaim: 'And verily Our host shall conquer.'[23] It was a voice from the unknown which still resounds in that desert.

The valiant heroes of God advanced one by one and all were put to death. They were so uplifted by spiritual fervour that they longed for nothing but to offer their lives to safeguard the covenant of God.

By noontide of the tenth of Muḥarram, not one of Ḥusayn's fighting men remained. For his final words with the army of Ibn Sa'd, Ḥusayn advanced towards them and addressed them in his melodious voice. With conviction and love, he exhorted the soldiers, reminded them of their letters to him, requested them to cease fighting and emphatically reiterated his appeal to withdraw from the scene of bloodshed. Individual soldiers were moved by his words and scarcely anyone dared to throw even a stone at him. The writer of *Muḥriqu'l-Qulúb* says that at this critical moment an arrow sank deep in Ḥusayn's body and then a thundering voice was heard. 'Inform Ibn Zíyád that I was the first to shoot an arrow!' Such was the claim of the chief commander, Ibn Sa'd.

How contemptible and disgraceful are often the standards set by men! To take pride in killing the grandson of the Prophet! To hope by this cowardly act to win the approval of Ibn Zíyád!

This first arrow aimed at the Imám opened a dam and released a flood which covered the plain of Karbilá – land of agony and disaster – and carried off the family and friends of Ḥusayn to captivity and martyrdom. An army of more than four thousand, to please the despots of Kúfah and Damascus and to ensure their own share of the booty of war, assailed seventy people and threatened their women and children. The army had every available means; Ḥusayn's companions had none. No supremacy of valour or audacity could be claimed for that victory.

At noon, Ḥusayn asked for a truce to say the noon prayers, which was granted. He chanted prayers, sang songs of heroism, and committed his family to the loving care and ever-abiding protection of God. As the hour of his death approached, an unbounded ecstasy transformed his pitiable plight and found expression in words of joy and exultation.

After prayers, he again counselled his opponents in gem-like words, but they surrounded him like beasts of prey, striking so many blows with iron bars, spears and swords that he could no longer support himself on his charger and fell to the ground. His horse galloped towards the tents where the Imám's family had taken shelter, paused there a little, then disappeared into the endless desert.

The full brunt of the wrath of that frantic mob fell heavily on the Imám. His face was streaming with blood. He lifted up his garment to wipe it away. In that moment an arrow sank deep in his chest, causing him to fall to his knees. The wounds were all on his chest and arms, for he never turned his back to his foes. Then a soldier gave the Imám such a severe blow on the head that he fell on his face. In the confusion, a group of soldiers, headed by the heartless Shimr, started to invade the Imám's tents for the purpose of looting and putting all to death. Ḥusayn shouted at them, 'If you do not follow the religion of God, behave, at least, as true Arabs, and spare the women and children!' Shimr turned back at once, ordering his soldiers to withdraw.

The hand of death was not yet on Ḥusayn, and although fallen, he inspired such awe in the hearts of the soldiers that no one dared to commit the heinous deed of decapitating him.

Some approached but shuddered in fear and rejoined their ranks. 'The remorseless Shamer, a name detested by the faithful, reproached their cowardice.'[24] Then this envoy of the governor of Kúfah fell like a thunderbolt on Ḥusayn's body and severed his head with nearly ten strokes.

This sealed the contemptible victory of four thousand over barely seventy. No historian could rightly attribute it to superior intelligence, bravery or manhood. The episode remains as it was, an irremovable stain upon the history of mankind. Yet, in its exquisite demonstration of the gallantry of a few firm and steadfast adherents, it breathes courage and life even into bare bones, while its example of magnanimity awakens in those who justly consider it a desire to attain new heights of conscious and active devotion.

The martyrdom of Ḥusayn occurred at midday of Friday, the tenth of Muḥarram, the first month in the lunar calendar, in the year sixty-one after Hijrah.

The soldiers stripped the Imám of his garments and carried them away as loot of war. Shimr, who was adamant in his determination to kill all the surviving members of Ḥusayn's family and plunder their possessions, hastened again at the head of a group of soldiers to the tents where the Imám's family were sorely lamenting the grievous loss of their dearest one. But Ibn Sa'd noted this and came up to prevent the massacre of those who survived and were captives in his hands.

The Imám had more than thirty wounds on his body and arms from the swords and spears of his enemies. To leave no trace of the martyrs, the commander ordered his cavalry to trample the corpses with their galloping horses. This done, the heads of the martyrs were raised aloft on long spears. The impoverished members of Ḥusayn's family were roped together and dragged to the bare camels which would carry them to the seat of the governor. Zaynu'l-'Ábidín was put in chains and treated ruthlessly, though he was ill and weak.

So Ibn Sa'd and his victorious army left the plain of Karbilá, which was strewn with the remains of the martyrs, and marched off to Kúfah with immense excitement and joy, anticipating the praise and rewards which the governor had promised.

What agony possessed the hearts of the Imám's family remains forever undescribed. Words and phrases fail any writer who attempts to portray such poignant sorrows in the history of Man's atrocities. As the family looked back, they could see the desert strewn with the mutilated bodies of their dear ones; and when they cast their eyes to the road ahead, they beheld nothing but a forest of lances and spears adorned with their heads. Khúlí was the carrier of Ḥusayn's head.[25] The only remaining son of

Ḥusayn was in chains, driven along with the rest of his family to an unknown fate and further humiliations. Their prayer was to gain the approval of their Lord and His acceptance of all they had so generously offered at the altar of faith, devotion and sacrifice.

Before the arrival of the army, Ibn Zíyád had stationed soldiers at various posts on their path to be on guard lest the disastrous condition of the family of the Prophet should drive the masses to revolt. When the inhabitants of Kúfah saw the humiliations heaped upon Ḥusayn's relatives, they wept. Zaynu'l-'Ábidín, seeing their tears, reproached them, saying, 'You slaughter the members of our family and now you shed tears!' A woman who was watching from the roof of her house as they passed was so bitterly moved that she brought pieces of cloth and veils to cover the barely-dressed bodies of the sisters and daughters of Ḥusayn.

Zaynab, daughter of 'Alí and sister of Ḥusayn, looked pityingly at the people of Kúfah and addressed them in a tone as vigorous and eloquent as her father's.

> O ye inhabitants of Kúfah! O ye people of deceit and dissension! You shed tears, but you do not feel ashamed before the Prophet of God! You raised the worst creature to be your sovereign and slaughtered the best of all men. You brought upon yourselves such disgrace that its effects will remain with you forever. No power can erase the evil consequences of your shameful deeds. Nothing can ever wash from your hands the stains of the sacred blood of the martyrs. The Imám was shield and shelter to all the believers, and the sole interpreter of the revealed words of God. Through him could we find our way to the religion of God.

One of the daughters of Ḥusayn exclaimed, 'They took us captive, forced us to ride on bare camels, exposed us to the burning heat of the sun and allowed us no shelter in the desert.'

Again Zaynu'l-'Ábidín addressed the watching crowds and, after words of praise and prayer to God, affirmed:

> ... I am the son of the one who exercised patience to the end of his life; to the time when you severed his head from his body. Woe be unto you, O inhabitants of Kúfah! You sent letters of invitation to Ḥusayn. You deceived him and placed him in the hands of his enemies. You helped the oppressors to rule over him. How, then, can you ever face the Apostle of God? What will your answers be when He asks you, 'Why did you kill the members of my family?'

That fateful day passed. Then Ibn Zíyád invited the inhabitants of the town to watch the final scene of this tragedy in which he was the chief actor. Crowds of people assembled in his very large house. It is incredible that some of those who had seats of honour in that court of crimes and cruelty were of the most erudite of the region, venerated and famous for their piety. When all were settled in their places, the governor raised his voice to order that the captives be brought into his presence.

But first, the head of Ḥusayn was carried in and placed at his feet. Unable to control his vindictive satisfaction, the governor began to beat the head with the stick he held in his hand. One of the veteran believers, a companion of the Prophet, was present. When he saw the governor's brutal act he was agitated and overcome by grief, and raised his voice in protest, calling out, 'O son of Marjánih! Raise your rod from those lips, for many a time have I seen the Prophet's lips caressing that face with tenderest affection, the while He assured us that Ḥasan and Ḥusayn were His twin trusts to the believers!'

When Zaynab and others of Ḥusayn's family were introduced to the court, not one of them saluted the governor. In anger and contempt, he arrogantly inquired, 'Who is that woman?' When told she was Zaynab, the sister of Ḥusayn, he observed, 'I praise God that He has disgraced you all and revealed your lies.'

Immediately Zaynab answered him in clearest terms. 'Praise be to God who honoured us by our relation to the Apostle of God. It is He who cleansed our hearts from the dust of doubts and sin. Know this of a certainty, that the wrong-doers and sinners are placed in disgrace but we are not of them.'

'See what God has wrought for your brother and his men', rejoined Ibn Zíyád.

'It was decreed by God that some of the best and dearest ones should give their lives in the path of His religion. Ere long the supreme Judge will call them and you to His presence, and He is indeed the best of all judges', Zaynab replied.

With mounting rage Ibn Zíyád retorted, 'Now that we have killed your brothers, my heart is calm and appeased.'

Quietly Zaynab replied, 'O son of Marjánih! You uprooted the tree of prophethood and cut off its branches and boughs. We hope that now your heart rests in peace and that your thirst for the blood of our family is quenched.'

Ibn Zíyád's glance then fell on Zaynu'l-'Ábidín, and he asked, 'Who is he?' The answer came, ''Alí, son of Ḥusayn.'

Furiously, Ibn Zíyád exclaimed, 'Did not God kill you and your brothers?' And the Imám answered, 'The death of each individual is by the decree of God.'

In a blaze of wrath the governor ordered that he, too, should be beheaded. Then Zaynab's voice rang through the room: 'This is the only male member left to our family. If you desire to kill him, kill all of us together!'

Zaynu'l-'Ábidín looked calmly at Ibn Zíyád. 'Do you threaten me with death? Do you not know that martyrdom in the path of God is our prerogative and our greatest aspiration?'

Impatiently, Ibn Zíyád shouted an order to place the members of Ḥusayn's family in the prison adjacent to the mosque. To cause them more suffering, he commanded that the head of Ḥusayn be raised on a spear and carried through the lanes and markets of Kúfah.

After some days, the governor ordered Shimr, accompanied by soldiers and helpers, to conduct the captives to the court of Yazíd in Damascus.

When Yazíd was informed of the approach of the mournful caravan from Mesopotamia he ordered the inhabitants of Damascus to decorate the doors of their homes and shops with all festive ornaments and to prepare themselves to celebrate the victory of his dynasty over Ḥusayn. Crowds gathered outside the gate of the town to watch the arrival of the dejected and afflicted captives, who were preceded by the severed heads of their martyrs. Then came the invalid son of Ḥusayn in chains, followed by all the others, fastened with ropes on the bare-backed camels. As they approached the seat of the tyrant of Syria, the caravan stopped near the great Mosque of Damascus.

Yazíd arranged a very large gathering in his mansion. Seated on his throne and wearing a special crown, he imitated the Persian and Roman Emperors. At his behest the captives were brought into his presence. First came a man who carried the head of Ḥusayn. Reaching the throne of Yazíd, he shouted, 'Load my horses with gold and silver. We have killed the noblest son of the most exalted parents.'

These complimentary words about the vanquished put Yazíd into a rage; he ordered the immediate death of the offender. In his hoarse, loud voice, he shouted at the culprit, 'If you believed they were the noblest, why did you kill them?'

The heads of the martyrs were placed in a row at the feet of Yazíd, with Ḥusayn's in the centre of a glittering tray of gold. The grandson of Abú-Sufyán fixed his gaze upon the heads of Háshim's descendants. Relief and satisfaction were reflected in his face. The long struggle for power was ended, and the Umayyads were safely settled on the throne of their earthly sovereignty.

Then the members of Ḥusayn's family were brought in. As they entered, one of the audience gave vent to his feelings and shouted, 'You did well, Yazíd! You exterminated the generation of the Prophet and raised to command the son of an adulteress.'

Yazíd, intoxicated with his victory over the Háshimites, and remembering the deep-rooted rivalry which the Umayyads had always harboured in their hearts, the jealousy which had always consumed them, could not but express joy at the vengeance his clan had now taken. He wished that his ancestors had lived to behold the avenging sword-strokes on the bodies of the Háshimites, could have viewed with him the members of Ḥusayn's household, now captive in his conquering hands.

Zaynab, watching him, raised her voice fearlessly in exhortation.

> Do you realize what you are doing? Though you keep the members of your own family behind curtains and veils, you expose the daughters of the Prophet to public gaze. You carry them from town to town, hold them in bonds and chains, exhibit their sufferings, look at them in anger, feel no shame in killing them, beat the mouth of Ḥusayn with joy ... Are you followers of the Apostle of God? You rule with the sword of Muḥammad, and are haughty and proud because of this transient sovereignty.

Yazíd turned to Zaynu'l-'Ábidín and said, 'Your father challenged my rule.'

The Imám replied with quiet force, 'Prophethood and kingship are given to our family. Tell me, in whose house were the verses of God revealed? In yours or ours? Did Gabriel descend to your house or to ours? Do the verses commanding respect and reverence for the divine family refer to yours or ours?'

With this, Yazíd attempted to be kind and lenient to the prisoners and sent them into his mansion where all bewailed their condition. He even offered them luxurious hospitality which was not accepted, for scions of the uncompromising Ḥusayn never deigned to curry favour with the despicable tyrant of Syria.

On one occasion, when soldiers began to play their drums and sound their trumpets and bugles, Yazíd said to Zaynu'l-'Ábidín, 'This is our regal music.' The Imám did not utter a word, but waited until midday when the *adhán* was sounded. 'This is the song of our family which will endure forever', he told Yazíd.

To win the favour and sympathy of his captives, Yazíd often expressed regret at what had taken place in Mesopotamia, asserting that it had not been by his instruction. He even requested them to adopt Damascus as their abode where all their needs would be met. But Zaynu'l-'Ábidín and his companions asked to return to Medina, the city of the Prophet, by way of Karbilá, where they would bury the heads of their dead. As to their needs, they never alluded to any, but asked only that their relics should be returned to them. Those objects of adoration had been entrusted to their grandmother Fáṭimah, the most exalted woman of the Islamic era. Though seemingly small and insignificant, each one of these silent objects conveyed to them assurance of the ultimate victory of the Faith of God, and would impart to the remaining members of the Holy Family the fragrance of love growing in their midst.

They reached the plain of Karbilá on the fortieth day after the martyrdom of Ḥusayn. To their great satisfaction, they found that the devoted members of a tribe called Banú-Asad had courageously gathered the bodies of the martyrs and interred them. Having buried the heads, they offered prayers and resumed their way towards Ḥijáz.

They took the same path as Ḥusayn had followed to Mesopotamia. They paused to watch the rippling Euphrates hasten towards the south, and they remembered those who had thirsted for even one cup of its water. Every pebble of the desert spoke to them of the days just past, and of Ḥusayn, whose brave march across the desert had led him to an apex of glory and spiritual conquest so exalted that none, even of the immortal heroes amongst the Imáms, could ever approach it.

As was said before, to attempt to recount the true story of Ḥusayn resembles the excavating of ancient towns from beneath layers of stone, sand and soil, heaped upon them by time and by Man. For centuries, the pure and stainless life of Ḥusayn has been buried and obliterated under mountains of false judgement on the part of the enemies of his cause, and by exaggerated accounts from the immature and ignorant among his followers. The little written here falls within the light shed upon Ḥusayn's life by the intense love shown for him by Bahá'u'lláh. This account is short, and very limited in scope, but the hope is that it will frame worthily a picture so exquisite and divine in beauty and grandeur.

Amongst the grandchildren of the Prophet Muḥammad, the one who resembled Him most was Imám Ḥusayn. He was of medium height, with an olive complexion. Dignity coupled with charm made him a magnet to whom all were drawn, even unbelievers. The most attractive of all his qualities and heavenly gifts were his bold and resolute eyes and his warm, penetrating and resonant voice which inspired awe and commanded respect. 'Hussain, the second son of 'Alí, had inherited his father's virtues and chivalrous disposition.'[26]

Like the Prophet, he loved the poor and destitute. Whatever gifts were brought to him by the believers were distributed among the poor and needy. In fact he was often seen in their humble abodes, sitting with their families in an attitude of natural and sincere love that made every pain-racked soul relieved, happy and proud.

He was the essence of piety. It was his noble and pious life which enhanced his judgement and authority.

Ḥusayn's fame as the most generous man of the Arabian peninsula spread far and wide. If his children were taught verses of the Qur'án, Ḥusayn would make a gift of one thousand dinars to their teacher.

Once a man approached Ḥusayn and requested his financial help. He gave the man enough to sustain himself and his family. He then counselled him with words even more valuable than the coins, asking the man to come to him whenever he stood in further need; and should he choose to approach another, to make sure that his benefactor believed in God, loved his kind, and, above all, was honest and true.

From early childhood Ḥusayn demonstrated such remarkable feats of chivalry, undaunted courage and erudition that people took pleasure in sitting at his feet to learn the heavenly lessons he was endowed to offer.

His words were plain and he expressed truth in uncompromising terms. His addresses were concise, cogent and timeless: they stand forever as standards of truth and examples of genuine eloquence.

Many people wrote to Ḥusayn and took pride in receiving his answers to their inquiries. When asked about God, the Imám explained that God could never be comprehended by our senses, nor should He ever be compared with Man. God is very near, he explained, but free of attachment. He is remote and aloof, but inseparable from His creation. He is known by His own proofs and identified by His own signs.[27]

He defined the people of the world and their religious beliefs by saying that they are in thraldom to their possessions, riches and luxuries. For many, religion is a word uttered by their tongues; and even when they profess belief, their real interest is to procure and secure a livelihood. When tested, the true believers are very few indeed.

When Abú-Dhar, one of the early believers in the Prophet Muḥammad and His staunch supporter, was exiled from Medina by order of the third Caliph, 'Uthmán, 'Alí became very sad and, accompanied by Ḥasan and Ḥusayn, went to bid him farewell. 'Alí asked his two sons to say goodbye to their 'uncle'. Ḥusayn, in that sorrowful moment, said to the exiled believer, 'the people withheld their luxuries from you, and you did not sell them your faith. How detached you are from that which was not given you; and how needful they are of what you did not sell them.'

When the agent of Mu'áwíyah endeavoured to take the oath of allegiance in favour of Yazíd, he used words as sweet as honey, but, as usual, his words were mixed with the venom of violation of the covenant of God. Ḥusayn, with characteristic audacity and frankness, warned the inhabitants of the city of the Prophet against the deeds of those who would lead them away from the true path of God. He declared that they attempted to cover falsehood with the garment of truth. To follow them, one would win this world and all its transient joys, but would surely lose the everlasting life in the Kingdom on high. This is indeed the greatest of all losses that Man can sustain.

Ḥusayn made an eternal statement about prayer, the gleaming truth of which will be understood increasingly by mankind as it approaches the age of maturity. He claimed that we should never pray to our Lord and Creator for fear of the tortures of hell, nor because we covet the joys and comforts of paradise. We must worship God, Ḥusayn said, because He is worthy of our praise and adoration.

Some of the believers, more than others, came to realize the magnitude of his rank as the spiritual leader of mankind; they devoted their lives and consecrated their wealth in service to him and sought always to be in his presence. Ibn 'Abbás was one of the most erudite men of his time, but he used to walk holding the stirrup of Ḥusayn's saddle while the Imám was riding.

Abú-Hurayrah was another of the pious and learned people of his age. He used to clean the Imám's shoes with his own shirt, saying, 'Should the people know what I know of him, they would certainly carry him on their shoulders.'

The story of Bilál and his love for Ḥusayn is indeed touching. Bilál was one of the earliest to believe in the Prophet Muḥammad. When the Prophet decided to call the believers to the prescribed prayers, He asked Bilál to go up on the roof and chant the verses of the *adhán*. After the passing of the Apostle of God, he left Ḥijáz for Jerusalem where he made his home. Once Imám Ḥusayn sighed and expressed a wish to hear once more the far-reaching, vibrant and vigorous voice of Bilál. Bilál saw the Prophet of God in his dream summoning him and remonstrating with him as to why he had forsaken His family. On the morrow, Bilál was on his way to Medina. The moment he arrived in the city of his Beloved, he hastened to His resting-place. No sooner had he reached there than he threw himself on that sacred tomb. Overwhelmed with sorrow and drowned in memories of the past, he pressed himself against the grave, crying and shedding bitter tears. When the Imám came to know of his arrival, he immediately went to the holy precincts where he found this faithful friend of his Grandfather. He lifted him up, embraced him with much affection, and surrounded him with compassion and tenderness. He wiped his tears, strengthened and consoled his heart and asked him to go to the mosque and sound the *adhán*. When the believers heard the golden voice of Bilál chanting the first verses of the *adhán*, their hearts leapt in their breasts. The middle verses brought them out of their houses; and by the time Bilál had concluded the call to prayer, they were already hastening to the mosque.

In the course of this short account of the Imám's life, we have come to know that he never ceased to guide people to the right path of God. Even in that moment when he had fallen from his horse, with his own death fast approaching, when he beheld Shimr and his unruly soldiers about to sack his tents where his family shrank in terror, he called out to them to behave as Arabs, even if not as Muslims.

On this day of his martyrdom, he addressed his friends and foes, urging them to safeguard themselves against the world and its manifold temptations. The world is always encircled by multifarious disasters, he told them. Its bounties vanish soon. Its joys grow dim and clouded. The best of all fortunes in this transient life is to be virtuous, to have the fear of God in one's heart, and to be faithful to God's Messengers, the worthiest and noblest Beings of the whole creation.

Not only did Ḥusayn, in his lifetime, firmly and compellingly exhort his friends and followers in beautiful and eloquent language, but he has remained an ever-glowing, ever-burning beacon of guidance, a fount of heavenly qualities and spiritual utterances.

Our account will not be complete without a tribute to Zaynab, the sister of Ḥusayn. Even now we can hear the echoes of her lamentations on the episode of Karbilá ringing throughout the centuries. When the terrible butcheries enacted on that plain were ended, what emotions must have surged in the heart of that great and noble lady! In the hours of loneliness, might she not have whispered to her own soul such words as these:

> I followed my brother and trudged the path of suffering and sacrifice. He had an inherent gift which, like a magic spell, commanded respect and admiration. We followed him and walked in his shadow and under his shelter. I bore the loss of my own sons, the loss of my nephews, the loss of my brother 'Abbás, and the loss of many of the young believers who, intoxicated by the love of God, hastened to tear the veils asunder in order to behold the beauty of their Lord and Creator. All these losses could be tolerated, but the loss of Ḥusayn is one which cannot be measured. He was the Imám and we were his followers, enthralled by his love. His grievous loss is a wound so deep that nothing will give us rest or peace.
>
> I remember the blazing heat of Arabia, the burning thirst of the children, the swift storms which swept sand into our eyes and dust across our parched lips. The winds were sometimes so ravaging that the tents, our flimsy shelters, would be shaken and often nearly swept away. In the stillness of the night, I heard voices of a ferocity no mortal has ever experienced, the howling of rapacious soldiers who could not wait for dawn to break. I saw with my own eyes young enthusiastic youths who offered their souls when embraced and caressed by my beloved brother.

> These giants of spiritual strength were cast down by pygmies moved by lust and greed. How can these weaklings ever fill their places? I was captive in Kúfah and Damascus and saw with my own eyes their tottering earthly rulership. Their triumph came not from a heavenly revelation, nor was it due to any supremacy of courage and devotion. No gentle and continuing effort sustained it; rather, it was a spiritual disaster that ravaged the whole of the Muslim world.
>
> Did I endure all these ordeals? Did my eyes behold and my ears hear? How can I live? How am I able to sustain all these tempests of tests and trials? Why am I alive? Why?

It was decreed by God that Zaynab should live to protect the fourth Imám and thus assure the continuation of the Imamate until the year 260 AH. She was the one who raised the cry of 'Yá Ḥusayn!', and rallied the friends who were faithful, addressing them in a language so eloquent and stormy that it reminded them of Imám 'Alí. Had it not been for her forbearance in adversity and her incessant efforts to recount the events of those first ten days of Muḥarram, we should not have a full story of the radiant Ḥusayn, the 'Prince of Martyrs'.

A dramatic and marked contrast exists between the Imám and Yazíd, who left no stone unturned in his efforts to subjugate Ḥusayn. Yazíd was tall, well-built, and had a robust constitution. His hoarse voice, when raised in anger, created fear in his palace and capital. He was absorbed in luxuries and frivolities and frequently engaged in idle pastimes, displaying a great affection for games and hunting.

In the words of Syed Ameer Ali:

> Yazid was both cruel and treacherous; his depraved nature knew no pity or justice. His pleasures were as degrading as his companions were low and vicious. He insulted the ministers of religion by dressing up a monkey as a learned divine and carrying the animal mounted on a beautifully caparisoned Syrian donkey wherever he went. Drunken riotousness prevailed at court, and was naturally imitated in the streets of the capital.[28]

When Ḥusayn rose in defence of the covenant of God and chose the path of sacrifice with longing and enthusiasm, some of the believers, instigated by agents of the Umayyad capital, dared to send him letters of protest, criticizing his action and interrogating him as to why he had become the cause of dispersion by creating innovation in the Faith of God. They even exhorted him to be silent, else he would ignite the fire of mischief.

Ibn Zíyád was, in the beginning, one of the followers of 'Alí; but his appointment by Yazíd as governor of the eastern provinces of the Empire caused him to forget 'Alí and his family and to commit atrocities beyond description.

Ibn Sa'd was the son of an avowed supporter of Islám, the commander who had conquered Persia under the flag of Islám. The promise of the rulership of Ray caused Ibn Sa'd to violate the covenant of God, and to pride himself on having discharged the first arrow to strike Ḥusayn.

Those who signed the death-warrant of the Imám were numbered among the judges, religious leaders and potentates of the mosques. But as Gibbon has clearly explained, the temptations were too great for people to resist; they could not stand firm and unmoved. Shorayh, the chief judge, was one who was seated in the government-house of Kúfah when the heads of the martyrs were brought into the presence of Ibn Zíyád. With him was the leader of the congregational prayers, who had won the admiration of the populace by his reading and study of the Qur'án, and his prayer vigils at night. The news of the ignominious death suffered by the grandson of the Prophet awakened in him no prick of conscience. As usual, he led the congregation in prayers and took not the least trouble to ponder upon what had taken place, nor to understand the station of the one who had accepted these afflictions in the path of God.

Shimr, the heartless beast whose mere name creates waves of horror in the hearts of the faithful, was one of the religious judges and so apparently pious that he would pick up thorns from the roads lest they prick the feet of the pedestrians. Yet it was he who stepped forward in a display of heroism to decapitate the Imám with ten strokes of his heavy sword.

When Ibn 'Uqbah and his Syrian mercenaries reached Medina, the soldiers' greed for the riches of the people, their butcheries, their self-indulgence and unbridled lust proved unlimited. Even the most revered believers, including the veteran companions and helpers of the Prophet, were mercilessly put to death by them. Their horses were tethered and fed in the great Mosque, the ornaments and relics of the shrines were confiscated, and having disastrously ruined the city of the Prophet, they hastened to the Qiblih of Islám in Mecca and caused severe damage to the most holy spot in the Islamic world. These uncontrolled savageries were stopped only by the news of the sudden death of Yazíd. The mercenaries rushed home, but the bitter remembrance of their cruelties remained as a permanent thorn in the hearts of the believers.

This insolent and disrespectful spirit, and this heedlessness towards Islám and its resuscitating powers prevailed throughout the Umayyad dynasty. Exceptions were rare indeed. Al-Walíd II, one of the Umayyad caliphs, was so intoxicated with his worldly power that he tore the Qur'án into pieces, and while singing poems addressed the Book of God in mocking terms: 'If God asks you as to who tore His Book, tell Him Walíd.'

In the light of these comparisons, let us refer to the statements of 'Abdu'l-Bahá about the destructive influence of the Umayyad caliphs. He gave these explanations at the time of His incarceration in the prison-city of 'Akká (Acre), then governed by rulers many of whom were not less cruel. When asked about the 'beast' mentioned in the eleventh chapter of the Revelation of St. John, He replied:

> The beast that ascendeth out of the bottomless pit shall war against them, and shall overcome them, and kill them' – this beast means the Baní-Umayyih[29] who attacked them from the pit of error, and who rose against the religion of Muḥammad and against the reality of 'Alí – in other words, the love of God.
>
> It is said, 'The beast made war against these two witnesses'[30] – that is to say, a spiritual war, meaning that the beast would act in entire opposition to the teachings, customs and institutions of these two witnesses, to such an extent that the virtues and perfections which were diffused by the power of those two witnesses[29] among the peoples and tribes would be entirely dispelled, and the animal nature and carnal desires would conquer. Therefore, this beast making war against them would gain the victory – meaning that the darkness of error coming from this beast was to have ascendency over the horizons of the world, and kill those two witnesses – in other words, that it would destroy the spiritual life which they spread abroad in the midst of the nation, and entirely remove the divine laws and teachings, treading under foot the Religion of God. Nothing would thereafter remain but a lifeless body without spirit.
>
> 'And their dead bodies shall lie in the street of the great city ...'

> 'Their bodies' means the Religion of God, and 'the street' means in public view … the nations, tribes and peoples would look at their bodies – that is to say, that they would make a spectacle of the Religion of God: though they would not act in accordance with it, still, they would not suffer their bodies – meaning the Religion of God – to be put in the grave. That is to say, that in appearance they would cling to the Religion of God and not allow it to completely disappear from their midst, nor the body of it to be entirely destroyed and annihilated. Nay, in reality they would leave it, while outwardly preserving its name and remembrance.[31]

These words epitomized the centuries of the Islamic Era and the disastrous blows the Muslim community suffered throughout its history. Following the sack of Medina, we are told, 'Paganism was once more triumphant, and "its reaction", says a European historian, "against Islám was cruel, terrible, and revolting" … The colleges, hospitals, and other public edifices built under the Caliphs were closed or demolished, and Arabia relapsed into a wilderness!'[32]

Little did Yazíd know how futile his ephemeral sovereignty would be! Steeped in viciousness, he could not have a clear vision of the future. Gradually the small dim light he had in his heart grew weaker and weaker and was finally extinguished. By his own deeds he rang the death-knell of his own rulership which lasted about four years. Ere the ending of his days and before the lusty songs were terminated, his image was hidden under the pall of death, forever shrouded in shame.

History reversed the tide of events to favour the one who had been so mercilessly wronged. In the course of decades and centuries, Ḥusayn snatched victory from the dreadful jaws of the 'beast' which, gradually losing vigour and its hold over the hearts and souls of the people, was left abandoned.

Great indeed was Ḥusayn's undertaking, and hard was the path he had to pursue amidst his ferocious enemies. It was a time of foolish and unfounded beliefs, which proliferated in the favourable climate prepared by the Umayyad dynasty. But to safeguard the Faith of his Grandfather, Ḥusayn accepted all atrocities.

As we review the history of those eventful years, we reach a page wherein we behold Ḥusayn's sacrifice emerging to cleave a path through the debris of cruelties and massacre. His figure comes forth from the mist of the past. His story re-echoes in sad and heavenly song. Minstrels, wandering from tent to tent and from town to town, sing tales of those intrepid souls who severed all their ties with the world, suffered with great tenacity, composure and dignity, and marched on and on, higher and higher, towards an apex which touches the zenith of the heavens of Glory.

POSTSCRIPT

Because of the treacherous acts of those who dared to flout the words of the Prophet Muḥammad, the two centres of Islám – the spiritual and the administrative – were forever separated. While the spiritual centre remained in Ḥijáz where the Qiblih of Islám is fixed, the administrative centre drifted away, shifting from Ḥijáz to Damascus, Mesopotamia, Egypt, and finally, the Ottoman Empire.

This factor, and the attitudes and actions of the caliphs, drained the vitality of the Faith. To retain the caliphate in their own hands, and heredity in their lineages, they spared no efforts to keep the Muslim world under their sway.

It is not the aim, nor is it a part of this essay, to analyze the spiritual damage resulting from their deeds, but the writer desires to draw the attention of readers to the fact that such innovations undermined the religion of God and its institutions, thus causing a gradual decline in the morale of its adherents and bringing the institution of the caliphate to its close in the year AD 1924, at the hands of that 'audacious man', Mustafá Kemal Atatúrk.

NOTES AND REFERENCES

1 Jáhilíya, before the advent of Muḥammad.

2 Gibbon, Edward. *The Decline and Fall of the Roman Empire*, ch. 50.

3 Bahá'u'lláh (1817–92) was the Founder of the Bahá'í Faith, the Báb (1819–50) its Forerunner, and 'Abdu'l-Bahá (1844–1921) its Exemplar.

4 Tradition has it that Adam built the Ka'bah, which was rebuilt in a later age by Abraham and Ishmael.

5 See 'Abdu'l-Bahá, *Some Answered Questions*, ch. XI. (Bahá'í Publishing Trust, Wilmette, Illinois, rev. edn. 1964.)

6 See *Gleanings from the Writings of Bahá'u'lláh*, section XXIII. (Bahá'í Publishing Trust, Wilmette, Illinois, rev. edn. 1952.)

7 Gibbon, Edward. *The Decline and Fall of the Roman Empire*, ch. 50.

8 The passages quoted in this paragraph and the next are from Gibbon, ibid. ch. 50.

9 The collection is called *Nahju'l-Balágh̲ah*, and is referred to by the great teachers of Islám as 'not the words of the Creator, but heaven above the words of man'.

10 Hitti, Philip K. *History of the Arabs*, p. 183. (Macmillan and Co. Ltd, London, 10th edn. 1070; also St. Martin's Press, Inc., New York.)

11 Passages quoted in this paragraph and the next are from Gibbon, Edward. *The Decline and Fall of the Roman Empire*, ch. 50.

12 Gibbon, ibid. ch. 50

13 Hitti, Philip K. *The Arabs, A Short History*, pp. 59–60. (Macmillan, London, 5th edn. 1968; also St. Martin's Press, New York.)

14 The book read in the presence of the Báb in the prison of Máh-Kú. See Nabíl, *The Dawn-Breakers*, p. 252. (Bahá'í Publishing Trust, Wilmette, Illinois, 1932.)

15 Cited by Syed Ameer Ali in *A Short History of the Saracens*, pp. 83–4. (Macmillan and Co. Ltd., London, repr. 1921.)

16 ibid. p. 84

17 Gibbon, Edward. *The Decline and Fall of the Roman Empire*, ch. 50.

18 In favour of 'Alí and his claim to be the first Imám. (A. Q. Faizí.)

19 Hitti, Philip K. *History of the Arabs*, p. 196. (Macmillan and Co. Ltd, London, 10th edn. 1070; also St. Martin's Press, Inc., New York.)

20 The birthday of Bahá'u'lláh, according to the lunar calendar, is the second of Muḥarram, in the year 1233 AH (after Hijrah).

21 This number does not include the women and children.

22 Gibbon, Edward. *The Decline and Fall of the Roman Empire*, ch. 50.

23 *Qur'án*, 37:173

24 Gibbon, Edward. *The Decline and Fall of the Roman Empire*, ch. 50.

25 See *Gleanings from the Writings of Bahá'u'lláh*, section XXXIX. (Bahá'í Publishing Trust, Wilmette, Illinois, rev. edn. 1952.)

26 Cited by Syed Ameer Ali in *A Short History of the Saracens*, pp. 83–4. (Macmillan and Co. Ltd., London, repr. 1921.)

27 The Persian mystic poet Rúmí says, 'The sun rose. Its rays are its own proofs and its light its own sign.'

28 Ameer Ali, Syed. *A Short History of the Saracens*, p. 83. (Macmillan and Co. Ltd., London, repr. 1921.)

29 Dynasty of the Umayyads.

30 These two witnesses were the Prophet Muḥammad and Imám 'Alí. (A. Q. Faizí.)

31 'Abdu'l-Bahá, *Some Answered Questions*, pp. 60–62. (Bahá'í Publishing Trust, Wilmette, Illinois.) Note: 51–53 in newer eds.

32 Ameer Ali, Syed. *A Short History of the Saracens*, p. 88. (Macmillan and Co. Ltd., London, repr. 1921.)

STORIES FROM
The Delight of Hearts
The Memoirs of Ḥájí Mírzá Ḥaydar-'Alí.
Translated and abridged by A. Q. Faizí

FOREWORD

One of the most thrilling aspects of Bahá'í history is the story of the many waiting souls who embraced the Faith manifested by the Báb and Bahá'u'lláh. These souls appear in every clime and in every stratum of life. For them it is sufficient merely to behold a ray of the Sun and they exclaim, 'We believe'. With the slightest movement of a finger, the veils are drawn aside and such souls become illumined by the light of the Divine Message.

Ḥájí Mírzá Ḥaydar-'Alí was one such person. He was born in Iṣfahán, where his father was one of the well-known dignitaries of the Muslim community and a prominent member of the Shaykhí sect. As such, he endeavoured to give his son the most suitable education of that time. The Ḥájí pursued the normal Islamic curriculum, which included the Qur'án, the Arabic language, interpretation, jurisprudence and rhetoric.

As a young man, the Ḥájí stood firm as he faced the baffling problems of life. It seemed that a certain mysterious power gave him the strength to remain steadfast and staunch against all sufferings and afflictions, including repeated exiles and imprisonment in horrible dungeons. When he reached the prime of his youth, there was no question about his moral strength and spiritual uprightness.

Someone mentioned to him the news of the advent of the Qá'im, and Ḥájí Mírzá Ḥaydar-'Alí plunged himself in the Ocean of the new Revelation. Thereafter, he faced nothing but tribulation, adversity, exile, and imprisonment. Never did he retaliate, nor did he manifest any sign of hostility or desire for retribution. Time and again, he faced the storms which raged about him and drew him into the vortex of misery. And yet, invariably, he was always ready to receive all blows with thanksgiving and radiant acquiescence.

Finally, the beloved Master, 'Abdu'l-Bahá, invited him to the Holy Land, where he lived to the end of his life. Letters often came to Haifa requesting the Ḥájí's presence in the eastern countries where the believers regarded with great affection this veteran soldier of the Army of Life. But 'Abdu'l-Bahá refused, often covering the Ḥájí with His own cloak and embracing him, repeating, 'Ḥájí is ours. Ḥájí is ours.'

During the long years of the Ḥájí's imprisonment, the attendants used to shave the heads of all the prisoners. And of course he was included. It became a habit of his to shave his head each day, and he continued to do so even after his release. One day, in Haifa, the Ḥájí complained of eye trouble. The beloved Master spontaneously advised him, 'Do not shave your head anymore. Try each day to write a few pages.'

Our Ḥájí followed these instructions strictly, and the sweet fruit of this daily exercise is the book which you are about to read.

A. Q. Faizí

A GROUP OF BELIEVERS AT THE TIME OF BAHÁ'U'LLÁH

Standing, from left to right: Ḥájí Mírzá Ḥaydar-'Alí, Jamál Effendi, Mírzá Abu'l-Qásim-i-Iṣfahání, Mi<u>sh</u>qín Qalam, Muḥammad-Riḍáy-i-<u>Sh</u>írází Qannád, and Mírzá Ja'far.

Seated from left to right: Mírzá Maḥmúd-i-Ká<u>sh</u>ání, Mírzá 'Abdu'l-Ra'úf, Mírzá Muḥsin Afnán, Mírzá Hádí Afnán (the father of Shoghi Effendi) and Zaynu'l-Muqarrabín.

A GROUP OF BAHÁ'ÍS IN THE HOLY LAND AT THE TIME OF 'ABDU'L-BAHÁ

Ḥájí Mírzá Ḥaydar-'Alí (second row, fourth from left).

The friends have often asked me how I first came in contact with the Faith and finally embraced it. The explanation is this: during my life in Iran, I often saw people mercilessly persecuted, often tortured and beaten to death. Sometimes I saw people hung by their ears or their hands and pelted with stones. Curious as to why such terrible punishments were being inflicted on these individuals, I approached many people and asked them about it. But the only answer I received was this: 'They are Bábís.'

My own spiritual quest had led me to many cities in Iran. I would enter a city and seek out all the religious leaders there. But I was always disappointed. While staying in Iṣfahán, I was invited one night to a garden. The men who were present talked about various subjects. Somehow the subject of the Báb and His religion was raised, and I took the opportunity to speak. 'This person made two great mistakes,' I said. 'Therefore, he was unable to accomplish his goals and was destroyed. First, he set himself against the established authorities, and, second, he tried to overturn the customs and beliefs of the masses. He should have allied himself with one or the other of these factions in order to gather support for his cause.'

One of those present responded politely, 'If this was a mistake, then it has been made by all the Prophets of God, including Muḥammad, the Seal of the Prophets, and all the Holy Imáms.'

I was surprised by this answer and also embarrassed that I had made such a false and simple-minded statement. I also realized that the one who answered me must be a Bábí and that there must be more to the Bábí Cause than I had previously thought.

I decided to become friends with this person, which was no easy task since all Bábís were in grave danger and had to be extremely cautious. Nevertheless, he eventually adopted me as his student, though he was at first afraid that I might be insincere in my quest. Fearful of the consequences of revealing his own inner convictions, he scarcely told me anything. Although he did not speak of the Cause, he was preparing the ground for a sacred and fruitful conversation, and gradually I won his confidence.

It happened one day that I saw a large crowd gathered in one of the squares of the city. I was attracted by the noise and commotion and drew closer. There I saw five siyyids, mullás, and merchants, well dressed and from the respectable classes. Their ears had been nailed to a post, and soldiers were beating them with sticks, demanding that they recant their faith. I was amazed that, even in that desperate condition, those believers were calm and patient and thankful. They refused to recant and quoted passages from the Qur'án to prove the claims of their Prophet, the Báb.

As I observed their steadfastness and submission to the Will of God, the fire of search was inflamed within me and I caught a glimpse of the grandeur of this Cause.

After I had become intimate with my friend, and when he was assured of my sincerity, he revealed to me that he was a Bábí, and we began to discuss the Faith. We were afraid of being discovered, so we could not meet openly. The times and places of our meetings kept shifting. Some nights he would invite me to his house – but always after midnight. When I entered the house, I had to hide myself in the corridor until we were sure that all the members of the household were in bed and sound asleep. Then, and only then, would my friend come for me and conduct me quietly to the kitchen. There we would study the Báb's Writings and chant prayers. At times, when it was too dark and we were unable to see the words, the only thing we could do was place a candle on the floor of the oven, then hold the Writings to the light and, with great difficulty, study them.

When my friend came to my house, it was with the same secrecy. Sometimes it would become even more difficult. We could not have meetings of more than three or four persons, and then only late at night. Once, I rented the upper room of a certain house. My room had a window that opened on the garden. So that the people in the house would not know where I went at night, I used to climb down from the window by a rope tied to the iron bars, and return to my room the same way before sunrise to sleep.

My father was not a believer. He was a Shaykhí and a follower of Ḥájí Muḥammad Karím Khán.[1] He was firmly against my Faith and would follow me to many places to voice his opposition to my beliefs. We exchanged some letters, but they did not help. Eventually he left Kirmán in quest of me and found me in the small town of Ná'ín. He hoped that there he would be able to educate and guide me, since most of the people of the town were followers of Karím Khán.

My father went to the governor of the town, whom he knew personally, and asked for me to be brought to him. I was summoned to the governor's house. But with the assistance of God, I was able to speak in a manner that pleased everyone. They all encouraged me and spoke words of approval. 'The grace of Ḥájí Muḥammad Karím Khán has encircled you and protected you', they said. 'He has not allowed you to go astray.'

Every morning it was their custom to recite verses from the Qur'án after prayers. It was my honour to recite these verses, and everyone was always pleased to hear those beautiful words. To open the way for our discussion, I began to include verses of the Báb with those from the Qur'án. No one criticized me – or even detected that verses other than those from the Qur'án were being chanted. This gave me an opportunity to present my argument to the people in the room, particularly my father.

An uncle of mine, Ḥájí Muḥammad-'Alí, lived in Ná'ín. He was a good friend of mine and knew of my correspondence with my father. So I asked him if he would be willing to hide me and protect me and take me secretly to Iṣfahán. He accepted, and I prepared to leave.

I went to the hall where my father and the governor and several other people were seated. I sat next to my father and said to him, 'Suppose I had been born blind and could not know you by sight. Could I not certainly recognize you by your voice?'

'What is your aim in asking this question?' he responded.

'Let me finish the premise, then you will comprehend the purpose of my question', I replied. 'Suppose, again, that you were to go on an extensive trip and return home only after a long time. I shall still know you by your voice and shall naturally run to you. When I receive kindness, compassion, and love, I shall know for certain that the newcomer is my father.'

All present agreed, 'This is true. It is obvious and understandable.'

'Now, here is my question', I continued. 'When I chanted the verses of the Qur'án for you, I often included in the texts verses revealed by the Báb. I am sure you recognize the verses of the Prophet Muḥammad by His words, tone, and style. Then, why did no one protest? Surely, only because the words revealed by the Báb have the same tone, vigour, and style, and come from the same Source.'

This concluded the discussion. I left the hall quickly and made for my uncle's house. I stayed in his house for a month, until all efforts to find me were exhausted. Then I secretly left Ná'ín and travelled to Iṣfahán.

My father and others came to Iṣfahán looking for me, and there they made efforts to have me killed or imprisoned. But the Ḥujjatu'l-Islám,[2] Siyyid Asadu'lláh, was a very influential man in Iṣfahán and was related to me through my mother. The followers of Karím Khán were rejected by the prominent 'ulamá in Iṣfahán, and the two groups were openly hostile to one another. Seeing only that I was opposed to these people whom they hated, the 'ulamá protected me. My enemies were defeated, and I was victorious. But when my father died, I learned that he had disinherited me.

In Iṣfahán, I spent most of my time in the presence of Zaynu'l-Muqarrabín.[3] We used to go to distant and desolate places far from the tumult of the towns and villages, just to be together, study the Writings, chant prayers, and discuss the Cause of God. These moments of joy kept us alive, but we longed to teach and make His Name known in any way we could.

We tried different methods of approach. We went to an Indian who claimed to have some medical knowledge, and Jináb-i-Zayn[4] opened the discussion by saying, 'I feel a painful sensation in my heart. I know of no physician who can help me.'

'What is the cause?' asked the physician.

Jináb-i-Zayn replied, 'A few days ago, I was walking in the street when suddenly I beheld a strange sight. Some people, held captive and helpless in the hands of a savage mob, were being tortured and mercilessly persecuted. I was so disturbed and alarmed that, ever since then, I have felt this pain in my heart.' Then Jináb-i-Zayn went on to tell the Indian doctor about the Revelation of the Báb, His tragic history, and His Writings.

One day we were outside the city of Iṣfahán in a very pleasant place where there was a mosque and a stream and a few trees. We had taken provisions to spend the night. We went to the mosque, where we planned to stay. A few of the inhabitants were curious, so they entered the mosque and someone asked me where I was from. I had a slight Iṣfahání accent, but I said that I was from Shíráz.

'Why are you lying?' the man replied. 'It is obvious that you are from Iṣfahán. Seventy thousand angels will curse a liar.'

'Have you seen those angels?' I asked, hoping to create an opportunity to teach the Faith.

'Why shouldn't I have seen them?' he replied. 'They are recorded in the authentic traditions of our Faith.'

I was rather incautious and said, 'Yes, I can tell that you have the spiritual discernment to have seen them.'

Then they guessed our secret and immediately cried out, 'These people are Bábís! Come and get them!' And we were forced to leave all of our belongings behind and run away.

These problems often occurred. There is one funny story about a certain siyyid who was a student in a religious school. I used to speak to him and I invited him to my home a few times. He claimed to have accepted the Faith. He got to know a few of the believers, and some of the Writings of the Báb were given to him.

Then someone informed me that the siyyid had said to him, 'I have got to know some Bábís. When I meet all of them and find out what their schemes are, I plan to inform the authorities and have them all arrested.'

The siyyid was living at the religious school at the time. So I went to the headmaster of the school and told him that he had a student who was a Bábí and was in possession of some of the Writings of the Báb. I also made sure that someone told the siyyid what I had done. When he heard this he was overtaken by fear, and, leaving all his belongings behind, he fled from the town and never returned.

A few years later, I was going from Shíráz to Búshihr. On the way, I stopped at a mosque in a small town, not knowing that this same siyyid now lived there. He saw me and recognized me. Seeing an opportunity to take his revenge, he approached me and said, 'Do you remember what you did to me in Iṣfahán?'

‘Yes’, I replied. ‘You are that same Bábí student who was going to be arrested and killed in Iṣfahán. Now you have come here and have become a leader of Muslims in this mosque.’

He was so frightened by my reply that the whole time I was in that place he would not leave my side, fearing that I would denounce him to others. He brought me food and tea until I left.

Although I was often persecuted in Iṣfahán and sometimes suffered great hardships, I was happy. I was in love with the Writings of the Báb, especially the Persian Bayán. Every day I would transcribe a portion of this book. In those days many were convinced that the advent of ‘Him Whom God shall make manifest’ could not be far off. I used to say that if the Báb had not manifested Himself, then the writings of Shaykh Aḥmad and Siyyid Káẓim[5] would have been left useless and unfulfilled. Now, similarly, if the Dispensation of the Báb were not followed by the Revelation of ‘Him Whom God shall make manifest’, then the Writings of the Báb would have no purpose.

I did not like Azal.[6] I used to say, ‘What is the difference between the “hidden Azal” and the Hidden Imám of Islám?’[7] Furthermore, I thought that his writings were just nonsense, except when he quoted from the Writings of the Báb. But I was confused and uncertain about these thoughts.

Then Jináb-i-Zayn brought me two Tablets of Bahá’u’lláh. I recognized a certain mysterious power and magic in every word. I fell in love with these Writings. Later, Ḥájí Siyyid Muḥammad Afnán, the uncle of the Báb, came to Iṣfahán and brought with him a precious gift – a copy of the Kitáb-i-Íqán, the Book of Certitude, which had been revealed in answer to his own questions. When I read this volume, I became a thousand times more attracted to Bahá’u’lláh, His Utterances, and His Writings. I would openly say that I regarded the Writings of Bahá’u’lláh as the greatest miracle ever performed. But some people were not happy with my views.

One of Azal’s supporters told me, ‘Bahá’u’lláh wants to take advantage of the prophecies of the Báb and claim the position of “Him Whom God shall make manifest”. Therefore, he has imprisoned Azal. Sometimes he beats him and forces him to produce books which Bahá’u’lláh then publishes in his own name.’

When he said these things I was amazed. I had never heard such nonsense. I protested that the Kitáb-i-Íqán was a matchless work, while the writings of Azal were neither significant nor well written. He claimed that the Íqán was written by Azal and that those writings which were attributed to him were not really his. This increased my amazement. However, since the conversation was friendly and confidential, I did not argue with him but kept the matter to myself.

I continued to transcribe the Bayán. But soon I became too well known in Iṣfahán, and my friends began to avoid me. Finally I was left alone and homeless.

There was a large, abandoned religious school where only a poor teacher conducted children's classes. I found lodging in a room in this old school. I had nothing with me but a copy of the Qur'án, the Bayán, the Kitáb-i-Íqán, and the Ma<u>th</u>naví.[8] I prepared myself for four months of retreat.

The caretaker used to prepare food for me, and as long as I lived in that dilapidated place, I met no one and no one knew I was there. Gradually I began to realize that seclusion is a waste of one's life. I reminded myself that one's actions should be pleasing to God, but this could not be accomplished unless one was of service and guided the people to the right path of God, that is, to His new Manifestation. Therefore, I decided to leave Iṣfahán.

For more than six years I journeyed from town to town and from village to village, across the length and breadth of central Iran. Although I travelled under the most difficult circumstances, I was in a state of the utmost joy. Everywhere, I proclaimed the advent of the Báb and the Expected One Whom God would make manifest. On many occasions people attacked me, beat me, imprisoned me, and caused me unbearable suffering. Very often I was beaten more than I had appetite for.

On one occasion, when I had been beaten most severely and my body was covered with wounds, one of the members of the 'Alíyu'lláhí sect came to my rescue. These people have peculiar and exaggerated ideas concerning the rank and position of 'Alí, the cousin of the Prophet Muḥammad. This man offered me hospitality until my wounds were healed. When I regained enough strength, I resumed my journey.

I went to <u>Sh</u>íráz and proceeded directly to the Ílk<u>h</u>ání Mosque, where Mullá Ḥusayn and his friends had once taken lodging. While I was there, I met Ḥájí Siyyid Muḥammad Afnán (the uncle of the Báb) and some other believers. I found the friends in Shíráz to be wholeheartedly attracted to Bahá'u'lláh. There was no mention of Azal. Jináb-i-Afnán's[9] countenance was always beaming with joy and sweet smiles.

One of the friends, Siyyid 'Abdu'l-Raḥím, who was well versed in the Bayán, had extracted many verses with which he would prove that the One Who would be manifested could be none other than Bahá'u'lláh, and that Azal was only a name without a reality. That same siyyid related the following story:

'After the martyrdom of the Báb, when Azal had become famous, I travelled to Ṭihrán just to meet him. But I remembered that, when I was in Badasht, I had seen manifest reverence paid to Bahá'u'lláh by no less than Quddús and Ṭáhirih, and, as a matter of fact, by every person in that great conference.

'When I reached Ṭihrán, I met Bahá'u'lláh in the bazaar. At this time, His glory was hidden under a myriad veils of light. He approached me and asked me if I had come to see Azal. I answered affirmatively. I went, in His company, to His house. Once there, He asked for tea to be served. Azal brought the samovar, served the tea, and remained standing in the presence of Bahá'u'lláh. Bahá'u'lláh spoke to me, and rivers of knowledge and wisdom flowed forth from His mouth. After drinking the tea, He stood up, turned to Azal, and said, "He has come to see you". Then He went into the inner court of the house. Azal sat down. I bowed low before him to express my respect. Naturally, I expected him to speak to me, but he said nothing at all.'

To earn my living, I would transcribe books for people. At times I became a doctor. At other times I wrote amulets and foretold the future. Sometimes I was an exorcist. By the grace of God, I was successful at whatever I attempted. The money I thus earned I divided in two parts: some to cover the bare necessities of my own life and the rest to feed the destitute. Some nights I had nothing but water.

In those days, one often met men called dervishes, who spent their time, wealth, and energy trying to discover what they called 'the elixir', a substance with which they would be able to change base metal into gold. They had many old manuscripts describing the process, and I was able to increase my income by copying some of these old books for them. They really believed that eventually they would be able to change mountains into masses of gold.

I am always astounded by the fact that the followers of the already established religions will deny whatever proof we offer them of the truth of the Message of God for this Day but will believe in all sorts of miracles performed not only by their own Prophets, but by mysterious forces emanating from the graves of some of their followers.

Eventually I made my way to Baghdád, travelling that great distance on foot. I traversed deserts and mountains, living very frugally. Although I endured many physical deprivations, I still remember, often and lovingly, the joy of those days. Sometimes I long for a moment of those intoxicating times.

I used to walk for several days before I would reach a village where I could rest to cure the blisters and regain strength to resume my journey. Some of the innkeepers were very hard. Either they would not allow me to enter or they would demand exorbitant prices. Nevertheless, I continued my long march toward the city of Baghdád.

I already knew that Jináb-i-Zayn was in Baghdád and that most of the friends did business in a marketplace called the Súqu'l-Ḥaráj. When I reached Baghdád, I immediately made for this market and, with the help of friends, sought Jináb-i-Zayn.

An uncle of mine, whom I had never seen, had decided to transfer his residence from Iran to the holy cities of Karbilá and Najaf. His name was Mírzá Muḥammad-i-Vakíl.[10] I did not know that he had become a believer. Through Jináb-i-Zayn we met each other. He took me to his house and showed me much kind hospitality. I later learned that among the more than eighty believers who had been imprisoned and exiled from Baghdád to Mosul, were my uncle and Jináb-i-Zayn. After some years my uncle returned to Baghdád, and Jináb-i-Zayn, on Bahá'u'lláh's instructions, made the Holy Land his home.

Ismu'lláh Munír[11] was in Baghdád when I arrived there. Munír was a great man adorned with all the heavenly virtues. I spent much of my time with this illumined and illustrious soul. A certain friend called Áqá Mírzá Javád also lived in that town. He had committed to memory the text of the entire Qayyúmu'l-Asmá', the Commentary on the Súra of Joseph written by the Báb. He used to recite it and explain the words of the Báb. He was faithful to Bahá'u'lláh and would not say anything about Azal.

After some time I returned to Shíráz by way of Baṣrih and Búshihr. In Shíráz I happened to meet Shujá'u'l-Mulk, one of the army chiefs who had fought against Vaḥíd in Nayríz. Though an enemy of the Cause, he confessed that Vaḥíd was the most erudite person of his time, particularly with regard to the Qur'án and its interpretation. He even went on to state that Vaḥíd and his followers had fought as courageously as the martyrs of Karbilá.[12]

I also met the treasurer of Prince Mihdí Qulí Mírzá, one of those who commanded the government forces in the Ṭabarsí upheavals.[13] He told me that there were three statements which he considered to be monstrous lies: 'One, that I embraced this religion and then recanted my faith. Whoever says this lies when he claims that I converted and lies when he claims that I recanted. Two, that Mullá Ḥusayn fought with me and wounded me. Anyone whom Mullá Ḥusayn struck in battle died immediately. Three, that I fought with Mullá Ḥusayn face to face. Actually, he was facing away from me, and I shot him in the back and killed him.'

In Ṭihrán I again met Jináb-i-Munír. Since he knew of my convictions and of my love for the Ancient Beauty,[14] he showed me a Tablet called the Súriy-i-Aṣḥáb, which had been revealed in his honour by Bahá'u'lláh. As I read this Tablet, I felt in every verse a fire of enthusiasm, and I could not control my feelings. So I turned to Jináb-i-Munír and asked him whether Siyyid Muḥammad[15] had deceived Azal, or Azal had deceived Siyyid Muḥammad, or whether the two of them had simply joined together in rebellion against Bahá'u'lláh. When Jináb-i-Munír heard these words he embraced me and kissed me and said, 'The enemies of Bahá'u'lláh are united in one thing alone, and that is to join forces against Him. They deceive and mislead each other in order to oppose Him.'

I was set on fire by reading the Súriy-i-Aṣḥáb. I felt such joy and spiritual exultation that even now, after fifty years, although I am getting older and all my senses are waning, the mere thought of those memorable moments sets my soul ablaze and ignites the lamp of my heart.

The Báb proclaimed the glad tidings of the advent of Bahá'u'lláh, and in the six years of His ministry He prepared the people perfectly, made the way clear, and planted the seeds of love and obedience to the Promised

One in the hearts of the Bábís. Bahá'u'lláh served the Bábí Faith and educated, protected, and nurtured the Bábís in such a way that eventually ninety-nine out of a hundred came to recognize in Him the fulfilment of all the promises of the Báb. Bahá'u'lláh sowed the seeds, provided them with the water they needed, protected them from the evil deeds of the enemies, attended them tenderly, and encouraged them to grow more vigorous each day. Therefore, when the hour decreed by God arrived and Bahá'u'lláh received His station, the true believers turned their hearts and souls to the Ancient Beauty and found no veil but light, and no hindrance but intense splendour.

Najaf-'Alí[16] was one of those true believers. At the time of his martyrdom he gave thanks and was heard to say, 'We have found Bahá and we hasten to offer our lives as a sacrifice to Him. He is our ransom.' He was so enkindled that he hastened to his death with the utmost joy and exultation. When the cup of martyrdom was brought to him and he saw it overflowing, he exclaimed, 'There is a custom in our province. The bride is taken on horseback to the house of her future husband. When the bridegroom sees his bride approaching, he gives the owner of the horse sumptuous gifts such as costly clothes and gold coins.' He then addressed the executioner, saying, 'I have long stored these gold coins for this day – the day of my greatest happiness. Here they are! Take them!' Then he pulled out a sack of coins from his pocket and with intense joy offered it to his executioner.

Another believer, being taken to his death, asked the executioner, 'Would you be so kind as to cut my vein first and give me time before the final blow?' The executioner, hoping that the old man would recant his faith, held his dagger to his victim's neck, making a wound. To his extreme surprise, he found the martyr holding his hands like a cup and filling them with his blood. The believer then cried out, 'O people, be my witness! Here I testify to the truth of my faith with my own blood.'

It was near Naw-Rúz when I made for Adrianople. On the way, I passed through Qazvín, where I went to the house of Mírzá Muḥammad-'Alí Kad-Khudá, who was one of the notables and dignitaries of the province. I met some of the friends there. My host related to me the following:

'I was a dervish and the follower of a mystic leader called Mírzá Kúchik-i-Shírází. He knew Ṭáhirih and had extraordinary power. Because of this I once asked my mystic leader, "What do you think of the Báb's claim?"

to which he retorted, "The Báb has written a unique and unsurpassed commentary on the Súra of Kawthar. Should He lay down His pen, no one of the past or present would ever dare to pick it up. But, unfortunately, He has not studied under or served any of the mystic leaders."

'This answer made me sad and forced me to contemplate the words he had spoken. I repeated to myself again and again, "He says that no one can ever dare to pick up His pen, yet He must be schooled and trained by a mystic leader like himself. How strange!" As a matter of fact, his answer drew me to the Báb and I embraced His Faith.'

In Zanján I met 'Abá-Basír, Siyyid Ashraf, and Mullá Ibráhím.

Mullá Ibráhím was from a village near Iṣfahán. This simple-hearted and innocent man had suffered so much in his own village that he was forced to forsake his home, friends, and relatives and seek refuge and shelter in this far-off district of Iran.

Before he left his village he had been in prison. As was the case in those days, the jailer constantly demanded bribes from the prisoners in exchange for providing them with the barest essentials of life. Mullá Ibráhím told the jailers that he had no money but was willing to work. So he earned his frugal living as a labourer in the prison. After he was released from prison, he went to his village to gather a little money from the sale of his house and property, but he learned that his relatives had taken everything. In order to find shelter and security, he left home, village, and relatives for a distant province in the north.

His joy was to work, earn a little money, spend very little on himself, and give the rest to the poor. He agreed to go with me on pilgrimage to Adrianople and promised to meet me in Tabríz. On his way there, two men clad as dervishes joined him, pretending to be believers on their way to Adrianople. They won his confidence; then they stole what little money he had and ran away. He reached Tabríz empty-handed but determined to go on with me despite his misfortune.

Now, on my way to Adrianople, many thoughts passed through my mind. In my childhood I had learned a tradition about how a man shall meet his Lord on the Day of Judgment. According to this tradition, those who are honoured with meeting their Lord on this Day will find themselves intoxicated with the wine of paradise and will experience such joy as is beyond description. I knew that the true meaning of this tradition was to attain the presence of the Manifestation of God and that such a meeting would be as heaven on earth. I was fond of this tradition, and by the grace of God I was permitted to discover for myself that it was true.

I also had a conversation with Ḥájí Siyyid Javád-i-Karbilá'í. This great man had the honour of meeting and studying with Shaykh Aḥmad and Siyyid Káẓim. He became one of the early believers in the Báb, and he embraced the Faith of Bahá'u'lláh and lived near Him during the Baghdád period. The Báb appointed him one of the Mirrors of the Dispensation of the Bayán. A follower of Azal once asked Siyyid Javád, in the presence of others, to describe the countenance of the Báb. He immediately said, 'He was unsurpassed in beauty and sweetness. Have you heard of the beauty of Joseph?[17] This is what I mean.' Fearing that his answer might be taken to mean that he was a follower of Azal, I asked him about Bahá'u'lláh, and he immediately replied, 'Know with certainty that if anyone, friend or enemy, claims to have looked directly into His eyes, he is a liar. I tested this again and again but all my attempts to look at Him were in vain. Sometimes the friends were so carried away in His presence that, in their bewilderment, they would forget the world within and without. Can one fix one's gaze upon the sun?'

During the seven months I stayed in Adrianople, I came to realize what those words of Ḥájí Siyyid Javád meant. Fifteen years after that, I went to 'Akká to visit Bahá'u'lláh. Often I desired to know what colour of táj He wore, and yet I forgot to think of it every time I was in His presence. One day, He was having His midday meal in a small room at the Garden of Riḍván. Some of the friends were inside, while others were standing in rows outside. From behind the crowd of believers, at last I could glimpse the marvellous táj on His head. Its colour was green.

What happened in my soul and heart while I was with Him was an inner and mysterious experience beyond the scope of my words to describe. One of the mullás of Iṣfahán once asked me, 'What did you see when you were in His presence?'

I said, 'I had expected to see all sorts of miracles. I also had several questions that I wanted to ask. But when I attained His presence, all this became unimportant. I had found the pure water which quenches thirst and gives true life.'

The mullá asked, 'What did you see?'

'I saw the form of a human being', I replied. 'But His every step and movement was like a miracle to me. I saw Him and my eyes could take in nothing else, for He is different from all others in His bearing and in His manner. He is unique by Himself. No one in the world can ever be compared to Him. He is the One Whom the Qur'án has declared to have neither father nor son.'[18]

'But Bahá'u'lláh's father was well known!' the man replied. 'And his son, 'Abbás Effendi, is renowned for his perfections!'

'I saw neither father nor son', was my response. 'Bahá'u'lláh alone is the Source of God's Revelation. He is the One Who "begetteth not, nor is He begotten." If you stand before a mirror and speak your name, your image will do likewise, but it is an illusion.' The clergyman was pleased with my answer and asked me more about the Faith.

One of the most famous merchants of Qazvín was Ḥájí Muḥammad-Báqir. Not only was he well known as a merchant, but he was also prominent in his service to the Cause, a service which was much appreciated by all the believers. Once he sent a letter to Bahá'u'lláh asking Him to bestow upon him the bounty of wealth so that he could serve the Cause with greater capacity. Bahá'u'lláh answered that the doors of wealth would be opened to him from all sides, but he must be ever vigilant lest material prosperity become a veil between him and his Creator.

Bahá'u'lláh also said to those in His presence at the time that Muḥammad-Báqir would soon be drowned in wealth, but material success would close his eyes to the realities of life to such a degree that he would turn his back on the Cause and even deny God. But he would suffer tremendous losses and would return to his Lord in repentance. Because of his repentance, God would change his losses into ample profits to such an extent as to enable him to become the leading merchant in Tabríz and Constantinople. This time, he would become even more proud and would again ignore the Faith, and then his wealth would be gone forever. He would no longer be able to trade and would become helpless. He would then return in repentance once more and remain poor but content. In this state, he would serve the Cause and achieve great success in his service to God. At the end of His wondrous and ominous statement, Bahá'u'lláh addressed me and advised that I should remember all the events as they unfolded.

After some time, Muḥammad-Báqir's brother was arrested and thrown into prison because of his Faith. Muḥammad-Báqir paid a large sum of money to obtain his brother's release. After that, Muḥammad-Báqir made his way to Constantinople. Upon his arrival, he recanted his faith and approached the court of the sulṭán and the Persian ambassador, begging them to consider him a true Muslim.

Bahá'u'lláh immediately remarked that this was the starting point of the chain of events he had described before.

I then went to Constantinople, where I stayed fourteen months. There, I learned that Muḥammad-Báqir had purchased great quantities of cotton. All of a sudden, the price of cotton dropped so low that our friend lost his wealth and became submerged in debt. In this deplorable condition, he again remembered his Lord and wrote a letter to Bahá'u'lláh in which he repented and begged Him to come to his aid. Bahá'u'lláh replied, assuring him that he would regain his wealth.

When I was in Egypt, I learned that the price of cotton had risen sharply. Muḥammad-Báqir's wealth grew to ten times more than ever before. Although he had been tested once, he fell a second time into the trap of greed and failed to know his Lord and Provider. Bahá'u'lláh wrote to him again and alerted him to the danger of material temptation. He exhorted him to remain steadfast in the Path of God and grateful for His bounties. But once more Muḥammad-Báqir ignored God and remained heedless.

When after many years I found him again in Tabríz, he told me, 'After I received the Tablet, it seemed to me that even the nails and curtains on the walls of my room had ears to hearken and obey. One by one, all of my possessions slipped quietly from me. I was reduced to poverty and was forced to leave Constantinople for Tabríz where I live in this house, which belongs to my wife, and wear clothes that are made by my children.'

Azal wrote a letter to the governor of Adrianople complaining about Bahá'u'lláh. He had no aim in doing so except to heap calumny on Bahá'u'lláh and attempt to place Him in an untenable position. The governor, who knew Bahá'u'lláh, took Azal's letter to His house and sought His instructions. The Ancient Beauty replied, 'Ask him to come and see Me. If he comes, then whatever he says is right.'

The governor asked Azal to go to the house where he could meet Bahá'u'lláh. To this simple request Azal answered, 'We do not go to each other's houses, and He will not come to the governor's house.' Eventually the Great Mosque of Sulṭán Salím was chosen as the meeting place for Bahá'u'lláh and Azal.

On a Friday morning, Bahá'u'lláh started out for the mosque. The people, anticipating His approach, thronged the way between His house and the mosque. All stood in reverence and awe to receive His blessing, hoping for even one glimpse of Him. The street was so full of people that all other travel was stopped. The people in the crowd spontaneously raised their voices in salutation and praise. They tried to approach Him, and some prostrated themselves in His path, hoping to kiss His feet. With great joy and respect for Bahá'u'lláh, they elbowed one another and made way for Him to pass through. In response to all these reverent salutations, Bahá'u'lláh raised His hand again and again and pronounced words of greeting: *Marḥabá! Marḥabá! Báraka'lláhu fíkum* (Greetings! Greetings! May God bless you all).

As soon as He entered the mosque, the preacher who was addressing the immense congregation from his high pulpit stopped the sermon and fell silent – either by choice or because he forgot what he had to say. Bahá'u'lláh took His seat and asked the man to continue. Time passed and everyone expected Azal to arrive also, but to their great surprise he never appeared.

There are dervishes who gather together, usually on Friday mornings, to sing the poems of the Mat͟hnaví, and to mention the names of God, repeating, 'He is God! O God!' To the rhythm of this chant and the sound of music and drums, the worshippers sing and sing, dance and dance, whirl and whirl, gradually increasing their speed until they become intoxicated with the mention of God and are attracted to Him, and His greatness and majesty. On that Friday morning, when Bahá'u'lláh left the mosque to return to His house, He heard the dervishes singing, and He said to His companions, 'Mawláná[19] needs a visit from Us.' The governor, his officials, and the notables of the town, finding this a great and unique opportunity, followed Bahá'u'lláh.

The mayor, Shaykhu'l-Islám, and the 'ulamá kept a distance of at least five paces behind Him. Every now and then Bahá'u'lláh would stop and ask them to approach, but they remained where they were, saluting Him in their fashion by placing their hands on their chests and bowing their heads in utter respect and reverence. In this order, they followed Bahá'u'lláh into the takyih.[20] The dervishes were in the midst of their shouting and rapid whirling, and the music was louder than ever. But when Bahá'u'lláh entered the takyih, the proceedings came to a stop and all fell absolutely silent. Bahá'u'lláh sat down and very graciously motioned to His companions to take a seat where they could; then He allowed the dervishes to resume their activities.

The night after that memorable day, I had the honour of being in His presence. Bahá'u'lláh said that when He entered the mosque, the preacher forgot his sermon; and when He entered the takyih, the dervishes stopped, awestruck, and were unable to continue singing and whirling. As the people of the world are brought up and trained in vain imaginings, they take such events as miracles, but God and His Prophets are in realms beyond Man's reach and comprehension.

In Adrianople, as well as in the Holy Land, I heard Him tell us about the events of His own life. He often remarked that should the people ponder the life of the Báb – His captivity, imprisonment, and martyrdom, and His Writings – they would surely realize what a gift He gave to the world, that throughout such an eventful life, the hand of God remained forever far above the understanding and reach of man.

Pondering His life, captivity, and exiles, one would surely come to realize that enemies of the Faith, their rulers, potentates, and kings, despite their well-equipped soldiers, well-organized plans, and cunning stratagems, were invariably turned into an army which caused the progress, proclamation, and solidarity of the Faith of God.

In the early days of the Faith in Iṣfahán, when I first became acquainted with the beautiful Writings of the Báb, I was captured by their power and majesty. The words were like a string of pearls. The proofs and arguments of the friends were so overwhelming that I felt no one could ever deny their truth. But when I was alone I would become the target of suspicions, vain imaginings, and evil whisperings. All that I had read and learned previously would then come before me. The purgatory implied in all the

Books of God surrounded me. To overcome this terrible period of testing was indeed difficult. Only God knows of my anguish and the many hours I wept. I passed many a sleepless night when rest and comfort abandoned me. Some days I concentrated so much on my own spiritual dilemma that I forgot to eat. Many a time I pushed away all evil thoughts and became a firm believer, but with the slightest negative thought I would once again retreat and almost deny my new-found belief.

Then, one night, I dreamed that a town crier appeared in the bazaar of Iṣfahán, announcing the advent of the Prophet Muḥammad and proclaiming that whoever wished to meet Him could go to a certain house and attain His presence. He said that a glimpse of His countenance was even more worthy than service in this world and the world to come. On hearing this, I hastened to the house wherein the Prophet Muḥammad was said to be, and, having entered, I prostrated myself at His feet. He lifted me up with utmost love, and then He addressed me, saying, 'One may claim that he has come here only for the sake of God, and has attained the presence of his Lord, only when he has stood firm against a world of enemies who have drawn their swords against him because he has embraced this Cause. Otherwise, he cannot say that his motive was to find God.'

I awoke and found myself in a state of joy and certitude. At that moment I came to understand the mystery of suffering and the reason why the followers of all the Prophets have suffered. I rebuked myself time and again, and said, 'I had read all those heavenly utterances of the Báb, yet I had to reach the state of belief and certitude through a dream.'

Fourteen years later, I found myself in Adrianople, where I stayed for about seven months. One night, when I was in the tearoom with Áqá Muḥammad-Qulí, I felt a longing to be in the presence of Bahá'u'lláh, even for a short while. I had not the courage to ask for such an audience since it was very late. Suddenly, 'Abdu'l-Bahá opened the door and asked me to follow Him. Having left the room, I found Bahá'u'lláh walking on the roofed area of the house. Some of the friends were standing and listening to His utterances.

Then I was admitted to the presence of the Ancient Beauty. I prostrated myself at His feet. He picked me up with love and gentleness and said, 'One may claim that he has come here only for the sake of God, and has attained the presence of his Lord, only when he has stood firm against a world of enemies who have drawn their swords against him because he has embraced this Cause.'

As I write this I have not the slightest intention of relating a miracle, but only wish to state the facts as they occurred. We cannot comprehend such confirmations from the Chosen Ones of God. The faculty of Man's understanding may be likened to a man who is lame or paralysed, while the minds of the Prophets of God move as swiftly as lightning through the firmament. How could these two forces ever come together?

That evening there was talk of my leaving Adrianople. Bahá'u'lláh sent a message to find out about my plans – whether I desired to stay or depart, and if the latter, when and to where. I hastened to the beloved Master, 'Abdu'l-Bahá, and begged Him, 'Please do not abandon me to myself. Do not ask me about my desire, plan, or will. Let His will be done. Let Him order me to go and confirm me to do whatever He desires. I am homeless, of simple needs, and have no one who depends upon me.' My plea was accepted and His instructions were conveyed to me that I should take up residence in Constantinople with the responsibility to receive Tablets and letters, and dispatch them to their destinations, and also to help the friends on their way to and from pilgrimage in Adrianople.

My companion in Constantinople was Mírzá Ḥusayn, and my joy and consolation was to have in my possession the Tablets I had brought in the handwriting of the Master and Mírzá Músá (Áqáy-i-Kalím).[21] What a joyful time was ours!

We had the honour of meeting the believers, receiving Tablets, dispatching them regularly to the friends, and preparing those things which were required for the household in Adrianople. I also had an opportunity to meet the pilgrims on their way to Adrianople. They had to remain a few days in Constantinople making preparations for the journey or seeking permission from Bahá'u'lláh for pilgrimage. They also stayed a few days on their way back.

Jináb-i-Kalím used to write regularly and keep us in touch with the glorious tidings from the presence of Bahá'u'lláh. And Áqá Muḥammad-'Alí would write concerning the purchase of things required for the House in Adrianople. Once he ordered some tea. I purchased some and sent it, but he was not satisfied with its quality and wrote me a very gentle letter pointing out that I should pay more attention because such goods were to be used by the Holy Family. Being young, haughty, and proud, I took offense at this small piece of kindly advice. In a state of bitterness I wrote an answer which was not courteous and, indeed, not even worthy of a believer.

A little time passed, and I received a Tablet from Bahá'u'lláh assuring me that all my services had been graciously accepted and expressing His approval and pleasure. When I read this Tablet, I realized that the letter I had written had been a grave mistake. Having lived seven months in His presence, I had come to know that this Supreme Manifestation of God chastises the souls of sinners with the scourge of love and compassion, for their own edification. He conceals our mistakes and forgives us so that the wrongdoers will receive divine education. In addition to that, His forgiving and merciful attitude to the people shows them by example the right path to tolerance and servitude.

When, through this bountiful attitude, I was awakened and came to realize what an impolite letter I had written to one of the servants of the Household, I turned to God, wept, and prayed fervently for forgiveness. I was in a deep state of distress and dismay. Again, I turned to 'Abdu'l-Bahá for help. I implored the Master to intervene and ask forgiveness for me. Then instructions came that I should go to Egypt. This assured me that I had been honoured with the garment of pardon and mercy. Before departing, I went to Adrianople on another pilgrimage. During the last moment of my audience with Bahá'u'lláh, He assured me that I would attain His presence again.

Before I had reached the continent of Africa, the Persians in Constantinople had written to those in Egypt warning them about the arrival of 'the Gabriel of the Bábís'. This made many of them hasten to my place of residence to behold such an unusual creature – a Bábí. Some came in and inquired, 'Why did you abandon Muḥammad, the Seal of the Prophets? Why did you withdraw your hand from the hem of the garment of our innocent Imáms? Why did you exclude yourselves from the Muslim community?'

I was at a loss for what to say or do! I had been instructed to be cautious and even to remain unknown. Now, if I hid myself and my faith, and did not utter a word in answer to these questions, they would accuse me of being a coward or of being ashamed of my beliefs. I knew there would be no end to such questions, but I felt that I needed to give some response, so they would not consider the followers of the Faith ignorant or unfaithful. Therefore, I answered them.

'We are not here to cause confusion or dissension', I said. 'Will you not show some kindness and let us discuss things on the basis of mutual understanding and good will? Let us fix our sole aim on finding out the truth.

'All that you have said so far consists of accusations and slander against us and has no basis at all. We believe wholeheartedly that the Qur'án is the Book of God, that obedience to it is compulsory, and that its verses are a guide to the path of truth. It is in this Book that we find the story in which a man from the family of Pharaoh, who was a believer and concealed his faith, said, "Will ye slay a man because he saith my lord is God, when He hath already come to you with signs from your Lord? If he be a liar, on him will be his lie, but if he be a man of truth, part of what he threatened will fall upon you. In truth, God guideth not him who is a transgressor, a liar."

'Surely you have heard of a certain notable from the lineage of the Prophet Muḥammad. Though this Siyyid was saintly in every aspect of His life and guided the people to God and His Prophets, He was severely persecuted, exiled, imprisoned, and finally put to death by a firing squad of many soldiers. You also have heard of thousands who followed His footsteps to persecution and martyrdom. Those who quaffed the cup of suffering and ignominious death were not of the ordinary people. There were among them the erudite, the chief clergy of the Islamic faith, philosophers, saints, mystic leaders, siyyids, and chieftains. Now the least that is incumbent upon the Muslims is to follow the example of that man from the family of Pharaoh and leave me in peace.'

They said, 'What shall we do? We said exactly what our religious leaders told us to say. They have even forbidden us to approach you, contact you, or talk to you.'

I told them, 'Have you ever heard or read anywhere that when a Prophet manifested Himself, the clergy told Him, "You are welcome"? The Prophet Muḥammad, Jesus Christ, Moses, and the others have been the targets of the most cruel accusations heaped upon them by the most learned of their times. The Imám Ḥusayn was put to death by a decree signed and sealed by the most prominent religious dignitaries of his era.

As for me, I do not even consider myself as equal to the dust of the footsteps of the least of Their lovers. I am not here to teach; I do not think of myself as worthy of such an exalted position.'

This discussion proved at least to be a good introduction. For three days the people remained hostile. But after that, they became friendly toward me. They even invited me into their houses. Ḥájí Mírzá Javád-i-Shírází was one of them and considered by all to be the most notable and honoured of the Persian merchants. He had seen the Báb in Shíráz and was full of admiration and reverence for Him. He often praised Him by saying that the Báb was unsurpassed in beauty, spirituality, and courtesy. There was no one equal to Him in nobility, accomplishments, and saintly qualities. He remained as One alone, unique in the age in which He lived.

Another one was Ḥájí Muḥammad-Ḥasan-i-Kázirúní. He eventually embraced the Faith, but did not reveal it to anyone. Ḥájí Muḥammad Rafí'á was also a well-known individual, famous for his truthfulness and laudable traits of character and manners.

Ḥájí Abu'l-Qásim-i-Shírází often used to come and meet me, but always in secret. The reason he gave for this was that he could not trust the friendship of his companions. But the time came when he could no longer hide his faith. He was seventy and became so ignited with the fire of certitude that he burned away all the veils separating him from his Beloved. He was totally transformed; that is to say, his fear was changed into audacity. He had been alone, but now he brought his family from Shíráz. He manifested such praiseworthy traits of character that his friends were astonished. He often said, 'Wealth and riches are good, but only when they are spent in the path of the Cause of God. Otherwise they will cause misery and the loss of one's own soul.'

He decided to go and behold the Countenance of the Ancient Beauty, but he had to get travelling documents from the Persian ambassador in Constantinople. It was extremely difficult, especially when they discovered that the applicant's intention was to go to Adrianople. He had to pay the ambassador a large sum of money, but he persevered and finally the difficulties were removed.

When he returned from his pilgrimage, he was utterly a new creation. Now he was steadfast in the Cause and could stand alone against the whole world. He was indeed like an unshakable mountain which had changed into a flowing river. His knowledge, love, and enthusiasm became exemplary. He could no longer remain silent. The stories of his pilgrimage were his favourite subject, and he always related them with the same joy and vigour.

It is worthwhile pondering the fact that he was seventy years old, and his thoughts, manners, and customs were deeply ingrained. It is a well-known saying that 'when a man becomes old, two characteristics will be reinvigorated in him – greed and ambition'. Yes, he became greedy, but to spend all that he had in the path of the propagation of the Cause. He also grew young in his hopes and ambitions, but these ambitions were to spread the Word of God.

The Persian consul advised many people to associate with me and even to pretend that they were believers. Ḥusayn Ḥakkák and Mírzá Ṣafá were among them. They would come to my room, and to win my confidence they would speak very highly of the Faith. Mírzá Ṣafá claimed that he had seen the Báb in Bú<u>sh</u>ihr, where he had recognized in Him the signs of the exalted station destined for Him. Afterwards I learned that these two had been the special agents of the consul sent to find out the names and addresses of all the believers in Egypt.

The day approached when all <u>Sh</u>í'ih Muslims would commemorate the martyrdom of the Imám 'Alí. The consul invited me to come to his house on this especially holy night. He told me that all the Persians in the city would be busy that night with prayers, and that he would send home the servants of his household. 'My house will be empty, and we will be alone to discuss whatever we wish', he explained.

A certain man, who was an old friend of mine, used to meet me very often. He was a man of no religion and, as a matter of fact, was against all of the Prophets. When I received the consul's invitation, he urged me not to accept, explaining that it was surely a device by which the consul could get me under his flag, in his office, and then arrest me and make me a prisoner. If this happened, he explained, the Egyptian government would not be able to protest. Even if they came to my aid, the consul would level accusations against me and slander me, and none of these charges would be challenged by anyone. He also reminded me that I had no one to stand on my side or to shield or defend me against such evil plots. I listened carefully to him, but I decided to accept the invitation because refusal would indicate weakness and fear, which are not worthy attributes for the followers of this great Faith.

I was reassured by remembering parts of the Tablets revealed by Bahá'u'lláh in my honour. In them He exhorted me to remember His exile, imprisonment, and hardship and to follow in His footsteps on the path of salvation. The believers should accept calamities and never be despondent in the face of persecution, but trust their Lord and remain happy, joyous, and steadfast as a mountain.

As I recalled the statements in my own Tablets, I became sure that imprisonment awaited me. Nevertheless, I went to the house of the consul at the appointed hour along with Mírzá Ḥusayn-i-Shírází and Darvísh Ḥasan. At first we behaved as Muslims, observing all the outward customs of Islám. But when the time came for the evening prayer, we demurred, saying, 'Congregational prayer is forbidden, except for the dead.' This led to a discussion of the Faith, and we spent the whole evening discussing the proofs of this Revelation. We even recited one of the Tablets of Bahá'u'lláh and related the sufferings of the heroes and martyrs of the Faith. The consul appeared to be impressed and even convinced.

Dawn was approaching when the consul retired. One of the servants came to convey our host's message that we should go home. This message astounded us because at first the consul had treated us very kindly, but now, at the hour of our departure, he rudely ordered us out of his house, not even having the manners to take leave of his guests. We left his house with a sense of foreboding. The consul had sent some people to carry lamps ahead of us to light the way through the dark and narrow lanes of the town. As we were treading the path toward my home, I discovered that, every few steps, more men joined our company. As I was thinking over this strange situation, we suddenly found ourselves surrounded by at least forty people who were indeed as devouring wolves.

We were dragged to the prison, where they robbed us of our clothing and placed all of us in chains and fetters, beating us with whatever was in their hands and cursing in the most horrible way. This continued until morning, when they closed the doors of the prison and went away. I was content, but my companions were rather despondent. I did what I could to raise their spirits.

The prison door remained closed to us the whole day. In the evening it opened, and we were allowed to go out for food and to say our prayers. At this time we learned that they had gone to my room and stolen all my possessions – clothes, books, works of calligraphy, and other precious articles. They gave me some old clothes, and when I said that the clothes did not belong to me, they became wild once again and began to torment us even more than before. Finally, they gave us a paper to sign. It was a receipt they had written explaining that, except for our books, all our belongings had been returned to us. We were forced to sign and seal this false document. They partially mentioned the names of certain books and Tablets, because they planned to show the receipt to the Egyptian authorities and tell them that we were in possession of strange and dangerous writings.

They grudged no effort to invent all sorts of false reports against us for submission to the Egyptian rulers, and their poisonous slander reached the members of the court. They represented themselves as the most sincere friends and well-wishers of the khedive[22] and stated that they were, in fact, protecting the Egyptians from the onslaught of the Bábís. They reported that the Bábís had made an attempt on the life of the shＨáh of Iran[23] and, having failed there, had dared to come to Egypt. The sovereign and the citizenry must be protected against such people, they argued, as they are sure to have friends and collaborators amongst the people of Egypt, Turkey, and Iran.

The khedive, who had no son to succeed him, became very fearful, and it was natural for him to be so under the circumstances. Unfortunately, we were not in a position to defend ourselves against these false accusations. We tried to explain that we were Bahá'ís and not Bábís, and that Bahá'ís are loyal and obedient to their government. But we were not even allowed to open our mouths to utter a word in our own defence.

For more than fifty years during the reign of Náṣiri'd-Dín Sháh, the courtiers and officials of his government in Egypt had nothing better to do than to make false reports against us to the sovereign. They even untruthfully told him that they had discovered caches of arms and equipment in the houses of the 'Bábís'.

A night came when I was taken to the consul's chambers. The consul and an Egyptian officer were seated and a group of jailers stood by. I observed also that there was a large group of people in chains. The consul suddenly became furious and, pointing his finger at me, shouted, 'All of the trouble has been caused by this man, their Gabriel and their Prophet!' No sooner were these words uttered than some men came and seized me, tied my hands behind my back, and put a chain around my neck. This accusation had the desired effect on the khedive of Egypt, who immediately ordered the consul to arrest anyone belonging to this religion.

It did not take the consul long to arrest some three hundred people. We learned that he even arrested a few Egyptian subjects. Ḥájí Abu'l-Qásim was arrested and when they brought the chain to be placed on his neck, he picked it up, kissed it, and, putting it around his neck, uttered the words, *Bismi'lláhi'l-Bahíyyi'l-Abhá*! (In the name of God, the Glory of the All-Glorious!)

The consul, under the pretext of persecuting the Bábís, had planned to collect large sums of money in bribes. My cell in the consulate was adjacent to a large room where these three hundred people were imprisoned – Jews and Christians and Muslims. In order to free themselves from the tortures of imprisonment, these victims had to offer him money. Thus an increasing flow of income found its way into the pocket of the consul. Each prisoner who was to be freed had to come to my cell, curse me, spit in my face, beat me, and abuse all of the Holy Ones of our Faith. This action would be taken as proof that the prisoner had not been, or was no longer, a Bábí. But, as previously mentioned, they had to pay large sums of money as well. Some of these victims were ashamed and would not even look upon my face. Their tormentors forced them to look into my eyes and do whatever they were ordered to do.

During the forty-five days I spent in that jail, we suffered as in hell because of the consul's staff and servants. But my soul was in a state of the utmost joy. Had it not been for this sense of inner tranquillity and composure, I could never have endured the savage acts, profane oaths, and the blasphemous remarks of these people.

I was very happy in prison. The only exception was in the early hours of the day, when the cruel persecutors would come to our room to beat, curse, and abuse us. This was the worst part of our daily life in prison.

One night the consul had invited some of the Persian dignitaries and some people from the Egyptian aristocracy to his home. The consul ordered that I should be taken in chains to that banquet. When I entered, it reminded me of the captivity of the Imám Ḥusayn's family and their arrival at the great gathering in the house of the governor of Kúfih.

Before the consul could speak, I sat down and addressed him, saying, 'Throughout the history of all religions, the Chosen Ones of God have been persecuted, chained, and forced to endure great hardships. It is a well-known saying that calamities are for the friends of God, and those who deny Him always follow the path of cruelty and injustice. Please ask all these people who are gathered here tonight what we have done that we must be subjected to so much humiliation and injustice. Remember the exhortation in the Qur'án which states that even if an evildoer brings you a message, it is your duty to investigate. What religion sanctions the type of treatment we have received from you? You only listen to those who accuse and never give the victims an opportunity to open their mouths and explain their case.' I spoke with such strength and authority that the consul ordered the jailers to take me back to my cell.

One time a group of Persians arrived who were on their way to Mecca. To show them how strong a person he was and how he protected and served his religion and country, the consul brought all the pilgrims to my prison cell. The moment he entered, he began to beat me with his cane. Then he said, 'Tell the truth. What is your name?'

'Ḥaydar-'Alí', I said.

'No!' he protested. 'You have other names. You have been called "The Gabriel of the Bábís", "The Amanuensis" and "The First Imám".'

'I have never said this', I responded. 'Someone has accused me of these things.'

'Yes', he said.

'Well, his name must be Satan', I immediately replied, 'because anyone who carries false reports and instigates people to act unjustly is none other than Satan. He always comes to people in such a way that they will not know him.'

He hit me again and said, 'Are you so presumptuous as to vilify the ambassador himself?'

They went out and brought back a man who accused me of theft. He demanded that I return to him the belongings of his brother. When he mentioned the name of his brother, I said that I did not know him. While we were arguing, all the others went out, leaving only the man and myself. No sooner were we alone than he embraced me and kissed me, saying, 'I am 'Abdu'lláh from Najaf-Ábád. I was in His presence. Now I am in Egypt on my way to Mecca. I heard about your imprisonment. Knowing that they have confiscated all your belongings, I had a little money and thought of bringing it to you.' He gave me the money and continued, 'I couldn't come into the prison to meet you unless I had some excuse. Therefore, I told the consul that his prisoner had the belongings of my brother. Now, whatever happens, I will be most grateful, even if he keeps me here with you in this prison cell. If he allows me to go, I will also be grateful to my Lord.'

This same 'Abdu'lláh made his way to Jiddih where he met Ḥájí Mírzá Ṣafá. There, he became the servant of this mystic leader. Some of the Persians knew 'Abdu'lláh and were extremely surprised that a man who was a religious leader had employed such a well-known Bábí as his close and trusted servant. The following conversation took place between Mírzá Ṣafá and 'Abdu'lláh:

'I heard that you have been to Adrianople?'

'Should I have any shortcomings or show any disloyalty in my services to you, you have every right to consider me a sinner and worthy of chastisement. But you have not employed my conscience. Yes, it is true that I had the honour of making a pilgrimage to His presence in Adrianople.'

'What did you see there?'

'All that I had heard about the past religions and the Prophets of God, I beheld in Him and in His Manifestation.'

'How is it that you saw such signs while the learned, the philosophers, and the mystic leaders have not seen such things?'

'It was the same in the days of the Prophet Muḥammad. The learned orators and philosophers denied Him, but the illiterate, the peddlers, and the slaves embraced His Faith.'

'Bravo! You answer well.'

After saying this, he gave 'Abdu'lláh his wages and some extra money, recommending to him that he go from Jiddih to Egypt, rather than to the resting place of the Prophet in the city of Medina. 'Abdu'lláh thought things over and said to himself, 'I have endured hardships, and now I am here where the feet of the Prophet Muḥammad have trodden and where I can behold the sights seen by His own eyes. Why should I deprive myself of all these bounties?'

He was then determined to experience the full pilgrimage, and in Medina he once again met Mírzá Ṣafá, who remonstrated, 'I told you to go to Egypt and not to come to Medina!'

'To pay homage to the Shrine of the Prophet Muḥammad is an act of worship and more important than obedience to you', 'Abdu'lláh responded.

'I want you to be in my employment again. You are an honest person, but at the same time I would like to give you some advice. Wise men never tread those paths on which they are perpetually confronted with many hardships, or on such roads where they are constantly faced with danger. They choose the highways that are well kept and secure, and along which are located many villages and towns. The path you have chosen for yourself will become, in time, a wonderful highway – but only after two hundred years or so. Now there are many dangers on it. You must avoid them.'

'It is absolutely true. But you must know that people like me must travel these dangerous roads and undergo difficulties and deprivation to pave the way for people like you.'

'How is it that you are so quick to answer and are so brave and daring in your response?' said Mírzá Ṣafá.

'In the Qur'án the Prophet Muḥammad has clearly said that those who long for death are always truthful. In order to tell the truth, no one requires meditation or careful thought, nor is the truthful man hesitant.'

A group of us were entrusted to the Egyptian officers to be taken to an unknown destination. One of the friends in chains became so excited and happy that he recited a poem which says:

> Against Thy Will not one complains,
> Lions are not ashamed of chains.

When the people heard us reciting joyous poems as a sign of faith and steadfastness, some burst into tears and others into laughter. We were conducted to another prison, where the chains were taken from our wrists and necks. We spent the night there.

The next morning our fellow prisoners asked us what charges had been brought against us. We said that we did not know what the Persian consul had accused us of.

'Have you killed anyone?' they asked. 'This prison is only for murderers and assassins.'

We were not accused of murder, however. The charges against us were that we had abandoned Islám and created a new religion. So the next day I was able to write a petition in Arabic to the Egyptian officer in charge of the prison.

In it I argued: 'The most basic principles of justice require that one should serve the sentence for the crime of which he is accused. The Persian consul, because of his personal animosity toward us, has accused us of establishing a new religion and discarding the laws of Islám. Yet, we are in a prison for murderers. Not everyone can be accused of establishing a new religion. Anyone so accused must at least be learned and resourceful and respected by many people. To imprison us with murderers is most unjust.'

The officer, fearing that we might lead the other prisoners astray, decided to move us to separate quarters. Our new room had carpets and a few other comforts, but the other prisoners were not allowed to speak to us.

A few days later the consul came to the prison and saw our new quarters. We knew from then on the conditions would be altered for the worse, and it was true.

Eight nights passed. On the ninth, shortly after midnight when all were asleep, soldiers came to our cell again, tied our hands behind our backs, and chained us all in one row. My hands were so tightly bound and so severely damaged that I felt the effect of those ropes for the rest of my life. Fifty soldiers, well armed and well equipped, took us on a stony road covered with thorns and thistles. Being ill and not sufficiently fed, we found walking very painful.

As we were going down the road, the soldiers fell into conversation with us. Gradually they realized that we were not violent prisoners and could not be any match for fifty soldiers. They asked us what we had done and we told them the truth. They began to feel pity for us. My hands were swollen and caused me much pain. First they released my hands, and then they became so kind and gentle that they even allowed us to ride horses in turn.

When we approached the famous prison of Famul-Baḥr, the soldiers again put us all in chains. They kept us outside the town and sent word to the governor, who specified our prison cell and ordered that we must be manacled together on one chain. He also emphasized that the prison cell must be dark and the doors should be bolted and locked. A hole was made in the door of our cell. The chain was stretched through this hole and was held firmly in the hands of the guards outside.

The day was almost as dark as the night, and when evening came no one gave us so much as a candle. We decided to chant the Tablet of Náqús, which had been revealed by Bahá'u'lláh for the celebration of the night on which the Báb had declared His mission. We were eight prisoners and our voices united in chanting the verses. When the soldiers heard this, they came in with a lamp for us. They thought we were dervishes and that we were chanting something which contained the mention of God. This attracted their kindness toward us. Thereafter, the soldiers kept the doors of our cell open during the day and unchained us all.

It was not long before officers, notables, merchants, and people of each and every class among the inhabitants of that area demonstrated a longing to be in our company and enter into discussion with us. Without exception these people showed us love and compassion. Some of them were indeed of noble nature. They did everything in their power to make us happy by their sincere love and often by their gifts. Some went so far as to ask us to give them the text of special prayers for the fulfilment of their wishes and the solution of their difficulties. During the fifty days of our imprisonment I was busy writing prayers, including verses that proclaimed the advent of the Báb and Bahá'u'lláh.

These fifty days enabled us to regain our energy, health, and strength. Every minute of those days we were far from the material world and very close to our Beloved because of the Tablets and prayers that we chanted. We were even ready to be martyred in His path. It would be better to be martyred here, we thought, than in the house of the Persian consul. In those days, because of the many cruelties we had suffered, our blood was thin and weak. After fifty days of rest and proper food, we felt that we had more and better blood to offer.

But all these were wishful thoughts, for the night arrived when the soldiers came to take us back to Egypt. Those soldiers proved to be very kind indeed. They did not cause us difficulties, nor did they torture us on the way back. On the contrary, they allowed us to ride on camels, horses, and whatever was available. They also stopped at two or three stations to have coffee and tea and allow us to rest before continuing on our journey.

When we approached a town, we were again put in chains, but the kind-hearted soldiers apologized by saying, 'We are under strict orders, and we have to surrender you to the authorities in chains.' We were then taken to the first place to which we had been sent in our exile. The officers told us, 'You are brought here for investigation.'

But after six days, we were again sent to the former prison in the same chains and along with the same guards and officers. We reached our prison, and on the sixteenth day the soldiers took us to ironsmiths and carpenters in order to place permanent fetters on our feet and chains around our necks. This process proved to be more painful than anything which we had previously endured. We could not control ourselves and cried out in pain. The soldiers, blacksmiths, and carpenters wept at our plight. This was particularly true of the blacksmiths and carpenters, who cursed their professions for making them instruments for the torture of innocent people.

The last operation was to put our hands in stocks. The heavy fetters on our feet, the terrible chains on our necks and hands made every little movement a torment. We could not move our hands much, nor was it possible for us to lift the chains on our feet in order to make their weight less painful while walking.

The fashioning of the chains and the stocks began about two o'clock in the afternoon and was finished a little after sunset. Then they took us to a steamer and delivered us to a group of a hundred officers and soldiers.

We began to understand the evil instigations of the consul. He had so terribly frightened the Egyptian government that the boat carrying us refused to accept commercial goods lest the people should come to the ports, see our plight, and discuss the inhuman manner of our treatment. Whenever the boat drew near the shore and dropped anchor, we were immediately pushed into a storeroom the windows of which were firmly shut.

During our captivity, our clothes had never been changed. We had worn them for months and they became so torn and dirty that they were intolerable. Now that we were chained, we could not even take them off to wash them.

Gradually, God inspired the hearts of the guards and soldiers, and they took a liking to us. Out of pity they prepared us long, white garments. They had to tear the clothes off our bodies. Then, they washed us with hot water and clothed us with the new long robes. We felt so happy that we thought it was New Year's Day and we were wearing clothes for the festivities.

We discovered that those soldiers had been told that this humble servant could control spirits and influence invisible creatures. Therefore, they approached me and asked me to give them amulets to protect them against the operations of the spirits called *jinn*, which they believed lived underground. I knew that the amulets which they were accustomed to contained the names of angels and numerological formulas. So I wrote some tablets for them in which I used the Greatest Name[24] and the anagrams for the names of Bahá'í friends. Sometimes I would add the names of the gifts which were brought to us, such as cheese, tobacco, bread, shirts, and tea. I write this particularly to show the reader that we were joyful and content in our imprisonment.

Ja'far Pá<u>sh</u>á, the governor general of the Sudan, came on board our ship. He sent for me, and I was taken to his presence. I asked him, 'What are the charges against us?'

'May God punish your consul', was his reply. 'He has created such fear in the hearts of the government officials that all are afraid of you. He has accused you of changing your religion, your Book, and the Holy Laws of Islám. He says that you are terrorists and that you intend to assassinate the heads of government. But it is obvious that you are people of the path[25] and that you do not meddle in politics.' He told us that he would see to it that we were made as comfortable as possible. However, we remained in that spot only three days.

On the third day, the guards were changed, and new ones came with camels for us to ride. But chained together as we were, our feet in one stock and our wrists joined by chains, how could we ride on camels? The guards were at a loss for what to do and how to carry us to our next destination. Eventually they brought some long pieces of strong, white cloth. They placed the hands and feet of each pair of us on the saddle, one person hanging on one side of the camel, and the other on the other side. Then they tied our hanging bodies to the camels with the white cloths.

A more torturous way to travel cannot be imagined!

Five or six times during the short journey they made the camels kneel down, and we were untied and permitted to have a little rest. The guards apologized to us, saying that previously they had taken a group of thieves and murderers to the Sudan in chains, but that these others had to walk all the way through the desert. Ja'far Páshá had instructed them to allow us to ride, and they could not think of any other way. Although we were in great pain and torture, as we watched each other hanging from the camels, the sight was so ridiculous that we could not help laughing.

In five or six hours we reached the banks of the Nile River where we were again sent to a ship. We boarded and set off. The ship deposited us at a place that was under the control of a very kindhearted Arab shaykh. We explained our situation to him and asked him to treat us with more mercy. We still had a long stretch of desert to cover by camel. When the shaykh learned of our plight, he ordered the camel drivers to have wooden seats provided for us on the camels and to carry enough food for all. The shaykh was well experienced and knew how severe the desert journey would be. We had to travel twelve days over an ocean of sand.

In place of Egyptian guards, we were now entrusted to Arabs who were cruel hearted, devoid of manners, and very hot tempered. The moment we were in their hands they made it clear to us that they possessed the power of life or death. No matter what they did, no one was to complain or utter a word. The shaykh had supplied them with enough provisions for all, but these people only gave us enough for one person and consumed the rest themselves. Their treatment called to mind the hardships we had endured in the house of the consul in Egypt. Still we remained happy and could always find something to laugh at. We made jokes about our guards in Persian and would laugh heartily. When we finally reached the Sudan, we thanked God that we were alive.

Our guards brought us to the prison of the Sudan and the jailers immediately put us into a small, dark, and putrid cell. There were so many people crowded together that we could not even breathe, let alone move. The slightest gesture would arouse the anger of the jailers. We were surrounded by darkness, mosquitoes, fleas, lice, all manner of filth, and prisoners who were worse than scorpions. This proved to be the worst place we had been imprisoned. We were absolutely at a loss for which way to turn and what to expect.

Eventually I mustered my courage and begged the guard to take a message to the officer in charge. Fortunately he did this for me, and I was taken to the officer. Upon entering his room I said to him, 'I am skilled in calligraphy and can write and arrange beautiful tablets. Would you kindly provide me with paper, ink, and pen?' He prepared everything for me, and I wrote a verse for him that said, 'I surrender all my affairs to God.' He was very pleased with the work and accepted it as a gift from me. After that he respected me. I told him that two of my companions were excellent calligraphers, another was a physician, and two were engravers. I also told him that we were prepared to do anything he might be pleased to order. So we were transferred to another room but still kept in chains. We rejoiced at the improvement in our condition.

Gradually we became known by the officers, guards, and prisoners. We transcribed many prayers for them, some of which would take us as much as two weeks to finish. Whatever gifts we received in return for our work, we immediately handed over to the jailer who had first taken our message to the officer. But he still kept us chained, two by two. No one can ever imagine the difficulties and hardships being chained in this position involved. To wash one's hands and face and attend to the other demands of nature was hell in itself.

After forty days they found that all the prisoners who were due to assemble there had arrived. A ship was made ready to take us to another prison in Khartoum.

Words fail to describe the foul language used by our fellow prisoners. Vile words and curses, epithets of blasphemy and damnation were freely, repeatedly, and shamelessly used by all. This group of bold, arrogant, and ferocious beasts took pride in exchanging stories of their thefts and escapes, their acts of murder and brutality toward others. They looked at us in disparagement and taunted us, saying, 'Look, we have done all these courageous things. What have you done? Nothing. We are ashamed to be on the same boat with you.'

There were some women prisoners on board, too. There was also a blind man who ceaselessly chanted the Qur'án. One day the women complained that someone had stolen their scissors. The guards searched everyone and everywhere. I could see that the blind man became pale and excited when the search began. Then the guards started beating the prisoners, one by one, in an effort to locate the scissors. So, to free the others from this misery, I told the soldiers that they should search the blind man. They found the missing scissors in his pantaloons.

Our trip was to have lasted six days, and enough provisions had been stored for this period. But because there was no favourable wind to fill the sails, we remained on board the ship for thirty-six days. Corn flour had been provided which we could bake, but with such malevolent companions, we were unable to approach the scanty provisions.

One day, while the boat was anchored, the guards told us that within two hours' walk there was a village where we could find some food. Because we had gone several days with nothing but water, we had become very weak. Now, walking in chains for more than two hours was a great challenge to our determination. Nevertheless, we set out on foot. Constantly falling down and pulling ourselves to our feet, we finally reached the village, where we fainted and remained unconscious. Some people took pity on us and gave us sweet coffee to drink. They gave us a paste which looked like flour and water to eat. We thought that we had to cook it, but they told us it was already cooked. As we ate, I asked someone in Arabic what it was. He answered in a funny manner, and we all laughed so much that we almost forgot about our condition. Still, we had to return to our ship on foot.

We sailed slowly and reached another port, where we stayed about twelve days waiting for favourable winds to blow. Some of these days were comparatively happy and comfortable. We wrote amulets for the inhabitants of the village where we were staying, and they gave us provisions for the rest of the trip. Eventually we reached our final destination, the city of Khartoum.

All the prisoners were afraid that they would be sent to the prison in Fashúdih, which was said to be the grave of prisoners. The weather there was supposed to be extremely unhealthy, and the prisoners were condemned to hard labour. We also learned of another prison close by called the 'Dungeon of Fear'. Since the ship to Fashúdih only travelled there every three or four months, prisoners were kept in this place until they could be transferred. It was indeed with sinking hearts that we heard about all these places.

Ja'far Pá<u>sh</u>á, the governor general, arrived and sent for us. He assured us that he would do his utmost to keep us happy and comfortable. He then ordered the officers to take us to the nearby prison, change our heavy chains for light ones, exempt us from work, and cause us no trouble. He also recommended that we be separated from the rest of the prisoners. Before he sent us away, he remarked, 'Love emanates from the heart. But a wise man must hide his love when he sees that others like him are cast into prison, and made to undergo grave difficulties, and have their property confiscated. One may love; but in case of danger, one should hide his feelings.'

I made no reply but returned to my prison room. There, I wrote a tablet for him. In large letters I wrote the following:

> O you who accuse me of love!
> If you understood my crime,
> you would not blame me.

Around the edges of these words, I transcribed two recognized Muslim traditions. The first read: 'Whosoever seeks Me, shall find Me. Whosoever finds Me, shall love Me. Whoso loves Me, him shall I also love. Whoso is loved by Me, him shall I slay. Whoso is slain by Me, I Myself shall be his ransom.'

Finally I wrote the second tradition: 'How can one deny his love while two witnesses are testifying – one's tears and the paleness of one's face?' I sent this tablet to the governor general through our guard. When the guard returned, he related the following: 'Ja'far Pá<u>sh</u>á says that the person who sent this tablet is a learned and accomplished man. He gives the correct answer to an argument and with a great deal of courtesy.' The governor general had also sent two gold coins to me.

The dungeon in which we found ourselves consisted of a large cell which had only two doors. Each of the four hundred prisoners there had no more than the space of two hand spans in which to sit, sleep, and live. We had no proper clothes; the long shirts we had been given on the journey were so badly torn in several places that they did not even cover us. In this filthy cell, malodorous and full of obscenity, we struggled to hold on to life.

One day Ja'far Páshá summoned the jailer and asked him about our condition. The jailer gave him a true reply: 'Because of the lack of space, intense heat, and filthy conditions, they are in grave danger.' On hearing this, Ja'far Páshá ordered the jailer to make us a cottage of mats, timbers, and dry grass, where we were allowed to sleep at night. But the heat in that cottage also proved to be unbearable.

In order to keep the guards awake all night, they were ordered to call out numbers in turn. If one failed to respond, he would be punished. We pitied our guard and told him to go to sleep – that we would guard in his place, answering the call of other guards by shouting, 'One! Two! Three!' for him. We were happy to replace the guard, for then we could stand outside under the canopy of the sky and enjoy the fresh air. But we still remained deprived of every comfort of life. No pots or pans were given us – not even a cup or glass for drinking water.

Our daily ration was a handful of kernels of corn. We had to grind and knead our own flour and then make a fire and bake the loaves. We did not even have a copper coin with which to buy salt. But after a while we were able to earn some money, and we could afford to have our corn baked for us. The first time we had this done, we rejoiced with a real celebration. We were even more joyful when we finally obtained cups for drinking, rugs, and sleeping benches. We spent eight or nine months in the 'Dungeon of Fear', and we were content and happy and thankful. From all sides, the doors of generosity were opened to us.

A Christian by the name of Búlus (Paul), who as the richest man in Sudan was the honorary consul of Persia, came to know of our condition. He was kind to us and sent us clothes, coffee, a lantern, and some mats. To express our thanks I wrote the name of Jesus Christ in Arabic calligraphy and arranged it in the shape of a cross. In the margin I wrote that since Jesus had found His way to His Beloved through the cross, this was a sacred and exalted form. I also made another one of these tablets for the German consul, who was also a Christian but of a Protestant sect. The German consul, in return, sent us a samovar and the means for preparing tea.

Now we had enough provisions and could even invite the other prisoners to tea. Gradually the people of Khartoum heard about us, and many of them from Muslim, Christian, and Jewish backgrounds came, individually and in groups, to see us. We even had visitors from among the army and civilian officials. Many of them came with different gifts. Whatever we received we shared with the guests and with our fellow prisoners.

Many strange events took place in that prison, some of which seem incredible. For example, there was a man named Joseph, who, because he committed thefts even in prison, had come to be known as 'Rat'. He was so shameless in his deeds and manners that I requested my friends not to associate with him. There was a woman, who had been caught in sin, who also lived in this prison. This same 'Rat' took her as his wife. There was no privacy, but they slept together regardless of the presence of four hundred other prisoners.

Once we learned that 'Rat' and his wife had been hungry for two days. As Bahá'ís we could not remain heedless of such a situation. I wrapped a gold coin in a piece of cigarette paper and offered it to him. When he saw the money, he became very courteous and even promised to reimburse us in the future. After that, he attached himself to me and I happily gave him a share of everything I had.

It then happened that some prisoners got together to devise a way to escape from the prison. They decided to cut the chains off each other's feet while they were grinding the corn. The noises were so mingled that none of the guards could detect the unusual sound of the file cutting through the fetters on the prisoners' feet. This took place at night, and eventually eight of them succeeded in ridding themselves of their chains. They rushed out suddenly, threw the guards to the floor, and ran away. The soldiers followed and caught four of them, but the remaining four threw themselves into the Nile, swam across the river, and disappeared.

The following day, the prison was a changed place. It was as if hell had opened its doors to us. The jailers and guards were changed, and new rules, regulations, and restrictions were instituted. Everyone was chained together. Harsh interrogations began, and those who were involved in the plot to escape were condemned to death by firing squad.

We were not even remotely involved in the plot. But all of a sudden the entire weight of this ill-fated venture fell upon our heads. Who had accused us? It was 'Rat', who had approached the officers and told them that the Persians owned a file and had given it to the prisoners to effect their escape. We could not sleep the whole night, fearing that fresh attacks and new cruelties would be heaped upon us. Finally, I opened the

Qur'án, and the first verse I saw, I read. It indicated that, on the morrow, the evildoers would be lined in a row in one chain. We took this as a sign that we ourselves would not be harmed. So we decided to try to be of service to others who were in trouble.

When the sun rose the next morning, we saw four gallows raised in front of our prison cell. All of the prisoners were taken out of the cell in chains, surrounded by guards; and we were among them. We were seated in a circle in front of the gallows. The commanding officer came forth with guards who had drawn swords in their hands. They marched up and down before the prisoners, ordering and shouting. Then there was silence, and the officer declared that the Persian prisoners had nothing to do with the escape. The soldiers removed our chains. We left the circle and immediately hastened inside because we could not bear the sight of the prisoners being hanged. For three days and nights thereafter, all the other people in the prison were chained together, and we served them with all our hearts and souls.

The benevolent Ja'far Páshá wrote favourably about us to his government, telling them that the Persians were well educated and of good breeding and manners, that they had never done any harm to the people, and that, on the contrary, they had proved to be very useful citizens. He therefore asked that we not be transferred from the 'Dungeon of Fear'. For this reason we were not sent to Fashúdih as about one hundred other prisoners, including 'Rat', were.

In Khartoum there was a blind man of extraordinary intelligence, by the name of Shaykh Amín, who had been appointed the Shaykhu'l-Islám of the city. I wrote him a letter which was quite a long dissertation on the history of the Cause. The concluding words were about ourselves imprisoned because of the cruel and unjust reports made by the Persian consul to the Egyptian government. This blind man saw that we had been treated with injustice. He took our letter to the governor, Ja'far Páshá, and requested him to see to our affairs. It was not long before the governor himself came to the prison and summoned us to his presence. He asked, Which of you wrote the letter to the Shaykhu'l-Islám?'

'We did', was our answer.

'I have heard that you are well educated and intelligent. But I asked you a question and you did not give me a proper answer.'

I answered him, saying, 'We are so overjoyed that such a high-ranking person should bestow such care and consideration on us that we do not know what we are saying. We know that in the presence of great ones such as yourself it is not proper to say very much. Moreover, we do not know your language, and therefore each of us may have a different idea of what you have said. And, finally, since we have all answered, one of us must be right, so we should not all be held responsible for a false answer.'

He was very happy with my reply and ordered chairs to be brought so we could sit. When we were seated he said, 'Ever since I first saw you, I have done my utmost to make life easier for you, and I will continue to do so.' Then he asked the guards to remove our chains and transport us to a jail in Khartoum. Out of kindness, he urged the custodian of the jail not to be very severe with us. He told the custodian that we should be permitted to be free during the daytime and be allowed to go into the streets and markets. Instead of the ration of corn, we now had wheat bread, which was given to us with some meat every day. When we reached Khartoum, we were allowed to open our own businesses. Two of us started engraving. Ḥájí 'Alí became a physician and 'Alí Effendi a teacher of English.

One of us, Ḥájí Abu'l-Qásim, kept to himself most of the time. He constantly recited prayers to himself. He was shrewd in business but also a bit miserly. When the rest of us went to Khartoum, he decided to remain in the prison. Since we were allowed to buy our food at the market, this friend would go to the prisoners, collect orders, and then visit the market. When he came back, he would sell them what they ordered, adding a good margin of profit for himself. Gradually he became rich, but he always satisfied himself with the corn given to the prisoners, selling his share of bread and meat to us.

Little by little, our prison cell became the town coffeehouse. Many people from different classes of society would come to us, and we entertained them with tea, coffee, sweetmeats, and even the water pipe. They asked me to make Persian rice for them. Because they brought me many gifts, I found it only fair to treat these guests with similar generosity.

Some of the most prominent people, and even some of the learned, believed that I had a strange mastery of witchcraft, capturing spirits, conquering the devil, and even ruling the sun. Once, while we were in the

'Dungeon of Fear', a s̲h̲aykh̲ was brought who had a reputation for being able to control spirits. I asked him how skilful he was at this art. He replied, 'I am able to write a verse on the fingernail of any person which will cause a *jinn* to visit him that very night.' 'You are not a master', I said. 'I can call for a *jinn* to come right now to attack you and beat you.' And I started to summon an evil spirit. He became very fearful and excited and begged me to stop. So, I forgave him. I told him that the spirit would visit him, but that he would not be harmed.

Innumerable and incredible superstitions prevailed among the inhabitants of this part of the world. For example, if someone, particularly a woman, became ill, they firmly believed that the patient's heart had been stolen. Groups of men and women would surround the patient's bed and spend hours playing music, singing songs, and telling stories. This was supposed to encourage a *jinn* to come and prompt one of the people to speak and say something like, 'Give so much money to such and such a man.' They believed that when the money was paid, the stolen heart would be returned.

Our benefactor, Ja'far Pás̲h̲á, was replaced by Ismá'íl Pás̲h̲á, who also proved to be very kind to us. He did his best to protect us from the onslaught of the ill-wishers. Although Ja'far Pás̲h̲á had written to the government recommending that we be released from the prison, given us permission to live in the town, and freed us to earn our own living, it was during the rule of his successor that the affirmative answer reached the Sudan. The new pás̲h̲á was very happy that during his regime we would be able to enjoy freedom from the prison and its hard labour, restrictions, and filthy atmosphere. He was so kind and gentle that he paid for the first year's rent on my house.

Unfortunately, his rule did not last longer than six months. He had more enemies than friends, and he found himself faced with a committee of investigation. This proved exceedingly hard for him to bear. During this very difficult period in his life, we approached his house and asked if we could see him. As he knew that we were sincere, he gave us an audience. In the course of the conversation we mentioned that should the charges laid against him by his enemies prove to be true, there was one door always left open by God, and that was the portal of repentance. For God has promised in His Book to be compassionate and forgiving to anyone who approaches Him in remorse and repentance. However, if he had been wrongly charged by his enemies, he must remain happy and contented and surrender his will and his affairs into the hands of the All-Merciful.

In the end, the pá<u>sh</u>á's assistant became the governor, but he retained all the military affairs under his control. He continued to be very kind and considerate to us and appointed me as a teacher of Arabic grammar in the government schools. I taught only in the mornings, and I spent my afternoons copying the Qur'án and several collections of prayers.

Through all these years, we remained ignorant of what had happened to Bahá'u'lláh. We did not know of His exile to the Holy Land. We longed to know something about Him, but we had no way of reaching His presence. We sent letters to Adrianople in care of our Jewish, Christian, and Muslim friends, but we had no confirmation that they were ever received.

There was, however, a Christian friend by the name of Ilyás (Elijah), who was very kind and fair-minded in his judgment. For example, in our discussions with him we learned that he believed the Qur'án was superior to all the Books of God preceding it. He knew of our deprivation and anxiety and promised to send our letters to Bahá'u'lláh in care of his friends, relatives, and business associates in Damascus, Beirut, and elsewhere.

How could we know that Bahá'u'lláh and his companions had been sent to 'Akká and had been living in very strict bondage? It was only afterwards that we learned that people such as Jináb-i-Nabíl had been trying for more than six months to have just a glimpse of him.

It was during this period of our anxiety that Ḥájí Jásim-i-Ba<u>gh</u>dádí arrived, clad in the robes of a dervish. He had travelled all the way from the Holy Land to the Sudan. As promised by Bahá'u'lláh, he found us in the Sudan. No words can describe the depths of our joy and gratitude. It was as if the Sun of Truth had sent the penetrating rays of His love into the darkness of our prison life. Ḥájí Jásim's stay lasted for forty days, during every moment of which we discussed nothing and heard nothing except the stories of His exiles, the restrictions of life in 'Akká, and news of the beloved friends.

When the people of Sudan learned that a messenger had come to us from the country of our Beloved, they were astonished at this unexpected expression of love. The Muslims described it as an act of the promised Qá'im, and the Christians said that only Jesus would perform such a loving act. The fame of this divine gesture went far and wide, and many prominent citizens from all backgrounds – Turks, Egyptians, Arabs, Christians, and Muslims – invited Ḥájí Jásim to their own houses. In all these gatherings, we spoke openly about Bahá'u'lláh, His exiles, and His plight in the Prison of 'Akká. They all knew that Ḥájí Jásim had been specially sent to the Sudan to inquire about our situation.

While Ḥájí Jásim was still with us, our friend Ilyás Effendi brought us a Tablet of Bahá'u'lláh which had been sent in answer to our supplication. Our happiness on receiving this Tablet was immeasurable. We read the Tablet to Ilyás Effendi, who was deeply affected by its contents. He said that he believed in whatever we said, but that if only he could believe in the lesser prophets of the Bible, he would believe that the author of this Tablet was the true Father of Jesus Christ. He often said that he longed to become like one of the believers. Once I wrote to him that it is said that the Prophet Elijah (Ilyás) is living. 'I believe with all my heart and soul that you are the living Elijah because you found my Beloved and brought me a message from Him.'

Ḥájí Jásim returned to the Holy Land, but ever afterwards we were honoured to receive at least five Tablets every year from the Blessed Beauty and regular news from the Holy Land and from His holy presence.

I feel obliged to mention Ḥájí Aḥmad of Mílán in Á<u>dh</u>irbáyján. It was because of the people who worked with him that we regularly received letters and news. All the friends knew of him and heard of his wonderful services to the Cause. His devotion, sacrifice, steadfastness, and detachment made him the unique servant of the Holy Threshold, and also to the Centre of His Covenant. Who am I to praise him?

Let me go back to Ismá'íl Pá<u>sh</u>á, who proved a benevolent ruler of the country. He gradually made his way to higher and higher positions. The more he was promoted, the more he showed kindness toward us. In his earlier positions, he had never deigned to come to our place of residence, but once he had reached the highest position in the government he would often come to our house just to show his kindness toward us.

For a short time he was absent, and an official who worked in the office of publications and supervised the religious school began to spread false rumours about this servant. He claimed that I turned my pupils away from Islám and so lodged a complaint against me, which he had many people sign. He did everything in his power to destroy me. He had almost the entire population leagued with him, and I had to depend upon God alone. Because of his evil machinations, many did not dare to come near us.

The reader will remember Shaykh Amín, the blind learned man of the Sudan. I had seen many such people, but none ever equal to him in learning and perceptive intelligence. Should a stranger pass by in the marketplace or in the street, he would immediately declare that a stranger had passed by, because he had not heard his footsteps before. He could open any book to the page he desired. At this time, when my name was on the lips of all, and many believed the accusations against me, this noble person arose to defend the oppressed ones. He openly proclaimed that the Persians were of true faith, were noble in their deeds, and that such slanderous accusations were absolutely false.

The páshá returned home, and the moment he heard about the accusations, he dismissed the official who had accused us and ordered an investigation of his affairs. It was soon discovered that this person had committed many unlawful things. He was then disgraced and lived all alone in his house. His own relatives would not go to see him, but they came to me and sought help for the management of the affairs of their household.

It was in the seventh or eighth year of our imprisonment in the Sudan that Ḥájí 'Alíy-i-Yazdí, accompanied by his brothers, came to visit us, as instructed by Bahá'u'lláh. This bounty of God was indeed overwhelming. By this time we were financially well settled. What we needed was the breeze of the Merciful wafting over us from the rose garden of His love. This was granted to us by the coming of these friends, who brought fresh news from the Holy Land.

We suggested that one of them should stay in Khartoum to open and manage a commercial centre. Ḥájí 'Alí accepted the proposal, and he himself became the head of this trading operation. The next year, I was in charge of this business, which in the course of time became very famous and a means by which many came to know about the Faith and its followers.

Once or twice a year someone would visit us from the Holy Land in the course of business. They would also bring the spiritual sustenance to keep us alive. We thanked God a thousand times that we had been favoured with the knowledge of this Revelation.

At this time, General Gordon became the governor of the Sudan. The person mentioned previously, who had falsely accused me in the past, now emerged from seclusion in his home to launch another attack against me, with more profane insults. He spared no efforts. Bribes were given in an attempt to poison the mind of the new governor against us. The first steps taken by this pernicious enemy seemed so injurious that we had cause to be alarmed. The governor, upon receiving these slanderous accounts, asked for reports from the English consul and others. All commended our small group and praised every one of us as noble citizens.

It was the custom at that time to set aside a special day when all the people would be invited to visit the new governor to welcome him and wish him a long and happy stay. When that day was announced, I prepared a mirror two and a half metres in length and one and a half metres in width. I had the mirror inscribed with mercury in large English letters: 'Long Live General Gordon'. I sent this mirror in care of the British Consulate. It was so warmly received that they ordered another one to be made for General Gordon's sister in England, and they sent a hundred pounds for the gifts we had offered.

Because Bahá'u'lláh had, both verbally and in some Tablets, promised that I would meet Him again, even during the most trying moments of my captivity and imprisonment, in the innermost part of my heart I felt certain that the day would dawn when I would make my way once more to His presence. When the second mirror was offered to General Gordon, he very kindly remarked, 'No amount of money could equal the excellence of your gift; therefore, you must tell me what I can do for you.'

It was a most opportune moment and I said to him, 'I want nothing except to free myself from this situation.'

'Write a petition and explain that you were imprisoned without any inquiry or investigation', he replied. I prepared a petition saying that we all abhorred what had been attributed to us, that kings and rulers have no sovereignty over the hearts and consciences of the people, and that no power except that of the Almighty could ever govern or control the hearts of men. Therefore, we requested to be set free and allowed to return to our homes. We concluded by stating that we would continue to pray for his just government. One of the other Bahá'ís wrote a similar petition.

This letter was dispatched to the general, and soon a cable was handed to us stating that we were free to return home, but we were not allowed to go to Egypt. The day of departure was indeed a great spectacle. All of the notables – Christians and Muslims – came to bid farewell and see us safely on board the ship bound for freedom.

After our departure, we learned that the consul general of Iran, Mírzá Ḥusayn Khán, who had committed so many iniquities and had been the cause of our imprisonment, eventually became the subject of the hatred of his own compatriots. The incessant plots he contrived against others for the purpose of depriving them of their possessions and money caused many oppressed individuals to lodge complaints against him to the Persian court. Officers investigated and soon his plans, plunders, and persecutions became known. First he was stripped of all the wealth he had so dishonestly gathered from Persian subjects. Then he was put in chains and dispatched to Persia. So he was punished for his evil deeds.

My boat was bound for Jiddih, the well-known Arabian port where thousands of pilgrims gather to approach Mecca and Medina. Wherever the boat docked, chiefs of the Arab tribes showed us much kindness and hospitality. When we landed in Jiddih, I turned toward Mecca and said, 'Yes, my Lord, I am here.'

In Mecca a great surprise awaited me. Upon my arrival I had the immense joy and honour of meeting two Bahá'ís, Salmán, 'the messenger of the Merciful', and Ḥájí Muḥammad-i-Yazdí.

After spending two months in quarantine, we left Mecca. Crossing the tempestuous sea, we saw at every moment the winds of death spread over us. After losing all hope of arriving anywhere, we finally reached Beirut. In this city we had the honour of meeting Muḥammad Muṣṭafá Baghdádí. He was one of the most distinguished followers of the Faith. From childhood he had faced the hardest tests and emerged stronger and with even more faith and certitude. He was staunch and steadfast, his heart filled with the intense heat of love and faithfulness. I have never met another person who could so perfectly offer the water of life to the friends, and at the same time the fire of God's wrath to the Covenant-breakers. His sons, Ḥusayn, 'Alí, and Ḍíá, carried the essence of their father.

They all stood as members of one body to serve the Cause of God and the people of Bahá. Even the children were adorned with the robe of servitude. It seems that their mother had fed them with the milk of eternal life and had brought them up in the bosom of love and compassion. Truly, the father of this noble family was a Bahá'í in name, deeds, life, and in every atom of his existence. While in the presence of this unique and wondrous family, I could inhale the sweet perfume of servitude to 'Abdu'l-Bahá.

It was in their house that I wrote a supplication to Bahá'u'lláh in the Holy Land. At the top of my letter I wrote a verse of the Qur'án which reads: 'Praised be the Lord Who has fulfilled His promise and granted us the earth as our inheritance and to live in Paradise as we wish.' But in the letter I changed 'as we wish' to 'as Thou desirest'. When my letter reached His merciful hands, He immediately said, 'We have invited him long ago. He is permitted to come.'

After three days we reached 'Akká, the city which is praised and extolled in the Holy Books of the past. There were three persons in the Pilgrim House who could be called the chosen ones of God and the essences of existence: Mírzá Muḥammad Ḥasan, the caretaker of the Pilgrim House and a true servant to all the visitors; Ḥusayn Áqá, who like a light of faithfulness constantly hovered near Bahá'u'lláh awaiting His every wish; and Mírzá Áqá Ján, who was in the presence of the Ancient Beauty.

The first two were never deceived by the rank and position given them, but the third one could not stand firm against the suggestion of self. Eventually, his nearness was changed into everlasting loss.

The first two had sacrificed themselves utterly to their Beloved and to the services granted them to perform. We never heard a word from them which could denote personal ambition. The Persian poet says:

> For their Beloved, the lovers die.
> They have no words to make reply.

Because of my long imprisonment, my eyes had become weak. For a considerable time it had been difficult for me to read and write. Once 'Abdu'l-Bahá entered our room at the Pilgrim House and asked me about the condition of my eyes and ears. When I explained, He recommended that I not shave my head.[26] He explained that it was against the explicit text of the Kitáb-i-Aqdas. He advised me to let my hair grow and to begin to write, even if only ten words a day. 'As you regain your eyesight, you should increase the amount of writing', was His loving recommendation to me. Now I am more than eighty years of age, but the weaknesses of my eyes and ears have never reached so low a condition as they were thirty-five years ago in the Sudan.

At night we were called upon to attend the presence of Bahá'u'lláh. As a Muslim I had learned that there are many categories of angels. Some constantly stand in prayer, while others sit, mentioning His names and attributes, and still others remain prostrated in front of Him. But the highest rank of angels are those who remain bewildered and awestruck by the beauty and splendour of the Beloved.

I found true examples of the last group of angels in the Bahá'í community of 'Akká. They numbered more than a hundred, each one united to the other like members of one body. They were proud of each other, and the bond which joined them together in perfect unity was nothing but their selfless love for the Glory of God. Most of them were busy during the day in their shops; but three hours before sunset, they gathered near the house of Bahá'u'lláh. Some would seat themselves on the steps, while others would walk slowly and talk of nothing but His words and His desires.

Sometimes they could behold Him walking on the balcony of His house. Their joy would know no bounds if He would beckon to them to hasten to His room. They were so united that they would sacrifice everything for each other. Whenever a group of them was granted permission to go to Him, all the others shared their spiritual ecstasy. It seemed that their exultation affected the whole surroundings. One could feel the effect of their rapturous state even in the atmosphere. And they had every right to reach such a state of intoxication because they were allowed to enter the Paradise of Reunion. It was extremely interesting to see them when they returned. For a long period of time they would remain quiet. When they were themselves again, they would report to the others the sweet words they had heard. Invariably they confessed that their words were not the exact utterances of Him in Whose presence they had stood, totally enraptured.

As far as I remember, there was no one who claimed to utter one complete sentence in His presence. Of course, there were some arrogant souls who reached the Land of Promise and sought His audience for the sake of argument, debate, or dispute. Even such people were graciously permitted to go to Him. Very often it happened, however, that the moment they heard His voice saying, 'Please come in', they would enter His room, prostrate themselves, and then remain seated, unable to utter a word. Thus they were transformed and went home sincere and full of love and faith. These were, of course, some exceptional cases. Some of the non-believers experienced the same feeling of overwhelming spiritual power but on going home declared, 'We were bewitched.'

Bahá'u'lláh's imprisonment in the walled city of 'Akká for nine years became a source of deep sorrow to the beloved Master, 'Abdu'l-Bahá. Therefore, He purchased land between two rivers and planted some flowers and trees there. Later this place became known as the Garden of Riḍván (Paradise).[27] The work involved in constructing this garden took six or seven years to complete. But Bahá'u'lláh would not accept the proposal of even visiting the place. Outwardly He was a prisoner and refused to go without the permission of the state. 'Abdu'l-Bahá asked the mufti of 'Akká to speak to Bahá'u'lláh. He instructed him to enter His room and not to leave unless and until He agreed to visit the garden. The officials of the government did not have the slightest objection to His going there.

The mufti obtained permission to enter Bahá'u'lláh's room. He approached, prostrated himself, and held the hem of the garment of the Blessed Beauty. Bahá'u'lláh tried to pull away the hem, but the mufti said, 'I will not let it go until you grant my wish.'

Bahá'u'lláh smiled and asked, 'What do you want?orwar

The mufti said, 'Nothing but this: that the garden become the Garden of Riḍván through the honour of your presence.' When He gave His consent, the mufti hastened out to give the good news to 'Abdu'l-Bahá and the government officials.

Three months passed and I was still a pilgrim. During this time, 'Abdu'l-Bahá arranged to rent the Mansion of Mazra'ih, where Bahá'u'lláh lived for two years. I remember that once the Riḍván Feast was celebrated in the house of Jináb-i-Kalím,[28] where I was living. A new pá<u>sh</u>á had arrived in 'Akká as the head of the Custom House. On that day he was sitting in a coffeehouse with many of his officers and other dignitaries of the town. Bahá'u'lláh was on His way to His brother's house. As He passed the coffeehouse, the páshá and all his retinue stood up and bowed before Him. As He passed by, He bestowed His loving benediction upon them. Then the páshá, bewildered, approached his friends and asked, 'Is this the Holy Spirit or the King of Kings? Who is He?'

'He is the father of 'Abbás Effendi',[29] was the unanimous reply.

I had such wonderful companions that I never wished to be separated from them. They were Jináb-i-Nabíl, the historian; Mírzá Muḥammad Ḥasan, the custodian of the Pilgrim House; and Darvísh Ṣidq-'Alí, one of the companions of Bahá'u'lláh in His exiles and imprisonment. We gathered together in the neighbourhood of our Beloved and spent the evenings in the mention of God. Because of our spiritual meetings, the night became more illumined for us than the day.

Darvísh Ṣidq-'Alí, before embracing the Faith, had been addicted to opium. Now that he had stopped using it, breathing became very difficult for him. Once, for an entire night he struggled to breathe. The doctors recommended that he return to opium, so he asked permission of Bahá'u'lláh to use a little. Instead, he was given a gold coin with which to purchase medicine. Fearing death, he came to us and said that it was contrary to detachment and absolute dependence on God to have such an amount of money in his purse. He could not reconcile himself to what he felt was a departure from spiritual law. But as Bahá'u'lláh had told him that He liked people to have some capital, he thought that the best investment for his money would be to purchase sugar and tea and offer them to the Holy Household. His offering was graciously accepted because his reasons were logical and acceptable.

The day came when I was to return home – but how could I leave the Paradise of Reunion? Twice I sent letters, and twice permission was granted me to stay another two weeks. When the third time came and I was asked to go, I went to 'Abdu'l-Bahá and explained how unbearable it was for me to leave the presence of Bahá'u'lláh. I was summoned to go to Bahá'u'lláh's room. He smiled and told me, 'You can stay fifteen days more, but on the condition that someone will guarantee your departure at that time. We want you to return home very happy, but do not forget the condition: someone must guarantee that you will leave!'

To this I promptly replied, 'The Master!'[30]

He smiled and agreed that I could stay fifteen days more. When I reached the Pilgrim House, I actually danced to show the uncontrollable joy that had overwhelmed me.

During my last fifteen days, I was very often in the presence of 'Abdu'l-Bahá. I have no words to explain the enchantment of my soul nor can I repeat the sweet utterances I heard. I can never be grateful enough for all the divine bounties which were abundantly showered upon me. I was sent to the Sudan as a humble prisoner and captive, and now I had emerged from the darkness of imprisonment to behold the wondrous countenance of Bahá'u'lláh and 'Abdu'l-Bahá. Then, I was poor and destitute; now, I had gold coins and material possessions. Spiritually and materially I was now in a perfect condition. How could I ever express my gratitude?

As I was pondering such thoughts in 'Akká, the beloved Master asked me, 'Would you be happy if you lost all that you now possess?'

I replied, 'I would be in the same position as when I left Persia years ago. I did not have a penny then – and now I will not mind if I am penniless when I return home. I do not care for anything, so long as I can keep my faith and love. You made me rich; when I offered my possessions to you, you accepted them and then returned them to me.' At that time I could not understand what the Master intended by this conversation.

Finally the day came when I had to leave 'Akká for Iran. Many Tablets were entrusted to me, but 'Abdu'l-Bahá's instructions were very explicit: 'When you reach the soil of Iran, you must give all the Tablets to a trusted friend and ask him to forward them to wherever you choose as your future address.'

I went to Iran by way of Mosul and Baghdád. In Mosul I had the great joy of visiting Jináb-i-Zayn and all the friends who had been captured in Baghdád and sent as prisoners to this northern district of Iraq. I lent the Tablets to Jináb-i-Zayn, who transcribed them. During my entire trip through various countries on my way to Iran, I was very courteously and respectfully received by the government officials, because they knew that I was an obedient servant of that illustrious person known as 'Abbás Effendi. Because of their loving attachment to the Master, the officials made every stage of my travel across their countries very comfortable and pleasant.

I also met my uncle, Jináb-i-Vakíl. As one of the captives, it was necessary for him to earn a living in order to provide for his family. At his advanced age he found no other way but to learn shoemaking. Though in a state of near poverty, he took me to his home. The love and hospitality that family showed put me to shame, especially when I could only express my gratitude in words – and promises of prayers on their behalf and on behalf of the deceased members of their family. These people lived in such unity, love, and peace that they mirrored forth the same light as one beheld in the Bahá'í community of 'Akká.

They vied with each other in serving the Cause and had no ultimate aim in life except to have a glance of His countenance. Though poor, they had established a fund to which the adults and children would contribute any extra amount from their daily income. In time of need the friends were allowed to borrow, but with the stipulation that they would pay back the loan with interest.

On the border between Iraq and Iran I met someone from 'Akká. When he learned that I had spent some time there, he introduced me to the Kurds, and they enveloped me with love and hospitality. Some venerable men of that district related to me stories of the sojourn of the Ancient Beauty in the mountainous districts of their country and of the spiritual impact He had on all the people. They were so enthralled with one of the Tablets 'Abdu'l-Bahá had written at the age of fourteen, in which He had expounded on divine love, that within a few days they made at least ten copies of that long commentary.

There was a Persian residing there named Áqá Ján-i-Naráqí. I learned that he had been a great opponent of the Cause and an enemy of the friends, for whom he had caused afflictions and persecutions. This man became a very firm believer during my stay amongst the Kurds, and he then arose to serve the Cause in order to compensate for his past errors. It happened that, on one of his trips, he and his companions were attacked by outlaws and robbed of their possessions. They found themselves penniless and with no means of livelihood. At that moment of distress and agony, he looked up to the heavens and said, 'O God, is this the way to treat Áqá Ján?'

After saying this, he continued walking home. Some time later he received a Tablet from Bahá'u'lláh. In it He stated, 'We heard your whisperings.

You are right! God will be with you and will confirm you.' From then on new doors were opened to him and to the other friends. They had great success in their services to the Cause which they had recently and very courageously embraced.

Áqá Ján and I spent many hours, together with other Bahá'ís, trying to teach the Faith to the Kurds. It was difficult, but four or five people became believers, and we held some meetings for prayers and discussion. Though we did not allow people to know about our meetings and everything was conducted in a very quiet manner, one night we heard a knocking at the door. When we opened it, a man entered and told us that he was thirsty to know about the Faith. He was in tears and said, 'You are known as the followers of a new religion. I have observed you and have found you to be people of purity, chastity, and piety. I nevertheless received reports of evil things about you. But when I observed those who spread those reports, I found them busy pursuing the material things of life. Sometimes I came across these people gambling or backbiting. In your conversation I heard nothing but the mention of God. Therefore, I believe that you are worshippers of God.' After some discussion this man embraced the Cause.

Another person came and asked for the Kitáb-i-Íqán. He returned the next day and said, 'When I went to my room and started reading the book, I stopped and decided that I would lock the door from within. I began to imagine all sorts of things: someone may have seen me lock the door and might guess I was reading a Bábí book. So I put out the light and retired early, in order to get up before dawn to read the book. Again an army of idle thoughts came to me: surely my neighbours will think that the reason for my going to bed in the early hours of the evening was to get up before dawn for no other purpose than to read Bábí books!

'I was beginning to feel at a loss for what to do and to wonder how I should ever have the courage to read this book. A verse from the Qur'án came to my mind. It says that assurance is granted to hearts only through the mention of God. I begged God, the Almighty, to strengthen my heart. As I was praying, something suddenly dawned upon me and I said to myself, "You are frightened to death at the thought of merely reading this book. Ponder then the strength of heart which belonged to the One Who first wrote it. This same courage has been imparted to many others who willingly hastened to the arena of martyrdom."'

These thoughts brought our friend to absolute faith. Though he was involved in extensive commercial enterprises, he spared no effort or time to copy Tablets and he was able to teach many others. The Persian poet says:

> Make no search for water. But find thirst.
> And water from the very ground will burst.

Since I had reached the soil of Persia, following the instructions of the Master, I found a reliable friend by the name of Asadu'lláh, and I entrusted him with all the holy Tablets. I asked him to dispatch them to Tabríz. As for my material possessions, I consulted with the friends on how best to invest my money so that the profit would enable me to travel and teach the Faith. The friends advised me to entrust my capital to the care of a respectable Bahá'í of Tabríz by the name of Ḥájí Aḥmad-i-Mílání. It never occurred to me to leave these material riches with those spiritual ones I had entrusted to Asadu'lláh. Neither I nor my advisors realized the reason for 'Abdu'l-Bahá's instructions. As the proverb says, 'When the end has come, the best physicians are but fools.'

One early morning we set off with a caravan heading for Tabríz. We had scarcely been on the way for more than half an hour when a group of thirty well-armed outlaws issued forth from the hills and spread themselves amongst the travellers. Everything we possessed was stolen – even our clothes were taken from us. We begged them to give us back enough clothing to cover ourselves, but they refused.

I had only one hope. As we had run away, I was able to throw a small pouch containing nineteen gold coins into a pit. After the outlaws abandoned us to our fate and the caravan drivers had scattered to rescue their mules, which had run away in different directions, I returned to the place where I had thrown the pouch and retrieved it. Then I made my way back to the house of friends where I had slept the night before. They brought me clothes to cover my nakedness.

Complaints were sent to the governor, but to no avail. I wrote a letter to the Holy Land and said in light-hearted fashion, 'I obeyed, and entrusted all the Tablets and Holy Writings to a friend upon arrival in Iran; but what would have happened if the same instructions had been given for the care and protection of the property of this servant?'

Many people came to our help, but none ever succeeded in locating the highway robbers nor in retrieving our possessions. The last one who came to help us was Mírzá 'Abdu'lláh Khán, the maternal grandfather of Jináb-i-Varqá. It was a great honour to be with this friend and to be aware of his spiritual excellence. As the days passed, I thanked God every moment that the loss of those ephemeral possessions gave me a chance to spend a few days with him.

I spent four months in that region, making every effort to recover my possessions. But there was no hope. During this time I continued to teach, and several people became Bahá'ís – Ṣúfís, merchants, and shop-keepers. These victories were only the result of being robbed and wronged, and of my suffering and poverty.

Afterwards, I travelled to Ṭihrán for a visit and also to earn a living and to teach the Faith. One Sunday I went to the service of a Protestant mission in the city. While there, I found an opportunity to talk about the Prophets of the past. The minister in charge was delighted and kept me after the service ended. We discussed different matters, and he found me to be sympathetic to the Protestant faith and so was kind to me.

But he was puzzled by my friendliness. He asked me who I knew among the noblemen of the city. I said that I had come to Ṭihrán only recently and that I was involved in cleansing my soul and therefore had met no one. This caused him to be even more curious about me. He appointed some people to spy on me and so discovered that I was a Bahá'í.

When I went to visit him again, he would not see me. 'We receive one hundred thousand tumáns a year from the United States to teach the Faith of Christ', he said. 'But you are a Bahá'í and have come here to infiltrate our group and hunt for converts.'

'I have not come here to hunt for converts from your congregation', I replied, 'but to find if you profess this faith for the sake of money or for the sake of God. Now I see that you love only money and power.'

After this encounter, I did not know what to do. I seemed to be a lost soul. I wanted to earn some money and to serve the Cause of God, but it seemed impossible. At my age, if I entered a profession, I would have no skills or experience, and my work would allow me no time to teach. Then I realized that if I became a scribe, I could satisfy my needs and study the

Sacred Writings as well. So I began to copy some of the Writings for a living. But I was entrapped in a spiritual dilemma.

I listened to the promptings of my own self, and it told me that in the Sudan we used to receive a Tablet at least every month or two. Then, Ḥájí 'Alí and Ḥájí Jásim were sent to convey messages of His love. Now, after all the sufferings that we had endured, ever since we had arrived in Iran there had been no message and no Tablet. Such vain imaginings caused me so much distress that I was nearly destroyed. I was immersed in a sea of despair. But soon I realized that my agony was due to nothing other than my own ignorance.

I continued to transcribe the Sacred Writings. One day, as I was copying the Hidden Words of Bahá'u'lláh, I came across the following verse:

> O Son of Man!
> Humble thyself before Me, that I may graciously visit thee. Arise for the triumph of My cause, that while yet on earth thou mayest obtain the victory.[31]

Suddenly all the past events of my life flashed before me. I examined them one by one, and as I found nothing except my lowliness, and the exaltedness of the bounties of God everywhere and in every instant of my life, I addressed myself saying, 'Act not like the beggars who expect wages for every insignificant deed.'

Fortunately, I was able to triumph over my despair and emerge with a new sense of happiness and responsibility. From then on I have refused to allow myself to feel sad and gloomy, even if all the friends should ignore me. This has never actually happened, but when the slightest suggestion of self would begin to overtake me, I would reproach my own self and say, 'It is your own mistake!'

Because of this inner struggle, I was gradually able to reach a world of tranquillity and immeasurable spiritual exaltation. I was revived, and with a new spirit I hastened to the friends. Many a night we gathered together. The friends were few in number, and we were never apart. These few believers were poor, and everyone earned a meagre living with great difficulty. One of them was Bábá-Ján, the gatekeeper of the house of the Amínu'd-Dawlih. His lunch was provided for him by his master. He would bring this home, and, adding to it a small amount of cheese and yogurt, he would invite the friends to partake of this banquet. It would feed seven.

At night he would provide us with *ábgúsht* (stew).

The only ones who were well off among the friends in Ṭihrán were Áqá Muḥammad Karím 'Aṭṭár and his brother, Ḥájí Muḥammad Raḥím. These two believers and their sisters were all devoted to the Cause of God. Whenever the friends desired to have a sumptuous meal, they would send them a message, and the family would comply with their wishes and send Persian rice and roast meat. One night the brothers themselves attended such a banquet, and the delicious food was followed by fresh fruit. We had a wonderful meeting together.

The time came when I decided to travel to towns and villages in Iran for the purpose of teaching the Cause. In order to be successful during such arduous trips, I adopted the most simple mode of life. I travelled with the caravans. My food consisted of ábgúsht and milk, whenever I could get that. Words fail to explain how all my affairs were arranged, but He hastened to me by miles whenever I drew myself near to Him even as much as one step! Should the whole world ponder this miracle, it would prove impossible to understand or appreciate such mysterious divine bounties. How can we then fittingly express our gratitude? His bounties are endless and our words of praise totally inadequate.

In the course of my Bahá'í tours and teaching sessions, I could feel His invisible and transforming force, which possessed all hearts. Transformation and confirmation are powers which belong to God alone. It is only through His grace and bounty that we weak children are enabled to crawl on the path of servitude. Yet He appreciates our feeble efforts and crowns them with the laurels of His pleasure and acceptance.

For about thirty years I travelled throughout Iran. Should I try to describe all the fallacious arguments and protestations of the people and their bitter disapproval, the love and assistance of the friends, the answers which were given only through divine confirmation and inspiration, this little epistle would become a voluminous book.

In Khurásán, the Shujá'u'd-Dawlih had met Fáḍil-i-Qá'iní (Nabíl-i-Akbar) and other illustrious Bahá'ís. But unfortunately some enemy of the Cause, under the pretence of being knowledgeable about the Faith, had met him and given him many wrong ideas about the Faith. Because of this, I very much desired to meet him so that I might dispel such false conceptions from the mind of this very powerful and influential governor.

One by one, his servants came to see me. I asked them to arrange a meeting between their master and me, and lest he would be disturbed, I emphasized that such a meeting should be held secretly.

A meeting was therefore arranged. When I was admitted to his home, I said that I was a traveller. He immediately asked me if I had been to 'Akká and if I had met Bahá'u'lláh. My answer was affirmative.

'What is His claim?' he asked.

'He claims to be the Promise of all the Prophets of God', I replied. Then I recited many of the verses revealed by His exalted Pen. In conclusion I said that I did not consider myself to be one of His true followers, but endeavoured to explain everything about them based on my own understanding and judgment.

He did not like my statement and he said, 'If you were not one of His followers, you could not speak so fluently about Him and would not have memorized so many passages from His Writings. I know you are one of them; therefore, unveil yourself and speak to me openly.'

When I confessed to him that I was one of the servants of the Cause, he showed me much kindness and commanded me to be in his presence every morning. He permitted me to withdraw only after the midday meal. During those days I explained every detail of the Faith to him – its history, principles, and precepts – and he embraced the Faith of God. Thereafter, people came to our meetings in large numbers.

Because of such victories, I wrote to Bahá'u'lláh and explained that I had spoken of the Faith openly. Soon I received a Tablet which was written in a joking style, yet was most alarming. Bahá'u'lláh stated that since I had confessed to Him that I had violated the principle of wisdom and had spoken openly about the Cause, I had made myself the object of sanction and must receive my punishment. But at the end of the Tablet He made me hopeful and happy by saying that God is always forgiving and compassionate. This Tablet warned me that certain unpleasant things were going to happen to me.

One of the friends told me that the governor had an extraordinary secretary. Should there be one hundred persons of outstanding intellectual faculties, he would surpass them all. But unfortunately he was an atheist and a drunkard.

My friend urged that I see this extraordinary person. It was therefore arranged that I should meet him.

We began talking at about sunset, and we continued throughout the entire night. During the conversation, I did my best to open up a discussion on the Faith, but he stubbornly turned the conversation toward some other subject each time it began to veer in the direction of religion. He was indeed a master of the art of conversation. I was utterly absorbed by the facility with which he directed the flow of our discussion in whatever way he chose. The more he rebuffed my efforts to introduce the subject of religion, the more I liked him and the more I longed to teach him the Faith of Bahá'u'lláh.

In the morning I finally asked him, 'Have you studied any of His Writings?' 'No!' was his immediate reply.

'Why not?' I asked. 'You have such a large library and yet you have not read any of His books.'

'I desire to live by my own free will', he answered.

I mustered my courage and, pointing to his books, said, 'I believe this is sheer prejudice and nothing else. You do not believe in the contents of all these books, and yet you have them and read them. Were it not for this prejudice against the Manifestation of God and His works, you would not refrain from knowing something about our literature.'

He said, 'You have overpowered me. After our long wrestling match, now you have me flat on the floor. You are right. Send me a book and I will read it.'

The Kitáb-i-Íqán was given to him. I saw him the next evening, and he told me that he had read the book at least ten times and was overcome with uncontrollable feelings for the revealed words and the One who had written such powerful utterances and mighty arguments. He wanted to copy it, but one of the friends gave him his book.

When he embraced the Faith, he broke all his barrels of wine and stopped using opium and other drugs. He became such a staunch supporter of the Cause that nothing could dampen his enthusiasm. He taught the Faith to his family and to many others; he met and openly challenged all the outstanding clerics of the province. No matter how we discouraged him, we could not prevent him from this open teaching.

The ‘ulamá grew desperate. Mullá Káẓim, who was the religious leader of the town, went to the Shujá’u’d-Dawlih and asked him to banish or imprison me. But the governor said, ‘Come and debate with him. If he cannot stand your challenges, I will agree to any punishment – even his execution. If I send him away now, the people will believe that I have punished someone who was innocent. I never want to be accused of such a grave error.’

The governor arranged for a meeting in his own presence. Many of the outstanding ‘ulamá were there, and government officials as well as other observers stood by watching the proceedings. I began the discussion by asking the following question:

‘Let us suppose that a Jew who, believing in the Old Testament, states that in more than fifty instances in that Book, God has mentioned that the Judaic dispensation would remain unchanged for eternity. Based on this, he does not believe in Jesus. There is also a Christian who says that it is explicitly stated in the Gospels that heaven and earth may pass away, but not a single word of this Book will ever be changed. This person denies anyone after Jesus. How does God judge such persons, and on what basis would they deserve the wrath of God and His punishment?’

‘There are no such references’, the ‘ulamá replied. The book was brought and references were shown, after which they said, ‘Their books were altered by their followers.’

I replied, ‘This is not possible. People who believe in a Holy Book will never change a single word of it. No thinking person could ever accept such an argument. Even if kings and divines join their forces to alter a word, it would prove absolutely impossible. This is because it is the Book of God and does not exist in only one town or one country. There are copies everywhere. So, even if a very powerful ruler changed some words in the books available in his own country, what about the copies of the same book in other countries and other continents of the world? Moreover, in all the revealed scriptures there is a promise given by God: “We reveal the Book and we protect it”. In many instances in the Qur’án, the Prophet Muḥammad, referring to the Jews and Christians, testifies that He approves and accepts the Books held in their hands.’

The ‘ulamá could not answer these proofs. They said, ‘Why do you speak only of pre-Islamic times and the Holy Books of the past?’ So proofs from the Holy Qur’án were also given.

The governor said, 'His proofs are sound and you cannot deny them.'

Mullá Káẓim became angry and left the room, saying, 'The governor supports the Bábís.' He was brought back. When seated, he said, 'What about the miracles?'

'In the Qur'án,' I started, 'the Prophet Muḥammad has declared that the revealed words of God are His miracles.'

'What about the moon which was split into two parts by just a movement of Muḥammad's finger?'

'Bahá'u'lláh declares that when He was in Adrianople, stars fell to the earth.'

The governor interrupted by saying, 'That is true. We were at the head of a very large army crossing the plains of Khurásán. During the night, suddenly, before our eyes stars began to pour down upon the earth. This spectacle continued for two hours. There were so many stars that the darkness of the night was changed to daylight.'

'If the stars fell,' Mullá Káẓim replied in a mocking tone, 'what are these stars that we see in the sky?'

I replied politely, 'If the moon was split, what is this round object that we see in the sky?' Everyone burst into laughter, and the governor prevented me from going on and asked me not to say anything more.

'We have gathered here to make things clear', he said. 'But I see that the matter has only become more confusing. I fear that the faith of some good Muslims here may be shaken.'

'Yes', Mullá Káẓim insisted. 'These people are masters at deceiving others and causing doubts in people's faith. They have memorized ten weak verses of the Qur'án and twenty doubtful traditions, and they are determined to mislead the whole population.

I replied, 'Although I am forbidden to speak, I hope you will excuse me. I must say this one thing. Why don't you recite the strong verses and the authentic traditions and stop the people from being deceived?' Everyone laughed again.

This discussion continued for more than seven hours, after which the 'ulamá arose to go home. But I could see that evil plots were already stirring in their minds against the Bahá'ís. I weighed the situation in my mind: if I stay here, the sleeping giant of malevolence will be awakened; and if I go, the people will think me a coward. What should I do? The governor was one of the strongest and most determined rulers of the provinces of Persia; because of the flame of his wrath, no one would dare agitate the people. Therefore, I stayed and readied myself for the worst that might occur. I was quite certain that whatever took place would bring only exaltation and prestige to the Cause and aid its propagation throughout those regions.

The next day, when the sun rose, people rushed to my house like locusts from every direction, all armed with sticks and clubs. I put on my clothes and decided to go forth and meet the attackers. I thought that in this way the Holy Scriptures which I had in my home would be spared. When I stepped out, I found myself attacked by no less than two hundred wolves. As they dragged me to the theological school, they spared no opportunity to beat me and utter curses and words of profanity against the Faith.

Mullá Káẓim was standing in the school, surrounded by the angry mob. I asked for a glass of water. I knew that, since they were Shí'ihs, they could not deny my request for water,[32] and I could take the opportunity to gain some respite from their tortures. So water was brought. But the mullá shouted, 'Shut his mouth!' They closed my mouth. Then the mullá approached and struck me on the head with his long stick.

'This is not enough', he told the mob. 'You must stone him.' I was forced out of the town and only God knows what befell me on the way to the outskirts of the city. They tortured me with sticks, clubs, stones, and fire. They finally imprisoned me in a small room situated far from the city walls.

After an hour, they returned and said, 'The mullá has decreed that you should give us your books, after which you will be free to go wherever you choose. If you do not obey, he has told us to tear you to pieces.' After a while the mullá himself came to my cell. He stood before the mob and ordered me to go wherever I desired. He would prevent the people from attacking me further, provided they could see me disappear over the horizon. The mullá and his followers stood and watched.

About noontime, I reached a village. But I was almost naked and covered with blood and wounds. The villagers thought that I had run away from the government prison, and their hearts melted with pity. They washed the blood from my body, applied balm to my wounds, and brought me food and tea. Out of pity they decided to hide me in their village.

In the middle of the night, I heard the galloping of horses. The horsemen asked about me, and I learned that they had been dispatched by the friends. They came in and informed me that the governor had sent twenty horsemen in different directions to find me and assist me to reach a safe destination. They had brought me some money and a cloak. I gave the money to the head of the village, thanked him and the villagers for their generous hospitality, and bade farewell to them. The horsemen told me that we had to reach the city of Qúchán before sunrise. But I was still in great pain, utterly exhausted, and could not ride a horse at great speed. Therefore, they decided to tie me to the horse and make it ride at a gallop until we reached our destination.

We arrived at the house of Mírzá Ḥusayn, and the people of his household, seeing me in that deplorable condition, burst into tears. They wept so bitterly that I could not control my own tears. When we were seated, I told them the whole story and explained that all such events had been foretold in a Tablet I had received from Bahá'u'lláh in which He stated that I would receive religious sanction and punishment.

They informed me that the mob had been aroused to such a frenzy that all the friends and their homes were in danger of attack. They also told me that the Shujá'u'd-Dawlih was furious. He had accused all the divines of conspiring against him. He sent them a message demanding to know why such events had taken place. The 'ulamá proved the worst of liars and the basest of cowards. They answered with the message, 'We know nothing about what the people have done.'

But the brave governor was not satisfied with this false reply. He dispatched soldiers to their town and ordered them to close the theological school, beat its occupants, and bring them all to his presence. Thirty-five siyyids and mullás were dragged to the governor's house. The Shujá'u'd-Dawlih issued an order to beat them all; it took the whole day. After that they were put in prison.

The governor sent a message to Mírzá Ḥusayn, in whose house I had taken refuge, telling both of us, 'You will not be able to withstand the onslaught of the wicked mullás and vicious inhabitants of this town.

Before sunrise, come to my house.' We went to the governor's house, where we beheld the evildoers of the town who had been beaten.

The news of our visit to see the prisoners went far and wide. Soon more than four hundred people who claimed to be the relatives of the prisoners came to me. They cried and begged me to intercede so that the mullás might be freed. Therefore, I approached the governor and asked him to permit the prisoners to go home. He graciously complied with my request.

But the fire of persecution was ignited everywhere. Soldiers went to the inns and announced that anyone who sheltered me would be severely punished and fined. I was in a room at one such inn when I heard the innkeeper ask the soldiers, 'Please tell me what kind of man he is. Is he tall or short; old or young?'

The answer was always the same: 'You should not give him shelter.'

Upon hearing this, I left the inn and became homeless. Wherever I sought lodging I knew that my hosts would be in serious danger because of me. I wavered between hope and fear – hope of reaching some place where I would not endanger the lives of the friends, and fear of the evil consequences which might be heaped upon the Bahá'í communities in small towns and villages where I stayed. I roamed to the east and west, the north and south, and finally came to Ṭihrán.

Mullá Riḍá, the famous preacher of Ṭihrán, spoke every day in the sh//áh's mosque. There was no topic which would please and excite his followers more than the condemnation of the Bahá'í Faith. He recounted to them all sorts of incredible, profane, and fallacious stories. He even dared to announce that the advent of the promised Qá'im, the Imám Mihdí, would definitely take place in the year 1300 AH (circa 1883 AD).

It happened that there was an outstanding Bahá'í by the name of Siyyid Mihdí. The governor of Ṭihrán used to show great respect and homage toward him. For example, once when Siyyid Mihdí desired to go out of the governor's room, the governor hastened to the door, bent down, picked up the siyyid's shoes and placed them at his feet. Such a gesture of respect and devotion was unheard of during the reign of the Qájárs, who were absolutely opposed to the Bahá'ís.

On one occasion this siyyid came to Ṭihrán, and many of the friends went to receive him upon his arrival. When I saw the majestic approach of Siyyid Mihdí, I told the friends, 'Go to Mullá Riḍá and tell him that his promised Mihdí is here now.' For a long time this became a standing joke among the friends. But alas! The same siyyid was soon overcome by his own self and gradually withdrew from the Faith of God, desiring nothing except to acquire material possessions.

In those days, hundreds of Bahá'ís in Ṭihrán were infatuated with this siyyid. But I could see that he manifested nothing but pride and self-importance. I could not bear this situation, so I left Ṭihrán for other provinces.

In the city of Qum, I had the pleasure of meeting the Naddáf family. The two Naddáf brothers had agreed to work long hours in order to earn as much money as possible. They spent some of their earnings for their daily living and offered the rest to the Cause of God, as a token of their gratitude for having attained the knowledge and acceptance of such a stupendous Cause. They were illiterate, but it was evident that their hearts had received innate knowledge through the grace of God. The other members of their families were not Bahá'ís, but the brothers did what they could to make them friendly to the Faith. For example, when people like myself would go to their house as guests, the two brothers would go to the market and purchase gifts. Upon returning home, they would go to the women of their household and give them whatever they had purchased, saying, 'Our friend has brought these gifts for you.' During the same year that I was in their house, they prepared to go to the Holy Land to visit the beloved Master.

Once, Ḥájí Siyyid Javád, a noble, dignified, and illumined believer, left Ṭihrán for Yazd and Kirmán. On his way he stayed in the city of Qum. The two Naddáf brothers found him in one of the inns and brought him some provisions. As they were having dinner together one night, the Naddáfs began to talk about the Faith. The siyyid warned them against talking loudly. 'Some people may hear and arouse the people to riot against us', he said.

One of the two brothers replied, 'You will be on your way home tomorrow. Our other guest will also leave us soon. No one will remain here except us. We are the ones who should be cautious, because the people here know us as Bahá'ís. Therefore, let us avail ourselves of this opportunity to meet you, hear your news, and listen to your exhortations. In this way the people will gradually learn about the Faith.

'Should they stand against us and begin to cause troubles, what shall we do? It is part of God's plan. Through affliction, difficulties, and tests He makes His Cause known. He is the All-Powerful. What can we do? We are the weakest of creatures, the most unknown, and the least significant. Can we go against His overwhelming power?'

The siyyid was astounded by their eloquence and deep understanding. 'Remember the days when the Prophet Muḥammad declared His Mission to His compatriots', one of them continued. 'The first ones who arrayed themselves against Him were His close relatives, the members of the Quraysh clan. One night they invited the Prophet to their abode and received Him with utmost courtesy, praise, and respect. When seated, one of them very disdainfully addressed Him: "Our clan is the most noble of Mecca and we have the privilege and honour to be servants of the Ka'bih.[33] Because of this custodianship, we are respected and revered by all the tribes of Arabia. Now, what you proclaim will become the cause of destruction to this shrine and will create such turmoil that our exalted position, rank, and honour will be totally destroyed. Therefore, we request that you forget your claim and have pity on your family, clan, and people. Otherwise you will gain nothing except persecution, poverty, humiliation, and grievous results in this life and in the life to come."

'When they finished their address, they found Muḥammad in tears. The arrogant members of the Quraysh family took these tears of compassion as a sign of His weakness and compliance with their disgraceful demands. Moved by His tears, they inquired as to the cause. He then opened His mouth and pearls of eternal truth were given them. "I believe in God, Who is the Ever-watchful, the All-Compelling", He said. "I have never claimed anything counter to His will, plan, or desire. He commanded me to rise and say, 'I am chosen by Him to be His Messenger.' I am a human being with the limitations of a man, but I am held in His grasp. How can I ever disobey the One Who is the King of all Kings and the sole Ruler of this world and the Kingdom above?"'

We all benefitted greatly from this deep and meaningful exposition. As they had said, we left the city of Qum for other destinations, and these two illustrious brothers stood steadfast for more than forty years against the cruel onslaught of the most prejudiced inhabitants of that city. Tempestuous opposition created by the oppressors could never shake them. Amidst storms of accusations they cried, 'We believe!' and remained unshaken and unmoved. They continued to teach and to receive all the Bahá'ís who passed through Qum.

To show the hazardous conditions under which the early believers lived and served, I would like to tell you another story which took place in the city of Qum. On one of my trips, the same Naddáf brothers told me of a Muslim friend they knew. He was essentially spiritual, upright, and trustworthy, but he would not accept anything which was not sanctioned by the 'ulamá. It was decided to meet this man in a garden far away from the tumult of the town. Our meeting was arranged and our conversation carried on with mutual love and courtesy. In the course of the conversation, I said something remotely concerned with the Faith. Our friend realized what my purpose was and he kindly said, 'What you say is true, but judgment of such matters lies in the hands of the 'ulamá. Let us talk about countries and climates and customs of tribes and nations.'

I asked him, 'Is it permissible for you to take a written question to the 'ulamá and request them to give you a concise and proper answer?'

'Yes, if you will kindly write it down.'

So I wrote on a piece of paper: 'What are the proofs by which we understand that the Qur'án is the everlasting miracle of the Prophet?' And our naive guest took the written question to the 'ulamá and requested an answer.

When the mullás read this one sentence, they immediately became angry and attacked our friend. They beat him and cursed him and humiliated him. They accused him of being a Bahá'í and tried to imprison him. But this injustice and weakness of the 'ulamá and their inability to answer one simple question awakened this pure-hearted seeker, and he embraced the Faith of God.

The next story took place in the city of Ká<u>sh</u>án, where there were many Bahá'ís whose profession was weaving. Because during these years there were not many customers for such handwoven goods, the friends were very poor. Jináb-i-<u>Gh</u>ulám 'Alí was the most outstanding member of the community. Though not rich, he was always ready to share what he had with the friends and their guests. At his home the favourite dish was a kind of soup to which water could be added when newcomers dropped in unexpectedly. The friends consumed the soup with pieces of bread while the host, who was a well-known humourist, told them jokes and stories. Very often we stayed together in his house until sunrise.

Though poor in material means, the beloved friends of Káshán took care of, protected, and served the poor and destitute, forsaken widows, invalids, and strangers. They were the very embodiment of the verses in the Qur'án in which the Prophet exhorts His people to always prefer others to their own selves and to sacrifice all to the service of their fellowmen.

In Shíráz, I had the honour of meeting three spiritual stars who shone from the horizon of unity. They were as one soul in three bodies. In their commercial dealings they shared profits and losses together, and they carried on this unity in their servitude to the Cause and to the beloved friends. When two of them – Ghulám Ḥusayn and Siyyid 'Alí – passed away, the third, Jináb-i-Dihqán, brought their families under the wing of his care and protection. He looked after the members of these two households as a devoted and affectionate friend and arranged the education of the children on a much higher level than they had enjoyed during the lifetimes of their own fathers. Jináb-i-Dihqán was a standard bearer of the Cause. He sacrificed every atom of his being to the Covenant of God. In addition to inviting me into his house, where I stayed for more than one year and received every day his loving hospitality, he volunteered to pay for my teaching trips. He regularly sent me all the money that I needed during my journeys in Iran.

We heard that Jináb-i-Varqá[34] had been on his way to Shíráz when the soldiers arrested him and took him back to Iṣfahán as a prisoner. One of the Afnán,[35] Siyyid Aḥmad, could not bear to hear about such senseless persecution, which afflicted the friends everywhere. He therefore wrote me a letter and asked me to gather a group of Bahá'ís to go to Russia and lodge complaints against the atrocities inflicted upon the Bahá'ís of Iran. I immediately wrote back and said that this suggestion was against the explicit text of Bahá'u'lláh's teachings. We, as Bahá'ís, must be obedient to our governments and abide by their decisions. Such proposals are wrong, I told him; if the enemies of the Faith learn of this plan, all the Bahá'ís will be in danger, especially people like yourself who are wealthy.

Siyyid Aḥmad wrote back and said, 'I knew that my proposal was fraught with danger. Now I will be happy and content if we are all sacrificed in the path of His Faith. It is certain that the news of such sacrifice will be heard by many. Thus the fame of the Cause will spread in all directions.'

I then wrote back to him and explained that the people of Bahá should not hope to sacrifice their lives by their own choice or plan. Martyrdom is a bounty which can be obtained only through the grace and pleasure of God.

I continued my journeys and reached Yazd. There I had the joyous experience of meeting Afnán Kabír, the maternal uncle of the Báb. He bore a great resemblance to the Exalted Báb in both countenance and character. He was known for his honesty and trustworthiness, his kindness and chastity, his charity and generosity. Though people knew him as one of the followers of the Faith, he remained the most trusted and respected individual in the province of Yazd. The 'ulamá and the government officials respected him to such a degree that the most difficult and frustrating cases were referred to him and his judgment sought and invariably obeyed. All the other Afnán lived under his shadow. Many believers were attracted to the Faith by his spiritual attainments.

The Afnán of Yazd and Shíráz received a Tablet from Bahá'u'lláh in which He expressed the desire that the friends should settle in 'Ishqábád, Russia. Two master masons arose to answer the call of their Lord. They set out for 'Ishqábád with the intention of building shops, houses, and an inn for the Afnán. I accompanied them, hoping that I could be of some service to the Faith.

On our way we reached Fárán where the illustrious Mír Muḥammad had his residence. He and his large family had been the pivot of affairs in that town, and thus the friends were well protected and lived in peace under the vigilant eye of this veteran general of the Army of Light. It was here that I received the answer to my letter sent from Shíráz. In this Tablet, Bahá'u'lláh praised the sacrificial spirit and devotion of Siyyid Aḥmad, but to his aforementioned plan He definitely said, 'No'. As to myself, He instructed me that it would not be wise for me to go to 'Ishqábád. The two masons were encouraged to go there, settle, and serve the Faith. I was told that I was also forbidden to go to Iṣfahán or Ṭihrán. Beyond this, the believers advised me not to go to Yazd or S͟híráz because I was too well known in those places, and my presence might cause disturbances.

I wrote back to the Holy Land and said, 'My God, what should I do? Ṭihrán, Iṣfahán, and 'Is͟hqábád are forbidden by You, and S͟híráz and Yazd by Your steadfast servants.' I was at a loss for what to do. The doors of all the provinces were closed to me. I wandered around the province of K͟hurásán, existing only by the generosity of the Afnán. I knew that I had no way out of this dilemma except to turn my face toward 'Akká and leave Iran for His holy presence.

Since one of the faithful maidservants of the Cause who lived in Ṭihrán had written to Bahá'u'lláh asking that she might marry me, the Blessed Perfection ordered me to travel to Ṭihrán to be married. Permission to go to the Holy Land came in the next Tablet. For the next fourteen or fifteen years that faithful maidservant who was inflamed with the love of Bahá'u'lláh served me with humility and selflessness. Her devoted services to me were so great that I am ashamed when I mention them.

I set out for the Holy Land, and part of the journey was by sea. On board ship I met someone from 'Akká who constantly talked of 'Abbás Effendi and His unique character. I told him that I knew that He had many followers in Iran, but asked him to tell me more. He was encouraged to relate more stories about 'Abdu'l-Bahá. He praised Him so highly that I eventually told him, 'Now, I must go to 'Akká and meet this exalted person.'

After disembarking in the Holy Land, this same man hastened to 'Abdu'l-Bahá before me and said, 'I have talked about the Faith to a Persian and he will be coming here to visit you. Surely he will become a Bahá'í!'

Before entering the presence of the Blessed Beauty, I prepared myself for a great spiritual feast. I repeated in my mind and heart: 'This is the day foretold by all the Prophets of God. This is the town praised and exalted by David. This is the plain of Sharon coveted by all the Holy Ones of the past. Now you are here with the burden of your sins and shortcomings.' When my eager eyes fell upon the countenance of my Lord, I was so overwhelmed that I could not describe my feelings to the friends. I was indeed like a dumb person who has a sweet dream and is powerless to describe it.

Bahá'u'lláh asked me about the friends in Iran, and He granted me the courage and power to speak in His presence. 'The beloved friends, though from widely different backgrounds, having grown up with different ideas, beliefs, and degrees of understanding, are united in one thing', I said, 'and that is to win the pleasure of God. Confined in prisons, kept in chains, beset by perpetual hardships and persecutions, they remain firm and steadfast so that the Ancient Beauty will be pleased with them.'

One night the beloved Master spoke about Mullá 'Alí-Ján. When I was travelling in the districts of Mázindarán, I had the honour of meeting this great and illumined soul. I discovered that Mullá 'Alí-Ján had taught more than five hundred people in Máhfurújak and its surrounding areas. Besides bringing them into the Cause, he had educated them and deepened them. He had instructed the women to dress modestly. He had taught the men to dress neatly and to be meticulously clean. It was absolutely forbidden for them to use vulgar or profane words. He instructed that in each house a special room be suitably furnished for prayer.

Upon their return home from a day's work, men and women alike would wash, change their clothes, and perform their prayers. After dinner the friends would be called to gather in one of the houses for a meeting to discuss Bahá'í matters. He had selected a few to teach and educate other believers. His wife and his three nephews helped him in these efforts by transcribing the Tablets and chanting them with melodious voices in the meetings. The Bahá'ís of Máhfurújak were so well trained that, although they were all well known, the 'ulamá could not find any reason to complain about their behaviour.

Mullá 'Alí-Ján was so deeply enthralled by the love of God that whenever he heard any Tablet read at the gatherings of the friends, he would take these words as a call inviting him to return to his Creator. Often he said to himself, "Alí! 'Alí! 'Alí! Are you still sitting here? Are you still living comfortably? Your Lord has written to you. Why don't you hasten to the arena of sacrifice? Why don't you raise your voice in His praise?'

The time came when the same Mullá 'Alí-Ján was taken captive because of a decree issued by the 'ulamá. He was taken in chains to Ṭihrán and brought to the house of Kámrán Mírzá, a high official. Kámrán Mírzá approached him and said, 'I have brought you good news! If you just tell me that you know nothing about this Cause, you will immediately be set free and allowed to return to your home and family. Furthermore, I will grant you a regular salary, special clothes adorned with the royal emblem, and a title from the sháh. Please have pity upon yourself and upon your children.'

'I will never agree to such a humiliating transaction', 'Alí-Ján replied. 'I will not barter my religion for gold, nor exchange eternal life for this ephemeral world. Tribulation in the path of God is to me far more exalted than anything in this mundane life.'

He was immediately put in heavy chains and sent to one of the squares of Ṭihrán to be killed. Under the burden of those heavy fetters, he walked so quickly that the executioners could not keep up with him. Many people who witnessed his execution became attracted to the Faith because of his courage, his inner joy, and his complete assurance.

Mullá 'Alí-Ján's wife, 'Alavíyyih Khánum, also had her share of suffering. After the martyrdom of her husband, she was arrested by the governor. He addressed her, saying, 'How dare you claim to be Fáṭimih, the daughter of the Prophet Muḥammad!'

'I have never claimed that', was her courageous reply. 'But now that you have made me a captive, I feel certain that I belong to her family.' Although she was only twenty-three years of age when she lost her husband, she never accepted another marriage. She expended her youth and all that she had in travelling and serving the Cause. She had the honour of attaining the presence of the Master.

The spiritual transformation experienced by those who have attained the presence of Bahá'u'lláh is so far above limited human experience that it cannot be described. It is that Paradise which is said never to have been seen by mortal eyes, nor experienced by earthly senses. The experience is like a tempestuous ocean, each wave of which brings forth pearls of beauty. Yet the waters of this ocean are so blissful that one does not even want to swim, but only wishes to be drowned in its ecstasy. This unbelievable joy often comes and passes like lightning. It is only granted to a few through a special bounty of the Lord, and then it will be manifested only as strongly as their spiritual capacity will allow.

Once I requested to be in Bahá'u'lláh's room when He was revealing Tablets. This request met with His approval. As I entered His room, I heard streams of words sweeping along in a torrential flow from His lips. It seemed that the atmosphere, the floor, the walls, and every atom in the room was filled with perfume. Only those who have had this indescribable experience can ever imagine what I mean. The flow of revelation continued for about five minutes. Then Bahá'u'lláh said to me, 'You have on several occasions been here when the revelation of Tablets has taken place. Should the people of the whole world wish to be present and hear the words of revelation, We would permit them. But since We have approved courtesy and ordained it upon men, we are reluctant to display this power publicly.'

The story is told that the brutal Shaykh Muḥammad-Báqir who was responsible for the martyrdom of so many Bahá'ís and whom Bahá'u'lláh named 'The Wolf' because of his evil plots, once shouted from his pulpit, 'Translate the chapter of the Qur'án in which the Prophet Muḥammad proclaims that God is one, has always existed, and can never be born. Give this to the Bahá'ís who have taken Bahá'u'lláh as their God.'

When the Ancient Beauty heard this, He said that Moses had heard the call of 'I am your God' from a burning bush. Why not from a man?

For a long time I carried the desire to prostrate myself at the feet of Bahá'u'lláh. Once I was admitted to His room as He was pacing the floor. When He came toward me, I flattened myself against the wall. As He walked away, I followed Him one or two steps in the hope of fulfilling my heart's desire. But then He turned, and I retreated and stood meekly against the wall.

'What is the matter?' He said, with a heavenly smile, 'I see that you are going back and forth.' Then He stretched forth His hand and commanded me, 'Stay where you are!' Though my wish was not fulfilled, the movement of His hand and that smile of pleasure brought me immeasurable joy.

On this pilgrimage also, when I was asked to depart, I requested that I be permitted to remain two more weeks. Bahá'u'lláh again asked for a guarantee. I immediately replied, 'The Master!' since we all knew that the Master's wish would be done. That evening I was admitted to the room of the Blessed Beauty where He told me, 'Stay one month more.

Your Guarantee is great, beloved, and precious. So you may stay more.'

Then He continued, 'In the days when We lived in Baghdád, We used to go to a coffeehouse where We would meet friends, strangers, and all sorts of people. This was the means by which the Word of God could be heard, and many souls were led into the Cause. But in Adrianople, and here in 'Akká, it is the Master who performs these services. He must face the same hardships which We faced previously. In Baghdád We were not imprisoned, and the fame of the Cause was not even a hundredth part of what it is today. Also, the enemies of the Cause were not as many or as powerful as they are now. In Adrianople We met many people, but in the Most Great Prison, We seldom receive visitors who are not believers. The burden of all these affairs has fallen upon the shoulders of the Master. To provide Us with some peace and comfort, He has made Himself Our shield, and thus He sees to Our affairs both with the government and with the people. He first prepared for Us the house at Mazra'ih, and then He procured this Mansion in Bahjí. He is so devoted to His services and so intensely occupied that sometimes weeks pass by and He cannot come here to visit Us. While We consort with the friends and reveal Tablets, He is immersed in the toils and troubles of the world.'

When I was permitted to come again into Bahá'u'lláh's presence, He said, 'The utterances of the Most Great Branch ('Abdu'l-Bahá) and His power are now concealed. Later it will be seen how He, singly and alone, will raise the banner of the Faith in the world. He will gather all mankind under the Tabernacle of peace and submission.' This was, of course, only the gist of His words, so far as I can remember them.

Bahá'u'lláh was usually in His room in the Mansion of Bahjí. From there He could see 'Abdu'l-Bahá as He approached the Mansion from 'Akká. When He would catch sight of Him, He would invariably ask all those in His presence to go out to meet Him.

One day Bahá'u'lláh was very sad. His sadness was caused by the behaviour of a few of the believers who lived in His household. In great sorrow He said, 'Were it possible, We would recommend that the pilgrims who enter the city of 'Akká go directly to the presence of the Most Great Branch, listen to Him, then meet some of the steadfast believers, and immediately afterwards leave 'Akká and return to their homes. This would be most conducive to their spiritual development. The reason is this: In the Master's presence the friends are not subjected to tainted human thoughts and deeds. All they experience is heavenly sanctity. If the people would open their eyes, they would see clearly the difference between the heavenly perfections of the Master and the human frailties and faults of others. Then, even if they witness odious deeds committed in My household, they will only utter words of praise about the greatness and patience of the True One Who is glorious, mighty, and compassionate. We are aware of their false words and lies. We know. But We must remain silent and cover their sins. Unfortunately, the liars think that We do not know the truth.'

A tailor by the name of Muḥammad-'Alí came on pilgrimage. He had a good character and a happy disposition, and he was endowed with quick understanding. He often circumambulated the Mansion of Bahjí. When he came to meet the friends, he would make them happy with his beautiful stories. Once he sent me a letter in which he related that a very famous mystic leader had said, 'O God! If I hear Thee calling me only once "My servant", I will ascend to heaven.' He told me that he had often walked around the gardens near the Mansion of Bahjí and felt immense joy. But never had he heard those sweet words.

I sent a letter to Bahá'u'lláh about this pilgrim, and we received a wonderful Tablet in which He calls each one of us 'My servant' not one, but nine times. In the Islamic traditions we had read the famous saying, 'Should the people approach Him only one yard, He will hasten to them by miles.' Now we saw the fulfilment of this promise.

Now there remained only three nights until the end of my pilgrimage, and I was summoned to the presence of Bahá'u'lláh. He spoke of His exiles and emphasized the fact that should the people ponder carefully on these different stages of His banishment, they would know that every step had been taken according to the Will of God. 'The hand of God is over all, and His might and power overwhelm the worlds of creation. Consider the case of those persons who, fearing the loss of their temporal powers, condemned Us to the Most Great Prison. Where are they now? What has befallen each and every one of them? God brought them down from their places and consigned them to their graves. Their names are never mentioned. But your Lord is established in this Mansion through the power of God, His might, and His sovereignty.'

He then asked someone to chant parts of the two Tablets addressed to the Sulṭán of the Ottoman Empire and to the shí́h of Persia. After that, the pilgrims were dismissed.

During our dinner someone brought sweets sent to us by Bahá'u'lláh. He also sent a message concerning me: 'Tell him to eat the sweets and say to himself, "I must go home."' This time I got ready to go and did not plan to ask the beloved Master to intervene on my behalf or to guarantee me. The sweet memory of His loving wit that I should tell myself, 'I must go home', remains fresh in my heart, and even more as I surrender my will to that of God.

The next day we had torrential rains. In the afternoon of that same day, I went to see Him. The moment I entered His room, He said, 'It seems that you expect the rain to intercede for you.' This tender joke helped to change all my despair into joy. When I returned to the Pilgrim House and reported my interview to the friends, they were all of the opinion that the next day there would again be rain, and that Bahá'u'lláh would not send me away.

But the day dawned with splendid sunshine, and I went to His room in the Mansion of Bahjí. He spoke about teaching. He said: 'A kindly approach and loving behaviour toward the people are the first requirements for teaching the Cause. The teacher must carefully listen to whatever a person has to say – even though his talk may consist only of vain imaginings and blind repetitions of the opinions of others. One should not resist or engage in argument. The teacher must avoid disputes which will end in stubborn refusal or hostility, because the other person will feel overpowered and defeated. Therefore, he will be more inclined to reject the Cause.

'One should rather say, "Maybe you are right, but kindly consider the question from this other point of view." Consideration, respect, and love encourage people to listen and do not force them to respond with hostility. They are convinced because they see that your purpose is not to defeat them, but to convey truth, or to manifest courtesy, and to show forth heavenly attributes. This will encourage the people to be fair. Their spiritual natures will respond, and, by the bounty of God, they will find themselves recreated.

‘Consider the way in which the Master teaches the people. He listens very carefully to the most hollow and senseless talk. He listens so intently that the speaker says to himself, “He is trying to learn from me.” Then the Master gradually and very carefully, by means that the other person does not perceive, puts him on the right path and endows him with a fresh power of understanding.’

When the final moment approached and I bade farewell to my Beloved, He approached the door and whispered in my ear, ‘I have entrusted you to the hands of the Master.’ Though these words were spoken with the utmost sweetness, and were a sign of His sublime consideration and love, they filled my heart with dark clouds of sorrow. They seemed to me to indicate clearly His imminent departure from this world.

Next I went to ‘Akká, to the presence of the Master. There was no end to His love. He had written a letter to Bahá’u’lláh requesting that I be permitted to stay, even outside the city of ‘Akká, because the sea had been rough and agitated. His letter had been returned with one sentence on the top: ‘It is better for him to go; God is the Protector – rest assured.’

From ‘Akká I went to Haifa and boarded a ship bound for Constantinople. After a short stay in that city I went on to Baku, in Russian Caucasia, and from there to Ṭihrán.

In Ṭihrán I learned that Muslims had attacked the friends in Ishtihárd, confiscated their property, beaten both men and women, imprisoned them, and destroyed their houses. More than fifty of these believers were now in Ṭihrán, and they gathered together to consult about this situation. They decided to send a petition to the court of the sháh asking for justice. Since they heard that I had been in the Holy Land, they asked to meet me in order to hear about the One in Whose path they had sacrificed their homes, their property, and their loved ones, and for Whom they were willing to offer up their own lives.

At this time it was not safe to hold large Bahá’í meetings in Ṭihrán. Therefore, after consultation, we agreed that every night only five of them would come, accompanied by the Hand of the Cause Mullá ‘Alí-Akbar. We made ready to receive five, but at the appointed hour fifty of them entered my room. Our joy knew no bounds. We chanted Tablets and prayers. We spoke of Bahá'u'lláh and consulted about their persecutions. For hours after sunset, thinking that there would not be enough food for the more than fifty people who had gathered, I refrained from inviting them for dinner and they all departed.

When my wife learned of this, she became very sad. With tears in her eyes, she rebuked me. 'I have prepared bread, cheese, and meat for more than fifty people', she said. 'These are the ones whose houses have been plundered in the path of God. Their families are dispersed because of their love for Bahá'u'lláh. Now, homeless and unsheltered as they are, they come to our humble home. What answer will we have if God asks us, "Why did you send them away unfed?"'

It was only then that I realized what a grave error I had committed. It is true that we must be prudent, but in this case I had been most uncharitable. To satisfy my wife and to make her dear heart happy and contented, we agreed that all of them would come again to our home, in groups of six, for dinner.

Not long after that I was instructed to go to Iṣfahán. I reached there when the families of the two illustrious believers, the King of Martyrs and the Beloved of Martyrs,[36] were preparing to go to the Holy Land. These dear friends were constantly in trouble. The governor and the 'ulamá, through their evil agents, were always ready to heap fresh persecutions upon them. Their departure from the tumultuous town of Iṣfahán seemed impossible.

The dreadful memory of the days when the force of hatred was set loose in Iṣfahán, and swallowed these two brothers in its flames, was still vivid in their minds. They were afraid that the same fate would befall the remaining members of their family. But their longing to reach His presence was stronger than their caution. Eventually their love overcame their fear, and they courageously made their way homeward – to the home of their hearts and souls. When they reached the Holy Land, the bounties they received were beyond measure. They were invited to remain in His presence for one year.

After their departure for the Holy Land, the sleeping giant awoke, and the inhabitants of Iṣfahán threatened to tear down their houses, plunder their riches, and cut the pilgrims themselves to pieces as soon as they might return. Anxiety and fear prevailed everywhere, and the other believers in the city lived in perpetual anxiety.

Eventually I wrote to the Holy Land, explained the situation, and suggested that the pilgrims stay in Ṭihrán for some months until, by the grace of God, this consuming fire might be extinguished. The reply was prompt and decisive. In a Tablet, Bahá'u'lláh assured the friends that the pilgrims would return safely. He revealed a prayer for them to chant upon their arrival home.

When our friends returned to Iṣfahán, they were accorded great respect by the people. Many of the 'ulamá and the notables came to their houses to welcome them home.

During this period, Mírzá Abu'l-Faḍl[37] blessed the soil of Iṣfahán with his presence. As he had been a student in Iṣfahán some years before, many of the divines and students of theology knew him well. But when they met him again, they discovered that this man was not the same Mírzá Abu'l-Faḍl whom they had known as a student in their theological schools. Then he was but a drop. Now they discovered that he had become an ocean. One of the famous teachers of the town, after visiting him, declared, 'If all the erudite leaders of our time surrounded Mírzá Abu'l-Faḍl, he would be a giant among pygmies. He is truly unique to our age, and eclipses any one of the 'ulamá in oration, in reasoning, and in his ability to explain philosophical questions.'

On one of my trips to Iṣfahán I arrived during the night and went directly to the house of one of the friends. It was almost midnight. The owner of the house prepared tea for me, but I saw signs of sorrow and anxiety on his face. When I inquired as to the reason, he said, 'Yesterday they killed Mullá A<u>sh</u>raf. And now they are looking for me.' I asked him to tell me more.

'Some days ago, A<u>sh</u>raf related a dream to us. In his dream he had seen the Báb, Who summoned him to His exalted presence. Immediately he found that he could fly. He began to soar higher and higher to reach Him. As he approached the Báb, his cloak fell off. When he reached His presence, the Báb said, "Look!" He looked, and found all the people illumined and united, with the light of love emanating from each. They were all singing songs in praise of the Greatest Name.

‘When he related this dream, Ashraf told us that he regarded it as a clear indication of his return to his Lord. He felt that this would take place very soon.’

Two or three days passed. He met a man, a wolf in sheep’s clothing, who pretended to be a true seeker after truth. Ashraf spoke about the Faith to him on four consecutive nights. Then the ‘seeker’ invited him to have tea with him in one of the schools of theology. Friends of Ashraf who knew this ‘seeker’ urged him not to accept the invitation. They warned that this man was a Judas Iscariot. In answer to their warnings, Ashraf said, ‘I leave my affairs in the hands of God.’ And he went. The moment he stepped into the school, three or four soldiers arrested him and dragged him to the seat of the governor. When he reached there, it was night and he was placed in prison.

In the morning the people of Iṣfahán saw a cross raised in the public square of their city. But they did not know why it had been erected. Ashraf was brought to the governor’s house. Although frail in body, he had been placed in chains. His dignified demeanour and his tranquil appearance so impressed the members of the government that even some of the princes arose to intervene on his behalf. ‘Do not stain your hands with the blood of this old man’, they warned. But their appeal fell on deaf ears. They raised this noble soul on the cross, but it broke. And so the day ended and Ashraf was returned to prison.

On the second day, the crowd gathered once more in the same square. All the notables pleaded on Ashraf’s behalf even more fervently than before. They insisted that the murder of this old man would be an evil omen for the governor. But the governor remained adamant. Finally he shouted, ‘Let the ‘ulamá gather and debate with him. Should his killing seem wrong and unjust, may God keep him safe from the fury of Áqá Najafí.’

On the third day, the ‘ulamá assembled in the presence of the governor. Two thousand people stood waiting for the arrival of Ashraf. He was brought in with heavy chains. They asked him questions, and he gave eloquent and courageous answers.

The ‘ulamá ordered him to recant his faith. He declared, ‘I abhor all lies, all deviations, and all false claims.’ But they were not satisfied.

‘Exonerate yourself by cursing the names of the founders of the Bahá’í religion’, Najafí demanded.

'The cursing of names is forbidden in the Qur'án even to denounce the gods of heathens', was A<u>sh</u>raf's firm answer. 'I believe in Islám. I greeted you with "Salám 'Alaykum". I am a mujtahid like yourselves; I know that it is the duty of every Muslim to investigate the fundamental principles of his own religion.' Many of the notables and dignitaries became disgusted with their unfair proceedings and so left the meeting in anger.

Najafí became more furious than ever and shouted, 'Let the people come in and bear witness to the fact that this man teaches the Bábí Faith!'

A<u>sh</u>raf immediately answered, 'It is very clear that people recruited from the market or the streets who come in and find me in chains will surely accuse me of whatever you wish. Remove the chains and then bring the people and have them point to who is guilty.' But they would not agree. At this point there was another exodus of government officials; even some of the 'ulamá left the meeting. Prince 'Abbás Qulí Mírzá became very angry. He stood up and as he left the room said, 'They are unjustly killing an old man, and yet they claim to be the religious leaders of the town.'

None of these remarks quenched the thirst of Áqá Najafí for the blood of Mullá A<u>sh</u>raf. He issued a decree that he must be put to death.

Though A<u>sh</u>raf was old, he hastened toward his cross so quickly that the soldiers could not overtake him. Upon his arrival at the cross, he kissed it and said, 'We are of God and to Him shall we return.' His highest wish was fulfilled, and his name became immortalized in one of the Tablets of Bahá'u'lláh. In this Tablet He says that the city of lovers became filled with love and exultation because one of the precious jewels decided to make its way back to His eternal treasure house, that one of His lovers hastened and attained the presence of his Beloved. The Exalted Pen expressed intense distress about the ignorant mob and the proud 'ulamá who remained unmoved at the sight of such a wondrous sacrifice.

After these dreadful days, the friends did not find it wise for me to prolong my stay in Iṣfahán. I left for other parts. For many months I journeyed through different provinces of Persia, staying longer in Kirmán where many strong and malignant enemies of the Cause were living. They had one, and only one, track to follow – to disprove and refute the teachings of the Faith. This they did constantly by every means which their wicked hearts could devise. Sometimes they forged tablets which they showed to people to discourage them from investigating the Faith. Association with such people was even more difficult than the tortures of prison.

In Khurásán I had the pleasure of meeting the lion-hearted Fáḍil-i-Furúghí. He was a treasure of learning and zeal. Many a time I proposed to him that such a staunch upholder of the Cause should leave his small town, travel around Persia, and impart to the friends his knowledge and love. The day came when he began his journeys. No sooner did he step into the arena of sacrifice and service outside his village than his fame went far and wide. Eventually he became a target for the jealousy and malevolence of the 'ulamá, who devised the most cunning plots against him.

Repeatedly the most outstanding members of the clergy decreed for him imprisonment, exile, and death. He became a wanderer and eventually was captured and put in chains. His life was in such danger that none of the friends had the slightest hope of his survival. However, after his release from prison, it seemed that some mysterious force protected him and enabled him to achieve great success in his teaching trips. The meetings held in his presence vibrated with his spiritual ardour. In one Tablet 'Abdu'l-Bahá calls him 'The Commander of the Great Army'. He made a pilgrimage and retuned to Persia with renewed courage, enthusiasm, and fervour.

I also had the honour of visiting the town of Bushrúyih, in Khurásán, the home of Mullá Ḥusayn. When I arrived there, I felt strong spiritual reverberations. It was as if the soil, the water, even the air itself vibrated with divine favours. The whole atmosphere seemed perfumed with the love of the Merciful. It was my joy and honour to visit the sister and nephew of Mullá Ḥusayn.

As the chosen ones were plentiful, so the enemies of the Cause were also many in number. They emerged with fanatic hatred whenever a stranger came to visit the small groups of solitary believers who had no share of life except bitter suffering. The enemies of the Cause were like wild beasts who sharpened their teeth and claws, waiting to pounce on the defenceless Bahá'ís scattered in isolated parts of the country.

My stay lasted one month. People gathered in large numbers to listen to the Writings and to listen to me speak of the Faith. After a while we learned that Muslims were joining forces against the small band of believers. Every morning and every evening we heard the voice of the imám from the top of the minaret of the mosque saying, 'Islám is dead. Heresy! Heresy! The people's faith is dead. Where is our religion? What has happened to our faith?'

I wrote to the leading mujtahid of the town and invited him to come to our meetings so that we could debate openly. I said that some government officials would also be asked to attend to witness the debate. This challenge quieted him effectively, and the fire subsided.

I can never forget one gifted woman by the name of Rúḥá. She had never been to school, but she was the pride of her sex. She was a heroic soul who, because of her audacious deeds, became known to the shah and his ministers. She was a living Ṭáhirih of those days. A weaver of cloth, her income was scanty, but whatever she earned she spent in travelling around to proclaim the name of Bahá'u'lláh. Her manners, her detachment, and her enterprising spirit are examples to be emulated by every aspiring teacher of the Cause.

In Ṭabas I met a very just and benevolent governor. He was known as 'Imádu'l-Mulk. He was fair and just to all his subjects. Under his rule all were taken care of and protected against ill-wishers. As a young man, he had met Bahá'u'lláh in Iraq, and he mentioned this very often. He had a pocketknife Bahá'u'lláh had given him, which he kept wrapped in a beautiful piece of velvet. He was very proud of the fact that he had had the opportunity of being in His presence.

When he passed away, his son inherited his father's title and position. In his love for the Cause, this son, who was now the governor, even went further than his father. He chose a very beautiful building as the place where the Bahá'í meetings were to be held. There was no end to the love and kindness he showed to the believers. Because of him many important people from the surrounding area became Bahá'ís. He was attracted to the Cause by the fundamental principles of the Faith. He very much admired the teaching that any controversy among the friends should be removed by referring the matter to the appointed and authorized Interpreter of the Word of God.

In Yazd and in many other provinces of Persia, I found that the distinguished behaviour of all the Afnán had won the admiration, wonder, and praise of all who knew them. The seeds sown and watered by the blood of the martyrs had grown under the sunshine of the love of these illustrious relatives of the Báb. 'They are perfect in everything', people would say. 'What a pity that they are Bahá'ís.'

When I was in Yazd, I lived in the house of Jináb-i-Afnán. During the summer, because of the intense heat, people would sleep on their roofs. Early one morning, when I descended from the roof, I found Afnán sitting immersed in thought. Because of the deep sadness on his face, I knew that something serious had happened. I did not dare to approach him, since I was still in my sleeping garment and not suitably dressed to attend the presence of such a venerable person. He withdrew, but sent a sealed envelope to me. When I opened it, I found the Tablet of 'Abdu'l-Bahá announcing the ascension of Bahá'u'lláh.

I was so stunned that I could not even cry. The friends gradually gathered in the house of the Afnán. They were so stricken with grief that no one talked. In the midst of this intense sorrow and bewilderment, Jináb-i-Afnán joined us. He wept openly, and all wept with him. He addressed us, saying, 'It was decreed that He would one day rid Himself of the endless suffering of this world. It was written that He would one day return to the Source of His glory. Praise be to God that He has left His sorrow-filled friends One Who will guide us. This is no less a person than the "Mystery of God".[38] We must hold fast to the hem of His mercy and arise to serve the Cause of God and be His true servants, sacrificing all that we have to uphold our beloved Faith.'

After hearing these consoling words, we again read the Tablet of 'Abdu'l-Bahá and decided to hold memorial meetings for nine consecutive days and nights where all the friends would gather together.

The news of His ascension spread everywhere and, though the population of Persia was at that time in the grip of a merciless attack of cholera, the people made merry and rejoiced and ridiculed the Bahá'ís.

A week after the news of His ascension had reached us, the friends received a copy of the Kitáb-i-'Ahd (the Book of the Covenant). Emphatically and explicitly, He had appointed the beloved Master as the sole Interpreter of His Word. When the friends received this great news, they were calmed, and, with hearts full of hope, they arose to raise the banner of servitude and uphold it with their utmost strength.

The ministry of 'Abdu'l-Bahá began so vigorously that Bahá'í communities everywhere were overwhelmed. Letters from the Master poured into every village, town, and country like the drops of the rains of spring. The friends were cheered and enamoured by His life-giving words. Whoever received a Tablet would make many copies and send them as precious gifts to friends throughout the length and breadth of the East. This opened a new field of activity, that of regular and informative correspondence amongst all the believers.

'Abdu'l-Bahá explained to the Bahá'ís that the physical body of the Prophet of God is like a cloud which covers the sun and which prevents its rays from reaching the earth. Because of their physical limitations, the Prophets of God must live by the rules of physical existence. For this reason, many people are tested. They will say, 'What kind of Prophet is He? He sleeps and eats and walks the streets like everyone else.' But when the cloud is removed, the rays of the sun reach the people directly, and the whole of creation is resuscitated by their life-giving light.

The friends became aware of their opportunities and bounties. Therefore, they arose in unprecedented numbers to proclaim the Faith and teach the Cause. Gradually, more enthusiasm, unity, and activity developed on every level of Bahá'í life. In a short time, lethargy, indifference, and coolness were replaced by intense teaching activities.

Such manifestations of zeal and ardour encouraged me also to act. At the urging of the Afnán, I wrote an open letter to the 'ulamá proclaiming the truth of this Cause. I then began fresh teaching tours in the days of the Covenant.

While I was in Ábádih I received a parcel from the Holy Land. It contained eighty-one Tablets written by 'Abdu'l-Bahá. But they came with unusual instructions: 'Do not read the Tablets. Choose eighteen believers. As you meet them, write their names on the Tablets and give them away. Do this also in Iṣfahán, Bavánát, and Yazd. Write the name of anyone you choose. You may also send the Tablets to some recipients, if you do not meet them in person.'

When I completed the task, I learned that whoever received one of the Master's Tablets found in it an expression responding to his own deepest longings. The fame of this event went everywhere. An Englishman who was the head of the telegraph office of Ábádih heard of this extraordinary occurrence. He said, 'It is very strange for me to learn of the spiritual powers of a human being. I wonder how He knew the secrets of these people's souls. The character and perfection of these believers are testimonies to the divine education they receive from Him.' This gentleman openly affirmed his belief in the Faith.[39]

I went to Iṣfahán, where I met Jináb-i-Vazír. He was the most outstanding person in that district. The finances of the province were under his jurisdiction, and practically everyone in the area knew that he and his family were Bahá'ís. Though the governor knew him better than anyone else, and knew that he was a follower of the Faith, he had absolute confidence in him. Shaykh Najafí, whose thirst for the blood of the Bahá'ís was never quenched, kept silent about Vazír. If he said anything about him, it was in praise. Jináb-i-Vazír treated the shaykh like a hungry wolf. Every now and then he would send him gifts, and this would appease him temporarily.

Ardistán was the home of Jináb-i-Fatḥ-i-A'zam.[40] I had visited him several times, and each time I had witnessed the wonderful signs of courage and steadfastness in him and in his son, Shaháb. This family and that of Jináb-i-Rafí'á were the pillars of the Cause in those regions. There were many Bahá'ís in this town, and most of them lived in one neighbourhood. Because of the shining example of these two families, all of the believers were strong and firm in the Covenant.

My tours of Ardistán, Iṣfahán, and the surrounding areas became so fruitful that they enraged Shaykh Najafí. He called for a general meeting in the Mosque of the Sháh. When the hall was packed, he ascended the pulpit and began, 'O faithful Muslims! To protect Islám is a duty incumbent upon every Muslim. We really did not do enough in the past to eradicate this misguided community of Bábís. Our only consolation was the belief that the one who called himself Bahá'u'lláh and led many people astray, would die one day. Then his cause would be forgotten, like those of all false claimants of the past.

Now we have learned that he has a son who in every respect is more learned and more audacious in the propagation of his religion than his father. He has risen with such might and power that he will soon eradicate Islám and will impose a tax on all Muslims.

'The shâh and his government captured, imprisoned, tortured, and killed as many followers of this false religion as they could. Many of them were expelled from the country. But now we see that the government is inactive. Therefore, it is your duty to arise and kill every Bahá'í by every means in your power. We pray that God will aid you and assist you. You may cleanse the country of this hated community. This will be considered as your greatest service to Islám, and your reward will be paradise, where spacious mansions, beautiful angels, and all that your hearts desire are awaiting you.'

In every community there are people who are eager to riot and wreak destruction. Such people, once aroused by the religious leaders, considered the worst crimes as acts of piety. This was particularly true in this case, when they could freely attack and kill Bahá'ís, as well as plunder and loot their property. When the believers, who had no means of defence, heard of the attacks of Shaykh Najafí, they could only raise their hands and their eyes to their Lord and beseech His protection.

It happened that the head of the telegraph office, in accordance with his duty, immediately informed the government in Ṭihrán of the way in which Najafí had incited the people to religious persecution. A cable soon reached Iṣfahán from the court of the shâh ordering a stop to all such harassment. Thus the friends remained unmolested.

There was a paper by the name of *Akhtar* which was printed and published in Constantinople. Some of the believers subscribed to it. In one of its issues, news was read that some of the members of Bahá'u'lláh's family had united against the beloved Master. We also heard reports of this kind from some of the foreign embassies. Such things were beyond our imagining, so we denied every such report. We knew that the editor of *Akhtar* was a very obstinate enemy of the Cause and had connections with the Azalís; therefore, we discounted the reports as mere slander.

For a long time I continued to travel from village to village and from town to town. Whenever I went I found the believers faithful to the Cause and actively engaged in teaching. Upon entering Ṭihrán, I received a Tablet from the beloved Master in which He instructed me to continue my travels and urge the friends to remain firm in the Covenant of God, lest they might be innocently entrapped in the deceitful plans of some ambitious souls. This Tablet was a clear indication that there were those near to Him who would pursue their own selfish aims rather than obey the One Bahá'u'lláh had appointed as the Centre of His Covenant.

My sorrow knew no bounds when I learned of the activities of Jamál in Ṭihrán. I knew him very well. He had always thought of himself as supreme over all the friends. He would use every means to gain leadership in the Bahá'í community. After the ascension of Bahá'u'lláh, he went to the Holy Land without first requesting permission from the Master. After he returned, he no longer hid his ambitions. All the evil thoughts and plans which he used to hint at, he now openly discussed with the friends. But he always embroidered them in the hypocritical design of steadfastness to the Covenant and service to the Master.

From the time that Bahá'u'lláh had been in Adrianople, Javád-i-Qazvíní had always been my connection for sending and receiving correspondence from the Holy Household. Now he wrote a secret letter to me from the Holy Land in which he gave me three instructions. He said that: (1) in my letters to 'Abdu'l-Bahá, or those that I might write on behalf of others, I should never use the phrase, 'May I be sacrificed for Thee', or other terms of high respect. Rather, letters should be addressed in the ordinary way. (2) I should not begin my correspondence with prayers. (3) I should never refer to 'The Branch', but always say, 'The Branches'.[41]

This letter was another indication for me that plots in opposition to 'Abdu'l-Bahá were underway in the Holy Land. Since I had seen signs of arrogance and sacrilege from Javád before, I supposed that Jamál and Javád were secretly opposing the Master. Therefore, I suspected that the letter had been written without authorization. I wrote back objecting to all three of the instructions and setting forth my reasons. I added that if these were orders from 'Abdu'l-Bahá, I wanted to receive them in a letter written by His own hand; and if not, I never wanted to receive another letter from Javád. Since I received no answer, I was sure that the birds of night had begun to gather.

It never occurred to me that the chief mover of all these intrigues could possibly be the half brother[42] of the Master. What vain imaginings the human heart can devise! Who could ever turn his face from the Mystery of God? For thirty years Bahá'u'lláh had trained the Bahá'ís to be steadfast in the Cause and in the Covenant. Now that He had taken His flight to the realm above, we were given the Kitáb-i-'Ahd, His Will and Testament, which placed 'Abdu'l-Bahá on the seat of His Covenant with all possible power and glory.

Strengthened by the Master, I travelled through to 'Ishqábád and Caucasia in order to raise the standard of the Covenant. I found the Bahá'ís in those places inflamed with the love of God. I warned them that no one, no matter how respected he may be, could claim a station equal to that of 'Abdu'l-Bahá. All agreed and were united, and signed a document confessing their faith.

From Russia, I travelled to Beirut on my way to the Holy Land. Here I again met Jináb-i-Muḥammad Muṣṭafá Baghdádí. He was a mountain of strength and steadfastness. During my stay in Beirut, this great soul (I owe my life to him) informed me of the secret plots against the Master in 'Akká. He revived my spirits and prepared me to attain the presence of the Centre of the Covenant.

In 'Akká, I did not go to visit anyone. My first action was to send a letter to 'Abdu'l-Bahá saying, 'I know no one except the Master and have no desire to meet anyone unless He permits. I will not even enter the Shrines or circumambulate them without His permission.' By the grace of God, on that very day I was able to make a pilgrimage to the Shrine of Bahá'u'lláh in the company of 'Abdu'l-Bahá and experienced the joy of hearing His melodious voice chanting the Tablet of Visitation.

The reader should know that Muḥammad-'Alí, the half brother of 'Abdu'l-Bahá, even during the lifetime of his Father, had transgressed against the station of servitude. Seeking to emerge from his relative obscurity and to claim some position for himself, he wrote letters and sent them secretly abroad. This caused the heart of Bahá'u'lláh infinite sorrow. The words of the Supreme Manifestation of God educated the whole of the Bahá'í world. He often remarked that Muḥammad-'Alí is a leaf on the Divine

Lote Tree,[43] which moves in accord with the breezes of God. Should it move away from this gentle breeze, it would wither and die.

Muḥammad-'Alí never wholeheartedly repented his action in writing these letters, but Bahá'u'lláh protected him and concealed his error. While he lived under the protection of Bahá'u'lláh, he remained relatively quiet, but the germ of dissension grew within him, and within some of his close associates.

When Jamál arrived in the Holy Land, after the ascension of Bahá'u'lláh, he met Muḥammad-'Alí. He also met Javád-i-Qazvíní, and they united in rebellion. They both assured Muḥammad-'Alí that all the Persian believers were obedient to Jamál and would be ready to turn to him at whatever moment he might choose. In this way, Muḥammad-'Alí could become the head of the Faith.

Such promptings fed the ego of Muḥammad-'Alí, and gradually he rose against his illustrious Brother. Those who were steadfast in the Covenant began to hear strange words. Whenever the plotters met with any of the Bahá'ís and found an opportunity to speak, they would warn: 'Be careful. Do not believe in two Gods.' This became like a frightening catchword. 'Who believes in two Gods?' the friends asked one another. 'Who has made this claim?'

The beloved Master showed increased love for the wavering souls and made life easier for them. But Muḥammad-'Alí and his companions did not pay any attention to the Master. They grudged no effort to humiliate Him and to create doubts in the hearts of those who were living in the Holy Land. Such champions of the Covenant as Muḥammad-Riḍá and Maḥmúd-i-Ká<u>sh</u>í repeatedly went to 'Abdu'l-Bahá's enemies and pointed out the explicit words revealed in the Will and Testament of Bahá'u'lláh. They openly and courageously warned Muḥammad-'Alí and his henchmen of the consequences of such nefarious deeds. They made it clear that disobedience is the fire of self-destruction, the smoke of which would inflame their own eyes.

'Abdu'l-Bahá suffered silently and never ceased His love and respectful treatment toward His enemies. At the banquets they all occupied the seats of honour around the table, while 'Abdu'l-Bahá stood and served. On many occasions we heard the Master give clear exhortations encouraging all to become united in the service of the Cause. He pleaded with them. But His words fell on deaf ears.

In those days, the friends' spiritual life, understanding, and growth depended upon the Tablets they received from the beloved Master, the visits of the pilgrims who gave them news of the Holy Land, and the letters from those who had the honour of living near the shrines and serving the Centre of the Covenant.

After the ascension of Bahá'u'lláh, a violent storm attacked the Faith of God and the believers everywhere. It created such a scorching fire and such suffocating smoke that many of the branches, boughs, and leaves which had grown on the Divine Lote Tree were burned and consumed. They had eyes that could not see, ears that were unable to hear, and hearts that could no longer respond. It is a most lamentable situation when Man becomes the captive of his own self. During His lifetime, Bahá'u'lláh taught the Bahá'ís to turn to Him when they did not understand any part of the Holy Writings. In His Will and Testament, He explicitly declared that in the absence of the Sun of Truth, the friends must turn to the Most Great Branch.[44] There were, however, a few who insisted on following their own egos and would not turn to 'Abdu'l-Bahá as the Centre of Bahá'u'lláh's Covenant.

Fire, once it is ignited, stretches out its fiery tongue and will consume whoever dares to approach it or stand in its way. The sons of Bahá'u'lláh were caught in this merciless conflagration, as were some believers who had been outstanding pillars of the Cause in the days of Bahá'u'lláh, and others who would not shun them. Finally the Master remained almost alone. But even in His solitude He stretched forth His loving hands to rescue whoever was endangered by that fire. Letters, messengers, and loving exhortations constantly flowed from His presence.

However, as 'Abdu'l-Bahá increased His love and consideration for His enemies, He remained watchful and vigilant lest their words and letters reach the far-off friends whose hopes and aspirations were centred on the Holy Land and were sustained by letters from the believers living near the Holy Precincts. He did not wish that the friends throughout the world should learn of the shameful rebellion against the Covenant, which was led by no less a person than His own half-brother, Muḥammad-'Alí. Therefore, He forbade the friends to open any envelope which did not bear His own well-known seal.

The believers were vigilant and alert. For example, there was a physician in the city of Qazvín who was given the name *Ḥakím Illáhí* (divine physician) by 'Abdu'l-Bahá. He received a letter which carried the seal of the Master and he opened it. When he read the contents, he doubted their authenticity. The writer of the letter gave special instructions on how to address correspondence and suggested some satanic plans intended to overthrow the authority of the Master. The physician sent this letter back to the Holy Land and asked the Master, 'Who is this person to instruct the friends? We all turn our hearts and souls to one point, and that is the beloved Master.'

This letter from Ḥakím Illáhí uncovered the fact that the writer, Javád-i-Qazvíní, had first written an acceptable letter and placed it in an envelope. After the Master had affixed His seal to it, Javád had opened the envelope and inserted a different letter containing his own suggestions and evil thoughts.

The ever-moving pen of 'Abdu'l-Bahá saved the situation everywhere. The friends in the smallest villages and towns, in far-off districts in various countries, regularly received His inspiring messages. In their joy, they would copy them and send them wherever they could. Thus a continuous exchange of divine gifts was carried on all over the East. The friends busied themselves reading and transcribing the Tablets, encouraging one another, and warning the communities against the merciless attacks of the Covenant-breakers.

Thus the believers were protected against the infiltration of Covenant-breakers, with their misinterpretations of the Writings and their selfish ambitions. Should the Cause of God be entrusted to the hands of the people, we would find many interpreters in every town and village, and the light of true guidance would be extinguished. It would be as if a proficient physician wrote a catalogue in which he listed the many kinds of illnesses and the herbs and medicines used to cure them. Would it then be enough to give this book to anyone who can read and ask him to attend a patient suffering from a serious disease? Would it be wise to follow the advice of anyone who could read this book? This is not enough. We need someone who can diagnose the illness and tell us what kind of medicine should be given – and how much, and at what times. Hence the Covenant of Bahá'u'lláh provides for the continuing guidance so necessary for the body of mankind.

There were many violators who vigorously attacked the Covenant and who travelled throughout the length and breadth of different countries. Yet they reaped no fruit but failure. Then odious arguments and evil attempts to undermine the Cause created some waves here and there, but ultimately the sea became calm, reflecting the shining Sun of Truth.

In Shíráz, I met Salmán, the messenger of the Merciful. To visit this great soul is a joy beyond measure for any of the believers. Though he was illiterate and his manner of life was extremely simple, he was the essence of intelligence and knowledge. Whenever the friends became entangled in some difficult question, he was able to answer the question and explain the matter under discussion in a few simple words. We never witnessed in him the slightest trace of self, which creeps so insidiously into the hearts of men. Salmán flattered no one, nor could he abide any compromise in matters pertaining to the Cause of God. The believers who were of pure character loved him and sought his presence. But there were a few who did not like him. During one of his many visits to the Holy Land, the Ancient Beauty spoke to Salmán and said, 'Respect the great ones in the meetings and do not belittle them.' To this he immediately replied, 'No one except the Ancient Beauty and the Master is great to me. They may be big, but they are not great.' His reward for this courageous reply was the sweet smile of Bahá'u'lláh.

Throughout the East, men and women of exceptional capacity and love arose to protect the friends of God against disunity and disobedience. Jináb-i-Afnán of Yazd stood like a mountain and never allowed the poisonous waters of the river of doubt to reach the tender shrubs which Bahá'u'lláh was cultivating. In Ardistán and the surrounding areas, the Rafí'á, Fatḥ-i-A'zam, and Majd families stood against the onslaught. In Iṣfahán, Jináb-i-Vazír was the champion of the Covenant of God.

The turbulent months passed, and the sun shone again on calmed and assured hearts. A new life began to stir. The Bahá'ís everywhere demonstrated signs of revival and joy after this destructive attack. Reports of unprecedented contributions and increasing teaching activity were heard from all sides. Under the sunshine of the Covenant, the friends began to grow into maturity.

In Iṣfahán, Shaykh Najafí's thirst for the blood of the Bahá'ís had not diminished. He issued a death warrant for Jináb-i-Majd, one of the outstanding Bahá'ís of Ardistán. Majd was a tall, strong man. He was extremely firm in his faith, and he had a daring spirit which could strike fear into the hearts of the enemies of the Faith. When he heard that Najafí had signed and sealed his death warrant, he left Ardistán for Iṣfahán and walked up and down the most crowded streets and squares of that town. When the shaykh learned of this courageous behaviour – how Majd had audaciously walked among the crowds in the most dangerous quarters of Iṣfahán – fear overtook him. He stopped going to the theological school, refused invitations, and even refrained from appearing in the mosque to lead the congregational prayers.

Some weeks passed, and Najafí continued to hear that his daring victim was still in Iṣfahán. Then he sent the believer a message: 'Go home and do not breathe a word of this event to anyone.' When Najafí was sure that Majd had returned to Ardistán, he renewed his public appearances.

It was about this time that I first witnessed the effect of the unifying power of the Word of God. During my teaching tour I reached Káshán where the friends came from many different backgrounds: Jewish, Christian, Zoroastrian, and Muslim. But one could not tell them apart. Their unity was like water and perfume of rose: once mixed, it is impossible to distinguish one from the other.

In the city of Qum, I again met the Naddáf brothers and their newly converted friends. Strangely enough, these Muslim believers had been taught through the efforts of some Bahá'ís of Zoroastrian background who did business in Qum. It was a great privilege to visit Jináb-i-Ibn-i-Aṣdaq, who had just returned from the Holy Land. He arose like a giant to confirm the believers in the Covenant and arranged meetings every night to deepen the friends in the Cause of God.

However, in that region Jamál was like a thorn in the flesh of the believers. He would have liked nothing better than to become the leader of the Bahá'í community. Not only that – he did everything possible to extract money from the friends to support his son and relatives, who were like leeches attached to the Cause. The Hands of the Cause, the teachers, and all the Bahá'ís did their utmost to keep Jamál satisfied, but to no avail. The more they gave, the more he desired.

Dr Muḥammad Khán, the son of Munajjim, was alert to the dangerous activities of Jamál. He warned the friends against him, saying, 'I have known this man ever since my childhood. Since my father was well known as a Bahá'í at that time, he seldom appeared on the streets. But he regularly sent me to visit Jamál, inquire after his well-being, and bring him gifts. My father was always sad and worried about Jamál and often said that Jamál did not believe in anything. His sole aim is to gather fame and wealth. My father tried to keep him pacified, but he believed that it would have been much better if Jamál had never heard of the Faith.

'My father said that the friends should try to keep Jamál appeased. Should the smallest thing happen contrary to his plans and wishes, he could cause a great deal of trouble. My father was sure that if Jamál felt the least bit slighted he would go immediately to the 'ulamá in Ṭihrán, denounce the Faith, and assist in shedding the blood of innocent Bahá'ís.'

Jináb-i-Afnán invited many friends to a meeting and requested that Jamál be present. The purpose of this meeting was to create unity and to inspire the friends to arise and serve the Cause. Jamál pretended to be steadfast in the Covenant and said, 'Let us all write a letter to the Master and ask that He not call Himself 'Abdu'l-Bahá (the Servant of Bahá). Let Him continue to be called Sirru'lláh (the Mystery of God) as He was in the days of Bahá'u'lláh.'

The friends were very much displeased with this presumptuous suggestion. One of them said, 'He is the Centre of the Covenant and He knows what to do. Who are we to tell Him what name or title He should adopt? We have accepted Bahá'u'lláh as the Supreme Manifestation of God. We know the Centre of His Covenant under any name He chooses to be called.'

In the Holy Land I found the Centre of Bahá'u'lláh's Covenant bereft of the companionship of the faithful. He was surrounded by those who desired nothing but to follow their own selfish desires and vain imaginings. I was astounded by the loving patience 'Abdu'l-Bahá showed toward these people. He never failed to provide them with whatever they demanded. Everyone knew that they made outrageous demands only for the purpose of forcing the Master into poverty and debt. Yet He accepted all such unkind treatment and met their demands, hoping only that they would not openly rise against the Faith and so cause unrest and distress in the infant Bahá'í communities around the world. Such a violent storm might prove fatal to the tender shoots growing in the vineyards of God.

The Master respected all of the members of His family, protected them, and sought to guide them on the true path of faith.

For example, when my visit to 'Akká came to an end, 'Abdu'l-Bahá instructed me to travel to Iran by way of India. But before I left, He asked me to go to the Mansion of Bahjí to bid farewell to Muḥammad-'Alí and the family. He said, 'You will be their guest during the whole night. About midnight, Muḥammad-'Alí will ask you to be with him alone, as he desires to talk to you in private. When you answer his questions, be sure that you first ask permission from him. You must talk to him with love, courtesy, and respect. Utter nothing but that with which you will be inspired by God.'

I went to Bahjí. It was late at night when Muḥammad-'Alí summoned me to his room. He asked his son to leave us alone and then stated, 'I have a very private question to ask you. Don't you think that whatever my brother has inherited from Bahá'u'lláh, I have inherited, too?'

'Would you kindly grant me permission to answer?'

'Yes', he replied.

'In the Kitáb-i-Aqdas and in His Will and Testament, Bahá'u'lláh emphatically commanded the Branches, the Afnán, and all without exception to be obedient and submissive to the Most Great Branch. The more you obey, the higher will be your rank and position in the hearts of the believers. The station of the Branches and the Afnán is conditioned on their obedience to the Centre of the Covenant. Since the Master was clearly given this great station, He must have something you do not have. Moreover, who is there in the world who can claim that he is comparable to the Master in any respect?'

At this point Muḥammad-'Alí got up and said, 'It is time to sleep.' Then he dismissed me. I slept in one of the lower rooms of the Mansion of Bahjí and returned to 'Akká the next day. I left Haifa for Bombay. But this experience showed me the crafty way in which the Covenant-breakers sowed the first seeds of doubt in the hearts of the believers.

In Ṭihrán, Jináb-i-Adíb was a new Bahá'í. He was very mature, learned, audacious, and staunch in his faith. He was appointed a Hand of the Cause by Bahá'u'lláh. After the ascension of Bahá'u'lláh, but before the

Kitáb-i-'Ahd had reached Iran, Adíb had approached Jamál and asked him about the future leadership of the Faith. The arrogant Jamál replied that he knew that the Branches would share the leadership of the Faith.

Jináb-i-Adíb immediately protested that in the Kitáb-i-Aqdas, and in some other Tablets, Bahá'u'lláh had specifically mentioned that, after His passing, the believers must turn to only one person as the head of the Faith.

Jamál insisted, 'There must be two Branches who will lead the believers and be the heads of the Faith.'

'Then one must be silent and submissive; and one will speak and be the leader of the community', Adíb replied.

'No, both will speak', was Jamál's answer.

'This is against all standards of logic and reason', Adíb replied. 'Even in worldly causes there cannot be two leaders at the head of any movement who share power between themselves. How much more must this be true of the Cause of God, which is based on a mighty foundation.'

Since he could see that Adíb would not be convinced by his arguments, Jamál began to deny his position and to say that this was only something that he had heard from others. And the more Adíb protested, the more Jamál denied and relied on the excuse of his faulty hearing.

Jináb-i-Adíb was a mountain of steadfastness and sacrifice. Once he wrote a letter to the Grand Vazír of Iran explaining the Bahá'í position and giving clear and obvious proofs that Bahá'ís shun all political activities and are obedient to their governments. He signed his name and his title to this letter and openly stated that it was his religious duty to report these things to the state.

I considered the fact that I had enjoyed fifty years of happiness in the shadow of the Faith, while Adíb was a new believer who had already sacrificed so much. So, since the danger was obvious, I proposed that this letter should be copied by Maḥmúd-i-Zarqání and sent in my name, because we needed Adíb and we did not want to run the risk of losing him, or having him become entangled with the many difficulties which could result from such a letter. My suggestion was agreed to, and the letter was sent through the mail. In due time we received an acknowledgment signed by the secretary of the Grand Vazír. The entire letter was eventually cabled to the crown prince who was then on his way to Ṭihrán.

This was one of the greatest services which Jináb-i-Adíb rendered to the Cause of God. His letter protected the Bahá'ís from suspicion and from the slanderous reports which, like torrents of hate, might cover the whole country during the times of convulsion and upheaval. Bahá'u'lláh later praised the justice of the Grand Vazír who received this letter and acted so fairly.

The Hand of the Cause, Mullá 'Alí-Akbar, was well known as a Bahá'í by the people. For years, whenever he passed through the streets or the public squares, he would be abused with curses and foul words. A certain Mullá Riḍá was a neighbour of this Hand of the Cause, and he started a campaign against the Faith. He maliciously attacked the Bahá'ís and encouraged the people to kill Bahá'ís and plunder their property. He singled out Mullá 'Alí-Akbar for special attack.

In order to protect this friend, the other Hands met in the house of Jináb-i-Ibn-i-Aṣdaq. They consulted on what to do and concluded that during the first part of the month of Muḥarram, when religious sentiment among Muslims would be high, Mullá 'Alí-Akbar should change his residence and make no public appearances until the period of commotion and chaos was over.

They then invited the Hand to attend this meeting, and one of those present explained the results of the consultation. Mullá 'Alí-Akbar showed himself to be the epitome of faith, devotion, and steadfastness. He smiled and said, 'In His many Tablets, 'Abdu'l-Bahá has advised us to observe wisdom. But this means submission, and not fear and hiding. It means solidarity in plans of action, truthfulness and forbearance, and that the seeds of faith should be sown in fertile soil.

'I have been arrested more than ten times, put in chains, and placed in prison. Often there did not appear to be any hope of my release. On one occasion I was in prison for three years. People who were less well known than I were honoured with the cup of martyrdom, while I am still alive. If martyrdom is to be my destiny, what greater end! If it is the decree and the will of God, why hide and be afraid?' All of us were greatly heartened by this explanation, every word of which gave us more understanding and assurance.

The time came when I had to leave Ṭihrán for other parts. I travelled to Qazvín and to Tabríz, and then to 'Is͟hqábád.

In Qazvín, though this city was the centre of Jamál's evil plots, I found the friends steadfast and faithful and firm in the Covenant. In Tabríz, with the exception of two persons, all others were steadfast in the Covenant. Bahá'í meetings were held every day. In some places, the friends had donated gardens, houses, and land to the Faith. Letters received from the Holy Land, which were not signed or sealed by the Master, would immediately be sent back to 'Akká. It seemed that Muḥammad-'Alí was doing his utmost to penetrate this citadel of the Covenant. But in all cases he met impenetrable barriers and found no way to disturb the beloved friends, who remained safe and secure in the shade of the Tree of Life, under the shadow of the Most Great Branch.

While in Caucasia I learned that Jamál had finally revealed his true self. The friends had begun to realize his burning ambition. It became known that he had written a letter to 'Abdu'l-Bahá and had demanded three things: that he be appointed as the head of the Faith in Persia, that 'Abdu'l-Bahá prepare a special house for him and his son, and that the Master rebuke the Hands of the Cause for their behaviour toward him. This letter remained unanswered.

Jamál became furious that the Bahá'ís of Persia did not turn to him and instead remained steadfast in the Covenant of Bahá'u'lláh. He wrote letters to the outstanding Bahá'ís of the country complaining and bewailing the fact that they would not assist him with his plans. Such deeds of pride and profanity made the Bahá'ís realize that Jamál never had a particle of faith. The friends from then on shunned him and would not even walk on the street where he lived.

There is an important lesson in the story of Jamál. In the eyes of the friends he had been a very important person. When he entered the homes of the friends, the bed he slept on and even the chairs he used would be regarded as special objects. The friends used to kiss his hand. He would say to the people, 'The kissing of hands is forbidden. But for the glory of the Cause, I will not prevent the believers from prostrating themselves in front of me and kissing my hand.' However, when these same people learned that the object of their adoration had become a Covenant-breaker, they did not even allow him to enter their homes.

When Jamál had failed in all his plans, I wrote him a short letter and said, 'An ignorant person may claim that there is no God. But God keeps the whole universe functioning in perfect order, without allowing anyone to break this order. Now reflect on the many schemes you have devised to reach your goal. Reflect also on the fact that all of these plans have been thwarted. None have produced the desired result. Is this not sufficient evidence that your aims and desires are opposed to the order of God, the Fashioner of the universe?' The friends gave him my note, but I received no reply.

After passing through Caucasia I went to Beirut. From there I made my way to the Holy Land. The beloved Master's first instruction to me was this: 'Do not mention Jamál and his misdeeds.'

I said, 'But he has written pamphlets to refute the Covenant of God and they are being spread everywhere.'

'Yes', 'Abdu'l-Bahá replied, 'but he has not signed them. As long as he does not openly proclaim himself as the author of these works, we will not denounce his name and his wrongdoing. We must always conceal the faults of others.'

Some days after my arrival, 'Abdu'l-Bahá instructed the pilgrims to go to Bahjí. The Master came by Himself on foot, and slowly approached the Shrine of Bahá'u'lláh. After tea, He instructed all of us to stand in a circle around the Shrine and wait for Him to come out. He said that even if we heard curses and foul words, or if we were pelted with stones, we must not pay any attention.

This actually happened. The Covenant-breakers who lived in the Mansion next to the Shrine, those people without God or religion, cursed us and stoned us. Even so, that day was so wondrous that it is an everlasting memory which, whenever I recall it, enkindles my heart and soul.

It was heartbreaking for us to learn about the evil work of the Covenant-breakers and their malicious attacks on the beloved Master. These things were never related to any of the friends abroad. But being in the Holy Land, I could see what burdens of sorrow they laid on the Master's shoulders every day.

These enemies were able to approach the mayor of 'Akká and bribe him. They asked that he exile 'Abdu'l-Bahá from the city of 'Akká, thinking that after His departure the pilgrims would come to them and would consider them as the centre of the Cause. However, the mayor of 'Akká was soon dismissed and sent back to his own country.

At another time they offered one of Bahá'u'lláh's cloaks and a pair of His spectacles to the governor of Haifa. They encouraged him to go and visit 'Abdu'l-Bahá with the cloak on his shoulders and with the glasses. When he came, 'Abdu'l-Bahá realized that he was wearing things which had belonged to His Father, and He was deeply grieved. However, He did not say a word and treated the man with His usual extreme courtesy and love. That day passed, but the time came when that same governor was put in prison and in chains. It was 'Abdu'l-Bahá who hastened to help and liberate him. After receiving such unexpected kindness, he begged for forgiveness saying, 'It was not my fault. Your enemies misled me into taking such a grievous step.'

During the first week of my pilgrimage, early one morning, Mírzá Áqá Ján, who had been the amanuensis of Bahá'u'lláh, came in and made funny gestures. He said, 'Alláh-u-Abhá! You have an illumined gathering.'

I left the room, but he followed me to another room and said the same thing. I went to another room, and he again followed and said the same thing. I returned to the first room and he came with me. Again he said, 'Alláh-u-Abhá! You have an illumined gathering.'

Another believer and I left the house and made our way to a shop in the street. Áqá Ján followed us, hopping up and down and saying the Greatest Name. We went to one of the shops which was owned by a believer, and he followed us and stood outside repeating the same thing. A crowd gathered before we had left the shop. But still Áqá Ján followed us, hopping and saying the Greatest Name. This continued until after midday.

When the mayor of 'Akká learned that Áqá Ján had disturbed us and others, he sent soldiers to arrest him. He was taken to the governor's house. The mayor sent the following message to the Master: 'We are sending soldiers to Yemen. The boat is anchored in the port and is ready to sail. If you approve, I will banish this person to Yemen.'

'Abdu'l-Bahá's response was immediate. 'This would not please me', He replied.

Mírzá Áqá Ján was released, but he never ceased to cause fresh troubles for the Master. At one time he even sent news to the Covenant-breakers and to the friends that Bahá'u'lláh had appeared to him in a dream and had promised to help him if he arose at the appointed hour to conquer the Bahá'í world and displace the Most Great Branch. Even the Covenant-breakers once decided to kill him and destroy his body with fire, but 'Abdu'l-Bahá always protected him.

It often happened that when the Master went to the Shrine of His Father, either riding or on foot, the governor and his officials would follow Him to the surrounding area of Bahjí. These people would have tea and refreshments while the Master, followed by the friends, would pay homage at the resting place of Bahá'u'lláh. Many times they observed the Master carrying loads of earth in His cloak for the gardens around the Shrine. At other times they observed Him carrying a water pot on His shoulders.

Twice a year for about six years, 'Abdu'l-Bahá would take at least one hundred flower pots from the Riḍván Garden to Bahjí. It was the most exciting procession. 'Abdu'l-Bahá would carry a flower pot on His shoulder, and all the friends and pilgrims would follow Him two by two with flower pots on their shoulders. Mírzá Maḥmúd-i-Ká<u>sh</u>í would walk in front of the friends and chant prayers in a loud and melodious voice. Once the commander of the army, accompanied by his officers, passed by and saw this spiritual procession. He said to the Master, 'This is the Army of the Kingdom, and these are the angels of the Exalted Realm.'

I remember one evening, as the commemoration of the Ascension of Bahá'u'lláh approached, the Master prepared two hundred lanterns. One of these contained twenty candles, and each of the others two candles. It was about sunset when the same procession of friends, carrying these lanterns, made their way to Bahjí. It happened that we passed a camp of soldiers. The officers stood in their places and paid their respect to the Master. We were all in tears. When we reached the Shrine, there were two rows of worshippers: the friends in one row, and the officers with their soldiers in the other. Everyone was in tears. When the pilgrimage came to an end, the officers encircled the Master. They were served tea and refreshments. This was one of the most memorable nights of my life.

Every particle in the air and on the earth seemed both to absorb and reflect the glory and majesty of the Kingdom of God.

The Covenant-breakers could not bear to see such glorious acts of servitude. They hastened to the Muslim clergy in 'Akká and expressed their objection to such demonstrations of homage to the resting place of Bahá'u'lláh.

On that evening, 'Abdu'l-Bahá remained awake all night. The friends could not separate themselves from Him and gathered in the Pilgrim House adjacent to the Shrine. Sometimes tea or coffee was served. But the most lamentable part of it was when dawn approached. We all went to the shrine for a second time. To our horror we discovered that Mírzá Áqá Ján was there and had taken up residence in the Shrine. It was evident that 'Abdu'l-Bahá's heart was burning with anguish, but He remained silent. He approached the Shrine but chose to sit in the sandy place that surrounded it. About two hundred friends sat in a circle with Him as we remembered the days we had all spent in the presence of the Ancient Beauty.

All of a sudden, Mírzá Áqá Ján dashed out of the Shrine, barefooted and bareheaded, and dressed in a shroud of mourning. He threw dust on his head and gesticulated wildly. He kept repeating, 'My Beloved! My Beloved! Where are you?' His behaviour was so silly that we could not control our laughter. The Covenant-breakers who had occupied the Mansion next door tried repeatedly to take him away, but he kept returning. Again and again he dashed into our circle, repeating some of the verses of Bahá'u'lláh. He seemed like a drunken man who could not keep his balance. He kept shouting, running, and reciting parts of the Tablets in an irreverent manner. A short while later we all dispersed. Yet despite all this, 'Abdu'l-Bahá continued to respect Áqá Ján, and protect him, and care for him.

One of 'Abdu'l-Bahá's major services to the Cause of God was to transfer the remains of the Báb from Persia to the Holy Land, and to place them in the Shrine on the side of Mount Carmel. This act was the fulfilment of the prophecies recorded in the Holy Books about the glory of Carmel and the surrounding areas.

The Báb's wooden casket had been placed in the house of Jináb-i-Vazír in Iṣfahán. It was well hidden in the house, and no one knew its location. When the time came, the beloved Master issued orders that the body should be transferred from Persia to the Holy Land.

Those responsible were advised to travel first to Iraq. They arrived in Baghdád with their sacred cargo, entrusted it to the hands of the friends there, and, after visiting the Shí'ih shrines, returned home. My cousin, Ḥusayn-i-Vakíl, acted as a custodian of the casket in Baghdád. Further instructions were received that the Báb's remains were to be sent to Beirut and others were given the honour of this task. Finally, the box containing the Divine Trust was placed in the hands of the Master.

Let us look back for a moment to the early days when the Master took the first steps to purchase the land on Mount Carmel where Bahá'u'lláh had indicated the Tomb of the Báb should stand. When the Covenant-breakers learned that He intended to purchase that land, their malicious opposition was aroused. They approached the owner of the land and persuaded him not to sell. They assured him that in a short time the land would be worth ten times its value. They instigated others to write letters to the government claiming possession of all the land on Mount Carmel. Therefore, it took the Master more than six months of persistent effort to purchase the desired piece of land. But even so, that land was situated like an island in the midst of other land which belonged to other people. There was no access to it. The Master was so weighted down with troubles that He decided not to pursue the matter. During His silence, the Covenant-breakers became more active than ever. But the Master left everything in the hands of God. Time passed, and the Covenant-breakers were happy because they thought that they had been completely successful.

One day a person who owned land adjacent to the land for the Shrine, of his own free will, sought the presence of 'Abdu'l-Bahá. When he met with the Master, he told Him of all the intrigues of the enemies of the Cause. He expressed his deep regrets, begged the forgiveness of 'Abdu'l-Bahá, and declared his readiness to sell whatever land was desired.

The Master immediately began making plans for the construction of the Báb's Tomb. When the enemies learned of these efforts, they wrote letters to the Ottoman court reporting that 'Abdu'l-Bahá was planning to build a huge fortress on the side of Mount Carmel. They asserted that this fort would be a great danger to the safety of the empire. The government immediately ordered all work on the construction of the Shrine to cease. Such orders were given, not once, but several times. The Master appealed the case to a government committee of investigation, which eventually gave permission for the construction to continue.

Some of the friends lost their patience and suggested to the Master, 'Why don't you explain the whole situation to the government?'

'Impossible!' the Master answered. 'How can I explain these things to anyone? I would have to complain against the members of my own family. Then what would people say? They would surely say that a great Prophet had come for the purpose of bringing all people to unity, but the members of His own family are now fighting among themselves.

'This fatal disease must be fought with patience and forgiveness. Whatever wrongdoing I mention in my Tablets is only to help the friends to become more steadfast, and to strengthen those who are weak, that they might become firm and courageous believers. God is the greatest of all helpers: we surrender our affairs into His hands. We must be occupied with our own work and tread the path of servitude, detached from all else but God. Whoever walks this path will surely reap the fruits of his patience and forbearance, and will be counted as my companion in the service of His Threshold. Those who deviate from this path will surely find regret.

'We must supplicate our Lord so that He, in His unlimited bounty, may forgive our sins, accept our prayers of repentance, and awaken all Men to the light of true understanding.'

'Abdu'l-Bahá undertook to prepare a suitable depository for the priceless remains of the Báb. He instructed the friends of Rangoon, Burma, to make a hardwood coffin and a marble sarcophagus. The marble was to be unique and of brilliant lustre. When these were prepared, the Master instructed that the top and sides of the sarcophagus were to be adorned with the Greatest Name. The designs were prepared in exquisite penmanship by the calligrapher, Mishkín-Qalam.

When the friends in Burma were ready to ship their work to 'Akká, they brought two carts and walked the whole distance to the seashore, pulling the carts and chanting along the way. Their procession was joined by many others. Then they placed their precious trusts in a mosque, and crowds of people were attracted by the jubilation. They inquired about the reason for such joyous ceremonies. One of the friends took the floor and told them of the life of the Báb, His martyrdom, and His burial on Mount Carmel. Many hearts were touched, and many entered the Faith and joined the friends in serving the Cause in Burma.

There was not a moment's rest for the Master. At times He seemed like a man on a ship in the middle of a tempestuous ocean. But this would never cause 'Abdu'l-Bahá to lose heart. He never appeared despondent or hopeless. That was not the Master. Out of the darkness He would emerge time and again with a new plan and a new victory.

Not even having finished the Shrine, He called on the friends to raise the first Bahá'í House of Worship in Asia, in 'Ishqábád, Russia. A cousin of the Báb, Jináb-i-Afnán,[45] was appointed by 'Abdu'l-Bahá to go to 'Ishqábád from his native town of Yazd to oversee the construction of the Temple. Upon his arrival, the consul general of Iran, the governor of the province, merchants, and other notables joined the Bahá'ís in receiving their honoured guest. The governor expressed joy and gratitude that the first Bahá'í House of Worship would be erected under his dominion.

Preparations for construction were soon under way. Once the plans had been approved, the friends immediately set to work to build the Temple. The cornerstone was laid in place by a representative of the Czar himself. Most of the Temple was completed within four years.

At this time, 'Abdu'l-Bahá instructed me to take a trip to Caucasia and to 'Ishqábád. I had the honour of visiting Jináb-i-Afnán and being in his presence. He was the embodiment of perfection and sanctity. He had both spiritual gifts and administrative skill. He spent all his gifts to carry out the mission conferred upon him by the Master. He sacrificed most of his fortune to erect the House of Worship. I could see clearly that Jináb-i-Afnán was hardly in this world and did not belong to it. He would pay only scant attention to his personal and worldly affairs. Yet he remained rich, and his wealth would always meet all his needs.

The time came when I decided to bid farewell to the friends in 'Ishqábád and travel to Mashhad. There I met Maḥmúd-i-Zarqání. We shared a house together and worked together for the Faith. We associated with all classes of people, and before long our teaching activities became so well known that people came to us with all kinds of problems which had nothing to do with the Faith. Whoever came in, by the grace of God, returned home happy and contented.

Our teaching was so successful that some people feared that within one year all the important people of the city would become Bahá'ís. Bahá'í teachers from other areas came to help with this effort. Meetings were held all over the city, and the believers formed committees to feed the poor and advance the public welfare.

We were still in Khurásán when we heard of the great upheaval in Yazd. This news caused uneasiness among the new believers of Mashhad. The disturbances lasted for more than two months during which 195 believers were mercilessly put to death. The governor of the province, instead of protecting the people under his care, ruthlessly helped the bloodthirsty mobs. Bahá'ís were killed, their houses destroyed, and their possessions plundered or confiscated.

During these disorders, a well-known maidservant of the Cause, 'Alavíyyih Khánum, reached the city of Yazd. As soon as she set foot in the town she was arrested and made to undergo all kinds of persecutions. Eventually the chief of police took her under his protection and gave her some advice: 'Won't you just speak one word of denial and rid yourself of all this suffering?'

'Under no circumstances', she replied. 'That one word would deprive me of all the eternal bounties of God. I will gladly sacrifice this ephemeral life for the supremacy of the Name of God.' The governor heard about her imprisonment and issued an order that she should be sent to Ábádih.

During all these disturbances no one in the whole of Iran, or in the neighbouring countries, would listen to the cries of the Bahá'ís for justice. The beloved friends were at the mercy of the irresponsible mobs who were encouraged by the bloodthirsty clergy and the most ignorant of governors. The only One who stretched forth His hand to assist the wronged and sorrow-stricken victims was the Master, Who was Himself a prisoner, incarcerated in the city of 'Akká and surrounded by the most despicable enemies. He looked after the urgent needs of the children and youth, the old men and women who were caught in the fire of persecution.

The Covenant-breakers continually conspired against 'Abdu'l-Bahá. They formed groups against Him and, like vipers, began to move in different directions. The groups approached the governor, the secret police, the outstanding 'ulamá, and any other person they could influence in Palestine, Syria, or Turkey. They did everything they could to arouse the officials against 'Abdu'l-Bahá.

The Master remained calm and serene. He never approached the authorities. He suffered in silence. He prayed fervently for His enemies, that they might open their eyes and cease committing iniquities against the innocent band of believers in 'Akká.

Whenever 'Abdu'l-Bahá received any gift, He would immediately send it to His family who had violated the Covenant of God. Far from being grateful, they in turn would offer these gifts to the governor, the commander of the army, or others, in an effort to convince them to take steps against 'Abdu'l-Bahá. Their aim was to have the Master exiled to a distant and unknown place. If this could be accomplished, they believed that, since they would be in possession of the Holy Shrines, all of the believers would regard them as the centre of the Faith.

The most active of the Covenant-breakers was Majdi'd-Dín, the cousin of the Master. He was the centre of abominable deeds. He would sneer at the pilgrims who visited 'Abdu'l-Bahá and declare, 'You are only here for a few days. Soon you will leave and everything will fall into our hands. All will seek shelter under our shadow.'

'Abdu'l-Bahá liked to visit the resting place of His Father every week. But in order to appease the enmity of Muḥammad-'Alí and his supporters, He decided to remain in 'Akká. When He desired to visit Bahjí, He would go up to the roof of His house, face the Shrine of Bahá'u'lláh, and pray. He would sometimes chant the Tablet of Visitation in a loud voice. We would hear Him chanting, and we were indeed heartbroken. This situation continued for two years.

The result of all the complaints and mischief of the Covenant-breakers was an upheaval of debris which buried everyone. An order came forth from the officials that all members of the family were to live in 'Akká, and no one was to step outside the city. The Master was already residing in 'Akká, so it was the Covenant-breakers living in Bahjí who were now forced to return to 'Akká and to live there. They were all taken to the city and placed under restriction. The officials soon realized that it was Muḥammad-'Alí and Majdi'd-Dín who had caused all the trouble. But 'Abdu'l-Bahá intervened on their behalf and requested the authorities to allow them to return to Bahjí.

One governor came to power who was the essence of courtesy and faith. He loved 'Abdu'l-Bahá to the point of worship. In addition, Badrí Big, the military commander, was very friendly to the Master. When the enemies of the Cause saw this state of affairs, they became furious and joined all their forces to bring about the downfall of 'Abdu'l-Bahá.

They decided to send false reports, containing the most alarming accusations, to the Ottoman court. They claimed that the governor, as well as the military commander and his officers, had all become the servants of 'Abdu'l-Bahá. They were accused of training thirty thousand soldiers, of raising a flag of rebellion inscribed with the Greatest Name, and of convincing the Arab tribes of the desert to join this rebellion. The Covenant-breakers claimed that 'Abdu'l-Bahá had proclaimed Himself to be the Return of Christ and, as such, claimed sovereignty over all the nations of the world and regarded all rulers as His vassals.

'Abdu'l-Bahá sent a single sentence in reply to these accusations: 'Listen to the reports, but ask the accusers to present their evidence and their witnesses.' But the court accepted the reports without investigation. The reason for this was that the accusing letters had been signed and sealed by the brothers and cousins of 'Abdu'l-Bahá.

Before long, the thick clouds of confusion and persecution again covered the horizon of 'Akká. The friends and supporters of the Master were unexpectedly dismissed from their posts. When the noble governor came to the Master to bid Him farewell, 'Abdu'l-Bahá assured him that the governor would return to high position in the future and that the bounties of God would rain down upon him. The military commander was also shorn of his rank, but he remained happy and content that he had served the Master.

New officials were placed in charge of the telegraph and post offices. All letters were opened and read, and every telegram was scrutinized. Secret police were everywhere. People were ordered to stay at home in the evening. The enemies of the Faith were jubilant.

The Master remained alone. He even asked the friends to leave 'Akká and to disperse in different directions. Danger threatened Him from all sides, yet He retained His tranquillity and fortitude. He began to repair the house in which He lived and to plant grape vines in His small garden.

Letters of accusation regularly found their way to the court of the sulṭán in Constantinople. Although such reports should have been investigated, not even one of the believers was consulted. All of the reports were taken to be true, and a committee of four men was dispatched to 'Akká to confirm the charges.

No sooner had these high officials set foot on the shore of 'Akká than the Covenant-breakers clustered around them. They entertained the committee members in the most flattering way and offered them costly presents. Gifts were constantly sent to them. Though the enemies received no promises, their hearts were full of hope. They expected that 'Abdu'l-Bahá would soon be exiled.

'Abdu'l-Bahá never approached the members of the committee. This enraged the officials. In order to show their contempt for the Master, they sent a summons for "Abbás' to appear before them. Upon receiving this order, 'Abdu'l-Bahá went to the place where the committee held its meetings. The room was crowded with the enemies of the Faith.

The Master said, 'I am happy and proud that you referred to me as simply "'Abbás". This is the way that the Prophets of God are addressed. Who has heard of Moses Pá<u>sh</u>á, or Jesus Big, or Muḥammad <u>Kh</u>án? They are called simply Moses, Jesus, and Muḥammad.'

The officials were astounded by this audacious statement. One of them inquired, 'We have heard that you have books in your house which are dangerous to the public welfare.'

'Abdu'l-Bahá answered, 'No such books are ever found in my possession.'

The same officer declared, 'But there are witnesses who have testified to this fact.'

'Abdu'l-Bahá rose from His seat. He said, 'I told you that I do not have such writings in my house, and that is all.' Then He left the room. The committee was amazed at the courage of this man whom they believed to be completely at their mercy.

The joy and excitement of the Covenant-breakers was unbounded. And the sorrow of the believers overflowed. A few of the friends and the faithful members of 'Abdu'l-Bahá's family urged Him to flee 'Akká by ship, and the captain of one boat expressed his readiness to carry Him to whatever port He wished. But the Master responded that the Báb did not run away and abandon the arena of sacrifice. Bahá'u'lláh did not run away. Neither would He try to flee from danger.

As the members of the committee of investigation boarded their ship to return to Constantinople, they were happy and satisfied. They were impatient to reach the sulṭán's court and relate the results of their investigation. They saw this as an opportunity to present themselves as the protectors of the throne and the defenders of the empire. One of them announced to his collaborators, 'My reward for this investigation will be the governorship of Damascus. The very first act I will perform after taking office will be to hang 'Abdu'l-Bahá from the gate of 'Akká.'

But before the committee could reach its destination and present its libellous report, the foundations of the Ottoman Empire began to crumble and the realm was thrown into confusion. The committee and all its reports were totally ignored. All the evil efforts of these corrupt officials were brought to naught.

We were amazed when we realized that thousands of persons were put to death all over the empire because of the mere accusation by a spy or secret agent that they were disloyal. What grave danger was caused for the Master by the accusations of His own family, the false reports and rumours circulated about Him, and the investigation of a hostile committee from the sulṭán's own court! It is the most astounding fact that 'Abdu'l-Bahá should have remained alive after these repeated attacks from all sides. Can we not see the hand of God operating in the whole universe?

Now, at the end of my life, all I possess is ignorance and weakness and unawareness and heedlessness and neglect and valuelessness and worthlessness and uselessness and poverty and shamelessness and destitution and powerlessness and disobedience and wrongdoing and sin and darkness and worldliness and transience and selfishness and corrupt desire. Any wrongdoing or sin which can be imagined is mine.

I do not write this from a sense of humility. This is only truth and honesty and reality. The bounties of God are obvious and apparent. Fifty years ago in Adrianople I attained the presence of that Sun of Truth before Whom all others must prostrate themselves. From that time, every breath I have taken I have tried to conform to His will, and every step I have taken I have directed toward Him. I do not know if my services were acceptable to Him, but His compassion and love and generosity have always surrounded me. My worst deeds were met with the greatest compassion. The more I transgressed, the more He concealed my faults. The more I sought after my own vain imaginings, the more He showed me the light of His Spirit. The more I erred, the more generous He was. He saved me from the greatest difficulties, and from the calamity of self.

All humanity must follow some occupation, from kings and sulṭáns to servants and slaves. Everyone is surrounded by misery and trouble. A just king will have more trouble than any of his subjects; a fair chief will face more difficulties than any of his underlings. Just to earn a living and to gain their daily bread, some people have chosen years of exile. Moreover, for the sake of greed, many of the rich and the learned have placed their lives in danger continually. And all this is only to follow their own ambitions in quest of the mirage of prestige and honour. How often have others, on account of their own crimes and corruption, been placed in prison and suffered exile or been captured, enslaved, or executed! And I am only one of these people. Whatever evil caused such ones to commit crimes for which they were punished was also part of me. How grateful I am that I was protected, and my sins were concealed, and I was not put to shame. If I burn every second, I can never repay His forgiveness and mercy. I am utterly impotent.

All that I have comes from the Cause of God. The believers respected me as a teacher, but I did not deserve such respect. They were all the true teachers of the Faith. They would face the problems of the world to earn a living, and then spend their earnings on those like me who could travel and teach. Then we were called the promulgators of the Faith. But we made no sacrifices; we only received. In the Name of God, those noble believers sacrificed everything for us. I, and others like me, reached the highest degree of honour and happiness without struggle or sacrifice. I can only pray that the mercy and generosity of God, which has followed me over thousands of miles, will also accompany me in the future.

Now it has been ten years, more or less, that, by the grace and bounty of the Master, I have lived under the shadow of mercy in the Holy Land, and have partaken every day of the manna from heaven, and have seen what Moses saw on Sinai. I thank God that I have attained and have witnessed the kindness and the generosity and the servitude of the believers – virtues which are but a drop when compared to the kindness and compassion of 'Abdu'l-Bahá and the Greatest Holy Leaf[46] and the Holy Mother.[47]

A true Bahá'í I am not. O God! Assist me and make my efforts fruitful. Assist the Master! This book I have written by His order. But I am so old and decrepit that many times while writing I have forgotten the order of my words and lost my train of thought. When this happened, I would have to get up and leave my work. But whenever I started to write again, my pen would carry on the story. This humble servant has never entered any school and is unaware of the rules of grammar and style.

I beseech all the Bahá'ís (may my soul be sacrificed for them) to beg for my forgiveness at the Holy Threshold, as I see nothing in myself but wrongdoing, and nothing among the servants of God but forgiveness and concealment.

With thanks to God, the Lord of the worlds.

17 May 1912

EPILOGUE

The author of these memoirs, Ḥájí Mírzá Ḥaydar-'Alí, who is known as the *Angel of Carmel* by the Bahá'ís of the West, was indeed close to the heart of 'Abdu'l-Bahá. During His journeys to America, the Master sent some of His most tender messages to this veteran soldier of the Cause. In one of them He describes the meetings which were held, the banquets, the newly recruited believers, and after each comment He repeats, 'I miss you very much.'

What finally happened to Ḥaydar-'Alí? There were many requests from all over the Bahá'í world for him to visit. But as he advanced in years, the

Master did not approve his going abroad. He would often wrap Ḥaydar-'Alí in His cloak and lovingly repeat, 'Ḥájí is ours! Ḥájí is ours!'

He was asked by the Master to teach the children of His household. All the grandsons of 'Abdu'l-Bahá attended these classes. Shoghi Effendi, who was later to become the Guardian of the Faith, was among his students. Ḥaydar-'Alí recognized his station even at this early age. Whenever the young Shoghi Effendi would enter the class, Ḥájí Mírzá Ḥaydar-'Alí would rise in respect for his student. He often whispered in his ear, 'Sufficient to you is the school of the Master.'

In many of the group photographs which were taken of the pilgrims in Haifa during the time of 'Abdu'l-Bahá, two old men can be seen standing on opposite sides of the group. One of these is Ḥájí Mírzá Ḥaydar-'Alí and the other is Mullá Abú-Ṭálib, a veteran believer from Caucasia.

Ḥaydar-'Alí and Abú-Ṭálib would often exchange jokes with one another in Haifa, to the delight of all of the friends. These two veteran soldiers in the twilight of their lives were still so lively that they could make everyone laugh.

When Ḥaydar-'Alí became ill and bedridden, the beloved Master would go to his room and inquire about his health and well-being. One day He asked him, 'How do you sleep at night?'

'Not very well', the Ḥájí replied.

Mullá Abú-Ṭálib immediately interrupted and said, 'He is wrong. He snores all night long!' And the Master and the friends laughed most heartily.

'Abdu'l-Bahá commanded that two of the believers should help Ḥájí Mírzá Ḥaydar-'Alí walk in the sunshine every morning. Once his cousin, Vakíl, took him by the arm to help him walk. He asked the Ḥájí, 'What else do you desire? The beloved Master comes to see you every day and grants you the strength to carry the burden of life.'

Ḥaydar-'Alí smiled and said, 'If you really love me, pray that I will die steadfast in the Covenant and ...'

Before he finished his sentence, his cousin interrupted and exclaimed, 'What do you mean, dear cousin! You are almost ninety years old, and so much loved and respected by the Master!'

'Yes, that is true', was the reply. 'But you cannot imagine how very cunning and insidious the self can be. It accompanies a man to the edge of the grave. The only thing that protects us from its deadly grasp is the divine assistance which is granted through prayer.'

The next day, when the Master visited the Ḥájí, He assured Ḥaydar-'Alí saying, 'You will sleep well. You will sleep well.'

NOTES AND REFERENCES

1 Ḥájí Muḥammad Karím K͟hán was a student of Siyyid Káẓim. He assumed a position of leadership among the S͟hayk͟hís in Iran after the siyyid's death, and became a bitter enemy of the Báb.

2 A title of the S͟hí'ih Muslim clergy.

3 Mullá Zaynu'l-'Ábidín, surnamed Zaynu'l-Muqarrabín (Ornament of Them that Are Nigh unto God) by Bahá'u'lláh, was a S͟hí'ih mujtahid before becoming a Bábí. He later became an outstanding follower of Bahá'u'lláh.

4 Jináb is a polite title meaning honourable. The name of the person referred to follows immediately after this title.

5 S͟hayk͟h Aḥmad and Siyyid Káẓim were the two leaders of the S͟hayk͟hí School who anticipated the imminent appearance of the Báb.

6 Ṣubḥ-i-Azal, Mírzá Yaḥyá, the half brother of Bahá'u'lláh who eventually rebelled against Him and became the 'Arch-Breaker of the Covenant of the Báb' (see *God Passes By*, p. 233). Azal was nominated by the Báb as His successor, 'as a figurehead pending the manifestation of the Promised One' (*God Passes By*, p. 28).

7 S͟hí'ih Muslims believe that the Imám Mihdí, the Twelfth Imám, did not die, but went into hiding for a thousand years. He lives in a secret place and will reappear at the time of the end to establish justice and righteousness on earth. The Báb fulfilled these prophecies with His declaration in 1844.

8 A classic epic of mystic poems, consisting of six volumes, composed in the thirteenth century by Jalálu'd-Dín Rúmí.

9 The surname Afnán (Twig) designates relatives of the Báb.

10 See *Memorials of the Faithful*, pp. 108–16.

11 See *Memorials of the Faithful*, pp. 5–8.

12 Now a city in Iraq. Karbilá is the place where the Imám Ḥusayn, the rightful successor of the Prophet Muḥammad, fought a hopeless battle against his enemies and was martyred, along with many of his followers, in 680 AD.

13 The Shrine of Shaykh Ṭabarsí is the place where a few hundred Bábís withstood the siege of the Persian army from October 1848 to May 1849. The Bábís were finally lured from their makeshift fort when the enemy swore an oath of peace on the Qur'án, and were massacred.

14 Bahá'u'lláh

15 Siyyid Muḥammad, the Antichrist of the Bahá'í Revelation, joined with Ṣubḥ-i-Azal in rebellion against Bahá'u'lláh.

16 See *Epistle to the Son of the Wolf*, p. 73, and *God Passes By*, p. 178.

17 The son of Jacob. See *Qur'án*, Súra 12, and Genesis, chapters 37–50. The Qur'án states: 'and when they saw him they were amazed at him, and cut their hands, and said, "God keep us! This is no man! This is no other than a noble angel!"' (Súra 12:31, Rodwell translation).

18 The verse of the Qur'án reads (Súra 112):
Say: He is God alone:
God the eternal!
He begetteth not, and He is not begotten;
And there is none like unto Him.
(Rodwell translation).

19 A reference to Jalálu'd-Dín Rúmí, who founded the order of dancing dervishes in the thirteenth century.

20 The house of retreat and worship for a dervish order of dancing dervishes in the thirteenth century.

21 The faithful brother of Bahá'u'lláh.

22 The ruler of Egypt who acted as a viceroy of the Sulṭán of Turkey.

23 Two Bábís attempted unsuccessfully to assassinate Náṣiri'd-Dín Sháh in 1852. See *God Passes By*, pp. 62-63.

24 The name Bahá'u'lláh (Bahá). The two most widely used forms of the Greatest Name are Yá Bahá'u'l-Abhá, an invocation, and Alláh-u-Abhá, a greeting. Both of these are referred to as the Greatest Name.

25 The phrase 'people of the path' is used here in the Islamic sense to denote people of true religion.

26 see Foreword, p. 224

27 This place should not be confused with the other garden (also known as the Garden of Riḍván) in Iraq where Bahá'u'lláh first revealed His Mission.

28 see note 21

29 'Abdu'l-Bahá

30 'Abdu'l-Bahá

31 *The Hidden Words of Bahá'u'lláh*, Arabic No. 42, p. 13.

32 When the Imám Ḥusayn and his band of warriors were besieged on the plains of Karbilá, their enemies denied them access to water, even though they were dying of thirst and the Euphrates River was within their sight. The Shí'ihs remember this as a heinous crime. (See note 12.)

33 A cube-like, stone building in Mecca. At the time of Muḥammad it was a pagan shrine. Muḥammad destroyed all the idols housed in it after His conquest of Mecca, and made it a place of pilgrimage for all Muslims.

34 Mírzá 'Alí-Muḥammad, surnamed Varqá (Dove) by Bahá'u'lláh. He was an outstanding Bahá'í poet and teacher. He and his twelve-year-old son, Rúḥu'lláh, were both eventually martyred.

35 see note 9

36 The honorific titles of two Bábí brothers who were prominent citizens of Iṣfahán. They were denounced by the Muslim clergy of the city and were martyred.

37 The illustrious Bahá'í scholar. He was sent to the United States by 'Abdu'l-Bahá and is well known as the author of The Bahá'í Proofs.

38 One of the titles of 'Abdu'l-Bahá.

39 See *'Abdu'l-Bahá: The Centre of the Covenant of Bahá'u'lláh* by H. M. Balyúzí, p. 526, note 58. Reference is made there to an Englishman who embraced the Faith in Persia, and who was an official of the Indo-European Telegraph Company. This may be the same individual mentioned here by Ḥájí Mírzá Ḥaydar-'Alí.

40 See *A Day When the Faithful Rejoiced* in this volume on page 9.

41 The term Branches (Aghṣán) refers to the male descendants of Bahá'u'lláh. One of the titles of 'Abdu'l-Bahá is 'The Most Great Branch'. Here, 'Branches' refers to Bahá'u'lláh's sons.

42 That is, Mírzá Muḥammad-'Alí, the Arch-Breaker of Bahá'u'lláh's Covenant.

43 'Divine Lote Tree' is a symbolic reference to the Manifestation of God, Bahá'u'lláh.

44 'Abdu'l-Bahá

45 Ḥájí Mírzá Muḥammad-Taqí-i-Afnán. See *Memorials of the Faithful*, pp. 126–29.

46 Bahíyyih Khánum, the sister of 'Abdu'l-Bahá.

47 Munírih Khánum, the wife of 'Abdu'l-Bahá.

Three
Meditations
on the Eve
of November
the Fourth

Shoghi Effendi, the Guardian of the Cause of God, referred to by 'Abdu'l-Bahá in His Will and Testament as 'the most wondrous, unique and priceless pearl that doth gleam from out the Twin surging seas', passed away on November 4th 1957 and these Three Meditations on the Eve of November the Fourth were those of Hand of the Cause of God Abu'l-Qásim Faizí as he stood on the shores of the Straits of Magellan at Punta Arenas looking across to Tierra del Fuego, the Land of Fire, at the southern extremity of the South American continent.

Dearly beloved friends at home and pioneers abroad:

Dear companions of my heart, solace of my eyes, and strength of my soul. When I am tired, sad and gloomy, I think of every one of you. At this hour, as I stand at the window of my hotel room and gaze at the beautiful stretch of water called 'The Straits of Magellan', I think of you; thousands, nay millions, of waves like unto white-feathered pigeons, emerge from the invisible horizons and approach the shores, I take them as messages of love and prayers which have taken wings throughout eternity.

Today as I was gazing at the picturesque work of nature, my memory turned to what I had read years ago about the discovery of this ocean path. Suddenly it seemed that an unseen hand tore asunder the veils which covered the past centuries, and a glorious vista stretched in front of me – the year 1520.

It was in this year that Magellan, despondent of procuring the means for an expedition in his own country, left Portugal for Spain.[1] He had one fixed idea, and of that he was so sure that he pleaded, with all his vigour and power, for the royal sanction and promise of financial support.

'I shall find the *paso*', he roared in the Spanish court. 'I alone know where to find it.'

Months passed before he was on his ship, leading four others with no less than the magic number of 260 sailors under his command.

It was one of the most arduous tasks that could be undertaken in those years, when no means of comfort and no wholesome provisions were available. It was an act of faith, vision and audacity. Nothing could be foreseen and no measure could ever be premeditated. Yet, they sailed on. Inhospitable climates, the wrath of nature in the form of tempests and gales, snow and hail, met them wherever they dared seek harbour.

Notwithstanding the incalculable disasters such as had rarely been inflicted upon any adventurer, or the schemes fraught with fear, consternation and threat, he, the captain of his fleet and the master of his soul, with indomitable courage and supreme audacity, always kept on sailing and commanding, 'To the South!'

Officers became dubious and reluctant, and influenced the sailors. The fleet was menaced by mutinous leaders and malcontented men. Everything forebode disastrous consequences – gloomy days one after the other dawned upon him and each augured hours of repining and rebelling. But the captain never flinched, never doubted, mastered every situation and held the reins of affairs in his iron grip. He kept on sailing 'To the South', never did he reverse course.

It is the law of God and the ocean that the disloyal ones should be punished lest their perfidious acts of unfaithfulness contaminate the whole atmosphere of hope and peace. Without such divine discipline, no boat can ever cross even a small lake.

High-ranking officers, like stars in the firmament of command, were cast down and sailors were marooned. Slow and painful death and the loss of every trace to posterity became the disgraceful fate of those who rebelled against the onward voyage of the ships to their destined goal.

One year passed. The last days were the gloomiest. One ship was lost. Stores and provisions dwindled. The coastal inlets they penetrated proved to be buoys of false hopes.

Fear of the unknown and uncharted south seas, fear of starvation and death, overtook everyone.

> What moments of paradoxical visions;
> What grave times to take great decisions;
> What a struggle within and without!
>
> He started the expedition with clear vision,
> Had faith in what he saw,
> Was brimful with zeal and enthusiasm,
> Braved all dangers,
> Weathered all storms,
> Surpassed mutiny,
> Created discipline and order and
> Travelled thousands of miles.
>
> But now he was all alone in his cabin and did not know that
> He was at the threshold of final victory,
> Had little more time to go,
> Two more degrees of latitude to cover,
> Two hundred more miles to travel and then
> To discover the *paso*.

He peered with his keen sight at the dark horizon and could discern nothing but darkness – darkness and nothing more.

He sighed and whispered that nothing was discovered, nothing was achieved, his quest ill fated, without the slightest hope of any future resumption, the work of all his yesterdays at the brink of ruin and destruction.

Had he been a man with less vision and faith, he would have followed the path of least resistance, yielded to the counsels of his companions and returned home.

At this juncture, however, when his fate and everlasting glory were hanging by a thread, he closed his ears to the repeated clamours and claims of men and patiently assessed the situation. Then, suddenly emerging from the depths of despair, free from the pangs of doubt and clutches of dismay, once more his command rang out: 'To the South!'

In the last act of this great drama, we see nothing but mute mountains, standing in eternal solitude, clad in the white robe of snow – desolate landscapes where no sign of living Man could be detected. No enchanting music could be heard from far-off shores, nothing except the howling of wind and the roaring of storms.

The disquieted, impatient voices raised again and again in restlessness never encroached upon the brave heart of that iron-willed man who had his goal clearly set in front of him.

Cruel nature never desires to open the veils and reveal the mysteries of its realm to Man. When the four remaining boats entered the labyrinth of endless twists and turns that was the passage, a tempest of unprecedented vigour and strength descended upon them. The hopes of the crews were shattered, but the faith of the captain remained unshaken and out of the darkness which covered all horizons and all hearts, heedless of the lightning and thunder, his voice echoed: 'Sail on, sail on, we are on the right *paso* – go on – steer on – on – on!'

From the window of my hotel room at this hour of the night, I can visualize those days of more than four centuries ago, when no one lived on these shores. The fumes and flames of the Land of Fire and threat of the gigantic Patagonians[2] were left behind on the far-off horizons.

Now the waves of the new ocean slowly surged to embrace for the first time the messengers of the old world. The ships were gliding in the silent path and opening a way – a new way – that dreamt-of *paso* from one ocean to another.

How immense must have been the relief and rejoicing which came to them. Tired but blissful, they reached their goal and for the first time the globe was circumnavigated.

What a great contrast is this to the position of the Bahá'ís in their fate-filled hours.

We have passed through many years of turmoil, toil and travail. A vow unprecedented in the history of mankind was taken by all the friends: never to retreat until all goals are won.

Hundreds and hundreds of our brave pioneers, men, women, young and old, children of all ages, left their homes and sailed their boats towards goals clearly set for them in the divine plans.

But we have still more distance to cover; the Ark will pass from one ocean to another and we will enter a new era in the history of our Faith. How very grateful every one of our dear and precious pioneers should feel that they remained firm and staunch, never flinched, never doubted and never turned their faces from their guiding star. How proud, extremely proud, all of us should feel that the Bahá'í Community throughout the world has produced such great and brave souls, in such a bitter period of history and in such a short space of time.

They heard harsh and unjust criticisms, experienced humiliation, scornful laughter and derision, underwent indescribable hardships, suffered premature deaths, sold lifetime savings, lost their children and relatives, entered into unknown lands and islands, crossed stormy seas and tempestuous oceans, climbed hills and mountains, penetrated the depths of deserts and forests, laboured in the most cruel and inhospitable climates, and settled amongst suspicious people, but nothing could ever shake their faith and determination. We are sure that in the future, too, they will remain undaunted and unshaken.

Bravo! Thousands of bravos and cheers for the Knights and heroes of Bahá'u'lláh who are scattered throughout the globe!

In the dark nights of despondent sorrows and dismay, let us rise in thought above the earth and penetrate with our own eyes the darkness of irreligion which has enveloped the whole earth; let us gaze on the summits of mountains; into the cottages of Africa; the huts of India; the Isles of all the seas and oceans and behold the most beautiful spectacle ever arranged by the hands of the Almighty. We are dazzling lights of heavenly beauty, as if gems of unimaginable splendour are strewn about the earth. They are the burning souls and hearts of our beloved pioneers who are lamps of guidance, fires of love, torches of divine knowledge, and crystal clear springs of the water of life to a bewildered mankind.

Even if the people are not thirsty, they proffer the cup, for they are sure that the day will come when even the seven seas will not suffice to slake their thirst.

No moth is to be seen near them although they burn brightly, yet they are certain that the time will come when thousands will cluster around them or their memories.

Thousands of praises to our dear pioneers who found *Pasos* – new *Pasos* – to the hearts of the people who for many, many centuries had been left in the catacombs of misery and oblivion; people who had never been approached and spoken to as members of Man's family, or as children of the One God, who is the Father of all.

Our pioneers went to them, to their houses, farms, cottages, huts and shelters; embraced them and made them understand and believe that they are also the leaves of one branch and the fruits of one tree, thus adding to the links of love which like a gold chain, are girdling the globe in the Name of Bahá'u'lláh.

Those men of four centuries ago sailed the pathless ocean full of fears and doubts, but we sail the oceans of sacrifice and service which are clearly charted by His mighty, powerful and inspired pen, with hearts of hope that the final victory will be for the Cause of God.

Look at the map of the divine plan where many circles are drawn. In His own powerful description, the circles are the wheels of Bahá'u'lláh's chariot. Let us walk beside His chariot when it passes from one era of victory to another era of greater victories. Let us walk with it when it passes through many rainbow arches of triumph and enters into wider and wider horizons of many stars and multifarious spectacles of majesty; let us remain with it and be rewarded by our nearness to the hem of His mercy and be intoxicated by the melodious music of the ever-rolling wheels of Bahá'u'lláh's chariot throughout eternity.

Let us remember that when sacks of wheat, barley and other grains were discovered in the tombs of ancient kings, many thought that such grains, which had remained for centuries under the earth, had lost their vitality of growth. But when they planted them, they grew. The same thing is true of the people who have been pushed to the mountain fastnesses, to the depths of forests and to the remote islands. They have not lost their vitality. They are alive. They have that potentiality of growth. Now the mighty hands of God are plunging into these forlorn and forsaken continents and are planting these souls into the fertile soil of the divine garden, and thus they will grow.

I am returning from a visit to your brothers and sisters – the pioneers of Bahá'u'lláh. I met them in their houses, their fields of service, in cities, villages and mountains. I saw them get ready to dash forward to deserts and woods, carrying the water of life for the thirsty souls scattered in the obscure corners of the world. I watched them passing through lanes, streets and densely populated areas of their towns, giving to the people roses of love fresh from the gardens of their hearts.

Theirs is not the fate of heroes and knights who are little known, recognized or appreciated in their own days; their brothers and sisters at home know them and praise them, although the people around them may look at them with suspicious eyes and sometimes, with scornful whisper or in raging anger, tell them, 'Go back home.' There are people also who, sometimes in mournful tones and sometimes in imperious manner, warn them of calamities and disasters which are looming near and then ask them again, 'Why are you still here?'

But at all times I found the pioneers like beacons built on solid rocks amidst the tempestuous seas. The waves attack them cruelly but only wash off the dirt and the lamp remains shining more brightly than ever before.

How can I forget them, and how can I ever describe to you the way they tread the stony path of sacrifice? Think of a meagre, slim maid-servant of Bahá'u'lláh who, single-handed and alone, goes to the valleys and villages and with a heart brimful with love for mankind, puts her hands on the foreheads of sick children, caresses their mothers and speaks some consoling words to the fathers and relatives. She takes rays of sunshine with her into the abyss of misery.

'Love's labour' is the label of the work of the other dear soul who, in the midst of teaching activities, patiently and persistently makes beautiful little picture books with some lines of explanation. When the little children recited their Bahá'í lessons, and I asked them how they learned these beautiful things, they showed me their books, which were made by this devoted pioneer.

My heart leaps up when I think of that family who always have groups of Indians in their house. They talk to them, teach them, entertain them and share with them their own daily bread. In these great services, father, mother and four children participate.

It was in a village that I found a mother with her only child. The mother works every possible hour to earn enough to support herself and her daughter. Both keep the fire burning in the fireside where many come to hear about our beloved Faith.

Think of two families united by the bonds of marriage but scattered all through the world in the Name of Bahá'u'lláh and each one an example of self-sacrifice and devotion.

I knew an Armenian family in Iran. Father, mother and small son embraced the Cause and started to serve it in a manner that amazed everyone. As it proved somewhat difficult to teach the Armenians in Iran and Turkey, I asked the father of this family, 'How did you become a Bahá'í?' In answer to this question, he taught me a beautiful lesson. He said, 'Have you ever seen a cobbler's shop? In the evening the floor of the shop is nothing but a heap of rubbish. The cobbler takes a magnet in his hand and moves it in the heap. All the clean, useful and shining nails jump to the magnet. The cobbler stores the nails and throws away the rubbish. The same is true with the Word of God. It is held up between heaven and earth and all who have the required intrinsic qualities are attracted to it. Now we are three Armenian nails.' How very true! They are as firm and steadfast as nails and are now working with many other pioneers in South America.

I cover my face because of my shortcomings in the service of the Cause when I contemplate the services of the dearly beloved Mother of South America, who for more than forty years did everything in her power for the propagation of the Cause, forged ahead in spite of all insurmountable obstacles and now, with bent back and grey hair, sees glorious edifices all around her in honour of the Faith she loves so sincerely and devotedly.

Dearest friends, I am certain you are all praying for your precious pioneers and know they are always in your hearts. Let us more closely than ever before follow the example of the Master who said that a king may attend the council of his ministers, summon his courtiers to his presence, order banquets and spread sumptuous tables, but at all times his mind and heart are turned towards the soldiers who are guarding or fighting in the far-flung frontiers of the country. He said that the same is true of 'Abdu'l-Bahá. He always thinks of the teachers and pioneers. He expects to receive news of their victories, to send them what they need and convey to them messages of love, assurance and encouragement.

This is not a story of ages gone by. It is a humble tribute to the pioneers and a poor description of the almost inexplicable conditions under which many of the new members of our world-wide Bahá'í family are living. This plaintive voice comes to you from the depths of human misery. I could not believe mine eyes when for the first time a group of indigenous believers emerged from their cottages with their arms open to greet and embrace me. Their clothes had been made many years ago from a piece of sackcloth, and I saw men and women wearing many-coloured patches held together to cover their dear bodies. Their hair was unkempt and dirty, their hands covered in layers of dust. Their feet changed into solid things after years of walking almost barefoot on the sharp, stony paths of the mountainsides. I consoled myself by thinking that only in that locality were believers the victims of so much poverty but afterwards, wherever I went, I found them under exactly the same burden, destitute and in the same deplorable, degraded plight.

But of their manners, politeness, purity of heart, strength of soul and their quick receptivity to the light of the New Day and comprehension of the fundamental verities of this World Faith, I have so many stories to tell.

It is clear that they are the remnants of a race once grand and glorious, civilized and cultured. All their material wealth had been taken from them by force, evil plots and atrocities. No way was left for them except to find shelter in the remote fastnesses of wild mountains as far as possible from the cunning hands of men from other parts of the world.

Their imperial pride and grandeur can still be easily discerned in their countenances, their large, black, penetrating eyes and graceful demeanour. They are very calm and reserved. They discuss for hours, but in a calm and quiet atmosphere. Never did they hurry for food, tea or anything else, no matter how late they were served or how hungry they were. They never hastened to have their share first but sat patiently until such time as the plates were served. No one expressed the desire for one more plate; even the children did not cry for more.

One of the most shining memories of my visit is the night when we had a large meeting. The only light we had was from two or three candles. The impression of the profiles of these men and women went deep into my heart. To me they were newly enrolled soldiers of Bahá'u'lláh's Army of Life, ready to accept discipline before entering the arena of service and taking charge of affairs.

A question was asked, 'What did you like the most in the Bahá'í teachings?' The following answers were given, 'Equality of the rights of men and women. Universal education. Prohibition of liquor', etc.

To hear these words from the lips of these people who have been pushed aside from the circle of the human family for centuries and in these very remote mountains of the world, took me back to the dark days of the desolate prison room of Bahá'u'lláh in 'Akká. And in that minute of ecstasy His words echoed in my mind. When in prison He said that He accepted the chains on His neck so that all chains would be broken into pieces and Man would become free. He accepted prison confinement so that Man will have liberty. He accepted to live in the most ruined city of the world so the ruined citadels of hearts would be repaired and made firm.

The chains are giving way day by day and we hear the resounding note of every link as they fall. Here I could behold the shimmering light of new life from the windows of the newly fortified citadels of the hearts of these dear and precious souls. In that darkness no one could see the pearls of tears shed at their feet.

Nothing will ever be prettier to me hereafter than this: Bahá'í women walk along with their men for hours or even days to attend a meeting. When they entered the meeting, they would open their arms and embrace me. I would see a bundle carried on their shoulders and in that bundle a little heavenly gift – a child, its two beautiful large black eyes gazing at me. They were the loveliest things that my eyes could behold. To me they were two sources of light – two windows through which one could peep into heavens of beauty and charm. They welcomed me with their innocent looks. By the slightest touch of a fingertip, their beautiful lips would open into smiles. How easily they are appeased – glimpses of light shone from the faces of the mother and child to make one understand that no stranger had ever touched their children before. Oh, how I loved them – adored them – picked them up, hugged and kissed them! But to see them in such depths of hunger, nakedness and misery is beyond human endurance.

We are rightly happy and proudly claim and proclaim, 'We love you and we embrace you!' But is this sufficient? When did embraces and kind words satisfy the hunger of the body and soul, satiate the thirsts of hearts and clothe the dying naked ones in the blizzards of the terrible cold seasons? They are our brothers and sisters, fragments of human families, which have been cast away by the hands of cruelty, covetousness and atrocity. They are our relatives who would have remained lost to us had it not been for the bounties of Bahá'u'lláh, who gathered them and placed them on our laps and told us that they are His trust.

What do we expect from people who have been utterly deprived even of the most rudimentary means of livelihood? What can they do if their provision consists of only wheat, corn and potatoes? A loaf of good bread is a prize to them, and a handful of sugar is considered a valuable gift. Their children die amidst plenty, there is no one to spend lavishly for their birthdays, and death to them is a relief. Men and women are so delicate and tender that the slightest touch of a disease takes them to their graves – I hardly ever saw any old women or old men amongst them.

Now that they have come to the tabernacle of love and unity, they consider it as the last haven and heaven for themselves. Should we fail to keep them, they will lose all hope and nothing will remain for them but to fall again to the lowest depths of deprivation.

They need everything, even the crumbs that we carelessly throw away can feed their hungry infants. Schools, centres, teachers and regular supervision are needed to keep them happy and hopeful.

What can you my dear pioneers do? What can we do if we do not truly realize in what period of Man's history we are living? If love is not translated in these days into tremendous sacrifices, it will remain unproductive forever. These are fleeting hours. Every minute and second is valuable. No sacrifice will be too great in the spiritualization of this planet.

Rest assured, beloved pioneers, that your brothers and sisters at home and throughout the world will not leave you forsaken. Streams of help will be flowing into the proper administrative channels. In these God-granted opportunities, be sure that the friends will give all that they have for the redemption of mankind and spiritualization of the globe.

Rest assured that your friends will never abandon you. Carry on and invite thousands and thousands to the banquet of Bahá'u'lláh and give them their share of the Bread of Life. Climb higher and higher on the ladder of success and awaken the people from their long spiritual lethargy. March on to the loftiest summits of victory and be certain that all your sacrifices and endeavours will bear splendid fruits, and the deprived members of the human family will emerge out of obscurity and will find their abode in the warm sunshine of universal love.

Pray that the hungry cries of the newly born babes in the Kingdom of God and the plaintive voices of the many recent settlers in the tabernacle of Bahá'u'lláh will reach thousands of souls and stir thousands of hearts in these opportune hours which, if lost, will remain irretrievable throughout eternity.

The hours of loneliness weigh heavily upon this humble traveller who finds the path too long and the cross too heavy. No wonder then if people see me strolling on the shores of this Strait, watching sunrises and sunsets and listening to the secrets that the ripples whisper in my ears.

When it dawned upon me that here – in this water path – two boundless oceans meet and mingle, I found myself spellbound by its glorious fate and function and it seemed to me then a bountiful and salubrious fountain of crystalline, fresh water, full of captivating beauty and charm. Often its ripples washed away the soils of sorrow from my aching heart and its waves dispelled the chains of melancholy from my waking soul.

Today I did not find solace in this solitude. The thin veil of dusk, through which the ruby of Mercury and the sapphire of Neptune were dimly discernible, fell solemnly upon all things. In the midst of my prayers and pleas I could hear the waves whisper again and again,

> Come … Come
> No voyager can pass
> But needs must hear my song.
> Then on he sails, o'erwhelmed with joy,
> With the knowledge of things unknown before.

The waves were no longer white-feathered pigeons conveying messages of love and prayers, but free and fearless giants who, heedless of 'mountains heaved to the heavens scraping the edges of the skies', whipped the sharp, stony shores and retreated only to return and combat more ferociously than before. They were mountainous, reckless monsters above and beyond the power of law and order, ruthlessly rocked by gales, ever rolling, ever rearing – the noise of their thundering echoed on all sides.

The forest-shaded eastern shores were established with such verdure as to seem covered by tapestries of many tinted turquoise while horizons to the west were enveloped in mists of crimson hue.

The ever-moving lantern of the heavens was gracefully gliding downward from the azure dome and, in its downward march, bestowed a drop of the lover's blood upon each wave and proudly looked beneath to find thousands, nay millions of its own reflections in the scarlet velvet of the ever-surging seas.

Rather than taste the bitterness of the approaching mysterious night, the sun, like unto a fast-fading flame, drowned itself amongst the mountainous waves, sinking deep into the infinite seas of solitude and thus putting its crimson seal on the death warrant of a day. Then when the red-rimmed scroll of the night was opened and unfurled, lids were taken off the inexhaustible treasures of the universe and myriads of diamonds and pearls were poured into the deep blue bowl of heaven; and the moon – floating like a dream – poured its mysterious blue lustre on these sparkling jewels.

The reflection of the moon formed a magic, transparent, silvered path beneath which the waves were seen, not yet subsided but still in constant commotion and fret, bathing all shores in showers of white foam.

The noises of the tumultuous town were gradually hushed. The exhausted fisherman, enfeebled by age, weary and bent by years of tireless toil, his head sunk into the collar of his threadbare coat, and his feet bleeding on the sharp rocky shores of the ever-surging sea, headed home to his mournful sleep. Plaintive songs of fast-flying sea birds echoed the lamentation and groans of another day rolled into the abyss of time, dead and doomed to eternal loss.

Oh sea, ever moving, ever surging! Pluck some gleaming pearls from the yet unseen fathoms and bestow them as souvenirs upon your homeless and humble companion. Tell him tales of terror and trouble, even if his blood runs cold. This is his last request while he still feels free and bold.

How can seas of emotion be poured into chalices of words, though they be of gold? Unlimited in their scope to contain, they are powerless in their capacities to convey.

But look around:

Are not these ravishing spectacles of majesty and might,
Immensity and height,

But a token of the two eternal oceans of spiritual lineage of that …
'most wondrous, unique and priceless pearl that doth gleam from out the twin surging seas'?

Are not the vast horizons, hued and framed in green and red, signs of the most cherished memories that he had of his Beloved, 'The Exalted One'?

Was it not through the lustre of this pearl that heroes and conquerors were made out of the commonest clay? Did not his words well up from the depths of his loving heart and pierce all hearts deep in the core, so that out of swamps of heedlessness, pioneers and knights were born?

Through the magic of his clarion-call, the spells of lethargy were broken and the dreamless dust became heaven-lit with the sweetest dreams, the realization of each one becoming the water of life to many a thirsty soul.

His love will shield generations from fear and will increasingly and permanently cause many legions of steadfast and stalwart knights to spring free from the snares and pursuit of material comfort to the arenas of honourable death or resplendent victory.

Through the ingenious application of his loving advice, the abandoned and distressed, the forlorn and forsaken, will find shelter in the sunshine of God's Universal Love.

We all remember the last melody he sang – it echoed the onward march of the intrepid soldiers of the Army of Life, whom we all watched while our eyes brimmed with tears of joy.

He invited mankind to many sumptuous joyful banquets spread in the Name of their Redeemer, but alas! Whoever suspected that at the zenith of his plan, the midway point of his crusade, there would creep a dark and dreary shadow which would break all cords, shatter all the golden bridges of hope, lay the harps broken and bruised at the feet of the guests and alter all the music meant for mirth and merriment into sobbing, buried in the bosom of long and lonesome nights of desperate separation?

Tortured to the quick by the speedy flight of the most precious hours of Man's life, the weary traveller uttered words to the night as if in delirium:

Oh Night!
Where is the depth of Man's ignorance?
Where is the abyss of his downfall?

Oh Night! Deep, mysterious night!

Reveal stories of the fateful hours which took wing from out
your bosom.

Grant them as gifts to this homeless and humble voyager.

Like unto ancient troubadours tell him some tales of old, even if
his blood runs cold. He ventures to request this while he still feels free
and bold.

The night mourned and groaned like a mortally-wounded bird:

Hold up your goblet – I see it brimming with tears. Receive this drop from the depths of the wild darkness of the past and then yours will be a nectar hitherto unheard of and untasted.

It was at a time when Man, the essence of negligence and pride, started sending satellites to probe into the silent realms above while,

His heaven and haven
His beloved and benevolent
true and sincere brother
was lying in bed unrecognized
and unsought for.

Yes, this is the sad story of a bewildered humanity.

It was during that summer when Man, victim to the ruthless scourging of his never-ending animal lusts and desires became enchanted, nay bewitched, by the song which he sang all the summer long. Consumed in the fire and flame of his wild pursuit of passion and shame, heedlessly he went on.

Thousands and thousands were hurled into their graves, but nothing could stop time from rolling on towards that gloomy dawn. Even if all would kneel and beg the Lord to accept them as sacrifices, that portentous moment could not be advanced or delayed. Seven seas of the blood of martyrs could not wash away the dust of despondency accumulated upon the illustrious pearl of the two divine oceans!

Yes, in that ominous hour came to pass that which dimmed all souls and devastated the rose garden of all hearts. Ever since then the tongues never stop uttering, 'Beloved', and souls burn in the fire of longing to touch the hem of his attire, or to have one – only one – glimpse of his heavenly countenance.

What heart can remain sterile rock, unmoved and untouched at this hour?

What soul has no zest and fervour and is not deeply moved at this moment, when, 'the most wondrous, unique and priceless pearl that doth gleam from out the twin surging seas', was quietly taken back to its eternal abode in the celestial treasure houses of the Lord?

NOTES AND REFERENCES

1 In the first of these three essays, Mr Faizí reflects on the historic expedition led by Portuguese explorer Ferdinand Magellan to chart a *paso* or passage from the Atlantic ocean to the Pacific ocean. Magellan left Portugal for Spain in 1517 and discovered the passage in 1520.

2 This refers to the stories of giant people that Magellan claimed to have encountered on his voyage.

A Village Scriptorium

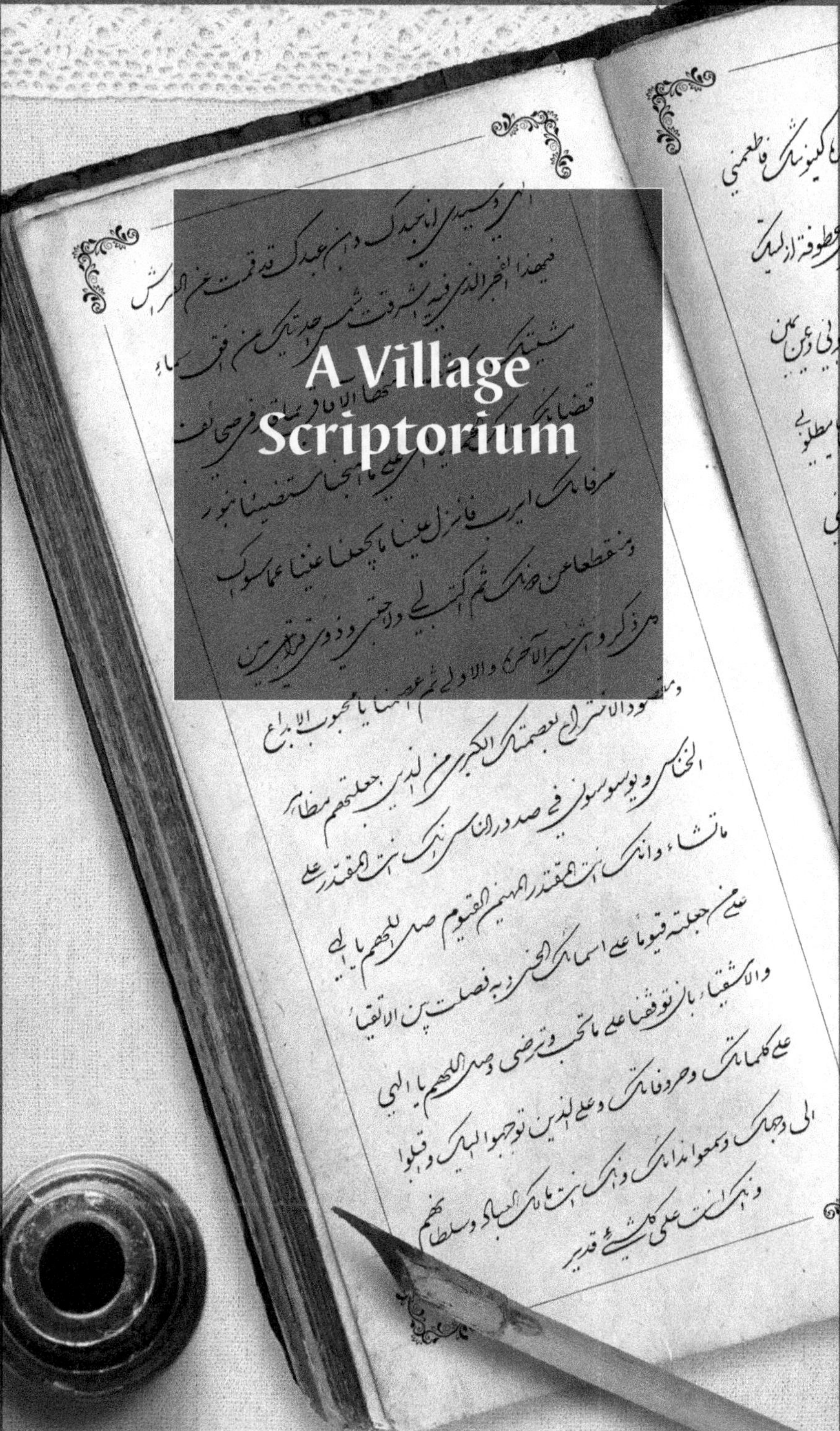

Publisher's note:

In this essay Mr Faizí refers to Alcuin of York, a prominent figure of the Carolingian Renaissance who ensured that the monastic scriptoria preserved classical texts by copying, distributing and storing them. The words that Mr Faizí quotes at the close are attributed to Alcuin.

The book *The Mysterious Forces of Civilization* (mentioned on page 366) was retranslated and published with a new title *The Secret of Divine Civilization* in 1957.

One's heart leaps up with joy and wonder when, reflecting on the events of history, it reaches Alcuin's laborious task of transcribing the ancient books. The monastic schools had labour-rooms wherein young monks marched solemnly to copy the works of Bede, Isidor or Augustine in the interval between periods of prayer and meditation.

One does not need to revert to those antique monasteries to search for the monks and nuns, secluded in their own private and individual cells, copying books or words of the Divine Law. If one is earnest and enthusiastic to behold those scriptoriums, one may even find them in this age of plenty, when copies of such a book as *The Bahá'í World* can be printed and bound in a few days.

Indeed the indefatigable efforts of those pious and conscientious men of religion preserved precious and costly manuscripts for the coming generations and they conferred great benefits on humanity up to the time of the rise of universities and the age of the printing press, when the scriptoriums were done away with.

In this portion of the world, there still exists such a condition and the need is so severely felt that scriptoriums were founded again. Everybody knows that there is a severe law due to which Bahá'í literature is absolutely forbidden entrance in Iran.

The Bahá'ís are eager to study their religious books, to propagate the teachings of their Cause for which they have long suffered, and are still giving their lives. The children and the youth are to be educated and familiarized with the works written in the Cause.

It is the most compulsory of all the Bahá'í obligations, to educate the children, imbue them with the ardour and love of obeying the Divine Precepts and create in them the feeling of participating in the many Bahá'í activities to bring about the World Order devised by the mighty pen of Bahá'u'lláh.

No book may be obtained from outside and there is no freedom of press inside. There remains only one alternative: to copy the books.

Everybody knows what a difficult and irksome task is the copying of books. The scribes should take the utmost care to not intersperse their own frivolities, nor make mistakes through haste. This is true of all kinds of books and especially true about the revealed Words of God.

In this village where I am living, there are classes of *Dars-i-Akhlágh* (Character Training Classes) where the following books are taught in different grades: *Some Answered Questions*, *Memorials of the Faithful*, *The Mysterious Forces of Civilization*, *Ishráqát*, Arabic and Persian Prayers, etc. There is only one copy of each of these books in the village library. Each group of students goes to the house of a friend where a teacher dictates the books and the children write down and study the materials therein.

Besides that, there are many Nineteen Day Feasts where the Tablets should be chanted and the history of the Cause must be explained and related. There is a special class for this purpose. The members write down the required Tablets, then study them very carefully and take notes from speeches made from *The Dawn-Breakers*.

The friends of this village are indeed attached to the Cause. They are very steadfast and have a long history coloured with the precious blood of their many martyrs. They are always looking forward to receiving a letter from the beloved Guardian or news from the friends in other hands. Whenever there is something new, the Nineteen Day Feast scriptorium gets entirely busy.

It is very touching to watch the busy work going on. The teacher reads slowly and clearly at a measured rate and corrects spelling mistakes of the students. Thus a score of copies are made at once.

The very enthusiastic and energetic children sit down at night to copy a book for their use in their character training classes. The students believe that by thus doing, they are doing their best in the path of God and it is their firm belief that 'Writing books is better than planting vines, for he who plants a vine serves his belly, but he who writes a book serves his soul.'

The Wonder Lamp

INTRODUCTION

Dearly loved friends of India,

In January 1969, when I was returning from an intensive tour in the Far East, I fell ill in Bombay, was taken to the hospital and confined to bed. The members of your National Assembly, yourselves and even your darling children showered me with so much love that despite all my efforts I remained speechless and unable to express the depth of my gratitude.

Then one day I thought of writing a story for your dearly loved children – it is an abiding testimony of my heartfelt thanks and appreciation.

The vision of a Wonder Lamp was written in a hospital room overlooking the Indian Ocean, the beautiful waves of which always reminded me of the many waves of your love, consideration and prayers which covered me and cured me.

Yours in the service of our beloved Guardian,

– A. Q. Faizí

Part I

A lonely traveller reached the top of the hills overlooking an endless space of land stretched towards the ever-surging sea. His silhouette against the deep blue sky was very graceful and charming. He gazed at the valleys, forests and mounds and found them barren and dead. Trees, bushes, herbs and grass, which once ornamented the skirts of the hills, had been mercilessly swept away by the last winter gales. The bare trees stood on the slopes of valleys as relics of luxurious treasures lavishly strewn everywhere in the days gone by, but now all seemed long forgotten, inaccessible and irretrievably lost.

The lonely voyager sighed deeply and, looking at all sides, whispered to himself, 'The winter has been devastating, but the spring is not far off. If only my people could comprehend!'

Having uttered these words, he took his way towards the sea which he reached at a time when the endless daily struggle between the moon and Mother Earth was at the highest tension. The moon, though pale and formless, was exerting a universe of power to pull the immense layers of water which covered the breast of Earth. On that particular day, the sea reflected the deep blue of heaven and rested beautifully all round the endless shores, looking like the prettiest blue gown with thousands of waves of white lace in constant rhythmic movement hitting against the rocks and sands with a roar which could reach the dome of heaven.

The struggle continued for hours but, eventually, Mother Earth gave way and the moon started to pull with all its power. It pulled and pulled and the beautiful white laces began to go farther away, leaving the breast of Mother Earth bare and exposed. The Earth beheld in grief and sorrow how the waves were running away and away. She no more could see the white foam and hear the roar of the giant waves. They diminished into ripples and looked like a vanquished army whose fighting soldiers were in captivity and were drawn to a foreign land in chains – no sound was heard from them. All, in the silence of shame, were heading far away – away from the breast of Mother towards their unknown fate.

Thousands of birds like unto hungry urchins were waiting impatiently for Mother Earth to open her breast and give them their daily food. These white-feathered birds soared up and up and up, until such time as they appeared like the tails of children's kites – white dots in the endless firmament floating to the music of the ever-roaring ocean. Then they would suddenly swoop down and down and touch the waves with their wings and make angry noises of hunger and impatience.

When the tremendous rush of waves subsided and they reached their unknown destiny in the far-off distance in the west, the birds came down on the breast of Mother Earth and perched on crevices where delicious food had been provided for them. They jumped up and down and consumed their share of the provision. They chirped and chirped and praised and thanked and manifested joy and gratitude.

Hours passed and Mother Earth could not sleep in peace and tranquillity being so bare and cold. Mother Earth was thinking of her children who had gone so far away from her bosom. She wanted them to come back to warm her body and to roll and roll on her bosom and fill the world with their roaring. She invited them to return and hit against the rocks and sands and make white foam as beautiful as the lace work of India, and waves delicate as the lines on the ancient swords of Japan.

The evening star appeared and it stood very near to the moon. The evening star became very sad when it found that the moon had, by force, drawn away all the children of Earth and had held them in captivity. The moon asked the evening star as to the cause of its sadness, and said, 'When I was a crescent, I held you in my heart. We looked like a ring in heaven's ear. When I grew in size, you went a bit further and still we both shed our two lines of light on the seas and made the sky and the oceans very beautiful for the lovers … and now you keep so much aloof that we look like two who had never been friends.'

'Why do you keep the waves away from their shores?' asked the evening star. 'Send them back.'

No sooner these words were uttered than the waves were set free. They began running like victorious armies returning home. They looked like a white belt around the Earth. As they approached, one would hear the cries of joy more and more. They reached the breast of Mother Earth at night. They slept there quietly. It took hours before they reached there, but it was very sweet when they were back home.

They calmly and slowly covered the breast of Mother Earth and roared and roared in a slow, sweet and steady tone. She slept in peace and wept no more.

It was there that our fellow traveller became a friend of the evening star. He then resumed his daily walk. He went from village to village and gave the people the glad news of the advent of the beautiful days of the Spring. Every evening, he would wash himself in the pure translucent waters of rivers or ponds or lakes and wait for the appearance of the evening star to offer his prayers.

PART II

It was in the first part of the spring that a wonderful lamp appeared. It was a huge, gigantic lantern, aglow with all the hues of the rainbow and the warmth of the sunshine. The lamp was not static. It was not hanging. It was placed upon a very beautiful pedestal which enabled the lamp to rotate and shed its mysterious light to all sides. It was not merely rotating, it seemed as if the lamp was moving to a mysterious music – low, sweet and utterly out of this world. The traveller was struck dumb with surprise and thrilled to the core of his bones. He could not take his eyes away from that Wonder Lamp.

As it turned, and its resuscitating rays were gradually spread, the light and heat penetrated every one of the living cells, and the endless forest thrived with the zest of a new life. There flowed into every branch fresh sap and into every vein fresh blood. The dark soil was covered with turquoise carpets interspersed with multi-coloured flowers. The fresh leaves on the trees glowed and became transparent crystals of all sizes, shapes and colours. Gradually the almond, the peach and the apple trees were completely transformed into most ravishingly beautiful umbrellas on the cover of which blossoms had been painted – blossoms of white, rose and pink.

A small child stealthily came and, with her beautiful large black eyes wide open with surprise, stared at the Wonder Lamp. Not knowing what it was, she timidly approached, stretched her arms bedecked with rings and bracelets and opening her fingers in front of the light, she moved them, like people who warm themselves in the wintertime standing near a furnace. In her childish ecstatic delight, she moved her arms, then her shoulders and then her whole body with so much grace and tenderness that even heaven enjoyed the scene and sent its soft music for the joy of the innocent.

The small girl tiptoed and beckoned the other children, who came clad in different colours and different dresses, some with bells on their ankles. They all started to go round the Wonder Lamp and danced and danced, their merriment and mirth became as boundless as the space and as pure as the joys in heaven.

While they were overwhelmed by their unending innocent intoxication, they heard the sound of drums, bugles and the footsteps of soldiers. The children became pale like people who were having a feeling of an impending storm fraught with unending perils. They ran to one another and nestled close to each other. They then came to know that all the drums and bugles were played as a prelude to the coming of a Prince.

The Prince reached the spot and looked with the greatest amazement at the Wonder Lamp and exclaimed, 'How beautiful! I have never seen one like it in seven climes.' He was still on his horse.

'Where is it made?' he asked his tutor.

'As far as I know,' the tutor replied, 'such things are usually made by the craftsmen of China.'

Fear-stricken, the helpless children were hiding behind the hills, praying that no harm would ever befall their beloved lamp. With their wide-open eyes they were also staring at the Prince, his ludicrous vanity and the petty and false pride of his flattering retinue who had arrayed themselves in such a way so that each one would be in the sight of the Prince.

There was a death-like silence when the Prince alighted. To break the silence, one of the courtiers bowed to the ground and proposed, 'Won't Your Highness leave some valuable object on this lamp as the souvenir of your visit here?'

The Prince exclaimed in contentment and joy, as he was walking on the green grass, 'How astonishingly alert!' Then as if haunted by a fresh thought he stopped, and addressing his treasurer commanded, 'Bring me the famous piece of silk sent to me from China. It is even finer than air and more translucent than fresh water.'

The treasurer immediately brought a parcel and after bowing several times, offered it to the Prince who, in turn, opened it and held it up in the air. It was indeed an exquisite piece of art, rarely to be found in these days. Such craftsmanship belonged to the days when men and women had more time, patience, endurance and peace of mind; therefore, much of the God given gifts found outlets and were manifested in such incomparable masterpieces. The Prince asked the help of his retinue and, with their assistance, the silk cloth was reverently laid on the lamp. It was an ethereal phenomenon to watch.

But alas! It diminished the light of the lamp.

Now a group of bashful, blossoming youth surrounded the lamp to bathe in its life-giving rays. The endless blue of the sky mixed and mingled with the shimmering green of grass while the leaves on fresh branches rustled and quivered in the pleasant mid-summer day breeze. Everything exhilarated with new life. Everything was adorable and God was manifested in all His majesty, beauty, glory, grandeur and love.

All of a sudden, the dancing circle of the youth stood still. They heard the galloping of horses as swift as lightning and as wild as the storms of the mid-winter nights. A Minister was approaching with all his pomp and glory. When they reached the spot, they breathed the fresh and perfumed air, gathered round the lamp and wondered at its beauty.

The Minister, holding his bejewelled belt, looked at the lamp again and again and said, 'Is this the lamp the fame of which has gone far and wide?' One of his attendants, lest someone else would come in with a new thought, pushed everyone aside and, drawing himself nigh to the Minister, bowed to the ground and said 'Yes, Your Excellency. This is that illustrious object of art, which I was the first one to report to you. Such lamps with so much lustre and even warmth are the work of far-off Cathay.'

An old man, not clad in the garment of gold, shy and with open and unblinking eyes, stepped forth and exclaimed, 'Your Excellency! Such mysterious lamps are manufactured in heaven.' No sooner had he mentioned this than all roared with laughter, obviously not to contradict the man, but to flatter the Minister. The Minister also laughed and said, 'Listen to the voice of a prophet!'

The man stood firm on his ground and resolutely said, 'I am not a prophet, but a follower of one.' Having uttered these words, he went on his way.

Someone who was feeling the silk on the lamp with his finger, suddenly jumped forward and said, 'Why not throw something on this lamp as the souvenir of your visit here?' 'Well said!' shouted the Minister. 'Let me see. What do I have worthy of this wonderful object?' He murmured to himself while walking up and down, and then called his private attendant.

'Bring me that shawl which is made in ancient India. It is embroidered, and it is sacred and old.'

The shawl was brought and with the greatest care and reverence it was spread over the lamp.

The young ones, in their pitiable plight heaving heavy sobs, burst into heart-breaking tears. They found their lamp still turning but with great difficulty. Its light was dimmer and its warmth had diminished a great deal. They could no more bathe in its rays and feel blissful and happy. That afternoon, the forest reflected the sorrow-stricken spirits of the children. The children raised their hands in supplication that their lamp might again regain its original splendour and lustre. But alas! A profound slumber prevailed everywhere. The green foliage which was once a solace to one's eyes withered and a death-like sorrow covered the small hearts of the deprived children.

Towards sunset, loud peals of soldiers' laughter were heard which announced the coming of no less a person than the Grand Vizier as a prelude to the advent of the King.

The first step taken by the Grand Vizier was to examine the two covers already spread on the lamp. Feeling certain that in the presence of the King, he would never have a chance to contribute his share to this object of beauty and wonder, he immediately covered the lamp with a third piece of cloth which proved to be even heavier and thicker than the previous ones.

It did not take long before the King dismounted from his stallion. Then in a voice even louder than thunder he shouted, 'Where is this renowned lamp?'

'Under these mantles, Your Majesty!' said the Grand Vizier. 'The top one is mine which indicates the extent of my heartfelt joy to welcome you here!' Then he lifted a part of the covers so as the King could have a glimpse of the glory and splendour of the lamp. When his eyes fell on it he exclaimed, 'Exquisite! Unique! The only one that I have ever beheld in my life! Now tell me, where it is made?'

'We heard from our erudite ancestors', said one of the attendants, 'that such lamps are made in China.'

At this moment a pedestrian clad in simple garments appeared on the stage and raised his hand to take permission to talk. He was our lonely traveller.

'Draw nigh', said the King very kindly, being attracted by the youthful appearance of the man and truthfulness of his attitude. His eyes flashed with the fever of love and sincerity. He bowed in great respect, and stood very straight with his eyes fixed on the King's face. Then he said, 'This lamp is made in heaven and brought down here by the angels of God. This is a part of the universal law of Creation.'

'Hear! Hear! A prophet speaks!' said the King. 'No, your Majesty,' retorted the wayfarer, 'only a humble believer in Him. May I continue?'

The Grand Vizier, who was listening with the utmost aversion, interrupted and pleaded, 'Your Majesty, the night is drawing near!' The King answered with great kindness, 'I know, I know, but let him continue. I want to listen to him.'

'Such a lamp', continued the disciple, 'is brought to the earth almost every one thousand years.'

'Every one thousand years!' exclaimed the King.

'Yes, Your Majesty. The same rule prevails in the movement of the stars in the boundless firmament. Every one of them has a definite time to appear, a period of duration and a fixed time to set. There is a perfect order in the whole of this universe. This cannot be an exception.'

The King smiled with joy and contentment and told him to continue.

'This lamp is ignited by invisible hands and reinforced from sources beyond our comprehension. It burns with such power and intensity that should the whole world unite together and pour on it the waters of the seven oceans, it will never be extinguished. Rather than being put off, it adds to its many rays of light.'

The Grand Vizier, whose face had become very ugly, was burning with the fire of jealousy. In order to destroy the castles of the young man's hopes and aspirations, he approached and started to talk. The following words were uttered, but each one like unto flames of hell which burned and destroyed: 'Where are you coming from?'

‘From yonder. I go from village to village.’

‘Do you teach the same things to our people?’

‘I carry water and supply it to whoever is thirsty.’

‘Who is behind this hill waiting for you?’

‘No one. I am alone.’

‘You lie! You have formed crowds of irresponsible mobs to overthrow the throne of our kingdom.’

The King was agitated and interrupted the interrogation of the Grand Vizier by saying, ‘But he seems very honest and loyal to us.’

The Grand Vizier: ‘Yes, Your Majesty, in words, sweet words …’

The young man: ‘May I continue?’

The crowd of courtiers: ‘Yes.’

The King: ‘By all means.’

The young man turned his large, black and very attractive eyes to all sides. They all seemed hypnotized. He resumed his elucidation, ‘As to myself, I am a lonely wayfarer in these dales and valleys, far from the tumult of insurgent maddening life. My heart is parched and thirsty, but I carry the water of life in my hands.

‘To you I am abjectly poor and miserable, but I stand on the inexhaustible treasures of our Creator. Lotus flowers: I possess many, but ponds and lakes refuse to receive them. Thousands of songs warble from my lips, but the lyres of hearts are broken and the harps of souls have no chords.

‘Beware! Beware! Wild blazing fires of desire and passion are raging. Souls are abandoned, forlorn, forsaken and famished. Hearts are burned and bruised with lust and greed. This unbroken, inflexible monotony of the pursuit of passion drags Man from his throne to the abyss of animal life.

‘This lamp burns and purifies the hearts of men. It is the same lamp in all ages, but comes under different names and in different spots of the earth. Sometimes it is called Krishna, sometimes Buddha … Zoroaster … Moses …’

The Grand Vizier interrupted with great rage and fury and said, ‘Names that we have never heard, never known and never recognized.’

‘Let him continue!’ shouted the King.

'We are not worshippers of names. I am just telling you these names so that everyone will be grateful for their zest and contributions to Man's life. Had it not been for people such as Krishna, Buddha, Zoroaster, Moses, Jesus and Muhammad, we would never be prepared for this great day of God.'

'You see, Your Majesty,' very strongly protested the Grand Vizier, 'he is putting the name of our Prophet along with the names of those who are profane, untrue and as yet unrecognized by us.'

'But he mentioned them with reverence', said the King, and addressing the young man he ordered him to continue.

'As I said, they are the same, essentially the same ... of the same magnitude, aim, ideal and mission ...'

'Do you preach the same principles to the people of the towns and villages?' asked the Grand Vizier, in manifest anger.

'The sun shines the same on the kings' mansions and on the peasants' cottages,' answered the man, 'therefore, the Message of God is the same everywhere.'

A young man from amongst the courtiers approached the King and pleaded with him, 'Allow me to accompany him.'

'Why?' asked the King.

The young man drew his sword and exclaimed, 'Up till now I believed that the highest honour was to kill, now I comprehend that I am wrong. We must give life. His message brings life ...'

The Grand Vizier pointed to the young man with derision and scorn and said: 'Therefore you must take off all your gold and silver attires and become a beggar like him.'

The soldier began to disarm himself and he felt so exhilarated and happy that he cried, 'I feel as light as air and I will soar with him through the firmaments.'

The Grand Vizier became inwardly very joyous, because he found a pretext to rouse the anger of the King and bring down the final blow on the man he loathed so intensely. He very cunningly and softly approached the King and whispered, 'Up till now I kept the country in peace and perfect order. But this man in front of your own eyes snatched one of your own and very loyal followers. I know their sole aim is to overthrow the throne and create confusion, therefore from now on, I will not be responsible.'

As dusk approached and the darkness grew deeper and deeper, the children, who had been already cramped with fear and felt chilled and desolate at heart, scattered and the ripple of their joyful laughter was no more echoed in the hills and valleys.

The King was bewildered and the Grand Vizier was in the utmost of wrath. At the spur of one fleeting moment, he could snatch from the King the fateful decree against the young man. As the King was speedily mounting his steed, he ordered, 'Cover the lamp and kill the young man with his companion.'

A mantle, as heavy as armour, carrying the initials of the Imperial Household, was immediately placed on the lamp. In the cruel darkness which had enveloped everywhere just like the flash of lightning, a sword swept across the sky, not once, but twice and two innocent young men dropped down dead.

Dear children, wherever you are, by sunset look towards the spot where the sun disappears and you will always find a very brilliant star. This star was there at the moment when the youthful disciple and his companion offered their innocent, pure and precious blood at the altar of truth in which their hearts firmly believed. This evening star watched the dreadful bloodshed and wept the whole night. It saw that their blood commingled and streamed forth, meandered through the forests and reached deep, deep into the roots of all trees. In memory of that fateful event, the evening star appears every sunset, before all other heavenly bodies. It appears early to remind us of the lovely story of the Wonder Lamp and the two audacious devotees.

Every spring at that spot, hundreds of children assemble to make bouquets of roses which are like the drops of the blood of those two beloved heroes.

Centuries passed. One of the most gigantic tempests swept the whole earth. Millions of houses were destroyed. Thousands of temples were dilapidated and perished. Hundreds of exalted abodes, castles and mansions were razed to dust. The whole surface of the planet was altered.

When the tempest reached the Wonder Lamp, the heavy mantles were taken far, far away into the corners of oblivion and were lost.

The lamp began to move again; this time with more light, more vigour and more warmth. New buildings were raised and temples were constructed and the whole world was bathed in the spring rains, and purged from the dirty soils of dissensions, hatreds and prejudices. The large planet shrank and knit together and humanity became so close to one another that, henceforth, they considered themselves members of one household. The forests, the meadows, and the prairies were all dressed in their green attires, decorated with the multi-coloured flowers to welcome the scattered children who were returning home. They were of all races, colours, creeds and climes and, hand in hand, went round and round the Wonder Lamp.

They danced and danced. Heaven and Earth accompanied the chanting of the innocent when they raised their tender voices to mention the most great Name of God, the Creator of the whole universe.

Photographs

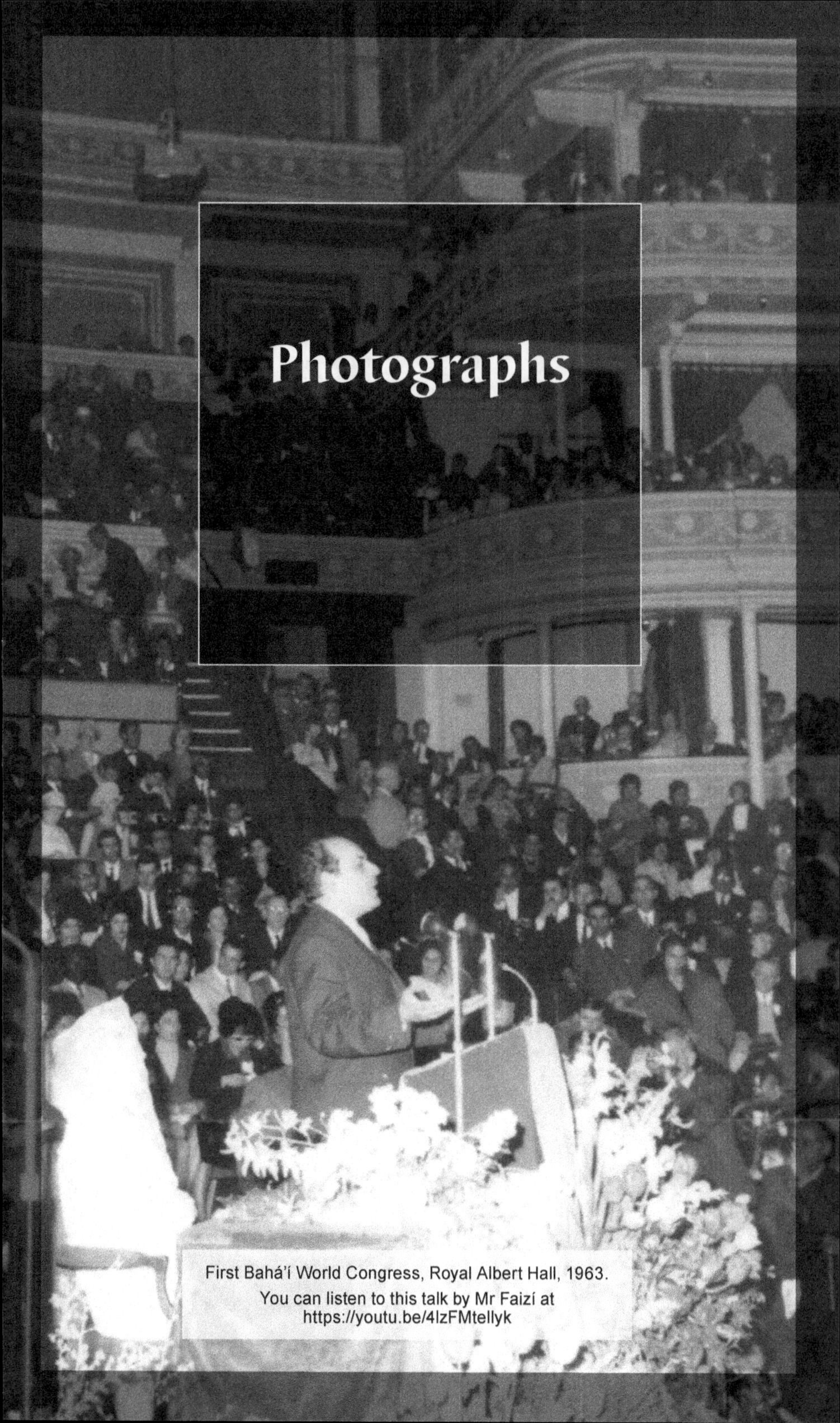

First Bahá'í World Congress, Royal Albert Hall, 1963.
You can listen to this talk by Mr Faizí at
https://youtu.be/4lzFMtellyk

1 Aged 18. **2** Tarbíyat School – Faizí standing middle row third from right. **3** Tarbíyat School – Faizí standing back row fourth from right. **4** As a young sportsman – top right. **5** Football match between the Tehran football team and a team from Russia, 29 November 1929 – Faizí is the middle figure. **6** Military service.

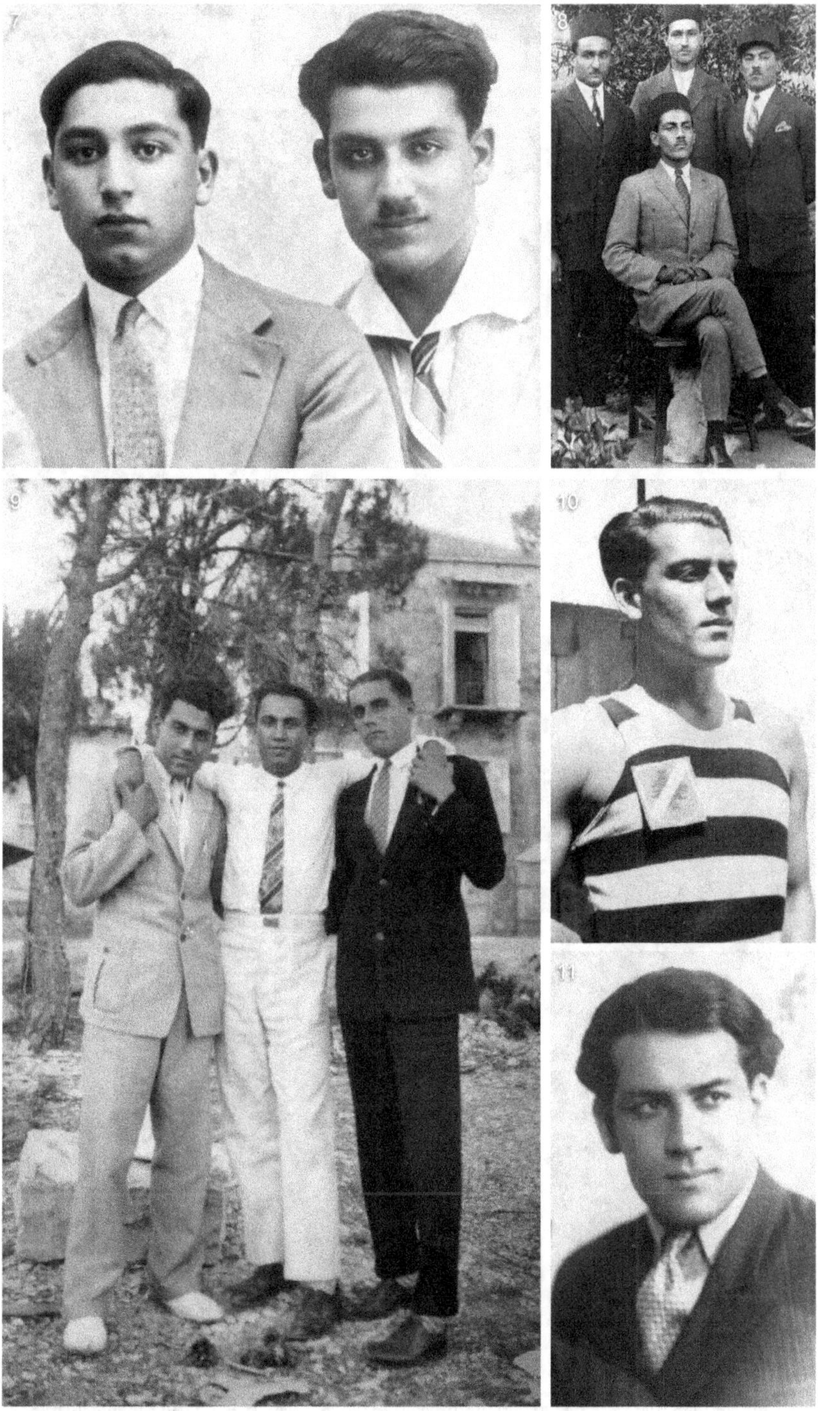

7–11 As a young man.

12

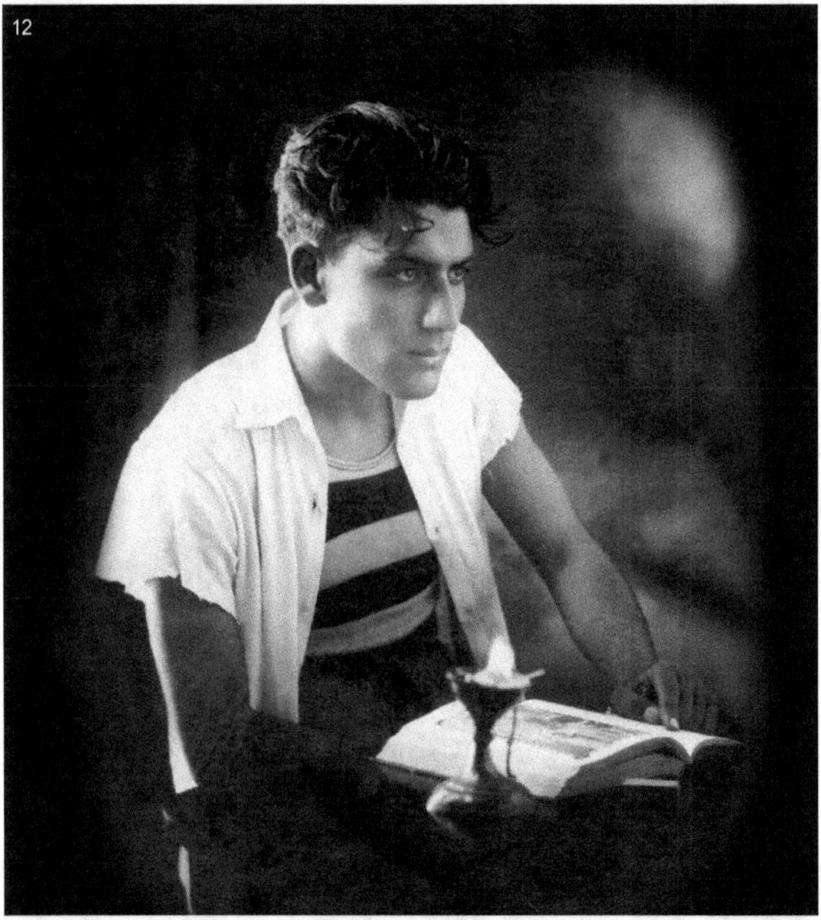

13

14

15

12–15 In various roles while studying drama as one of his subjects at the American University of Beirut – circa 1928.

16 Tutorial group with Professor Seeley at the American University of Beirut. **17** With fellow students – Ḥasan Balyúzí in centre. **18–22** In various roles while studying drama. **23** Recently graduated.

24 Special youth study group in Qazvín – standing left to right: Shaháb Zahrá'í, H. Hezárí, R. Samandarí. Seated left to right: Ehsán Zahrá'í (Zohreh's father), A.Q. Faizí, and B. Hamedání. **25** With some of the students in Qazvín. **26** With some of the Bahá'í community in Qazvín – **a**) Azíz Zahrá'í and **b**) Ezzat Zahrá'í (Zohreh's uncles).

27–31 With the Bahá'í community and some of his students in Najafábád.

32 National Youth Committee of Iran, 1941. Seated right to left: 'Alí-Muḥammad Varqá, 'Alí Nakhjavání, Mihrángíz Vaḥíd-Ṭihrání, Mihdí Samandarí, Muḥammad Yazdání. Standing right to left: 'Abdu'lláh Mesbah, Salím Noonoo, Mihdí Varqá, Zikru'lláh Khádem, Faizí (guest).

33 Faizí (middle back row) translating for visiting American Bahá'í, Jim McCormack. Shíráz, 1938. Seated far right, front row, 'Alí-Muḥammad Varqá.

34 Youth Committee, Baghdad, 1942 – Faizí standing on left. **35** At summer school with Nadím Bá<u>sh</u>í, one of the judges in Iran who became a Bahá'í. **36** First Summer School in Iran held near Tehran – Mr Mesbah sitting on left. **37** & **38** Tutoring during summer school – 1930s.

39 Bahá'í undergraduates at Beirut University, 1928 – Faizí standing second from left and Gloria in centre. **40** Gloria. **41** Faizí tutoring Gloria in Beirut. **42** & **43** Newly married couple, Najafábád. **44** Newly married couple and Faizí's mother.

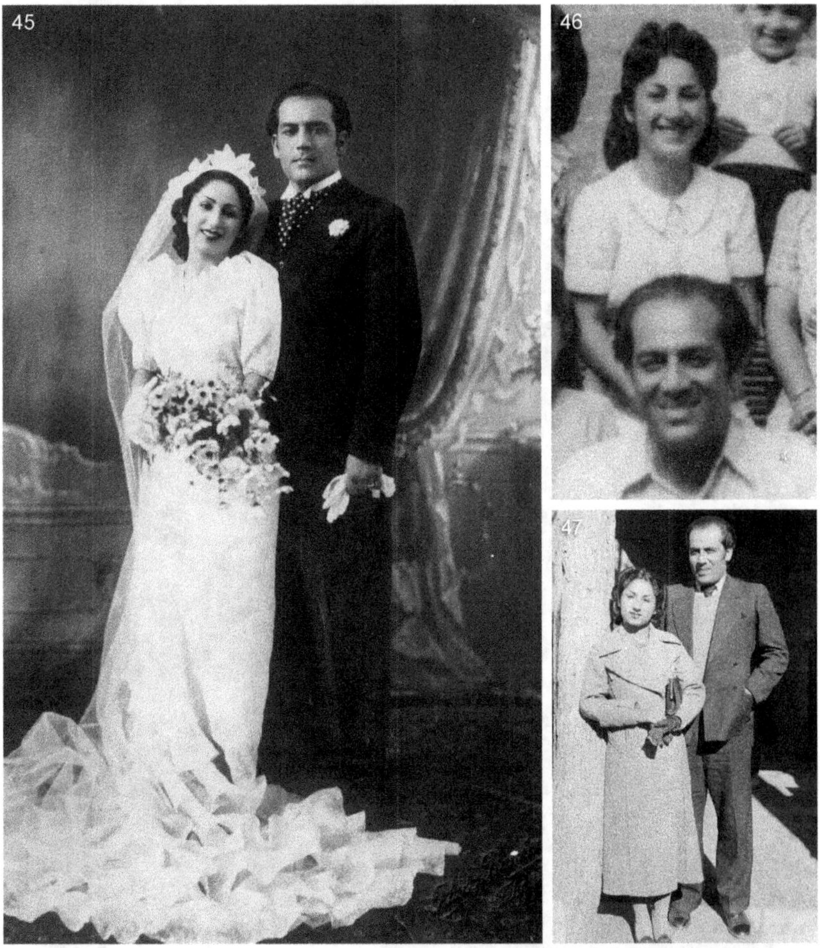

45 Wedding – 26 September 1939. **46–49** As a young couple.

50

51

52

50 Exercising with Persian dumbbells. **51** & **52** Exercising with Naysán.

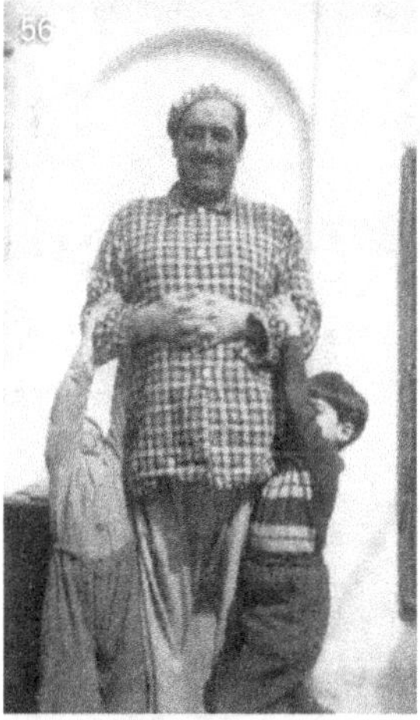

53 Exercising with some of the children in Najafábád. **54** At the Zurkhaneh (traditional Persian martial arts). **55** With Pahlaván Khalíl Oghab, also known as the 'Iron Man from Iran'. **56** Exercising with Naysán. **57** & **58** Naysán as cowboy and swashbuckler.

59 Photograph taken in Beirut to send to his mother for Naw-Rúz. **60** With May and Naysán. **61, 62** & **63** With Gloria, May and Naysán.

64 In traditional Arab garments. **65** & **66** Studying and researching. **67** Faizí and Ehsán Zahrá'í with a group of Bahá'ís in Kuwait. **68** With some of his students in Bahrain. **69** The first National Spiritual Assembly of Arabia (one member absent) – with Hand of the Cause Mr Samandarí and General Sohráb (Zohreh's grandfather).

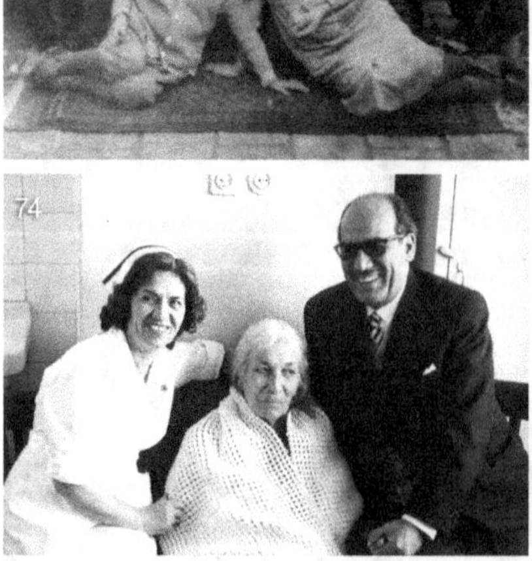

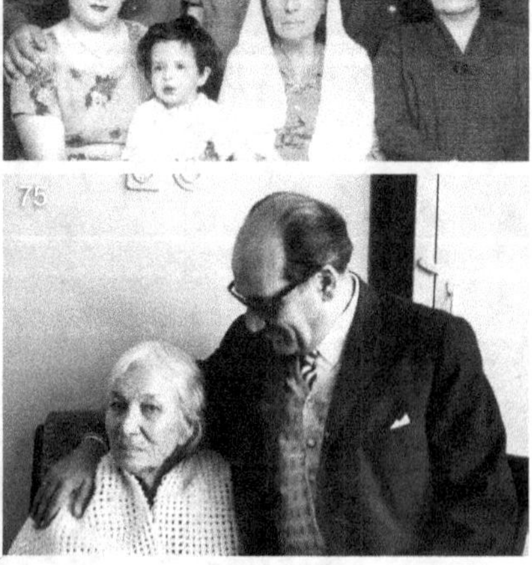

70 The Faizí brothers with their wives, children and relatives. **71** Daoud Toeg's (seated in centre) visit to Iran in 1936 – with Salím Noonoo, Raḥmat 'Alá'í, Najmieh 'Alá'í and Mr Aḥmadpour. On the floor: Gloria and Manuchehr. **72** With his mother and Gloria. **73** With his brother's family. **74** & **75** With his mother, Ṣiddíqih Khánum and mother-in-law, Najmieh 'Alá'í.

76 With his brother, Muḥammad ʻAlí Faizí. **77** With his cousin, Reza Jahángírí. **78** With Gloria, May and Naysán in Haifa, 1962. **79** With his adopted son, Húshang Mosaed. **80** With Ehsán and Soraya Zahrá'í – who became like loving parents to their son-in-law Naysán.

81 The Hands of the Cause and the members of the Universal House of Justice – circa 1965. Faizí standing seventh from left. **82** With Collis Featherstone, Bill Sears and Rúḥíyyih Khánum. **83** With Paul Haney. **84** With Mr Samandarí. **85** With Rúḥíyyih Khánum.

86 With Raḥmat Muhájir. **87** With Agnes Alexander. **88** With Hú<u>sh</u>mand Fatḥ-i-A‘ẓam. **89** With ‘Alí Akbar Furútan in Australia, 1953–54. **90** With ‘Alí-Muḥammad Varqá and Luṭfu’lláh Ḥakím. **91** With Enoch Olinga and Adelbert Mühlschlegel. **92** With Ḥasan Balyúzí.

93 With the Hands of the Cause, Jalál Ḵházeh, 'Alí Akbar Furútan, Músá Banání, Ṭaráẓu'lláh Samandarí and Raḥmat Muhájir. **94** With His Highness Malietoa Tanumafili II and Suhayl 'Alá'í, 1977. **95** With Enoch Olinga and Elizabeth Olinga at a conference in Plön, Germany, August 1972. **96** The Hands of the Cause with Counsellors of the International Teaching Centre, 1973: (front row, left to right) 'Alí Akbar Furútan, Florence Mayberry, Rúḥíyyih Khánum, A. Q. Faizí, (back row, left to right) Paul Haney, 'Azíz Yazdí, Hooper Dunbar. **97** With the National Spiritual Assembly of Australia, 1969. From left to right: Joy Vohradsky, Stanley Bolton Jr, Elizabeth Hindson, John Davidson, A. Q. Faizí, David Hoffman, John Walker, Joy Stevenson, Grenville Kirton, Pieter de Vogel.

98 With Panamanian Bahá'ís, 1974. **99** With Bolivian Bahá'ís, 1963. **100** In India, 1955 – Hú<u>sh</u>mand Faṭh-i-A'ẓam standing on the right.

101 In Karachi, 1955–56. **102** In Dahomey (now Benin), 1970. **103** With Gloria in the New Era School in Panchgani, India, 1976–77.

104

105

106

107

108

104 Arriving in Hawaii, January 1974, one of the many destinations to which he travelled. **105** Deep in thought. **106** Faizí's heartfelt and infectious laughter. **107** On board a launch going out to passenger ships anchored offshore to greet arriving Bahá'ís – Bahrain. **108** On board the ship from India to Australia, 25 October 1953.

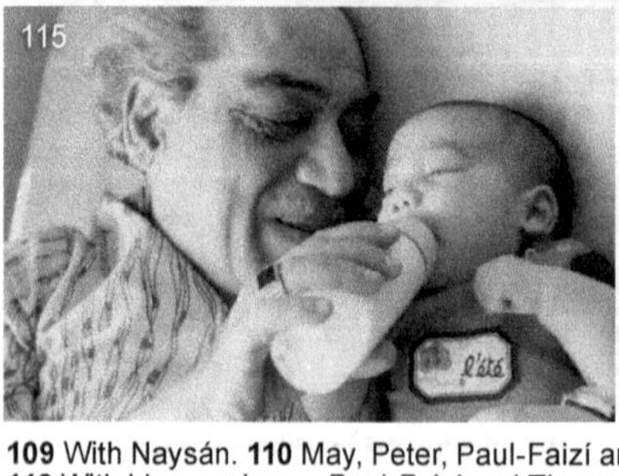

109 With Naysán. **110** May, Peter, Paul-Faizí and Thomas. **111** With Zohreh and Cherry. **112** With his grandsons, Paul-Faizí and Thomas Moore. **113** With his granddaughter, Cherry Gloria Faizí. **114** With Gloria – one of the last photographs of Faizí before his passing in 1980. **115** With his grandson, Aram Amoz Faizí.

www.ingramcontent.com/pod-product-compliance
Lightning Source LLC
Chambersburg PA
CBHW060549230426
43670CB00011B/1752
9780853986379